GW01079969

2007

# CONTEMPORARY MUSICIANS

ISSN 1044-2197

# CONTEMPORARY MUSICIANS

## PROFILES OF THE PEOPLE IN MUSIC

**Tracie Ratiner,** Project Editor

VOLUME 60
Includes Cumulative Indexes

THOMSON

GALE

Detroit • New York • San Francisco • New Haven, Conn. • Waterville, Maine • London

## Contemporary Musicians, Vol. 60

**Project Editor**
Tracie Ratiner

**Editorial**
Angela Pilchak
Dana Barnes

**Rights Acquisition and Management**
Margaret Abendroth, Tracie Richardson,
Tim Sisler

**Imaging and Multimedia**
Lezlie Light

**Image Research and Acquisitions**
Dean Dauphinais

**Cover Illustration**
John Kleber

**Composition and Electronic Capture**
Tracey L. Matthews

ISBN 13: ISBN 978-0-7876-8073-2
ISBN 10: 0-7876-8073-7
ISSN 1044-2197

This title is also available as an e-book.
ISBN 13: 978-1-4144-1025-8
ISBN 10: 1-4144-1025-5
Please contact your Thomson Gale sales
representative for ordering information.

Printed in the United States of America
10 9 8 7 6 5 4 3 2 1

# Contents

# Introduction

## Fills in the Information Gap on Today's Musicians

*Contemporary Musicians* profiles the colorful personalities in the music industry who create or influence the music we hear today. Prior to *Contemporary Musicians,* no quality reference series provided comprehensive information on such a wide range of artists despite keen and ongoing public interest. To find biographical and critical coverage, an information seeker had little choice but to wade through the offerings of the popular press, scan television "infotainment" programs, and search for the occasional published biography. *Contemporary Musicians* is designed to serve that information seeker, providing in one ongoing source in-depth coverage of the important names on the modern music scene in a format that is both informative and entertaining. Students, researchers, and casual browsers alike can use *Contemporary Musicians* to meet their needs for personal information about music figures; find a selected discography of a musician's recordings; and uncover an insightful essay offering biographical and critical information.

## Provides Broad Coverage

Single-volume biographical sources on musicians are limited in scope, often focusing on a handful of performers from a specific musical genre or era. In contrast, *Contemporary Musicians* offers researchers and music devotees a comprehensive, informative, and entertaining alternative. *Contemporary Musicians* is published twice per year, with each volume providing information on about 70 musical artists and record-industry luminaries from all the genres that form the broad spectrum of contemporary music—pop, rock, jazz, blues, country, New Age, folk, rhythm and blues, Latin, gospel, bluegrass, rap, and reggae, to name a few—as well as selected classical artists who have achieved "crossover" success with the general public. *Contemporary Musicians* will also occasionally include profiles of influential nonperforming members of the music community, including producers, promoters, and record company executives. Additionally, beginning with *Contemporary Musicians 11,* each volume features new profiles of a selection of previous *Contemporary Musicians* listees who remain of interest to today's readers and who have been active enough to require completely revised entries.

## Includes Popular Features

In *Contemporary Musicians* you'll find popular features that users value:

*Easy-to-locate data sections:* Vital personal statistics, chronological career summaries, listings of major awards, and mailing addresses, when available, are prominently displayed in a clearly marked box on the second page of each entry.

*Biographical/critical essays:* Colorful and informative essays trace each subject's personal and professional life, offer representative examples of critical response to the artist's work, and provide entertaining personal sidelights.

*Selected discographies:* Each entry provides a comprehensive listing of the artist's major recorded works.

*Photographs:* Many entries include portraits of the subject profiled.

*Sources for additional information:* This invaluable feature directs the user to selected books, magazines, newspapers, and online sources where more information can be obtained.

## Helpful Indexes Make It Easy to Find the Information You Need

Each volume of *Contemporary Musicians* features a cumulative Musicians Index, listing names of individual performers and musical groups, and a cumulative Subject Index, which provides the user with a break-down by primary musical instruments played and by musical genre.

## Available in Electronic Formats

*Licensing.* *Contemporary Musicians* is available for licensing. The complete database is provided in a fielded format and is deliverable on such media as disk or CD-ROM. For more information, contact Thomson Gale's Business Development Group at (800) 877-GALE, or visit our website at www.gale.com/bizdev.

*Online.* *Contemporary Musicians* is accessible online as part of the Thomson Gale Biographies (GALBIO) database accessible through LexisNexis, P.O. Box 933, Dayton, OH 45401-0933; phone: (937) 865-6800, toll-free: (800) 227-4908.

## We Welcome Your Suggestions

The editors welcome your comments and suggestions for enhancing and improving *Contemporary Musicians.* If you would like to suggest subjects for inclusion, please submit these names to the editor. Mail comments or suggestions to:

The Editor

*Contemporary Musicians*

Thomson Gale

27500 Drake Rd.

Farmington Hills, MI 48331-3535

Or call toll free: (800) 877-GALE

# Clay
# Aiken

**Singer**

AP Images

Although Clay Aiken is a multiplatinum-selling singer, he didn't plan to have a singing career. He originally wanted to become a teacher, and earned a degree in special education from the University of North Carolina at Charlotte. He planned to teach, get a master's degree in administration, then become a school principal when he hit the age of 50. He truly loved teaching children with developmental disabilities, and worked one-on-one with a boy who had autism, Mike Bubel. Bubel's mother, Diane, had seen the singing-contest television show *American Idol,* and knew that Aiken had a big voice. She encouraged him to audition for the show, and it changed his life forever.

### "You Don't Look Like a Pop Star"

Aiken came to the attention of millions of TV viewers during the second season of the show in 2003, when he startled viewers with the contrast between his lanky, red-haired, big-eared looks and his large, resonant voice. The show's judge, Simon Cowell, remarked, "You don't look like a pop star." Not only did he not look like a pop star, he didn't act like one. Aiken, a Christian, spoke openly about his beliefs, didn't drink, smoke, or swear, did not sing sexual songs, and wore a bracelet with the letters WWJD (What Would Jesus Do). Despite his unlikely appearance, Aiken came in second by less than 1 percent of the viewer vote, launching his singing career.

Aiken's debut album, *Measure of a Man,* released in 2003, went double platinum. He was named Fan's Choice at the American Music Awards, was one of *People*'s Top Entertainers of the Year, and was chosen as *TV Guide*'s Fan's Favorite Reality Star. With the money he made from the album, Aiken surprised his mother by paying off the mortgage on her home.

In that same year Aiken founded the Bubel/Aiken Foundation, a nonprofit group that helps children with special needs. Many fans of his singing became supporters of the foundation. Aiken told Holly Vicente Robaina in *Today's Christian,* "Through [the fans] we have been able to do a great deal of work in spreading the word about the need for and the benefits of inclusion for children with disabilities."

In 2005 Aiken published an autobiographical book, *Learning to Sing.* In the book, he wrote about his life and faith. He commented, "Some people have argued that I'm too religious and that I talk about my faith too much. Other people have criticized me because I don't stand up for my beliefs enough. But my position is that there's a fine line that has to be walked. There are a lot of people who have given Christians a really bad name by being overly aggressive."

He also commented that although he won't talk about sex or sing songs that use sexual innuendo, he doesn't

## For the Record . . .

**B**orn Clayton Holmes Grissom (later changed his name to Aiken, his mother's maiden name) on November 30, 1978, in Raleigh, NC; son of Faye Aiken and Vernon Grissom; stepson of Ray Parker, who raised him and his brother Brett. *Education:* University of North Carolina at Charlotte, degree in special education.

Won second place on TV talent show *American Idol,* 2003; released debut album, *Measure of a Man,* 2003; released *Merry Christmas With Love,* 2005; released *A Thousand Different Ways,* 2006.

Addresses: *Record company*—Sony BMG Music Entertainment, 550 Madison Ave., New York, NY 10022.

often sing songs with overtly Christian lyrics either. He told Robaino that although he enjoyed listening to Christian radio, he also knew people who did not listen to it, and those were the people he wanted to reach out to: "If I can put a secular love song on an album, and someone can interpret it in a way that makes them think of God's love for them or the power of Jesus' sacrifice, then I think I've fulfilled my purpose."

In a review of the book in *Entertainment Weekly,* Kristen Baldwin wrote, "Clay Aiken is far more interesting as a person than a pop star—and, God bless him, he's smart enough to know it." She praised Aiken for spending little time discussing his experiences on television and telling more about his working-class upbringing in North Carolina. "Behind the polite narration emerges a complex guy with a folksy sense of humor and an endearing ambivalence about his own insta-celebrity."

Aiken did not expect this "insta-celebrity," or the rush of publicity he would get as a result of his *American Idol* performances and his album, and he was startled to be mobbed by fans whenever he left his house. He began having panic attacks, and finally decided to ask his doctor for help. He began taking Paxil, an antianxiety medication, although he did not go to therapy for this problem. The medication helped him deal with publicity, but it also blunted some of his emotions. He told Michelle Tauber in *People* that when his stepbrother, Brett, left to fight with the Marines in Iraq in July of 2006, "I was trying to make myself cry and I couldn't. I started thinking, 'Do I not have emotions anymore?' It was kind of weird for me."

Aiken also found that as his fame grew, it became increasingly harder to maintain old friendships or to make new, true ones. Robaina noted, "There are plenty of 'friends' who've come out of the woodwork from every direction. Former classmates who never spoke to him in high school now ask him to sing at their weddings."

Like any celebrity, Aiken was often the target of tabloid gossip, and in 2006 he spoke up about persistent rumors that he was gay. He told Tauber, "It doesn't matter what I say. People are going to believe what they want." He added that his mother had always advised him that when faced with negativity, he could always "leave it alone." He added, "I think certain people and certain magazines have had enough publicity. I have always been told to let the negative stuff fall away." Aiken also told Tauber that he had matured and learned a lot over the past few years. "I learned this year that you can't make people like you or care about you or love you."

Aiken has spent increasing time on his work with charities, most notably the Buber/Aiken Foundation and UNICEF. With UNICEF, he traveled to Uganda and Indonesia, and he testified before Congress on UNICEF's behalf. He has considered adopting a child, or setting up a way to pay for an underprivileged child to go to college. He told Tauber, "I want to be a father so badly. I want [kids] one day. Not now." In addition to having children, Aiken is also thinking of going back to school to get a master's degree in education. About his life, Aiken told Robaina, "My life has been guided by Provident direction more than anything else. I was really in the place God wanted me to be, at the time He wanted me to be there."

## Selected discography

*Measure of a Man,* RCA Records, 2003.
*Merry Christmas With Love,* RCA Records, 2004.
*A Thousand Different Ways,* RCA Records, 2006.

## Sources

### Periodicals

*Billboard,* September 16, 2006, p. 56.
*Entertainment Weekly,* November 19, 2004, p. 87; September 16, 2005, p. 74; September 29, 2006, p. 80.
*People,* July 26, 2004, p. 24; December 3, 2004, p. 48; December 13, 2004, p. 36; August 8, 2005, p. 26; October 22, 2006, p. 122.
*Today's Christian,* November-December 2005, p. 18.

—Kelly Winters

# Anggun

**Singer**

AP Images

As a child singing star in Indonesia, Anggun recorded her first album when she was nine years old. She has since become known on the international scene, and has had platinum and gold albums in both Europe and Asia.

## A Singing Prodigy

Anggun was born in Jakarta, Indonesia, the daughter of prominent parents. Her full name, Anggun Cipta Sasmi, means "a grace created in a dream." Anggun's father, Darto Singo, was a well-known writer and journalist in Indonesia, and her mother came from a wealthy family in Java. Like most children in Indonesia, she learned to sing and dance as a very young child. She told Adrian Brown in *Mahasathi,* "It's a part of the culture, everybody can do it." However, her father noted that she could do it better than most other children, and he encouraged her to train her voice and become a singer. Her father had a book on voice training and he read to her, chapter by chapter, while she practiced the techniques. In an interview posted on *Planetmole* she told T. Sima Gunawan, "I think my real vocal teacher was Freddy Mercury because I used to listen to his songs. I should sing like him, with a similar technique." She added, "I love the Beatles and I was into rock music."

When she was nine years old she recorded an album of children's songs, moving on to rock as she grew into her early teens. When she was 19, she founded her own record label in Indonesia. In 1986 Anggun recorded a rock album, *Dunia Aku Punya,* which became a big hit in Indonesia and brought her widespread attention in that country and throughout Asia.

In the following years she recorded more albums: *Tua Tua Keladi* (1990), *Anak Putih Abu Abu* (1991), *Noc Turno* (1992), and *Anggun C. Sasmi...Lah!* (1993). During these years she also performed throughout Asia.

While touring in Borneo, Anggun met a young French engineer, Michel Georgea. They met again in Singapore when her tour was over, and soon developed a serious relationship. Anggun's family disapproved of their relationship, but they were married anyway. In 1994 they moved to London, but soon decided to move to an apartment in Paris. She would later divorce Georgea and marry another French national, Oliver Maury. Anggun told Gunawan that she was not bothered by the cultural differences between herself and her husband: "I prefer someone who is different so that I can enrich myself, so that there are more things to talk about."

Although Anggun was completely unknown in Paris, she didn't let this stop her. She met French musician and producer Erick Benzi, who had worked with several international stars, including Celine Dion, Johnny Hallyday, and Jean-Jacques Goldman. Benzi told Anggun he would cowrite an album with her, but only if she forsook her original rock style for a softer, more romantic style.

## For the Record . . .

Born Anggun Cipta Sasmi on April 26, 1974, in Jakarta, Indonesia; daughter of Darto Singo (a songwriter, and producer) and a homemaker; married Michel Georgea (divorced); married Oliver Maury.

Began recording career at age nine; released *Dunia Aku Punya,* 1986; released *Tua Tua Keladi,* 1990; released *Anak Putih Abu Abu,* 1991; released *Noc Turno,* 1992; released *Anggun C. Sasmi…Lah!,* 1993; released *Au nom de la lune* (also released as *Anggun*), 1997; released *Luminescence,* 2005.

Addresses: *Record company*—Sony BMG Music Entertainment France, 26 Rue Morel, 92110 Clichy, France.

## Snow on the Sahara

Her new style was what French listeners were looking for, and the album she and Benzi produced, *Au nom de la lune* (1997), had one track, "La neige au Sahara" (Snow on the Sahara), that became a big hit. The song featured a variety of musical influences and a range of instruments, including flutes and electric guitars. According to Catherine Curran in *WWD,* Anggun said this album was "more intimate and mellow" than her previous work, and added that "many of the songs talk about femininity in a soft way." The song shot to the top of the European charts and brought her to the attention of listeners all over Europe. The album sold over 150,000 copies in France and Belgium alone. The album was also released in Indonesia with the title *Anggun,* and sold over 100,000 copies. Ultimately the album went triple platinum in Indonesia, double platinum in Italy, and gold in France and Malaysia.

In 2000 Anggun was invited to sing at a Christmas concert at the Vatican. She followed this with a 2001 Asian tour, and worked with a variety of musicians, including DJ Cam and Serge Lama. In the same year, she appeared on the soundtrack to the Scandinavian film *Anja and Viktor,* and in 2002 she sang on the soundtrack of another Scandinavian film, *Open Hearts.*

In 2003 Anggun was one of many international performers to contribute to the 21-track album *Gaia.* Proceeds from the album were to be used to finance education programs in schools all over the world.

Anggun was honored in 2004 with a French Chevalier des Arts et des Lettres award. She also became an official spokesperson for the United Nations' Microcredit program, which is designed to help eliminate debt in underdeveloped countries. She told Leony Aurora in the *Jakarta Post,* as reprinted on the International Year of Microcredit website, that the concept of microcredit reminded her of her maternal grandmother, who had a small business making and selling batik-dyed cloth. She said, "Microcredit is important because it helps women to play a greater role in supporting their families, as my grandmother did. It provides knowledge, motivation and, most of all, an opportunity for poor people to break away from poverty." In that same year, she experienced tragedy when her beloved father died. In 2005 Anggun released a new album, *Luminescence,* and began extensive touring in support of it.

Anggun told Christian Lorenz in *Music and Media,* "I really wanted to have an international career as a singer, and that wouldn't have happened if I stayed in Indonesia. Nobody would have come and looked me up."

## Selected discography

*Dunia Aku Punya,* 1986.
*Tua Tua Keladi,* 1990.
*Anak Putih Abu Abu,* 1991.
*Noc Turno,* 1992.
*Anggun C. Sasmi…Lah!,* 1993.
*Au nom de la lune* (also released as *Anggun*), Sony Music France, 1997.
*Luminescence,* Sony Music France, 2005.

## Sources

### Periodicals

*Billboard,* May 8, 1999, p. 47.
*Billboard Bulletin,* September 29, 2001, p. 41; January 3, 2003, p. 2; March 22, 2003, p. 73.
*Music and Media,* July 10, 1999, p. 3; April 7, 2001, p. 30.

### Online

"Anggun," *RFI Musique,* http://www.rfimusique.com/siteen/biographie/biographie_6085.asp (November 6, 2006).
"Anggun's Driving Ambition," *Asiaweek,* http://www.asiaweek.com/asiaweek/magazine/2000/0901/as.people.html (November 6, 2006).
"Creating Her Own Destiny: Anggun Cipta Sasmi," *Mahasathi,* September, 2005, http://www.freelists.org/archives/mahasathi/09-2005/msg00058.html (November 6, 2006).
"Indonesians in Focus," *Planet Mole,* http://www.planetmole.org/06-05/indonesians-in-focus-anggun-cipta-sasmi.html (November 6, 2006).
"It's Better to Provide a Fishing Rod Than Fish," *Year of Microcredit,* January, 2005, http://www.yearofmicrocredit.org/pages/reslib/reslib_interviews_jan05.asp (November 6, 2006).

—Kelly Winters

# Ray Anthony

## Bandleader

**B**and leader Ray Anthony has been an immense presence on the swing scene for over 50 years. He cut his teeth as a trumpeter, performing first with Glenn Miller and Tommy Dorsey during the 1940s before embarking on a successful solo career. During the 1950s and 1960s he appeared in numerous movies and on television shows, and became well known for recording the theme to *Dragnet*. He also wrote novelty tunes such as "The Bunny Hop," and modern classics, including "Dancing in the Dark."

Ray Anthony was born Raymond Antonioni on January 20, 1922, in Bentleyville, Pennsylvania, one of six brothers. His family later moved to Cleveland, Ohio, and Anthony, at the age of five, learned to play trumpet from his father. Soon Anthony began performing in the family orchestra. As a teen he formed his own band in Cleveland, and soon came to the attention of jazz great Glenn Miller. At only 18, Anthony was asked to join Miller's band.

Anthony performed with Miller's band in 1940-41, but with the advent of World War II he joined the U.S. Navy. He returned to Cleveland awaiting assignment, and temporarily joined the Jimmy Dorsey Band. "In the case of Jimmy," Anthony later recalled to Christopher Popa at *Big Band Library,* "he was almost like one of the guys in the band." In the Navy, he served as the head of a show band in the Pacific arena that would later be recognized as one of the top service bands. "That's where I did most of my growing with the band," Anthony told Popa, "and eventually took it into civilian life, when the War was over."

After his discharge in 1946, he formed the Ray Anthony Orchestra, an outfit that would impact the American music scene for the next 50 years. The band traveled widely and played before large audiences, earning Anthony a contract with Capitol Records in 1949 that would last for 19 years. The orchestra also helped feed a national dance craze with the release of the "Bunny Hop" and the "Hokey Pokey."

The success of the band led to multiple opportunities in Hollywood. In 1953-54, Anthony served as the director of the orchestra for the series *TV's Top Tunes,* and in 1953 he recorded one of his best known pieces, the theme to *Dragnet.* For 13 weeks in the summer of 1953, *The Ray Anthony Show* served as a summer replacement to the *Perry Como Show,* and the program returned for another eight weeks the following summer. The Ray Anthony Orchestra appeared in the Fred Astaire movie *Daddy Long Legs* in 1955 and in *The Girl Can't Help It* the following year. In 1955 Anthony married Mamie Van Doren, an actress and noted sex symbol of the era.

Anthony's television and film work continued to evolve through the remainder of the 1950s and into the 1960s. He was known for his handsome Cary Grant-like looks, and found it easy to move into acting roles. He played an undercover agent in *High School Confidential* in 1958 and a hotel clerk in *Night of the Quarter Moon* a year later. The Ray Anthony Orchestra also continued to work in films, appearing in *This Could Be the Night* in 1957. Interestingly, Anthony landed the role of fellow bandleader Jimmy Dorsey in *The Five Pennies* in 1959. A new version of *The Ray Anthony Show* appeared in 1956-57 and ran for 30 weeks. Syndicated versions of *The Ray Anthony Show* reappeared in 1963 and 1969-70.

Jazz critics often dismissed much of Anthony's recorded work, categorizing it as a popular, watered-down version of jazz. During the 1950s, however, he recorded two albums that rose to a much higher mark in their estimation: *Anthony Plays Allen* and *Swing's The Thing.* Anthony's recorded work, despite his lukewarm acceptance by critics, experienced an enthusiastic response from the listening public, sending a number of his singles and LPs onto the pop charts in the 1950s and early 1960s. *Golden Horn,* an album from 1955, rose to number 10 on the pop charts, while 1962's *Worried Mind* reached number 14. The single "Melody of Love" reached number 19 in 1955, while "Peter Gunn," the theme to a television series, rose to number 8.

Aside from his occasional movie and television appearances, Anthony's public popularity declined during he 1960s. In 1961 he and Van Doren divorced, and his film career came to an end. Although Anthony's career in movies was fairly short, he received a star on the Hollywood Walk of Fame. Anthony's music also ap-

## For the Record . . .

Born Raymond Antonioni on January 20, 1922, in Bentleyville, Pennsylvania.

Joined Glenn Miller band as trumpeter, 1940-41, and Jimmy Dorsey Band, 1941; formed the Ray Anthony Orchestra, 1946; signed with Capital Records, 1949; served as director of the orchestra for the series *TV's Top Tunes,* and recorded the theme to *Dragnet,* 1953; appeared with Ray Anthony Orchestra in *Daddy Long Legs,* 1955, and *The Girl Can't Help It,* 1956; played Jimmy Dorsey in *The Five Pennies,* 1959; appeared in various productions of *The Ray Anthony Show,* 1950s-60s; performed at the Presidential Inaugural Ball, 1985; performs for charities and private parties, 1980s–.

Addresses: Record Company—Aerospace Records, 9288 Kinglet Drive, Los Angeles, CA 90069, phone: (800)-845-2263, website: http://bigbandcdstore.com/aerospacerecordssite.html.

peared less frequently on the popular charts after the early 1960s. The album *Worried Mind* reached the charts in 1962, and two singles, "Let Me Entertain You" and "Worried Mind," broke the top 100.

A number of Anthony compilations have been issued. In 1991 Capitol reissued the *Capitol Collectors Series,* a collection that included some of Anthony's best-known songs, including "The Bunny Hop," "The Theme to Peter Gunn," and "Dragnet." In 2005 Lone Hill Jazz released *Plays the Arrangements of George Williams,* a collection derived from 1950-55. "Most importantly," wrote *All Music Guide,* "this music is fun. Nothing too serious or complicated here—just good clean fun." Anthony also took advantage of a resurgent interest in Swing Jazz during the 1980s and 1990s. He opened the Big Band Record Library and started a mail order service. "People hear this music and they want to buy it, but there's no place to buy it," he told Popa. "The record stores have stopped selling it. So we've started a sort of a clearinghouse." Anthony also released *Boogies Blues and Ballads* and *Dream Dancing in Hawaii* on Aerospace.

Anthony continued to pursue his vocation during the 1980s, 1990s, and beyond. He performed at the Presidential Inaugural Ball in 1985, and has loaned his talent to numerous charity events. He has continued to front his orchestra, and the band remains active at private parties in Beverly Hills. "I can't remember a time when music wasn't part of my life," Anthony was quoted on his website. "Music puts wings on the human soul. Nothing can touch people the way music can. And every day is a new opportunity to create, change, stretch and reach for new heights doing something that I absolutely love—entertaining people through great music."

## Selected discography

*I Remember Glenn Miller,* Capitol, 1955.
*Golden Horn,* Capitol, 1955.
*Dream Dancing,* Capitol, 1956.
*Dancing Over the Waves,* Capitol, 1958.
*Dream Dancing Medley,* Capitol, 1961.
*Capital Collectors Series,* Capitol, 1991.
*Plays the Arrangements of George Williams,* Lone Hill Jazz, 2001.

## Sources

### Online

"Ray Anthony," *All Music Guide,* http://www.allmusic.com/ (October 9, 2006).
"Ray Anthony: A Man and His Music," *Big Band CD Store,* http://www.bigbandcdstore.com/rayanthonysite.html (October 9, 2006).
"Ray Anthony: 'Mr. Anthony's Band,'" *Big Band Library,* http://www.bigbandlibrary.com/ (October 9, 2006).

—*Ronnie D. Lankford, Jr.*

# Lloyd Banks

**Rap musician**

In the world of East Coast rap music, rhyming about gangs, gunshots, and drugs wasn't just a trend; it was the life of New York rappers like 50 Cent and his friend Lloyd Banks. At the start of the new millennium, Banks, 50 Cent, and their group G-Unit thrived in the city's mixtape scene. After rap star Eminem signed 50 Cent to Interscope Records imprint, Shady/Aftermath, G-Unit's life, including Banks', was never the same. G-Unit's first major-label release went double platinum before Banks released two successful solo albums. "To define yourself as a complex individual in the G-Unit clan is a difficult task, but here's a rapper who can do it," David Jeffries of *All Music Guide* wrote about Banks.

Born Christopher Lloyd, in 1982, in Baltimore, Maryland, Banks was raised in Jamaica, Queens, by his Puerto Rican mother and African-American father. His mother did most of the work as Banks' father spent much of his childhood behind bars. Growing up in the extremely tough and dangerous Southside Jamaica, Queens, Banks saw early on the effect that drugs, money, and violence had on his family. At 10, Banks saw his first murder when one of his father's close friends was shot and killed right outside his own house. When Banks' father was out of jail, he would lavish his son with gifts he couldn't afford before usually ending up back behind bars. Banks never paid attention to his studies, instead he kept a notebook of lyrics. "I always wrote a notebook," he told *I Like Music*. "The books I was supposed to use at school I was writing in them what was going on around me. It wasn't even rapping up to that point, it was just me jotting down things real fast and after a long period of time I started to take the rap thing more seriously. It started off in 6th or 7th grade just me sitting there and writing in the classroom." With the nickname "Lazy," Banks dropped out of high school when he was 16.

Partnering with Queens' friends 50 Cent and Tony Yayo, the trio formed a rap group G-Unit. Banks was a legend on local mixtapes, dropping rhymes about his neighborhood. Banks and G-Unit didn't just rap about gunshots, they also received them. On September 10, 2001, Banks was shot outside of a nightclub. The aspiring rapper had a bullet hole in his liver, but quickly recovered. G-Unit never beat down any doors or pestered record labels with their demos; their skill was just undeniable, something Detroit's star Eminem realized early on. But before G-Unit was ready for the big time, 50 Cent became the crew's biggest star. In 2003, 50 Cent released his multiplatinum solo record *Get Rich or Die Tryin'* on Interscope/Shady/Aftermath. G-Unit's album was put on hold, but they toured behind 50 on his solo tour and multiple group tours with Eminem. Also in 2003, Banks said goodbye to many loved ones, including his grandfather, his uncle to a stroke, and two friends who were murdered.

Supporting 50 Cent at every turn, Banks and G-Unit took time to finally record their debut album. Much of

## For the Record . . .

Born Christopher Lloyd on April 30, 1982, in Baltimore, MD.

Formed rap group G-Unit with 50 Cent and Tony Yayo, group released *Beg for Mercy,* Interscope/G-Unit, 2003; released solo debut *Hunger for More,* Interscope/G-Unit, 2004; *Rotten Apple,* Interscope/G-Unit, 2006.

Addresses: *Record company*—Interscope/G-Unit, 2220 Colorado Ave., Santa Monica, CA 90404, 1755 Broadway, 8th Fl., New York, NY 10019, website, http://www.interscope.com. *Website*—Lloyd Banks Official Website: http://www.lloydbanks.com.

the 2003 double-platinum release *Beg for Mercy* was recorded on a bus while the group toured with 50 for the Roc the Mic Tour. As Banks toured with G-Unit, he began releasing a selection of mixtapes with DJ Whoo Kid. In 2003, Banks won the honor of Mixtape Artist of the Year at Justo Faison's Mixtape Awards. Banks soon began to compile ideas for his own solo album. Banks knew New York City up and down, and sang about it to a tee, but touring with G-Unit and Eminem gave the rapper a new outlook on his music. "If you stay in one place, you can only rap about one thing because that's all you know," Banks told *Newsweek's* Allison Samuels. "... I've seen and learned enough to keep my music fresh and spread out." Watching and learning from 50 Cent, Banks grew smarter about the industry and his music. "I always wanted to be complex, not too complex, but complex enough to excite people and make them want to rewind and hear what you said again,...." he told *I Like Music.* "If you've got a style and a certain swagger to you, people respect you for it. I never wanted to be or sound like anybody else, so I think I'm really in my own zone.... You just have to practice your craft."

With producers like Eminem, Kwame, and Timbaland, Banks' June 2004 solo debut *Hunger for More,* debuted at Number 1. Much of the Interscope record was, once again, recorded on the tour bus while Banks was on the road. The album's first single, "On Fire," was produced by Eminem, and reminiscent of G-Unit and 50 Cent's style. "From G-Unit's early mixtape days, he's specialized in rewind-worthy quotables marked by an assassin's cold heart, an ironist's savage humor, and a willingness to say what others won't. Or perhaps shouldn't," Chris Ryan of *Vibe* wrote about Banks' skill.

With six tours under his belt, for Banks' first solo tour, unlike the big productions of G-Unit or 50's tours, he performed most shows on stage with only DJ Whoo Kid to back him. "My whole life we've been tryin' to get out and just see things. Just to be on the road, it makes me feel like I'm alive," he told *Pollstar.* "Being able to get out there and perform in front of these people who buy my CD, it's a whole other feeling. And to be able to leave with that impression that they're gonna go home and talk about your show for the next two weeks ... that's what it's about."

With the triumph of *Hunger for More,* Banks was soon ready to do it again with a new album. He continued his series of underground mixtapes releasing *Money in Da Bank, Vol. 4* with DJ Whoo Kid. For his sophomore album, Banks rounded up a more eclectic group of producers and singers. In addition to producers Eminem, Timbaland, and Havoc (of Mobb Deep), R&B singers Alicia Keys and Musiq Soulchild, and rap artists Rakim, Scarface, 8 Ball, and of course members of G-Unit produced a well-rounded collection of songs. In October of 2006, Banks issued his second solo album, *Rotten Apple.* In an interview with Alexander Fruchter of *SoundSlam* the rapper explained the meaning behind the more aggressive album, *Rotten Apple,* as a flip on the city's nickname the Big Apple. "I'm giving them what they see with the naked eye, but I'm also giving them what it takes for you to ride through these neighborhoods for you to see," he told Fruchter. "For you to see police harassment, for you to see the murders, and the teen pregnancy, and the broken homes ... and situations that we're put through every day.... This is a continuous struggle that's not gonna stop. People think that just because I'm a rapper and I live a certain lifestyle based off success, that changes you. It doesn't change you. I lived 21 years in Southside Jamaica, Queens. It's hard for ... success to erase all of that negativity, and that's still going on today."

## Selected discography

(With G-Unit) *Beg For Mercy,* Interscope/G-Unit, 2003.
*Hunger for More,* Interscope/G-Unit, 2004.
*Rotten Apple,* Interscope/G-Unit, 2006.

## Sources

### Periodicals

*Newsweek,* June 28, 2004, p. 54.
*Vibe,* September 19, 2006.
*XXL Magazine,* May 4, 2004.

## Online

"Lloyd Banks," *All Music Guide,* http://www.allmusicguide.com (November 11, 2006).

"Lloyd Banks," *Pollstar,* http://www.pollstar.com/news/viewhotstar.pl?Artist=LLOBAN (November 11, 2006).

"Lloyd Banks Interview," *I Like Music,* http://www.ilikemusic.com/interviews/Lloyd_Banks_interview_2006_G_unit-3033 (November 11, 2006).

*SoundSlam,* http://www.soundslam.com/articles/interviews/interviews.php?interviews=in060604lloydb (November 11, 2006).

—*Shannon McCarthy*

# Basement Jaxx

**Rock group**

With the release of 1999's *Remedy,* the British house music duo Basement Jaxx—DJs Felix Buxton and Simon Ratcliffe—set the dance world on fire with a sound they call punk garage, turning the pair into club land messiahs. Given the pair's diverse musical influences—Timbaland, Larry Heard, George Duke, Lonnie Liston-Smith, and Thomas Bangalter—Basement Jaxx's music has reflected a myriad of musical styles. And as illustrated by their album *Remedy,* Buxton and Ratcliffe have displayed a penchant for creating original, exciting music. "There's the ragga and the Latin, and a bit of disco, funk and noise," Buxton explained in *Rolling Stone.* "We were tired of music that didn't have any joy about being alive at all—just dreary going-on music."

Not only did the full-length debut sell millions of copies worldwide, but *Remedy* also turned out to be one of the most critically acclaimed albums of the year, garnering the kind of positive reviews usually reserved for traditional rock groups. *Rolling Stone* gave it a four-star "excellent" rating, and *Spin* named it as one of the top albums of the 1990s. Upon the LP's release in America, the first single from the album, "Red Alert," hit number one on the *Billboard* Dance Music/Club Play chart. According to the music press, Basement Jaxx's

## For the Record . . .

**M**embers include **Felix Buxton** (born in 1971 in London, England; son of an Anglican church vicar); **Simon Ratcliffe** (born in 1970; raised in Holland and Wales).

Formed Basement Jaxx in Brixton, South London, England, 1993; founded Atlantic Jaxx Records, 1994; signed with XL Recordings, released *Remedy,* 1999; released *Rooty,* 2001, *Kish Kash,* 2003, the compilation *Singles,* 2005, and *Crazy Itch Radio,* 2006; toured United Kingdom, including dates with Robbie Williams, 2006.

Awards: Awards for Best Newcomers and Best Dance Act, Winter Music Conference 2000 (WMC2000) in Miami, FL; Grammy Award, for Best Electronic/Dance Album, 2004.

Addresses: *Record company*—XL, 625 Broadway, 12th Fl., New York 10012, telephone: (212) 886-7500, website: http://www.xlrecordings.com/. *Management*—Andrew Mansi and Mark Pickin, West Management, London, England. Booking for North America—Sam Kirby, Renaissance Entertainment, New York, NY. Booking for other markets—Peter Elliott, Primary Talent, London, England.

success arose because, unlike other techno outfits who focus primarily on drum loops and samples, Buxton and Ratcliffe decided to reintroduce melody, structured songs, and real vocalists onto the world's dance floors.

And while Basement Jaxx's music does resemble other house music imports such as the Chemical Brothers or Fatboy Slim, there nonetheless exists a noticeable difference. "It's music of this moment. Our music is less throwaway," said Buxton in an interview with *Boston Globe* correspondent Christopher Muther, describing the difference between Basement Jaxx's sound and that of other techno-styled music. "For me, music needs to move you, that's what it's all about. That's what we're trying to do."

### A Passion for House Music

Although unrecognized among mainstream audiences until the phenomenal arrival of *Remedy,* the hard-working team had already made a name for themselves behind the scenes. The pair first met in 1993, when Buxton, the son of a vicar in the Anglican Church, was employed by a publicity firm, although what he really wanted to do was make house and garage music. Ratcliffe, who grew up in Holland and Wales, was a student at the University of London and working, like Buxton, outside of the music business in an electronics store, although he had recently begun creating his own jungle and house records in his basement studio.

Not long after their initial meeting, the duo started recording together at Ratcliffe's flat, combining their musical inspirations into a single ideal: to return to the roots of house music. Whereas Ratcliffe gravitated to the deep Latin funk of groups like War and George Duke, Buxton found his inspiration in Chicago house music. This resulted in Basement Jaxx, a mixture of several different styles. In 1994 the pair formed their own label, Atlantic Jaxx Records, and recorded their first two EPs. Although they went unnoticed in England, the recordings attracted recognition from some of their heroes, including DJ legend Tony Humphries.

### Jaxx Night Set in Motion

In addition to receiving complimentary words from other DJs, the pair also earned a reputation for their live performances. A crucial factor in their eventual success, the two held regular "Basement Jaxx" nights at various locales around Brixton. As word spread about the duo, Jaxx night at various small venues became popular attractions, with more than 100 people from all walks of life crammed into dimly lit rooms built to hold just 50 patrons.

A typical show would include Basement Jaxx spinning all types of music, from Whitney Houston and Public Enemy to the duo's own originals. "Posh people, people off the street, drug dealers, everyone came together. The system was booming, and it was really raw. It was wicked," Buxton told Matt Hendrickson of *Rolling Stone.* However, the two decided to quit holding Jaxx nights in the late-1990s, at the peak of the events' popularity. From the beginning, Basement Jaxx had held strong to the ethos: "Check your attitude at the door, and throw your coat on the floor." So, when Jaxx night later became known as the "cool place to go," Buxton and Ratcliffe thought it best to pull the plug. "Before, we could just play the music we wanted. That disappeared," explained Ratcliffe. "Everyone started coming with this attitude of 'You're cool, let's see what you can do.' … We could see it changing. So you have to move on."

Meanwhile, Basement Jaxx had concentrated on recording, too, and in 1995 their club classic "Samba Magic" caught the attention of Virgin Records. After the label picked up the song for distribution, the duo started drawing praise from both the American and British house communities as one of the top production units around. As a result, Basement Jaxx spent much of 1996 remixing songs for several well-known acts such as the Pet Shop Boys, Roger Sanchez, and Lil' Mo Yin Yang. That same year they also released a third EP containing the club favorite "Flylife," which reached the British Top 20 and was one of the most popular dance anthems of the year after the Multiply label re-released the single in 1997. Soon thereafter, the pair released a compilation of their best Atlantic Jaxx efforts that led to offers from several major record companies.

### A Four-star Album

Weighing their long list of options, Buxton and Ratcliffe decided to sign to the independent XL Recordings, with Astralwerks distributing Basement Jaxx's records in the United States. In May of 1999, after the arrival of "Red Alert," Basement Jaxx released *Remedy* in the United Kingdom. In August of that year, the duo's full-length debut arrived in America to rave reviews. *USA Today* listed *Remedy* on its list of the ten best albums of the year, while *Rolling Stone* reviewer Rob Sheffield described Basement Jaxx as "a pair of daft punks whose wholly original 'punk garage' style melds old-school Chicago house with Latin salsa, ragga, jazz discord and anything else that isn't nailed down." Sheffield added, "For these guys, dance music belongs to the true believers, and on *Remedy* they take you to church."

The success of the unique Basement Jaxx sound brought Buxton and Ratcliffe's live act—featuring a live band, dancers, and singers—to fans across the globe, from Japan and Australia to California, New York, and Canada. The duo's popularity continued to escalate, and they scored their second number one *Billboard* Dance Chart hit with "Rendez-Vu." In 2000 Basement Jaxx earned three Brit Award nominations: Best British Album for *Remedy*, Best Dance Act, and Best British Single for "Red Alert." They picked up two awards at the Winter Music Conference 2000 (WMC2000) in Miami, Florida, taking home honors for Best Newcomers and Best Dance Act.

In 2001 Basement Jaxx released its sophomore album, *Rooty*, a name derived from a club night held by the duo. "*Rooty* is an excellent dance record," wrote Jeff Magill in the *News Letter*, "every track makes you want to catapult onto a dance-floor or simply close your eyes to be transported to a state of bliss." *Rooty* reached number five on the Top Electronic Albums chart, and both "Romeo" and "Where's Your Head At" climbed the Hot Dance Music/Club Play charts. In 2003 Basement Jaxx followed with *Kish Kash*, featuring guest appearances by punk rocker Siouxsie Sioux, JC Chasez (from NSYNC), and rapper Dizzee Rascal. While *All Music Guide*'s John Bush believed the album less effective than the duo's earlier efforts, he nonetheless wrote, "Still, *Kish Kash* may be the best dance record of

2003." Burton and Ratcliffe received a Grammy Award for Best Electronic/Dance Album, for *Kish Kash.*

In 2005 Basement Jaxx released the compilation *Singles*, a stop-gap between albums that included two new tracks. "Even if mainstream dance music is on the ropes," Stephen Dalton wrote in the London *Times*, "Basement Jaxx are making sure it does not go down without a fight." In 2006 the duo issued *Crazy Itch Radio*, and by November the album had risen to number four on the Electronic Albums chart. "We thought we might go off in a totally different direction with this album," Felix Buxton told Si Hawkins in the London *Evening Standard*, "but we didn't. We just went in and did the usual stuff really. Good solid music, with quirky bits." Reviewers singled out "Take Me Back to Your House," while "Hush Boy" broke into the European Hot 100.

In 2006 Basement Jaxx toured widely, supporting Robbie Williams in a number of venues and announcing a tour of the United Kingdom in November. The duo have also continued to remix other artists' work, including Missy Elliot's "4 My People" and Justin Timberlake's "Like I Love You." As recording artists, live performers, and contributors to the work of their peers, Basement Jaxx have left a deep impression on the contemporary music scene. "They are to house what Miles Davis is to jazz, what Chuck Berry is to rock, what Public Enemy is to rap," wrote Andy Kellman in *All Music Guide.*

## Selected discography

"Red Alert" (maxi single), XL/Astralwerks, 1999.
*Remedy*, XL/Astralwerks, 1999.
"Bingo Bango" (single), XL, 2000.
*Rooty*, Astralwerks, 2001.
*Kish Kash*, Astralwerks, 2003.
*Singles*, XL, 2005.
*Crazy Itch Radio*, XL, 2006.

## Sources

### Periodicals

*Atlanta Journal-Constitution,* August 5, 1999; December 26, 1999.
*Billboard,* May 29, 1999; July 3, 1999; August 14, 1999; October 9, 1999; October 30, 1999; November 6, 1999; January 1, 2000; February 12, 2000; March 4, 2000; March 18, 2000.
*Boston Globe,* September 10, 1999; September 16, 1999.
*Evening Standard* (London, England), September 4, 2006.
*Los Angeles Times,* June 27, 1999; October 4, 1999; December 12, 1999; January 2, 2000.
*Melody Maker,* July 10, 1999; July 24, 1999; October 23, 1999.
*News Letter* (Belfast, Northern Ireland), June 29, 2001.
*Rolling Stone,* August 19, 1999; September 22, 1999; December 16-23, 1999.
*Times* (London, England), August 6, 2004.

*USA Today,* August 31, 1999; December 28, 1999.
*Village Voice,* March 2, 1999; August 3, 1999.
*Washington Post,* August 22, 1999; October 24, 1999.

## Online

"Basement Jaxx," *All Music Guide,* http://www.allmusic.com/ (October 9, 2006).

"Basement Jaxx," *Contact Music,* http://www.contactmusic.com/ (October 9, 2006).

Basement Jaxx at Astralwerks, http://www.astralwerks.com/ basementjaxx/ (May 17, 2000).

Sonicnet.com, http://www.sonicnet.com (May 17, 2000).

*—Laura Hightower and Ronnie Lankford*

# Cameo

Rhythm and blues group

© S.I.N./CORBIS

The R&B vocal group Cameo broke through to pop chart success with several singles in the 1980s, most notably the top-ten hit "Word Up!" in 1986. Their list of top-level R&B hits is somewhat longer. But listeners who know Cameo only through a group of hit singles are missing the qualities that have made them among the most durable African-American vocal groups of the modern era. Cameo has remained among the last active survivors of the funk movement of the 1970s because they have not only kept up with the times musically but also, for many years, have tended to anticipate major trends. They were among the first African-American acts to make Atlanta, Georgia, their headquarters, and songwriter and frequent lead vocalist Larry Blackmon has shown a knack for putting various strands of contemporary black music together in original and entertaining ways.

At the core of Cameo lie three musicians: Blackmon, Tomi Jenkins, and Nathan Leftnant. In performance the group has varied in size from those three to as many as 13 members, with rotating groups of musicians added as necessary to fulfill the requirements of particular tours or of the styles current at a particular point in time. The founder and longtime creative sparkplug of the group is Blackmon, who came from New York City's Harlem neighborhood and grew up near the famed Apollo Theater. Starting at age four, he was taken to the Apollo by an aunt and uncle, and he kept going on his own. He saw, as he told Geoffrey Himes of the *Washington Post,* "everyone from Otis Redding to King Curtis, Bill Cosby to Sam Cooke, Pigmeat Markham, Jackie Wilson, Flip Wilson, Marvin Gaye, even the Jackson 5 when they were babies. It gave me a real sense of history and the importance of keeping that tradition going."

Another influence on Blackmon, one that showed up in the complex arrangements of many Cameo songs, was classical music; he studied at New York's Julliard School. Working as a tailor by day and frequenting New York clubs at night, Blackmon was inspired by the Ohio Players and other horn-heavy funk bands of the early 1970s to create a group of his own in 1974. At first the group was called the New York City Players, but soon they changed their name to Cameo; the new name referred to the cameo-style (raised-relief portrait) jewelry that was popular in urban communities at the time, often bearing images of African figures. With a full horn section in action, the group numbered 13 players at its largest, and after a few years of playing New York dance clubs, they were signed in 1976 to the Chocolate City label, a subsidiary of the larger urban independent label Casablanca.

## Love That Funk

At this point, just before the rise of the lush, mechanical disco style, funk music with a big beat and a slightly skewed attitude was at a creative high-water mark,

**For the Record . . .**

Formed in 1974 as New York City Players in New York, NY; changed name to Cameo; signed to Chocolate City label, 1976; released debut LP, *Cardiac Arrest*, 1977; moved to Atlanta, GA, 1982; formed and recorded for Atlanta Artists label; leader Larry Blackmon became artists-and-repertoire executive at Warner Brothers label, 1992–94; group signed to Reprise subsidiary, 1992; recorded for Intersound and other labels, continued to tour, 1990s–2000s.

Addresses: *Booking*—Universal Attractions, 145 West 57th St., 15th Fl., New York, NY 10019. *Record company*—Polygram Records, c/o Universal Music Group, 2220 Colorado Ave., Santa Monica, CA 90404.

thanks to the efforts of the related Parliament and Funkadelic groups, for whom Cameo sometimes opened while on tour. The stage antics of classic funk acts like Bootsy Collins would shape Blackmon's own emerging stage personality; his trademark over the next three decades of touring would be a bright red codpiece that he tried several times to retire but was consistently forced by popular demand to continue wearing. Cameo released their debut LP, *Cardiac Arrest,* in 1977. Three singles from the album landed on *Billboard* magazine's R&B chart, and when Blackmon heard the first one, "Rigor Mortis," on the radio at the tailor shop where he was still working, he put down the chalk with which he had just marked the cuffs of a customer's jacket for alteration, and walked out, never to return.

With disco in full flower in the late 1970s, Cameo still managed to swim against the tide, mixing ballads with uptempo numbers. They scored several more R&B top-ten hits, including "Sparkle" (1979), from the album *Secret Omen.* Two decades later Alex Henderson of the *All Music Guide* praised the album's "sweaty, gutsy, horn-powered funk" and opined that the album was "among Cameo's most essential releases." Cameo albums such as *Knights of the Sound Table* (1981) remained moderate hitmakers ("Freaky Dancing" and "Flirt" were urban dance-club staples of the early 1980s), but Blackmon was ready for a change. He found it by relocating Cameo from New York to Atlanta in 1982. Blackmon was ahead of the curve not only musically but also socially—a large migration of African Americans southward accelerated over the course of the 1980s and 1990s. "[W]e made the bold move, and subsequently made [Atlanta] a capital of black music," he explained to the *Washington Post.* "[I] find the North

and South have switched roles. If I walk into an elevator in a northern city with people of a different color, they jump back three feet; I don't find that so much down here. If you spend a lot of days on the road like we do, you want to be able to relax when you get home."

## Masters of Fun

Cameo set up its own label, Atlanta Artists, and landed a distribution deal with the large Polygram conglomerate. With Cameo's sound revamped to take advantage of 1980s synthesizer technology but not losing sight of its funkier roots, Blackmon entered a creative songwriting period. It did not take long for the Atlanta move to begin to pay off. "She's Strange," the title track of a 1984 album, was one of the first singles from outside the rap sphere to feature rapped passages; the song topped R&B charts and cracked the pop top 50. The title track of 1985's *Single Life* album drew on the style of Minneapolis-based funk-rock fusion star Prince, and Blackmon took to describing Cameo's style as "Black Rock." *Single Life* reached the number two spot on the *Billboard* R&B chart, and Cameo's popularity built steadily.

Cameo finally hit the big time in 1986 with "Word Up!," again the title track of the album on which it appeared. Blackmon, using an exaggerated version of his usual nasal singing voice, collected a sequence of stock dance-floor song phrases ("with your hands in the air like you just don't care") and deployed them over a ferocious funk beat in such a way that they landed on the then-new slang phrase of the song's title (it meant "that's right"). The song topped R&B charts, reached high levels on pop charts, and remained a staple of party and wedding DJ dance mixes two decades later. For a year or so, Blackmon was a major star, and newspapers reported on attention-getting antics like an episode in which he allegedly had the roof of his limousine raised to accommodate his growing Afro. The *Word Up!* album spawned another major hit, "Candy."

Cameo never quite matched that album's level of success again, although the albums *Machismo* (1988), *Real Men Wear Black* (1990), and *Emotional Violence* (1992) continued to spawn moderate urban hits. Blackmon thought about making the usual career move behind the scenes in the music industry, and he did production work for jazz trumpeter Miles Davis on some of the recordings the jazzman released near the end of his life. From 1992 to 1994, Blackmon worked as a vice president for artists and repertoire at the Warner Brothers label.

His heart remained in performing, however. Davis pointed to the group's strengths as a live act when he wrote in his autobiography (as quoted in the *Post*) that "I'm still learning every day. I learn things from Prince and Cameo. For example, I like the way Cameo does their live shows. The live performances start slow, but you have to watch the middle of their concerts because that's where their [stuff] starts picking up unbelievable speed and just flies on out from there."

### Lasting Influence

With nearly 20 years of high-quality music-making behind them, Cameo had amassed several generations of fans, and they garnered new ones when hip-hop artists began sampling their recordings extensively. Cameo returned to the road in the mid-1990s, releasing new albums every few years, and as of mid-2000 they were still a major concert draw; a spate of compilations of their ever-infectious singles appeared in the early 2000s. Tributes ranged beyond hip-hop as the heavy-rock group Korn recorded a cover version of "Word Up." "Korn? Who would have thought?" Blackmon mused to Jordan Zivitz of the *Montreal Gazette*. "But to go and do our song says that they're either very inspired, or—well, were looking for things to do. Either way, the greatest form of flattery is imitation, and we get that all the time."

## Selected discography

*Cardiac Arrest,* Chocolate City, 1977.
*We All Know Who We Are,* Chocolate City, 1978.
*Secret Omen,* Chocolate City, 1979.
*Ugly Ego,* Chocolate City, 1979.
*Cameosis,* Chocolate City, 1980.
*Feel Me,* Chocolate City, 1980.
*Knights of the Sound Table,* Chocolate City, 1981.
*Alligator Woman,* Atlanta Artists, 1982.
*Style,* Atlanta Artists, 1983.
*She's Strange,* Atlanta Artists, 1984.
*Single Life,* Atlanta Artists, 1985.
*Word Up!,* Atlanta Artists, 1986.
*Machismo,* Atlanta Artists, 1988.
*Real Men Wear Black,* Atlanta Artists, 1990.
*Emotional Violence,* Reprise, 1992.
*Money,* Warner Bros., 1992.

*In the Face of Funk,* Way 2 Funky, 1994.
*Nasty,* Intersound, 1996.
*Ballads Collection,* Polygram, 1998.
*Sexy Sweet Thing,* Universal, 2000.
*20th Century Masters—The Millennium Collection: The Best of Cameo,* Mercury, 2001.
*Anthology,* Mercury, 2002.
*Best of Cameo,* Collectables, 2004.
*Gold,* Mercury, 2005.
*The Definitive Collection,* Mercury, 2006.

## Sources

### Books

George-Warren, Holly, and Patricia Romanowski, eds., *The Rolling Stone Encyclopedia of Rock & Roll,* 3rd ed., Fireside, 2001.
Slonimsky, Nicolas, editor emeritus, *Baker's Biographical Dictionary of Music and Musicians,* Schirmer, 2001.

### Periodicals

*Billboard,* March 7, 1992, p. 12.
*Detroit News,* August 21, 2002.
*Gazette* (Montreal, Canada), September 16, 2004, p. D1.
*Herald* (Sydney, Australia), July 9, 1987.
*Milwaukee Journal Sentinel,* November 17, 2000, p. 20E.
*New York Times,* May 17, 1987, p. 65.
*People,* May 28, 1984, p. 31; October 31, 1988, p. 26; July 16, 1990, p. 15.
*Washington Post,* March 10, 1995, p. N13; November 29, 1996, p. N15.

### Online

"Cameo," All Music Guide, http://www.allmusic.com (November 8, 2006).
"Freaky Forever," Montreal Mirror, http://www.montrealmirror.com/2004/091604/music1.html (November 8, 2006).
"Word Up: Cameo Is Still Kicking," *Ottawa Sun,* http://jam.canoe.ca/Music/Artists/C/Cameo/2005/01/12/896053.html (November 8, 2006).

—James M. Manheim

# Beth Carvalho

## Singer

Having been born and raised in the middle-class neighborhoods on the south side of Rio de Janeiro, it would seem unlikely that Beth Carvalho would grow up to become one of Brazil's most famous and well-loved samba performers. But for more than 30 years, Carvalho has been that person. She fell in love at an early age with the spirit, passion, and style represented by the traditional samba performers and dedicated her career to making it more accessible. Her dedication and talent have made her one of Brazil's most valued and acclaimed musical celebrities. Not only has she introduced millions of people to the sound of samba, but she has just as generously worked for the social justice in a country with a long history of inequality.

Born Elizabeth Santos Leal de Carvalho on May 5, 1946, in Rio de Janeiro, Brazil, Carvalho's father was a lawyer with liberal political ideals that put him under a great deal of stress during the years of Brazilian dictatorship. He and his wife appreciated music of many different styles and introduced Carvalho to classical music as well as the more homegrown Brazilian music performed at *serestas* (backyard serenades) and the samba school rehearsals.

Around age seven, Carvalho started attending school at the Brazilian Academy of Music. There she learned how to play guitar and became quite good at it. She briefly attended Rio University to study psychology, but the lure of performing was too much and she started a career in music. At that time, Brazil was in the midst of a bossa nova craze. Carvalho sang with a bossa nova group called Conjunto 3-D. Her first recorded single was "Por Quem Morrer De Amor," a famous bossa nova tune.

### Committed to Samba

In 1968, she competed in the III Festival Internacional da Cancao (International Song Festival). She placed third with her version of the song "Andanca." She recorded her first album, *Andanca,* the following year and launched her career as one of Brazil's most successful singers. Even though bossa nova was extremely popular at the time, she found that she was drawn to samba music, and by 1971 she had committed herself to that style. That year found her recording the song "Rio Grande Do Sul Festo Do Preto Forro," a samba-enredo, which was performed by the samba school Unidos de Sao Carlos during the annual carnival festivities.

That same year her song "So Quero Ver" became a huge hit. When she saw that it was being sung and performed throughout the poor areas of the city in "rodas de samba," informal groups singing songs in a form of competition, she decided that she would begin recording her music in a more casual manner. In this way, she felt she would be paying homage to the communities that birthed and formed this style of music. She explained to the *Christian Science Monitor,* "Everybody knows the word 'samba.' But I think that samba itself, its essence, is not known, even in Brazil. Samba isn't just a rhythm; it's a … resistance." She explained further that samba's origins stem from a group of people who are self-trained and usually very poor.

In 1974 she released the album *Pra Seu Governo,* which contained the hit song "1800 Colinas." The song was not only popular in Brazil but also in France where she performed in support of the album. In 1977, she had two hit songs, "Saco do Feijao" and "Olho Por Olho." Their popularity led to more than 400,000 sales of her album *Nos Botequins Da Vida.* The following year she had another hit song with "Vou Festejar," from her album *De Pe No Chao.* Then in 1979, she released what would become her biggest hit ever, "Coisinha Do Pai," from the album *Beth Carvalho No Pagode.* Other hit songs from that album included "Pedi Ao Ceu" and "Tem Nada Nao," but nothing topped "Coisinha Do Pai." In 1997, the song would be included along with a selection of music sent on the Mars Pathfinder mission.

In 1987, she released the album *Beth Carvalho Ao Vivo No Festival de Montreaux,* which was recorded at her performance at the Montreaux Festival in Switzerland. Her other live albums include *Ao Vivo No Olympia* (1991) and *Pagode de Mesa Ao Vivo* (1999).

## For the Record . . .

Born on May 5, 1946, in Rio de Janeiro, Brazil. *Education:* Attended Brazilian Academy of Music; attended Rio University.

Won TV talent competition, 1965; finished third place, III Festival Internacional da Cancao, 1968; won her first Carnival competition, 1971; released *Pra Seu Governo,* 1974; released *Nos Botequins Da Vida,* 1977; released *De Pe No Chao,* 1978; released *Beth Carvalho No Pagode,* 1979; released live album *Pagode de Mesa,* 1999; headlined 12th annual Brazilian Summer Festival, Los Angeles, CA, 2005.

Awards: Premio Sharp Award (defunct music award equivalent to Brazilian Grammy), six years; TIM (current equivalent to Brazilian Grammy), for *Beth Carvalho Canta Nelson Cavaquinho,* 2003; Latin Grammy Award, Best Samba Album for *Beth Carvalho A Madrinha do Samba: Ao Vivo,* 2006.

Addresses: *Management*—Afonso Carvalho, phone: 55-21-7817-7102. *Website*—Beth Carvalho Official Website, http://www.bethcarvalho.com.br/.

## Discovering the Next Generation

With her career as the godmother of samba firmly established, the late 1970s saw Carvalho working to bring outstanding samba artists to public attention. She explained her passion for finding new talent to John Wright of the *Las Vegas Review,* "I have the attributes of a discoverer…. I discover and rescue. That's my objective…. The composers and musicians I've discovered are the new generation of samba." The list of composers and artists that she has discovered include singer Luiz Carlos da Vila, singer and composer Jorge Aragao (who composed her 1978 hit song "Vou Festejar"), and composer and musician Arlindo Cruz. Carvalho has also distinguished herself as a composer with the song "Cancao de Esperar Nenem," from her 1980 album *Sentimento Brasileiro.*

Throughout the years Carvalho has been intimately involved in the celebrations and performances surrounding Rio de Janeiro's world famous carnival events. In 1971, her song for the samba school Unidos de Sao Carlos won the prestigious award for best vocalist. Soon afterward she joined the Mangueira Samba School and has remained a member for more than thirty years. In 1984, to honor her contributions to samba and carnival, the samba school Unidos do Cabucu chose as their song to perform during competition "Beth Carvalho, a Enamorada Do Samba."

In Brazil she is known as the "Godmother of Samba" and the "Queen of Carnival," namesakes that she has earned from her years of dedication to the art forms born of Brazil's unique cultural mix. She has used her influence as one of Brazil's most prized performers to bring injustice to light and support causes that serve the underdog. Her energetic presence shines and entertains as she continues to tour and perform. In 2005 she headlined for the 12th Annual Brazilian Summer Festival in Los Angeles, California. Don Heckman who reviewed the show for the *Los Angeles Times* described her performance, "Carvalho has been a star of Brazilian music for 40 years, but she performed with the dynamic energy of a new arrival."

## Selected discography

*Andanca,* Odeon, 1969.
*Canto Por Um Novo Dia,* Tapecar, 1973.
*Pra Seu Governo,* Tapecar, 1974.
*Pandeiro e Viola,* Tapecar, 1975.
*Mundo Melhor,* RCA, 1976.
*Nos Botequins da Vida,* RCA, 1977.
*De Pe No Chao,* RCA, 1978.
*Beth Carvalho No Pogode,* RCA, 1979.
*Sentimento Brasileiro,* RCA, 1980.
*Na Fonte,* RCA, 1981.
*Traco de Uniao,* RCA, 1982.
*Suor No Rosto,* RCA, 1983.
*Coracao Feliz,* RCA, 1984.
*Das Bencaos Que Virao Com os Novos Amanhas,* RCA, 1985.
*Beth,* RCA, 1986.
*Beth Carvalho Ao Vivo (Montreaux),* RCA, 1987.
*Almo do Brasil,* Polygram, 1988.
*Saudades da Guanabara,* Polygram, 1989.
*Interprete,* Polygram, 1991.
*Ao Vivo no Olympia,* Som Livre, 1991.
*Perolas: 25 Anos de Samba,* Som Livre, 1992.
*Beth Carvalho Canto o Samba de Sao Paulo,* Velas, 1993.
*Brasileira da Gema,* Polygram, 1996.
*Perolas do Pagode,* Globo/Polydor, 1998.
*Pagode de Mesa Ao Vivo,* Universal Music, 1999.
*Pagode de Mesa Ao Vivo 2,* Universal Music, 2000.
*Nome Sagrado: Beth Carvalho Canta Nelson Cavaquinho,* Jam, 2001.
*Beth Carvalho Canta Cartola,* BMG, 2003.
*Beth Carvalho A Madrinha do Samba: Ao Vivo,* Indie, 2004.

## Sources

### Periodicals

*Christian Science Monitor,* October 25, 1990, p. 10.
*Las Vegas Review,* March 19, 1993, p. 15d.
*Los Angeles Times,* June 28, 2005, p. E.2.

## Online

"Beth Carvalho," *All Music Guide,* http://www.allmusicguide. com (October 29, 2006).

"Brazil's Emissary of Samba," *Brazzil Magazine,* http://www. brazzil.com/content/view/9295/79/ (November 5, 2006).

"Mrs. Samba," *Brazzil,* http://www.brazzil.com/mussep95. htm (November 6, 2006).

*—Eve Hermann*

# The Church

Rock group

Critics' descriptions of the Church's sound have varied with the band's ever-changing albums, but the group's distinctive style and ambience remain a constant. The group was formed in Sydney, Australia, in 1980 and over the years has garnered international attention. "Once upon a time," vocalist Steve Kilbey recalled in *Raygun,* "we were four young fellows starting a band in Sydney in 1980, and we all ate the same things, and looked the same way, and wore the same clothes."

Those four young fellows—Kilbey, guitarists Marty Willson-Piper and Peter Koppes, and drummer Richard Ploog—made up the Church's original lineup. The year following their formation, the band released *Of Skins and Heart,* their debut album on Australia's Parlophone Records, featuring the single "The Unguarded Moment." In 1982 they landed a deal in the United States with Capitol Records and released *The Church,* which included most of the cuts from their first Australian release plus three other songs from a double-45 single.

The Church stopped making records for Capitol after their self-titled U.S. debut; instead they continued to produce albums in Australia, including 1982's *Blurred*

Paul Natkin/Photo Reserve, Inc.

## For the Record . . .

Members include **Jay Dee Daugherty** (member 1988-93), drums; **Steve Kilbey**, vocals, bass guitar; **Peter Koppes** (left group 1993; rejoined 1996), guitar; **Richard Ploog** (member, 1980-88), drums; **Tim Powles** (joined 1996), drums; **Marty Willson-Piper**, guitar.

Band formed in Sydney, Australia, 1980; released first album, *Of Skins and Heart,* in Australia on Parlophone Records, 1981; released self-titled debut album in U.S. on Capitol label, 1982; recorded for Carrere Records in Australia, 1982-83, and Warner Bros. in the U.S., 1984-86; signed with Arista Records, 1987; Willson-Piper and Kilbey released first album as a duo, 1994; released *Uninvited, Like the Clouds* and embarked on acoustic tour, 2006.Member 1988–93.Left group, 1993.Member 1980–88.

Addresses: *Record company*—Cooking Vinyl USA LLC, P.O. Box 246, Huntingtion, NY 11743, e-mail—infousa@cookingvinyl.com.

*Crusade,* with critically acclaimed tunes like "I'm Almost with You" and "Come Up and See Me," and 1983's *Seance,* featuring the tracks "Travel by Thought," "Fly," and "Dropping Names." Then, in 1984, the Church signed a deal with Warner Brothers and released their next album in the United States, *Remote Luxury.* With "Constant in Opal," the hit single and video from the album, they started developing a dedicated cult following in the States.

That same year, the band went into the studio with producer Peter Walsh to record *Heyday,* which landed in record stores two years later. The Church moved toward stronger and catchier melodies with songs like "Tristesse" and "Myrrh."

Though the Church's following had built steadily, they had yet to attain hit status or gain widespread recognition in the United States. They opted to switch record labels once again, and in 1987 inked a deal with Arista. In the meantime, Kilbey, Willson-Piper, and Koppes each signed solo deals with Rykodisc and began working on their own material.

Determined to promote the Church, Arista suggested that producers Greg Ladanyi and Waddy Wachtel work with them on their next album. A year later, Starfish got

them the attention they were waiting for. "*Starfish* is the best in a long line of great Church hymnals," wrote a *Rolling Stone* contributor, "thanks to the band's refined studio poise and a bumper crop of jangle-and-strum jewels like 'Blood Money,' 'Reptile,' and Marty Willson-Piper's 'Spark.'" In addition, their hit single "Under the Milky Way" received significant radio airplay, and the Church made their first major tour of the United States. Arista re-released the band's entire back catalog that same year, and the band developed a whole new fan base. The song also became a mainstay of television and film soundtracks meant to evoke the quintessential sound of the 1980s. Kilbey said in an interview for Michigan's *Royal Oak Daily Tribune* that the inspiration for "Under the Milky Way" came to him in a flash, recalling that the song "just came falling out of the air." The subsequent exposure of the song in the film *Donnie Darko* and *The O.C.* even earned Kilbey fans in his own household. "The exposure has helped us gain interest from newer people," he told the *Royal Oak* newspaper. "My 15-year-old twin girls are now really interested in what I do. They tell me, 'Hey, dad, you're alright. You're in 'The O.C.' You're in a great band!'"

After touring to support the album, the Church went back into the studio to work on their next album, *Gold Afternoon Fix.* When they finished recording, they booted drummer Richard Ploog out of the band and recruited Jay Dee Daugherty to replace him. *Gold Afternoon Fix,* released in 1990, featured the singles "Metropolis" and "You're Still Beautiful," but failed to live up to the popularity of *Starfish.* However, the band's goals didn't necessarily include getting the top spots on the charts. "I feel that it's really important to just write songs without worrying whether it's going to be a hit or not," Willson-Piper noted in the band's Arista Records press biography. Chris Mundy, writing in *Rolling Stone,* described *Gold Afternoon Fix* as "the Church's invitation to visit its murky, ethereal world. It's an invitation that should not be refused."

As a conceptual lyric writer, Kilbey has often been asked to define the songs on the Church's albums, and *Gold Afternoon Fix* stimulated the question with cuts like "Pharaoh," "Terra Nova Cain," and "Russian Autumn Heart." "Simple pleasure is the most important thing," Kilbey stated in *Musician.*

More than any other ingredient, the chemistry existing between band members seems to have sparked the Church's creative output. Kilbey, Willson-Piper, and Koppes all had their solo projects to express their individual creativity, so when the band came together, they concentrated on unifying their ideas. In 1992 they produced *Priest=Aura,* featuring the single "Ripple." "It was the classic, introspective, ambiguous Church album," Willson-Piper said in the *Boston Phoenix.* Moving away from the more commercial sound of their last two albums, the Church seemed to head in a darker direction with *Priest=Aura.* "Set against this elegant soundscape, not so quiet storms add a glint of savagery, bringing moments of drama and beauty to stately songs," proclaimed Ira Robbins in a *Rolling Stone* review of the album.

The Church toured worldwide once again, with a last stop on their home turf in Australia. Just hours before their tour of Australia began, Koppes announced his intention to leave the band. He agreed to finish the tour, but quit as soon as they completed their last set. Kilbey and Willson-Piper dismissed Jay Dee Daugherty not long after Koppes's departure. "We weren't sure if the band was going to exist anymore," Willson-Piper said in the band's press biography. "I figured we would just know if and when the time was right to get back into the studio."

In the middle of 1993, Willson-Piper left his home in Stockholm to join Kilbey in Australia, and the two of them started working on the next Church album. "Originally, we were worried about the chemistry being different after all that time together as a four-man band," Willson-Piper explained in their press biography. "So we just started messing about together in the studio. Once we recorded "Lost My Touch" we knew everything was going to fall into place." *Sometime Anywhere*—written, recorded, and mixed in two months during the summer of 1993 and released in 1994— became the first Church album produced by the two remaining members.

"Two Places at Once," the first single from the album, reflected a true collaborative effort by Willson-Piper and Kilbey. After they had cowritten the music for the song, they each penned separate lyrics and then decided to combine the two, with each member singing his own version until the end of the song, when the two would combine. *Pulse!* contributor Scott Schinder considered the material on *Sometime Anywhere* to be "denser, darker territory" than the band's earlier releases, and Brian Q. Newcomb commented in the *Riverfront Times* that in its new incarnation, the Church was still aiming to deliver "contemporary, intelligent rock."

The group re-formed in 1996 with the return of Koppes and the addition of drummer Tim Powles, and by the middle of the next decade, the Church had released material that continued to display their creative vitality.

The Church's 2006 tour followed the release of one of their strongest albums since their first decade. *Uninvited, Like the Clouds* returned the group to its neo-psychedelic heyday without a whiff of nostalgia. Instead, the songs sounded fresh and contemporary, beginning with the kickoff track "Block." Kilbey took particular pride in the song, telling the *Royal Oak Daily Tribune*, "All the songs feature the same thematic elements that have concerned me for a long time, including space, time, dreams and surrealism."

Kilbey has said he believes that the band's longevity is due to "the promise of what we could do with the music, which is what kept us together at first and keeps bringing us together to make good music."

## Selected discography

*Of Skins and Heart,* Parlophone, 1981; reissued, Arista, 1988.
*The Church,* Capitol, 1982.
*The Blurred Crusade,* Carrere, 1982; reissued, Arista, 1988.
*Seance,* Carrere, 1983; reissued, Arista, 1988.
*Remote Luxury,* Warner Bros., 1984, reissued, Arista, 1988.
*Heyday,* Warner Bros., 1986; reissued, Arista, 1988.
*Starfish,* Arista, 1988.
*Gold Afternoon Fix,* Arista, 1990.
*Priest=Aura,* Arista, 1992.
*Sometime Anywhere,* Arista, 1994.
*Magician Among the Spirits,* Griffin Music, 1996.
*Hologram of Baal,* Thirsty Ear, 1998.
*A Box of Birds,* Thirsty Ear, 1999.
*Under the Milky Way: The Best of the Church,* Buddha, 2000.
*After Everything Now This,* Thirsty Ear, 2002.
*Parallel Universe,* Thirsty Ear, 2002.
*Forget Yourself,* Cooking Vinyl, 2003.
*El Momento Descuidado,* Liberation Blue, 2005.
*Uninvited, Like the Clouds,* Cooking Vinyl, 2006.

## Sources

### Books

*The Trouser Press Record Guide,* Ira A. Robbins, editor, Collier Books, 1991.

### Periodicals

*Billboard,* November 10, 1984; March 5, 1988; April 23, 1988.
*Boston Phoenix,* May 20, 1994.
*Flagpole,* May 11, 1994.
*Honey,* May 1994.
*Melody Maker,* February 13, 1982; July 10, 1982; August 7, 1982; December 15, 1984; April 6, 1985; May 31, 1986; March 12, 1988; March 19, 1988; April 23, 1988; March 24, 1990; May 19, 1990.
*Musician,* October 1988, September 1990.
*Pulse!,* July 1994.
*Raygun,* June 1994.
*Riverfront Times,* June 1, 1994.
*Rolling Stone,* April 21, 1988; May 19, 1988; December 15, 1988; May 17, 1990; April 16, 1992.
*Royal Oak Daily Tribune* (Michigan), Aug. 11, 2006.
*Scene,* May 19, 1994.
*Variety,* June 22, 1988; June 20, 1990.

Additional information for this profile was obtained from Arista Records publicity materials, 1994.

—*Sonya Shelton and Bruce Walker*

# Coope, Boyes & Simpson

## Vocal group

The British trio of Coope, Boyes & Simpson has brought an originality of content and a new spirit of social and political commitment to the art of unaccompanied vocal harmony. Technically, the group amazes audiences and wins critical raves for its intricate trio arrangements, and, like other a cappella groups around the world, they have sung their share of traditional material. More often, however, Coope, Boyes & Simpson apply their harmonies to original songs about historical events and about life in modern England, focusing on war and on the lives of working people. Forging an entirely distinctive sound themselves, they have also been active as collaborators with other musicians, both in England and abroad.

Barry Coope, Jim Boyes, and Lester Simpson were all working consistently as musicians in Northern England's folk scene in the late 1980s, and their paths occasionally crossed. Boyes performed with a group called Swan Arcade that sometimes joined up with another group, Blue Murder, which included British folk pioneers Norma Waterson and Martin Carthy. Blue Murder would later grow to include Coope, Boyes & Simpson as a trio. Boyes also performed with Simpson in a vocal harmony group called Tup and in the Irish trio band Ramsbottom, which signed Coope as a keyboardist after Boyes left the group. In 1990, when all three musicians found themselves temporarily unattached, it made sense to singer John Tams to bring them together. "It was luck," Boyes told Vic Smith of *Folk Roots.* "When you are singing with other people that you are not related to, it's a matter of great fortune to find people that you can sing with. We knew instantly that this was going to work."

All three members combined a love of harmony singing with an appreciation for the seriousness of traditional folk songs, such as sea shanties, that addressed the life of trouble that England's poor had faced all through history. Coope and Boyes grew up singing hymns in Methodist churches, and Simpson had sung in an Anglican church. All three also soaked up influences from African-American gospel and soul music. By the time Coope, Boyes & Simpson began touring and recording in 1993, they had developed a unique harmony style, one that John L. Walters of the *Guardian* described as "in the folk-country tradition, but with a twist that mirrors the barbed lyrics, a wide pitch range, and thrilling bass sonorities swapped between all three." The group gained exposure with two appearances on BBC Radio; one was on the widely heard series *Kershaw Comes Home* and featured new songs specially commissioned for the program.

Those "barbed lyrics" marked another innovative contribution on the trio's part. Although a cappella singing in both England and America was strongly associated with traditional or at least old-fashioned material, Coope, Boyes & Simpson wrote most of their own songs. "It's strange, when we first started, and we hadn't recorded any traditional material, only our own songs," Boyes told Chris Nickson of *Sing Out!* "But we were still advertised as traditional." In fact, the group showed an early ability to create music tailored to specific events. In 1994 they were commissioned to write songs for a concert at Passendale Church in Belgium to commemorate the three Battles of Passchendaele ("Passschendaele" is an older spelling of the town's name, Passendale) in 1917, during World War I. Almost 600,000 soldiers lost their lives in a battle that lasted a little more than three months. The concert turned into an album, *We're Here Because We're Here,* recorded with Belgian musicians Willem Vermandere and Norbert Detaeye.

Later Coope, Boyes & Simpson would record other material related to Passendale and to the antiwar cause more generally. With another Belgian group, the octet Panta Rhei, they recorded an original song cycle, the *Passchendaele Suite,* in 1996, and they became involved with an annual peace concert held in the area. But they also followed other musical avenues. After another album of mostly original material, 1996's *Falling Slowly,* they turned to traditional British folk music with *Hindsight* in 1998. Critics quoted on the group's website described "the compelling unity of their voices and the enchantment of their adventurous chords" (*The Folk Diary*), performances "never short of ear boggling" (*Surrey Folk News*), and "an object lesson in the art of harmony singing" (*Shreds and Patches*).

In 1998, the group released the Christmas album *A Garland of Carols,* which was composed of regional

## For the Record . . .

**M**embers include **Jim Boyes**, vocals; **Barry Coope**, vocals; **Lester Simpson**, vocals.

A cappella folk vocal trio; formed 1990 in Sheffield, England; signed to No Masters recording cooperative; released debut album *Funny Old World,* 1993; released *Falling Slowly,* 1996; toured Belgium; recorded (with Belgian octet Panta Rhei) *Passchendaele Suite,* 1996; recorded other music based on experiences of World War I; released *A Garland of Carols,* 1998; released *Where You Belong,* 1999; (with Blue Murder) released *No One Stands Alone,* 2002; released *Fire and Sleet and Candlelight,* 2003; released *Triple Echo,* 2005; released *Voices at the Door: Midwinter Songs & Carols,* 2006.

Addresses: *Record company*—No Masters, 78 Moorgate Rd., Rotherham, S60 2AY, UK, phone: 44-0-1709-375063, fax: 44-0-1709-327164, website: http://www.nomasters.co.uk. *Website*—Coope, Boyes & Simpson Official Website: http://www.coopeboyesandsimpson.co.uk/

of their music, whether traditional or not. They recorded for the No Masters label, a cooperative organization that grew out of a period of labor agitation in Britain associated with a bitter miners' strike in the 1980s. The group's war songs also led to an association with antiwar activities. "The more things you find out, the more you're dragged back to the same area," Boyes observed to Nickson. "For most families [in Europe], there are World War I connections: great uncles and great grandfathers who fought in the war. It's because of that we've continued with it, and we continue to be invited back to do even more."

Coope, Boyes & Simpson shifted gears once again in 2005 with *Triple Echo,* the closest they had come to a traditional, archival British folk release. The album featured songs collected by three classical composers who also worked as folklorists in the early 20th century: Ralph Vaughan Williams, Percy Grainger, and George Butterworth. *Sing Out!* called the trio "remarkable singers with a chilling blend" who "keep these unaccompanied songs interesting with inventive arrangements, and a vocal energy that seems effortless." With a new album of seasonal music, *Voices at the Door,* appearing at the end of 2006, Coope, Boyes & Simpson were continuing to broaden both their audience and musical reach.

folk Christmas songs. The following year they joined with the Belgian group Wak Maar Proper for a Christmas album of a different kind, *The Christmas Truce,* on the theme of the temporary Christmas cessation of hostilities between German and British troops in 1914. Also in 1999 Coope, Boyes & Simpson released *Where You Belong,* a unique song cycle commissioned by and concerning the town of Belper in the Derbyshire region. The year 1999 saw the release of yet another album, the compilation *What We Sing.* Coope, Boyes & Simpson appeared with Blue Murder at the Beverley Folk Festival in 2000 and also made their first appearances in the United States as part of the Vocal Chords Tour, a New England series featuring a cappella groups from various traditions. They toured Britain, Belgium, and the Netherlands in 2001, featuring the *Christmas Truce* and *Garland of Carols* material, and they also joined a group of other folk musicians in a sort of social-critique review of songs about coal mining, *Hearts of Coal.*

In 2002, the collaboration with Blue Murder grew into a new album, *No One Stands Alone.* That same year, Coope, Boyes & Simpson also issued a new album of their own, *Twenty-four Seven.* The album consisted of edgy songs on social and environmental themes, and in general the trio expressed left-wing attitudes in most

## Selected discography

*Funny Old World,* No Masters, 1993.
(With Willem Vermandere and Norbert Detaeye) *We're Here Because We're Here,* No Masters, 1995.
*Falling Slowly,* No Masters, 1996.
(With Panta Rhei) *Passchendaele Suite,* No Masters, 1996.
*A Garland of Carols,* No Masters, 1998.
*Hindsight,* No Masters, 1998.
(With Wak Maar Proper) *Christmas Truce,* No Masters, 1999.
*What We Sing,* No Masters, 1999.
*Where You Belong,* No Masters, 1999.
(With Blue Murder) *No One Stands Alone,* No Masters, 2002.
*Twenty-four Seven,* No Masters, 2002.
*Fire and Sleet and Candlelight,* No Masters, 2003.
*Triple Echo,* No Masters, 2005.
*Voices at the Door: Midwinter Songs & Carols,* No Masters, 2006.

## Sources

### Periodicals

*Coventry Evening Telegraph* (Coventry, England), January 19, 2001, p. 55.
*Folk Roots* (now *FRoots*), June 1998, p. 29.
*Guardian* (London, England), September 22, 2003, p. 22.
*Sing Out!,* Fall 2005, p. 55; Winter 2006, p. 150.

## Online

Coope, Boyes & Simpson Official Website, http://www. coopeboyesandsimpson.co.uk (November 21, 2006).

"Coope, Boyes & Simpson," No Masters, http://www. nomasters.co.uk/coope_boyes_&_simpson.htm (November 21, 2006).

—*James M. Manheim*

# Cosmic Psychos

## Punk rock band

Melbourne, Australia-based punk rock band Cosmic Psychos became known for their hard-drinking, rowdy behavior and vulgar lyrics. Although they never received widespread international recognition, they became an important influence on the grunge scene in Seattle in the 1990s, and also influenced both Mahoney and Pearl Jam. Their sound is simple, with repetitive lyrics, fuzzy bass, and wah-wah guitar.

The band began in 1982 under the name Spring Plains. The four-piece band performed until 1985, when members Bill Walsh and Peter Jones fired their singer and asked bassist Peter Knight to form a new band with them. Thus the Cosmic Psychos were born. Their first recording was an EP, *Down on the Farm,* and it was followed by a self-titled debut album in 1987.

### "A Real Fuzzed-Out Sound"

In 1989 the Cosmic Psychos released *Go the Hack,* which received widespread attention and distribution outside Australia. In 1990 they released *Slave to the Crave,* a live album that showcased the energy of their live shows and included material from all three of their earlier albums. Soon after this release, however, guitarist Peter Jones left the group. He was replaced by Robbie Watts.

Next the band traveled to the United States to record their fourth album, *Blokes You Can Trust,* with well-known producer Butch Vig. Their next release was an EP, *Palomino Pizza,* which had three new tracks and three covers of Australian pub classics.

In 1995 the Cosmic Psychos released *Self Totaled.* This album had a notably fuzzy sound, so much so that Bill Walsh told an interviewer in *Cousin Creep,* "People who listen to it have said, 'Is there something wrong with the speakers?'" He added, "It's got a real fuzzed out sound which I really like actually. I think that when you see the band live we are very fuzzy." He explained that the album's producer, Lindsay Gravina, intentionally caught the fuzzy sound. The cover of the album, which featured the band disguised as old men, was nominated for an ARIA award. Walsh told *Cousin Creep* that if the band ever actually won such an award, "I think it would spell the end of the band." He added, "When you're considered serious in that sense then there are a huge new set of expectations on a band."

*Self Totalled* was followed in 1997 by *Oh What a Lovely Pie.* According to the Cosmic Psychos' website, this album "has become known as the Psychos' greatest record to date." One track, "Chainsaw," was picked up by an Australian serial-killer sitcom and used for its theme song.

A long studio hiatus followed, during which the band toured and played. They were offered $150,000 to sign with Sony, but refused. They learned quite a bit about working with a major label when they played with the American band Pearl Jam in a concert in Canberra. In *Cousin Creep,* Bill Walsh explained why the band was so adamantly opposed to signing with a big label: "You just don't have a life. You end up having to erect a ten foot high brick fence around your house to keep people out." He added, "I'm quite happy for the Cosmic Psychos to go on in their Cosmic Psychos way."

After nine years outside the studio, the band came back in 2006 to record *Off Ya Cruet!,* described by *Australian Music Online* as "10 tracks of balls-out and grunged-up punk rock equipped with a chip on the shoulder and a healthy thirst for amber ale." On the website for Australian radio station PBS 106.7 FM, Steven Rhall wrote that the album showed a certain maturity that had been lacking in the band's earlier work: "This album is more varied than what I'm used to, with each song having some quality that is unto itself. It is almost as if the band's influences have come through and mixed it up with their own style."

### A Big Loss

After the release of *Off Ya Cruet!,* guitarist Robbie Watts was found dead in a friend's kitchen in Bendigo, Australia, the morning after a show. In an obituary in *Undercover,* Andrew Tijs wrote that in contrast to the rowdy image of the band, Watts was "a quiet and gentle man, a respected rocker and well-loved father." He was also an accomplished banjo player and often played to entertain fans outside Melbourne soccer games. He had four children: Rani, Billy, Dan, and Lily, and was 47

## For the Record . . .

**M**embers include **Peter Jones** (guitar, vocals; left group in 1990), **Ross Knight** (bass, vocals), **Dean Muller** (joined group, 2006); **Bill Walsh** (drums, vocals), **Robbie Watts** (joined group in 1990; died in 2006).

Group formed in 1985; released *Down on the Farm*, 1985; released *Cosmic Psychos*, 1987; released *Go the Hack*, 1989; released *Slave to the Crave*, 1990; *Blokes You Can Trust*, 1991; released *Palomino Pizza*, 1993; released *Self Totalled*, 1995; released *Oh What a Lovely Pie*, 1997; *15 Years—A Million Beers*, 2000; released *Off Ya Cruet!*, 2006.

Addresses: *Office*—Cosmic Psychos, P.O. Box 158, Albert Park, Vic 3206, Australia.

years old at the time of his death. The band had been touring to promote *Off Ya Cruet,* but canceled all remaining tour dates after this.

After Watts's death, Dean Muller took his place in the lineup. In an interview in *Australian Music Online,* Muller described his job: "There are no challenges involved in writing and recording, it's easy! Can't understand why people think it's so hard to write and record songs. … It's paying for it or finding someone to release the product that is the hard part." Muller also commented on the band's loyalty to Australia and said the worst thing about the Australian music industry was Australian bands "that pretend they are too good for this joint and … moan about breaking into the overseas markets."

Bill Walsh summed up the band's achievements and goals to *Cousin Creep*: "We are beginning to be credited by people for having some kind of impact on our musical peers or whatever…. I just hope we continue to do things that younger people kind of like, and tell us their parents are really irritated by us when they play the records at home."

## Selected discography

*Down on the Farm* (EP), Mr. Spaceman, 1985.
*Cosmic Psychos,* Mr. Spaceman, 1987.
*Go the Hack,* Megadisc/Normal Records, 1989.
*Slave to the Crave,* Normal Records, 1990.
*Blokes You Can Trust,* Amphetamine Reptile, 1991.
*Palomino Pizza* (EP), Amphetamine Reptile, 1993.
*Self Totalled,* Amphetamine Reptile, 1995.
*Oh What a Lovely Pie,* Amphetamine Reptile, 1997.
*15 Years—A Million Beers,* Dropkick Records, 2000.
*Off Ya Cruet!,* Shock, 2006.

## Sources

### Online

"Cosmic Psychos," *Australian Music Online,* http://www.amo. org.au/artist.asp?id=1413; http://www.amo.org.au/qa_interview.asp?id=1142 (November 13, 2006).
"Cosmic Psychos: Bill Walsh," *Cousin Creep,* http://www. cousincreep.com/cosmic.htm (November 14, 2006).
"Cosmic Psychos Guitarist Robbie Watts Dies," *Undercover,* http://www.undercover.com.au/news/2006/jul06/ 20060703_cosmicpsychos.html (October 23, 2006).
Cosmic Psychos Official Website, http://www. cosmicpsychos.com/ (October 23, 2006).
"Cosmic Psychos: Off Ya Cruet!," PBS FM Website, http:// www.pbsfm.org.au/ (October 23, 2006).

—*Kelly Winters*

# Christopher Cross

**Singer, songwriter**

© Henry Diltz/CORBIS

Christopher Cross's star rose quickly in 1980. Both "Ride Like the Wind" and "Sailing" ascended the charts rapidly, and his self-titled debut sold millions of records. But no one, including Cross, was prepared for the young singer's sweep at the 1981 Grammy Awards ceremony. Over the span of the evening he won five awards, and is one of only two artists to sweep the "big four" categories: record of the year, album of the year, song of the year, and best new artist. Christopher Cross and Michael Omartian also won a Grammy for best arrangement for "Sailing." In 1981 Cross also won a Golden Globe Award and an Oscar for the co-written "Arthur's Theme (Best That You Can Do)." In 1983 he released his sophomore effort, *Another Page,* and "All Right," "No Time for Talk," and "Think of Laura" all placed on the charts.

Cross's meteoritic rise to fame, however, came to an abrupt halt after 1983. While several of his songs entered the charts in 1984, none rose to the top ten; after 1986, his chart success came to an end. Cross nonetheless continued to record and tour, and was determined to pursue his craft and make sure that his new songs would be heard by a wider audience. "I'm not bitter," Cross later told Sue Merrell in the *Grand Rapids Press,* of his quick rise and fall. "I'm blessed to have had the success I have."

Cross was born Christopher Geppert in San Antonio, Texas, on May 3, 1951. His father was a U.S. Army doctor, and Cross lived in Japan for five years as a child. As a teen in Texas, a friend invited him to go sailing, an activity that helped Cross escape from his problems. Later, these sailing expeditions served as an inspiration for his best known song, "Sailing." As he later confessed to radio talk show host Howard Stern, if his friend had taken him bowling instead, he probably would have written a song about bowling. In the 1970s Cross played in a band called Flash, in Austin, Texas, before signing a solo contract with Warner Brothers in 1978.

In 1979 Warner Brothers released *Christopher Cross,* and both "Ride Like the Wind" and "Sailing" quickly climbed the charts. "Soft rock albums hardly ever came better than this," noted Stephen Thomas Erlewine in *All Music Guide,* "and it remains one of the best mainstream albums of its time." After "Sailing" reached number one, two more songs from the album, "Never Be the Same" and "Say You'll Be Mine," appeared on the charts. "*Christopher Cross* was a huge, runaway success, the kind of success that either kicks off or derails an entire career," noted the website *Jefito.* Cross's phenomenal chart success in 1980 paved his way to five Grammy Awards in 1981, a feat that would not be repeated until 2003 with Norah Jones.

Cross returned to the charts in 1981 with "Arthur's Theme (Best That You Can Do)," for the Dudley Moore film *Arthur,* co-written by Burt Bacharach, Carole Baer

**For the Record . . .**

Born Christopher Geppert on May 3, 1951, in San Antonio, Texas; son of Leo Joseph and Edith Ann (Guderman) Geppert; married Jan Coker, May 14, 1988; children: Rain, Madison; one child from previous marriage, Justin.

Performed in Flash, 1970s; signed to Warner Brothers, 1978; released *Christopher Cross*, 1980; co-wrote "Arthur's Theme (Best That You Can Do)," for *Arthur*, 1981; issued *Another Page*, 1983; "Think of Laura" adapted for a plotline on *General Hospital*, 1983; released *Every Turn of the World*, 1985, and *Back of My Mind*, 1988; dropped from Warner Brothers; issued *Rendezvous* (1993), *Window* (1995), *Walking in Avalon* (1998), and *The Red Room* (2000).

Awards: Grammy Awards, Record of the Year, Album of the Year, Song of the Year, Best New Artist, and Best Instrumental Arrangement, 1981; Golden Globe Award, Best Original Song, 1981; Oscar, Best Original Song, 1981.

Addresses: *Record company*—Warner Brothers Records, 3300 Warner Blvd., Burbank, CA 91505-4694, phone: 818-846-9090, website: http://www.warnerbrosrecords.com/.

Sager, and Peter Allen. The song reached number one, and earned Cross a Golden Globe Award and an Oscar. Following his rapid rise to fame in 1980-81, Cross was ready for some time away from the stage lights and pressures of stardom. Personal problems, including a divorce, also complicated his life. "I got into auto racing for a while and did some things to escape the expectations and pressure of all that," he told Nick Krewen in the *Kitchener-Waterloo Record.*

Cross released his sophomore effort, *Another Page,* in 1983, three years after his debut. "By the time *Another Page* came out in 1983," noted *Jefito,* Cross's label "was faced with the unenviable task of reintroducing him as an artist." Whereas his debut had been an eclectic recording, featuring both upbeat material and ballads, the follow-up relied heavily on ballads. Both "All Right" and "No Time for Talk" reached numbers 12 and 33 respectively on *Billboard*'s Pop Singles chart, and *Another Page* reached number eleven on *Billboard*'s Pop Albums and achieved gold status. Later

in 1983, "Think of Laura" from *Another Page* became another number one hit on the Adult Contemporary chart, after the soap opera *General Hospital* began playing the song to accompany a plot line featuring a character named Laura. Many listeners mistakenly believed that the song had in fact been written about the character. Instead, "Think of Laura" was about an acquaintance who had been killed by a stray bullet while driving.

In 1985 Cross released *Every Turn of the World,* an album that added a new rock element. But his third release never reached higher than 158 on the *Billboard* 200, and the single "Charm the Snake" did poorly on the charts. Cross followed with *Back of My Mind* in 1988, concentrating once again on ballads, but the album failed to chart and Warner Brothers dropped him from the roster. After leaving Warner, Cross remained out of the spotlight, although he recorded four subsequent albums: *Rendezvous* (1993), *Window* (1995), *Walking in Avalon* (1998), and *The Red Room* (2000).

While commentators have been quick to call attention to the rise and fall of Cross's popularity, the singer is unbothered by his career trajectory. He has continued to tour on weekends, playing both his hits from the early 1980s and his later, less familiar material. "I've got to keep touring so fans can hear these other songs," he told Merrell. After one 2005 concert, Rachel Recker noted in Michigan's *Grand Rapids Press* that Cross's vocals remained strong, and "sounded just like their initial recordings." He has also, she noted, kept his sense of humor, joking about the "sweet young thing[s]" that arrive backstage to ask for autographs—for their grandmothers.

While he continues to record, he admitted to Krewen that his primary focus had changed. "It's just I've got other priorities. I've got kids and I want to spend time with them. And the public isn't clamoring for a record. That's just the way it is." Even short-lived fame, however, makes Cross a familiar figure today. "Sailing" and "Ride Like the Wind" continue in heavy rotation on Oldies' radio. "I had a nice 15 minutes," Cross told Krewen. "A nice byproduct of that is that my name is somewhat known. Most people on the street, if you ask them who I am, they'll say, 'Oh yeah, he did that Sailing song,' so I have some legacy."

## Selected discography

*Christopher Cross,* Warner Brothers, 1980.
*Another Page,* Warner Brothers, 1983.
*Every Turn of the World,* Warner Brothers, 1985.
*Back of My Mind,* Warner Brothers, 1988.
*Rendezvous,* BMG, 1993.
*Window,* Priority, 1995.
*Walking in Avalon,* CMC International, 1998.
*Red Room,* CMC International, 2000.

# Sources

## Periodicals

*Grand Rapids Press* (Michigan), August 10, 2005; August 12, 2005.

*Kitchener-Waterloo Record,* December 1, 2005.

## Online

"Christopher Cross," *All Music Guide,* http://www.allmusic.com/ (June 9, 2006).

"Complete Idiot's Guide to Christopher Cross," *Jefito,* http://www.jefitoblog.com/ (June 9, 2006).

—Ronnie D. Lankford, Jr.

# Mac
# Davis

**Singer, songwriter, guitarist**

Mat Szwajkos/Getty Images

Best known for such songs as "Baby Don't Get Hooked on Me" and "It's Hard to Be Humble," singer-songwriter Mac Davis parlayed a modest string of hit records into national fame as a recording artist, TV star, concert draw and, for a brief time, a movie star. Initially a music executive, he first gained fame penning hits for the likes of Bobby Goldsboro, Kenny Rogers, and Elvis Presley. As a recording artist in his own right, Davis's work is characterized by a sincere vocal blending of soft pop, gospel and country, lyrics that embrace a positive romantic outlook and a Roger Miller-influenced sense of humor. At his late-1970s peak, he garnered favorable notice as the drawling playboy quarterback in the film *North Dallas Forty.* However, *The Sting II,* an ill-advised sequel to the Paul Newman-Robert Redford classic, failed miserably, ending his days as a Hollywood leading man. Nothing if not a trouper, he made a successful return to songwriting during the mid-1990s, and parlayed his country charm into a starring role in the successful Broadway musical *The Will Rogers Follies.*

## Born in Lubbock, Texas

Born Scott Davis on January 21, 1942, in Lubbock, Texas, Mac Davis's father had to coerce him into singing in the church choir at age ten, but the youngster liked it so well that he ended up singing in various choirs throughout high school. That said, growing up in Buddy Holly's hometown during the frenzied years of early rock 'n' roll made an even bigger impression on him. "I saw Buddy Holly driving down the street with a bunch of girls in his car," Davis told Joey Kirk of the *Daily Toreador.* "I knew that's what I wanted to be." Another big early influence was Elvis Presley, whom Davis saw singing "That's All Right Mama" on the back of a flat bed truck at the Hub Motor Company. Little did he suspect that someday Presley would score major radio hits with Davis's own songs.

Davis started his first band after he moved to Atlanta, Georgia. While working for the Georgia State Board of Parole, he took night classes at Emory University, and fronted a rock 'n' roll combo dubbed Zotz. Performing covers of Jimmy Reed songs at area roller rinks, the band recorded a single for a local label called "Rock a Bongo" before Davis decided in 1961 that he wasn't cut out to be a full-fledged rocker.

Atlanta was a hot music town during the early 1960s and, like many artists before him, Davis decided to work his way up the ladder through music promotion, management, and publishing. Mostly he worked as a regional manager for Vee Jay Records during this era, handling area promotions of such popular artists as Jimmy Reed, Gene Chandler, and the Four Seasons.

### Wrote Hits For Elvis Presley

By 1966 Davis had left Vee Jay, which was undergoing financial upheaval and reorganization, and began working for the West Coast-based Liberty Records. His interest in songwriting eventually resulted in a job with the label's publishing imprint, Metric. He caught a big break when smooth baritone R&B singer Lou Rawls recorded his tune "You're Good For Me" and the then-red-hot Glen Campbell waxed "Within My Memory." However, it was his association with Elvis Presley that made his name as a songwriter.

Working with producer/arranger Billy Strange, Davis wrote ditties for the soundtracks of Presley's later films *Live a Little, Love a Little* (1968), *The Trouble With Girls* (1969), and *Charro* (1969). Strange and Davis tried to help the fading rock king redraft his sound into something more contemporary with the anti-hypocrisy gospel rock of "Clean Up Your Own Backyard" (1969). Yet, it was the danceable rocker "A Little Less Conversation, A Little More Action" that proved to be the more enduring movie song. Thirty-four years after its initial release, a clever disc jockey remixed the record, added fresh jams, and it became a worldwide hit all over again.

Davis provided important material for Presley's fertile comeback period of 1968-69. In addition to co-writing "Memories" along with Strange for the rock king's *Singer Presents—Elvis* TV special, Davis contributed the hits "In the Ghetto" and "Don't Cry Daddy" (1969).

Presley's chart smashes with Davis's songs provided opportunities to work with other major artists as well. Soul balladeer O.C. Smith scored hits with the Davis-penned "Friend, Lover, Wife" and "Daddy's Little Man," both in 1969. He also composed the politically aware "Something's Burning" (1970) for Kenny Rogers and the First Edition. The tune that eventually became his personal theme song, "I Believe in Music" (1972), was initially done in chipper style by the pop group Gallery. However, Davis's biggest non-Presley contribution as a songwriter was his authorship of "Watching Scotty Grow" (1971) for Bobby Goldsboro, a song inspired by the writer's eldest son.

### Became a Star During the 1970's

Appearances on network television shows hosted by Johnny Carson, David Frost, and the Smothers Brothers led to a 1970 signing with Columbia Records as an artist in his own right. He became a headliner in major concert venues nationwide, but hit records were not immediately forthcoming. Such earnest, well-crafted efforts as "I'll Paint You a Song" and "Whoever Finds This, I Love You" in 1970 didn't exactly burn up the charts. *The Billboard Book of Number One Hits* recalled that Davis's producer, Rick Hall, instigated the conditions of his first breakthrough smash: "[He] asked me to write a hook song, one with a repeat phrase which is singles oriented," Davis told *Billboard* in 1978. "So I came up with this phrase and melody line, baby don't get hooked on me." The song "Baby Don't Get Hooked on Me" spent three weeks at number one. Many subsequent singles charted on the pop, country, and adult contemporary charts, the most successful of which were "Stop and Smell the Roses" (1974) and "Rock 'N Roll (I Gave You the Best Years of My Life)" (1975).

After switching to the Casablanca label in 1979, Davis began to write songs that were more overtly country. Such 1980 hits as "Let's Keep it That Way," "Texas in My Rear View Mirror," and the comedic "It's Hard to Be Humble" personified his country-meets-adult-contemporary approach. But as the age of hip-hop took hold, Davis found he was no longer as welcome on pop radio, and his final Top Ten records—"You re My Bestest Friend" (1982) and "I Never Made Love (Till I Made it With You)" (1985)—benefitted from country airplay only.

### A Multimedia Star

Loaded with folksy charm and sly wit, Davis has always been welcome on television. Besides guest appearances on nearly every major variety and talk show produced over the last three decades, he has appeared as an actor on programs ranging from *Webster* and *Lois & Clark: The New Adventures of Superman* to *Murder She Wrote* and *Rodney*. His grinning, curly-headed presence was especially put to good use on NBC's *The Mac Davis Show,* which ran as a summer and spring replacement series from 1974-76.

Davis made a strong impression with his acting debut in the 1979 film *North Dallas Forty.* Portraying a "Dandy" Don Meredith-type quarterback, his boyish charm worked well next to co-star Nick Nolte's wry cynicism. However, follow-up films such as the lightweight divorce comedy *Cheaper to Keep Her* and the implausible sequel *The Sting II* were unmitigated flops that only served to curtail his big screen acting career.

Largely an in-concert attraction, Davis's star fell during the late 1980s and early 1990s, when he co-wrote "White Limozeen" for his friend Dolly Parton (1990). He rebounded during the mid-1990s with his first album of original material in a decade, the puckishly titled *Will Write Songs for Food.* More important, he enjoyed a well-received two-year run starring in the Broadway musical *The Will Roger Follies.*

With his curly locks now shorn, Davis has entered the senior phase of his career and is now regarded more for his past achievements than his future promise. He has been honored by his home town with a Mac Davis Day and presented with a star on the Hollywood Walk of Fame, and his craftsmanship as a songwriter was honored in 2006 when he was inducted into the Songwriters Hall of Fame in New York City.

## Selected discography

### Singles

"Baby Don't Get Hooked on Me," Columbia, 1972.
"Kiss it and Make it Better," Columbia, 1973.
"One Hell of a Woman," Columbia, 1974.
"Stop and Smell the Roses," Columbia, 1975.
"Burnin' Thing," Columbia, 1975.
"Rock 'N Roll (I Gave You the Best Years of My Life)," Columbia, 1975.
"Forever Lovers," Columbia, 1976.
"Every Now and Then," Columbia, 1976.
"It's Hard to Be Humble," Casablanca, 1980.
"Let's Keep it That Way," Casablanca, 1980.
"Texas in My Rear View Mirror," Casablanca, 1980.
"Hooked on Music," Casablanca, 1981.
"You're My Bestest Friend," Casablanca, 1981.
"Rodeo Clown," Casablanca, 1982.
"I Never Made Love (Till I Made Love With You)," MCA, 1985.
"I Feel the Country Callin Me," MCA, 1985.

### Albums

*Song Painter,* Columbia, 1971.
*Baby Don't Get Hooked On Me,* Columbia, 1972.
*I Believe in Music,* Columbia, 1973.
*All the Love in the World,* Columbia, 1974.
*Stop & Smell the Roses,* Columbia, 1974.
*Burnin' Thing,* Columbia, 1975.
*Forever Lovers,* Columbia, 1976.
*Thunder in the Afternoon,* Columbia, 1977.
*Fantasy,* Columbia, 1978.
*It's Hard to Be Humble,* Casablanca, 1980.
*Texas in My Rear View Mirror,* Casablanca, 1980.
*Midnight Crazy,* Casablanca, 1981.
*Forty 82,* Casablanca, 1982.
*Soft Talk,* Casablanca, 1984.
*Very Best & More,* Casablanca, 1984.
*Till I Made It With You,* MCA, 1985.
*Will Write Songs for Food,* Sony, 1994.
*A Man Don't Cry,* Combo, 1995.
*Baby Don't Get Hooked On Me/Stop and Smell the Roses,* Collectables, 1997.
*The Best of Mac Davis,* Razor & Tie, 2000.
*20th Century Masters,* Universal Music, 2006.

## Sources

### Books

Bronson, Fred, *The Billboard Book of Number One Hits,* Billboard, 1997.
Hyatt, Wesley, *The Billboard Book of Number One Adult Contemporary Hits,* Billboard, 1999.
McCloud, Barry, *Definitive Country—The Ultimate Encyclopedia of Country Music and Its Makers,* Perigree, 1995.
Stambler, Irwin & Grelun Landon, *Country Music—the Encyclopedia,* St. Martin's Griffin, 1997.

## Online

"Gary James Interview with Bobby Goldsboro," *Classic Bands.com,* http://www.classicbands.com/BobbyGoldsboroInterview.html. (November 7, 2006).

"Interview with Mac Davis," *Elvis Australia,* http://www.elvis.com.au/presley/printer_interview_mac_davis.shtml. (November 7, 2006).

"Mac Davis," *All Music Guide,* http://www.allmusic.com (November 7, 2006).

"Mac Davis," *Internet Movie Database,* http://www.imdb.com. (November 7, 2006).

"Mac Davis on life: put it into song," *Daily Toreador,* http://www.daileytoreador.com. (July 30, 2004).

Additional information for this profile was drawn from a 2005 interview with producer/songwriter Billy Strange.

*—Ken Burke*

# Taylor Dayne

**Singer, songwriter**

Steve Snowden/Getty Images

Pop vocalist Taylor Dayne first came to many music fans' attention with her 1988 debut album on Arista, *Tell It to My Heart.* The title track rocketed to top ten status, and the album garnered her four New York Music Award nominations. Her follow-up songs "Prove Your Love" and "I'll Always Love You" also received a fair amount of radio airplay, but Dayne's second album, *Can't Fight Fate,* brought her another smash hit with the single "With Every Beat of My Heart." Edwin Miller summed up the singer's powerful vocal style in *Seventeen:* "Personality she's got."

Born Lesley Wunderman on March 7, 1963, Dayne grew up in Long Island, New York. Her earliest ambition was to be a singer, and she was active in her elementary school choruses, often performing solos. She began listening to rock music when she was in junior high, and when she reached high school, Dayne sang with her boyfriend's band. She confided to Miller: "The other boys [in the band] didn't like me. They were intimidated because I sang better than they rocked." The group entertained at school dances, and performed songs made famous by the Allman Brothers, Joni Mitchell, and Joe Walsh.

When Dayne went to Nassau Community College to study philosophy, she hooked up with a band called Felony, where she sang duets with a male vocalist. Felony played its own compositions, and Dayne told Miller that she "loved getting away from singing somebody else's music … That was my introduction to original music, learning how to write and interpret." Though Dayne has made her mark in the pop genre, she offered this advice for aspiring singers, as quoted by Miller: "Never study with somebody who says they can teach you how to sing pop correctly. What's pop? Get to the fundamentals. Do the basics!"

After Felony broke up, Dayne had a stint with a pop group called the Next, and eventually decided to forsake philosophy, deciding that the only thing she could do in the field was teach. She started working harder on her music career, cutting a demo tape in Los Angeles and singing in New York City for record-company talent scouts, but with few results. Somewhere along the line she recorded two singles under the name Leslee; these also went nowhere. Dayne was performing in a Russian-American nightclub in Brighton Beach, New York, "belting bawdy Russian songs," in the words of *People* magazine, when she came to the attention of Arista Records. Anxious to distance herself from her previous unsuccessful recordings, she was aided in her search for a new stage name by friend Dee Snider of the rock group Twisted Sister, who suggested she use a male-sounding one and helped her come up with Taylor. Dayne found the last name in a baby book, according to Miller.

Once Dayne was under contract with Arista, things moved quickly. *Tell It to My Heart* was recorded in six

## For the Record . . .

Born Lesley Wunderman on March 7, 1963; daughter of a rare coin dealer and an actress. *Education:* Attended Nassau Community College.

Sang with rock bands since high school, including Felony and the Next; sang in Russian-American nightclub in Brooklyn, N.Y., c. 1987; recording artist, 1988–; also recorded two songs under the name Leslee.

Addresses: *Record company*—Arista Records, 6. W. 57th St., New York, NY 10019.

*Shadow.*

In 1986 Dayne released *Greatest Hits* and appeared in two more movies, *Fools Paradise* and *Stag.* She went back to the recording studio, cowriting and producing her next album, *Naked Without You,* and followed this with a live album in 2000. Also in 2000, she recorded the title song for the Robert DeNiro film *Flawless.*

In 2000 and 2001 Dayne appeared as a guest on the Showtime television series *Rude Awakenings.* In 2001 she moved to Broadway, playing Princess Amneris in the musical *Aida* for nine months. She continued to write and record music for soundtracks, including those of *Circuit, Lizzy McGuire,* and *Win a Date With Ted Hamilton.* Dayne has continued to compose new work and record tracks for television and film.

weeks. The title cut was described in *People* as a "catchy dance tune," and "Prove Your Love" was in a similar vein. "I'll Always Love You," according to *People,* was "an R&B-flavored ballad that Dayne hopes … will establish her as the white soul singer she longs to be." Aside from the hit "With Every Beat of My Heart," *Can't Fight Fate* also included the ballad "Love Will Lead You Back."

Dayne took a break after a world tour in support of the album. In 1992 she returned with *Soul Dancing,* which soared up the charts with "Can't Get Enough of Your Love," a remake of a Barry White classic. The song topped the charts in the United States, United Kingdom, and Australia, and stayed on the charts for more than 20 weeks.

Dayne branched out into movies when she appeared in the 1992 film *Love Affair,* starring Warran Beatty and Annette Bening. She also played Mehitabel in a Mel Brooks production of "Archie and Mehitabel," and recorded "Original Sin," the theme song for the film *The*

## Selected discography

*Tell It to My Heart,* Arista, 1988.
*Can't Fight Fate,* Arista, 1989.
*Soul Dancing,* Arista, 1992.
*Greatest Hits,* Arista, 1986.
*Naked Without You,* Neptune, 1988.
*Live,* Neptune, 2000.
Also released two singles on another label under the name Leslee.

## Sources

### Periodicals

*People,* May 23, 1988.
*Seventeen,* August 1988.

### Online

Taylor Dayne Official Website, http://www.taylordayne.com/ (November 6, 2007).

—*Elizabeth Thomas and Kelly Winters*

# Manu Dibango

**Saxophonist**

© Tony Frank/Sygma/Corbis

The most widely known musician from the French West African nation of Cameroon, Manu Dibango was one of the pioneers of world music in the early 1970s and remained one of the most internationally celebrated African musicians into the mid-2000s. The *Boston Globe* considered his 1994 hit *Wakafrika* to be his "best album in years." *Wakafrika* also brought together African and European stars, including King Sunny Adé, Ladysmith Black Mambazo, Peter Gabriel, and Sinead O'Connor.

Long recognized for combining African, American, European, and techno sounds, Dibango first achieved global fame in 1973 with *Soul Makossa,* through which he popularized makossa music, a Cameroonian form of early-century West African dance music. Living in Paris, in Douala, Cameroon, around Western and Central Africa, and later in Jamaica and New York, Dibango has experimented with jazz, reggae, hip hop, and electric music throughout his prolific career.

Although Dibango has been criticized at times for having a foreign sound—foreign from African, European, and American perspectives—he has strived for a musical universality inflected by his own identity. "What contribution have I made?," he asked himself in an interview by the *UNESCO Courier.* "I have built a bridge between my starting point and my curiosity. I contribute a sound which is unmistakably African. I add my difference."

## Music was Discovered

Born Emmanuel Dibango on December 12, 1933, in Douala, Cameroon, to a civil servant and a dressmaker, Dibango first discovered his interest in music as a boy at home and in church. His mother led the women's choir in their Protestant chapel and sang with her dressmaker's apprentices and Dibango, while working during the days. "We sang all day long," recalled Dibango in an interview with the *UNESCO Courier.* "I was the conductor. What I liked most of all was to marshall the voices into a human instrument that sounded right and true."

In addition to church music, which included many classical European scores, Dibango also listened without his parents' knowledge or approval to modern music on their gramophone. There and at performances in Douala, the young Dibango heard African musicians playing an assortment of modern Western music and Cameroonian styles, including initiation music, with drums and wooden instruments, and "assico," percussive dance music played by guitar bands.

Hearing these bands, Dibango gained early exposure to "makossa," a modern Cameroonian version of West African highlife music. Highlife developed in the 1920s and 1930s from African musicians who incorporated original dance tunes into their performances for colo-

kossa did not gain international prominence until Dibango introduced the sounds in 1973 on his globally popular album Soul Makossa.

## Love of Jazz

After moving to France with his family at 15 to study for a diploma, Dibango heard American jazz and began to consider himself a musician for his love of the art form. "How happy I was the first time I heard Louis Armstrong humming on the radio!" he told the *UNESCO Courier.* "Here was a black voice singing tunes that reminded me of those I had learned at the temple." For Dibango, jazz meant "a kind of freedom, fresh scope for the imagination."

In Paris during the 1940s, Dibango redirected his efforts from the piano toward the saxophone and absorbed, with a number of African musicians, the jazz, Latin American mambo and samba, Caribbean beguine, and Creole music permeating the city. At the end of the 1950s, Dibango moved to Brussels, Belgium, where during the 1960 negotiations for the independence of the Congo, he "experienced the tensions and clashes between whites and Africans," he stated in the *UNESCO Courier* interview.

Dibango also played with leading African musicians living in Europe, including Joseph Kabasele, a star singer from the Congo whose album, *Independence Cha-Cha,* became a hit in both Africa and Brussels when the Congo gained its independence in 1960 and became Zaire. Dibango performed in Zaire with Kabasele in 1961 and with the band African Jazz until 1963, when Dibango returned to his native Cameroon after a 12-year absence. Dibango began composing in Zaire, made his first recording there as a pianist for African Jazz, and appeared on over 100 singles.

In 1965 soul music was flourishing in Paris, and Dibango returned there to begin an international ascent as a saxophonist. After three albums, including his 1968 debut, *Manu Dibango,* Dibango's fourth record caught on big in the United States and across Europe and Africa. Released on Atlantic Records in 1973, *Soul Makossa* rode the phenomenal success of its title track to win a gold record for sales in the United States and a Grammy Award nomination for Dibango for Best Rhythm and Blues Instrumental Performance of the year.

## Influenced World Music

Henri Kala-Lobe described the album's stylistic success and enduring achievement in West Africa: "When *Soul Makossa* happened, it was a new lease of life for the eternal stylistic quarrel between traditional and modern. Its new sound, more electric and ragging, the using of alto-sax as main instrument, the jerky and

nial audiences. The form drew on Western music, including jazz. As a West African response to merchant trade under colonial rule during the first half of the twentieth century, highlife represented an early accomplishment for modern Africa. "[Seen] in historical perspective the music ... assumes enhanced status as a cultural achievement," wrote West African music critics and historians John Collins and Paul Richards in their essay "Popular Music in West Africa." As a form, ma-

spare rhythm and the horn riffs, gave a modern African soul approach to makossa." Similarly, on the basis of *Soul Makossa* and Dibango's earlier work in Paris and Brussels, *Billboard*'s Emmanuel Legrand deemed Dibango "one of the founders of the world music movement."

Since that success, Dibango has released numerous albums of African dance music combined with jazz and rhythm and blues. In 1979 he experimented also with reggae, recording with some of the Wailers in Jamaica. In 1984 he celebrated 30 years in the music industry with an "electric-pop" album called *Abele Dance*. The album exhibited the new hip-hop style from New York and was produced by Martin Meissonnier, whom *Vogue* described as "France's most active proponent of world music." The title single quickly became one of the top African songs of the year.

Still, Dibango received some criticism of his shows following *Abele Dance*. Lynden Barber of *Melody Maker* noted that Dibango's music was "less pure in source than … other big-name African artists." In response to such questions about his authenticity as an African musician, Dibango asserted the freedom of all musicians to absorb and mix influences. "The musician, even more than the composer, hears agreeable sounds around him and digests them," he told the *UNESCO Courier*. "The voices of [Luciano] Pavarotti and Barbara Hendricks have taught me to love opera. In my imaginary museum they join Louis Armstrong, Duke Ellington, and Charlie Parker. I haven't found anyone better. Mozart doesn't stop me from being African. I like mixtures."

His 1991 album, *Live '91,* on FNAC Music, featured Dibango's jazz saxophone along with an African chorus, drums, and south London rap. The U.K.'s Sinead O'Connor and Peter Gabriel joined with African stars Youssou N'Dour, King Sunny Ade, and Ladysmith Black Mambazo to record with Dibango on his 1994 album *Wakafrika,* released on the Giant label. This collaboration helped establish *Wakafrika* as "his best album in years," according to the *Boston Globe,* and "shows that Dibango can hold his own with the best of the younger generation."

Incorporating a remake of Gabriel's "Biko" and new versions of Dibango originals including "Soul Makossa" and "Ca Va Chouia," the album "dazzles in its vitality," wrote Paul Evans of *Rolling Stone. Wakafrika* reached number seven on *Billboard*'s Top World Music Albums chart in 1994.

Entering the mid-1990s, Dibango continued to grow as a musician. Hailed in the *Boston Globe* as "perhaps the most consistent African pop artist working at cross-cultural experimentation," his high level of energy remained apparent. "Now 60, having generated more than 20 albums, Dibango hardly sounds like he's slow-ing down at all," Evans wrote. Reviewing a performance at the Central Park Summerstage in July of 1994 in New York City, Jon Pareles of the *New York Times* agreed, noting, "He's still creating Afro-global fusions that are both slick and enjoyable." Judging also by the host of younger stars who joined him on his 1994 album, Dibango had begun to exert a lasting influence on the world music scene.

That influence deepened as Dibango continued to perform and record, slowing down very little as he passed 65 and then 70 years of age. His 1996 release *Lamastabastani* had a nostalgic tone inspired by his wife's death the previous year. In 1998 he organized an African music series called Soirs au village in Saint-Calais, France, and he continued to divide his time between Cameroon and his adopted homeland.

The year 2000 brought Dibango the honor of being named Cameroon of the Century; he shared the award with soccer player Roger Milla. He kicked off the new millennium with major concerts in Paris and London and with a new album, *Mboa'su,* that confirmed his status as an elder statesman of Cameroonian music; he brought several generations of younger musicians from his home country on board as guests. In 2003 he released a new album, *Africadelic,* with international distribution on the Mercury label, and the following year the box set *Voyage anthologique* summed up three decades of Dibango music-making. He returned to soundtrack composition in 2005 with a score for the French animated film *Kirikou et les bêtes sauvages,* and developed a DVD of his performance in London with his Maraboutik Big Band. By 2006 Dibango had lived long enough to accumulate a host of honors. One of those, the UNESCO Artist for Peace award bestowed in 2004, indicated the reach of Dibango's contribution to cross-cultural understanding.

# Selected discography

*Manu Dibango,* 1968.
*O Boso,* 1971.
*Soma Loba,* 1972.
*Soul Makossa,* Atlantic, 1973.
*Super Kumba,* 1974.
*Africadelic,* 1975.
(with Sly Dunbar and Robbie Shakespeare) *Gone Clear,* Island, 1979.
(with Dunbar and Shakespeare) *Ambassador,* Island, 1981.
*Waka Juju,* Sonodisc, 1982.
*Soft and Sweet,* 1983.
(as solo pianist)*Mélodies Africaines,* Volumes 1 & 2, 1983.
*Abele Dance,* RCA, 1984.
(with Herbie Hancock and Wally Badarou) *Electric Africa,* Celluloid, 1985.
*Afrijazzy,* Soul Paris, 1986.
*Polysonic,* Bird Productions, 1990.
*Live '91,* FNAC Music, 1991.
(with others) *Wakafrika* (includes "Soul Makossa," "Ç va chouia," and "Biko"), Giant, 1994.

*Lambastabastani,* Soul Paris, 1996.
*African Soul: The Very Best of Manu Dibango,* Mercury, 1997.
(with Cuarteto Patria) *Cubafrica,* 1997.
*Manu Dibango: Collection Légende,* 1998 (unreleased titles).
*Mboa'su,* JPS, 1999.
*Africadelic,* Mercury, 2003.
*Voyage anthologique,* Mercury, 2005 (box set).

## Film scores

*L'herbe sauvage,* Cote d'Ivoire, 1976.
*Ceddo,* Senegal, 1976.
*Le prix de la liberté,* Cameroon, 1976.
*Kirikou et les bêtes sauvages,* France, 2005.

## Sources

### Books

Collins, John, Musicmakers of West Africa, Three Continents Press, 1985.

Collins, John, West African Pop Roots, Temple University Press, 1992.
Collins, John, and Paul Richards, "Popular Music in West Africa," World Music, Politics, and Social Change, edited by Simon Frith, Manchester University Press, 1989.
Dibango, Manu, with Danièle Rouard, *Trois kilos de café* (English trans.), University of Chicago Press, 1994.

### Periodicals

*Atlanta Journal and Constitution,* July 31, 1994.
*Billboard,* November 30, 1991; February 13, 1993; July 23, 1994.
*Boston Globe,* July 12, 1992.
*Evening Standard* (London, England), October 29, 2003, p. 44.
*Guardian* (London, England), May 21, 1992; March 15, 1994.
*Melody Maker,* November 24, 1984.
*Nation,* October 24, 1994, p. 469.
*New York Times,* July 29, 1994.
*Rolling Stone,* August 11, 1994.
*UNESCO Courier,* March 1991.
*Vogue,* May 1989.
*West Africa,* November 8, 1982.

—*Nicholas Patti and James M. Manheim*

# DJ Krush

**Disc jockey, music producer**

China Photos/Getty Images

Hip-hop pioneers aren't what one would usually expect to come out of Japan. Growing up in Tokyo, Japan, turntabalist and producer DJ Krush has forged new ground with his jazz infused, hip-hop style of electronica music since the early '90s. Unlike many of his peers and followers, DJ Krush's career has prospered not only in Japan but in the United States and all over the world. His entrancing music and production aesthetics have earned him the credentials to work with some of the world's finest MCs and singers. *Remix*'s Bill Murphy summed up DJ Krush's admirable career by stating that the DJ has "established a sound that extended the DJ lexicon of backspins, samples and loops into new areas … molding live musicians and a lush, orchestral production style into what could easily be identified as the first real recorded instances of hip-hop composition, almost in the classical sense." Murphy continued writing that, "Krush has been at the forefront of innovation in hip-hop, lending his distinctive touch not only to his own albums but also to remixes for Herbie Hancock, Miles Davis, Bill Laswell, Galliano, Method Man…."

Born Hideaki Ishii in Tokyo, Japan, in 1962, as a young child, Krush would hear the jazz records his father played in the house on a regular basis. He couldn't have known at the time that years later, jazz would be one of his biggest musical influences. In grade school, like many of his peers, Krush listened to loud rock music on his headphones, while daydreaming of playing guitar on stage in front of thousands of people. His love for rock 'n' roll only lasted through his early teens, after which he began to ditch school to hang out with his friends and get into loads of trouble. In 1983, Krush's world would change forever after watching the hip-hop/breakdancing/graffiti documentary film *Wild Style.* Krush credits the film for his venture into hip-hop, which would become a lasting obsession. "There is no one word that can express my fascination with hip-hop," Krush told *Billboard*'s Rashaun Hall. "It isn't an exaggeration to say that hip-hop is my life."

It would be another four years before Krush debuted as a hip-hop artist in a group called Krush Posse. In 1992, after Krush Posse disbanded, Krush went off on his own and reinvented himself as a solo DJ. He quickly gained a name for himself as one of the first prominent DJs to use turntables as live instruments, performing sets with live musicians. "The hip-hop I want to do is different from U.S. hip-hop because I am Japanese," Krush relayed to Hall. "I continue to look for 'DJ Krush hip-hop.' So the best way to express my appreciation for hip-hop music was to create my own hip-hop." Krush released his debut solo album, *Krush,* in the early part of 1994. As soon as he started in the field, he kept on going. Later in the year, London label Mo' Wax put out *Strictly Turntablized* and followed that with his next release, *Meiso.*

Featuring a collaboration with DJ Shadow, *Meiso* foreshadowed the beginnings of the burgeoning trip-hop

## For the Record . . .

Born Hideaki Ishii in 1962, in Tokyo, Japan.

Joined hip-hop group Krush Posse, 1987; debuted as a solo artist, DJ, and producer with *Krush* and *Strictly Turntablized*, 1994; released *Meiso*, 1996; *MiLight*, 1997; *Zen*, 2001; *Shinsou: The Message at the Depth*, 2003; *Jaku*, 2004; released his own remixed album of his greatest tracks as *Stepping Stones: The Self-Remixed Best*, 2006.

Awards: AIFM Award, Best Electronica Album, 2002.

Addresses: *Record company*—Sony Music, 550 Madison Ave., New York, NY 10022. *Website*—DJ Krush Official Website: http://www.mmjp.or.jp/sus/krush/.

The Brand New Heavies) all appeared on what *Remix*'s Ken Micallef called "a set of ruptured beats and brooding productions." The album's title was a culmination of the formation of the record's tracks. "By Zen, I mean slowly or gradually—little by little," Krush said in his interview with Hall. "The 20th century was the century of destruction for man. In the 21st century, we have to re-create what we've destroyed slowly and gradually. I explained the concept to all the guest artists, so the tracks are the outcome of their interpretations of their own Zen." *Zen* was awarded Best Electronica Album at the AIFM Awards in the United States in 2002.

Inspired by the September 11 tragedy, Krush's 2003 output, *Shinsou: The Message at the Depth*, was as much a spiritual journey as it was musical. Collaborations with Anti-Pop Consortium, underground rapper Anticon, and Sly & Robbie made for a heavy collection of songs. *Shinsou* also marked the beginning of Krush using more computers in his work; something he consciously stayed away from in the past. In a review of *Shinsou*, *All Music Guide*'s John Bush wrote, "His beats are digital, heavily resampled and quantized, splintering off like drum'n'bass patterns but possessing a depth and clarity not seen since the heyday of Massive Attack."

With moody and mellow atmospheres, Krush quickly followed up *Shinsou* with the release of *Jaku*, an album that *Creative Loafing*'s Tony Ware said was "fraught with delicious tension." Def Jux rappers Mr. Lif and Aesop Rock put some hip sounds into the now legendary DJ's productions. Still performing live and recording albums, in 2006, Krush remixed 25 of some of his best tracks of all time, releasing a record titled *Stepping Stones: The Self-Remixed Best*. In his 40s, Krush sees no sign of stopping what he's doing. "I think back to when I first started playing for people in Harajuku [a district in Tokyo] and how exciting that felt. It stills feels the same way today," he admitted to *Remix*. "But I wouldn't still be doing this if it weren't satisfying creatively and if there weren't still people out there who seem to enjoy what I'm doing. So I'm grateful for all of that."

sound—a down tempo, jazz and soul-affected ambient style of hip-hop-beat driven music. With 1997's *MiLight*, Krush enlisted a score of guest MCs and female soul singers. *Salon*'s Michelle Goldberg wrote that *MiLight* had a "deliciously narcotic groove," with "dense complexity." Writer Justin Hardison summed up Krush's unique and prolific style in the online magazine *Hybrid* as, "Like a minimalist, he is able to express so much with a small amount of sound, only the essential gear and a close attention to detail."

With collaborations left and right for his own records as well as others', Krush continued to release a score of impressive albums that showcased his originality in the field. "Lots of artists take a famous song, loop it, and rap over that. That's fine for other people but I'm not satisfied," he told Hardison. "I want to do the total opposite and create something different in which I come up with the idea that I'm going to bring to the track. I don't sample sounds directly. I always want to tweak them and make them different."

In 1998, *Ki-Oku*, an entire album partnership with trumpeter Toshinori Kondo, hit and was soon followed by *Kakusei* in 1999 and the mix albums *Code 4109* and *Tragicomic* in 2000. That same year Krush spent six months recording his next record in cities all over the world including, Tokyo, Los Angeles, and New York. *Zen* appeared in 2001 to international rave reviews. With album cover art designed by Krush himself, the album was a mélange of sounds and included a bevy of respected vocalists. Guest singers like Zap Mama, The Roots' Black Thought, and singer N'Dea Davenport (of

## Selected discography

*Krush*, Shadow, 1994.
*Strictly Turntablized*, Mo' Wax, 1994.
*Meiso*, Mo' Wax, 1996.
*MiLight*, A&M/Mo' Wax, 1997.
(With Toshinori Kondo)*Ki-Oku*, R&S, 1998.
*Holonic: The Self Megamix*, Mo' Wax, 1998.
*Kakusei*, Columbia, 1999.
*Code 4109*, Red Ink, 2000.
*Tragicomic*, Sony, 2000.

*Zen,* Red Ink, 2001.
*Shinsou: The Message at the Depth,* Red Ink, 2003.
*Jaku,* Red Ink, 2004.
*Stepping Stones: The Self-Remixed Best,* Sony Japan, 2006.

# Sources

## Periodicals

*Billboard,* September 15, 2001, p. 43.
*Creative Loafing,* October 21, 2004.
*Remix,* February 1, 2003; December 1, 2004.

## Online

"DJ Krush," *All Music Guide,* http://www.allmusic.com (October 30, 2006).
"DJ Krush," *Salon,* http://www.salon.com/music/sharps/1997/11/24sharps.html (October 30, 2006).
"DJ Krush: A Conversation with the Zen Master," *Hybrid Magazine,* http://www.hybridmagazine.com/level/interviews/1101/djkrush.shtml (October 30, 2006).
DJ Krush Official Website, http://www.mmjp.or.jp/sus/krush/ (October 30, 2006).

—*Shannon McCarthy*

# Mike Doughty

## Singer, songwriter

© David Atlas

Singer, guitarist, and songwriter Mike Doughty (pronounced "doe-ee") first gained recognition as the vocalist and lyricist for the 1990s New York musical group Soul Coughing, whose jazz-inflected instrumentals were perfectly matched to Doughty's grainy vocals and abstract lyrics. When the group disbanded in 2000, Doughty embarked on a solo career. He self-released two albums before recording 2005's *Haughty Melodic* for friend Dave Matthews's ATO Records label.

Doughty was born June 10, 1970, in Fort Knox, Kentucky. His parents served in the military and raised him in various places in Europe and the United States, including the military academy at West Point. Doughty attended Simon's Rock College of Bard, an exclusive liberal arts college in Massachusetts. He later studied poetry at the New School for Social Research in New York City, where feminist singer Ani DiFranco was one of his classmates.

In June of 1992, under the moniker "M. Doughty," he founded the band Soul Coughing, along with sample player Mark De Gli Antoni, upright bassist Sebastian Steinberg, and drummer Yuval Gabay. He coined the term "deep slacker jazz" to describe the band's sound, which featured Doughty's voice, samples of various jazz elements, cool acoustic bass lines, and precise drum work. His emphatic, muscular vocals were melodic enough to suit the band's jazz flavor, but were delivered in a Beatnik style that showed off his humor and poetic sense. At its peak, Soul Coughing opened for the Dave Matthews Band on two national tours. On the strength of these and other performances, Warner Brothers signed them to a deal and issued three albums: *Ruby Vroom* in 1994, *Irresistible Bliss* in 1996, and *El Oso* in 1998. Three singles attracted significant attention: "Screenwriter's Blues" from their first album, "Super Bon Bon" from *Irresistible Bliss,* and the catchy "Circles" from *El Oso.* Soul Coughing tunes were showcased in the movies *Batman and Robin, Tommy Boy,* and *Spawn,* and were featured in the television programs *Homicide: Life on the Street* and *The X-Files.* Despite the band's successes and cult status, financial and proprietary disputes took their toll, and in 2000 Soul Coughing folded. Mark De Gi Antoni took on a series of soundtrack projects, Sebastian Steinberg began working with David Byrne and Neil Finn, and Yuval Gabay formed the band UV Ray. Soul Coughing's best work was compiled on the 2002 release *Lust in Phaze.*

The period immediately following Soul Coughing's break-up was personally and financially rough for Doughty. He fought heroin addiction and enjoyed only modest success in concert. Operating out of a rental car, he played to small audiences around the country and sold copies of a self-recorded CD titled *Skittish.* The collection was recorded in a single day and remained on the shelf for several years before Doughty decided to test the market. Thanks to file sharing on the Internet, it became known to a core group of diehard fans. More than 25,000 copies later, Doughty had es-

**For the Record . . .**

Born in Fort Knox, KY, in 1970.

Member of Soul Coughing, 1992-2000; released solo effort, *Skittish*, 2000; released *Haughty Melodic*, 2005.

Addresses: *Record company*—ATO Records, Publicist Little Big Man Publicist, andy@littlebigman.com. Mike Doughty e-mail: md@mikedoughty.com.

tablished enough of a following to play larger venues. "In Soul Coughing, there was always the question of whether or not I was the songwriter; whether the song was more important than the playing," Doughty was quoted in the biography on his website. "Even stuff that I really loved, songs that I wrote in a very traditional way and brought to the band, I didn't really feel a sense of ownership towards. So just to make something and wholeheartedly own it as a writer, as a performer, as a singer—that is incredible."

While he continued to perform Soul Coughing favorites like "Circles" and "Janine," Doughty used his time on the road to hone his solo act. The 2002 release *Smofe + Smang: Live in Minneapolis* documented his growing abilities as a songwriter, singer and guitarist. He skillfully interacted with his audience, filling the gaps between numbers with witty pop culture references and personal observations. He followed this with a self-recorded studio EP entitled *Rockity Roll,* which added a Roland Groovebox to the mix. The original releases of *Smofe* and *Rockity* eventually went out of print, but a double set of *Skittish* and *Rockity Roll* was reissued.

During the period between 2003 and 2005, Doughty painstakingly recorded *Haughty Melodic* (an anagram of Michael Doughty) with the help of Dan Wilson, whose production work included the Dixie Chicks as well as his own band, Semisonic. Unlike his earlier work, this set was lavishly produced, with multi-tracked vocals, guitars, keyboards, and horns. Some critics found that *Haughty Melodic* lacked the spontaneity and raw feeling of the artist's earlier material, but most agreed the extra polish helped Doughty secure a wider audience. The album produced a hit single and video, "Looking at the World from the Bottom of a Well," and featured benefactor Dave Matthews's vocals on "Tremendous Brunettes." The lyrics on *Haughty* were more positive and reflective, possibly due to Doughty's personal growth and his recovery from heroin addiction. He described the difference in an article in the *Reno Gazette-Journal*: "I used to get stoned a lot, and now I

don't. That's a very earthy explanation, I guess. I was wasted. Also, I've gotten older. Things change. You kinda chill out."

In 2005 he opened his "Small Rock World Tour" in Washington, D.C., and cemented the success of four solo CD's into a record contract on Dave Matthews's label. As he explained to the *Denver Westword,* "I was playing Bonnaroo in a little tiny tent and Dave was playing on this big gigantic stage in front of 70,000 people. I bumped into his wife and she brought me backstage to meet him. I handed him some rough mixes, he called me a genius, and he signed me to his label."

Having made the transition from hip-hop front man to solo genius, Doughty's next move was to hit the road with new keyboardist Jack Kirby, a gifted Fender Rhodes player. Doughty announced plans to perform and record several songs accompanied only by Kirby. Doughty also earned a spot as the opening act for cheeky Canadian pop group Bare Naked Ladies on their 2006 tour. In the meantime, he actively blogged on all topics and maintained a website announcing concert and recording release dates.

## Selected discography

### With Soul Coughing

*Ruby Vroom,* Slash/Warner Brothers, 1994.
*Irresistable Bliss,* Slash/Warner Brothers, 1996.
*El Oso,* Warner Brothers, 1998.
*Live Tokyo: Japan 03.02.97,* Kufala, 2003.
*Berlin/Amsterdam 1997,* Kufala, 2005.
*Live Rarities,* Kufala, 2005.
*New York, NY: 16.08.99,* Kufala, 2005.
*Rennes, France,* Kufala, 2005.

### Solo Releases

*Smofe + Smang: Live in Minneapolis,* 2002.
*Skittish and Rockity Roll* (reissue), ATO, 2004.
*Haughty Melodic,* ATO, 2005.

## Sources

### Periodicals

*Buffalo News,* June 14, 2006.
*Denver Westword,* September 7, 2006.
*Reno Gazette-Journal,* September 8, 2006.

### Online

*All Music Guide,* http://www.allmusic.com (Nov. 1, 2006).
Mike Doughty Official Website, http://www.mikedoughty.com (Nov. 1, 2006).

—Bruce Walker

# Fred Eaglesmith

## Singer, songwriter

The roots-oriented Canadian singer and songwriter Fred Eaglesmith has charted an independent career path that has rarely intersected with the mainstream activities of the music industry. For the most part he has distributed his own recordings and made a living touring a circuit of small venues in Canada and the United States. Eaglesmith's music has been difficult to keep in one pigeonhole for long, although the label of country music, broadly defined, will fit most of it—his songs mostly deal with the hardscrabble life of farms and small towns. Eaglesmith's powerful voice, energetic live shows, and uncompromising attitudes have earned him an unusually faithful following; his fans, known as Fredheads, will often travel long distances to see him perform.

Eaglesmith was born Fred Elgersma in 1957 in Brantford, Ontario, Canada. The sixth of nine children, he grew up on a 200-acre farm near Brantford. The atmosphere was strict. Day in and day out he helped with farm chores, and his evangelical minister father took the family to church five times a week. Eaglesmith grew up hearing country music on small-town U.S. stations whose signals crossed Lake Erie. When he was nine, he saw Elvis Presley perform on television. "I thought, 'Man, this is all this guy has to do and he's rich and happy? That's what I'm gonna do,'" Eaglesmith told Joshua Ostroff of JAM! Music. "I wrote my first song that day." By the time he was 16, he had had enough of farm life. He took off on a cross-Canada hitchhiking and rail-riding trip, performing in youth hostels or wherever else he could.

Friends had already given Fred Elgersma the easier-to-pronounce nickname of Eaglesmith, and when he was 18 he adopted that name for professional use. Dreaming of a music career, and seeing his parents lose their farm and possessions in a foreclosure auction, he wrote songs prolifically, a habit that never left him. Eaglesmith once quipped that for him, having writer's block meant that he hadn't written a song for two weeks, and he could write several dozen during a short burst of activity. In 1980 he released the album *Fred J. Eaglesmith* on his own label.

By that time Eaglesmith was married to his high school sweetheart, Mary, and the pair were soon raising three children. They bought a 100-acre farm near Alberton, Ontario, and to make it pay they began raising flowers to sell wholesale in the farmers' markets of Toronto. The flower business grew, eventually employing 28 people and reaching $6 million (Canadian) in annual sales. The family's move to Toronto gave Eaglesmith the chance to perform in clubs a couple of nights a week and to hone his songwriting skills by listening to Toronto folk performers like David Essig. He released the albums *The Boy That Just Went Wrong* in 1983 and *Indiana Road* in 1987.

Eaglesmith's leap to making music full time came after his flower business went bankrupt in 1991. Although the family's financial condition deteriorated, Eaglesmith took the career change in stride. "I believe you can't write good material when you're on safe ground," he explained to Susan Beyer of the *Ottawa Citizen*. "You have to live on the edge to write on the edge." With country music on the rise in popularity, Eaglesmith began traveling to the country music capital of Nashville, Tennessee, trying to sell songs to performers and publishers. His bleak, hard-edged songs about farm families in trouble found few takers, although one song, "Thirty Years of Farming," later became a top bluegrass success for vocalist James King. But Eaglesmith's songs and his soulful roar of a voice began to earn him fans in small U.S. venues, especially in songwriter-loving Texas. He released several more independent albums; 1994's *From the Paradise Motel* was drawn from a concert he gave at the La Casa folk music series in Birmingham, Michigan, outside Detroit.

By the mid-1990s Eaglesmith was trying to broaden his songwriting beyond farm themes. Touring with his band, the Flying Squirrels (who included Canadian songwriter Willie P. Bennett on harmonica and the wildly spontaneous Washboard Hank on percussion), he began to add a rock edge to his songs. Eaglesmith still had little success in cracking the mainstream country market, but with the albums *Drive-In Movie* in 1995 (voted one of the top 50 releases of the century in a Dutch poll) and the grim *Lipstick Lies & Gasoline* (1997), he gained wider recognition. "Wilder Than Her," from *Drive-In Movie,* gained airplay with its edgy yet catchy chorus (I'm wilder than her/Drives her out of her mind/I guess she thought that she/Was just one of a

war. "It got a tough reaction from the old guard," Eaglesmith admitted to Greg Quill of the *Toronto Star.* "They prefer the raw stuff I play with the Flying Squirrels. They want the jokester. A lot of them think the songs are too sad, too dark. But what's the point of writing positive songs when democracy has been cancelled and we're staring down the apocalypse? ... The people I'm writing about, the rural working poor, are really tired. ... all this war stuff is just one more burden for them."

Eaglesmith returned to more familiar territory with the reflective 2006 release *Milly's Café,* which featured the Flying Squirrels and once again reached the Americana top ten. Selling his albums mostly on his own and keeping the profits, Eaglesmith had prospered financially. But that year his world seemed to be overturned once more: his home and studio in Port Dover burned to the ground one night in February, with Eaglesmith himself narrowly escaping death—he was asleep on the building's second story when the fire broke out. An adherent of the Buddhist faith, Eaglesmith was philosophical about his loss. "It's a reminder that I don't need all this crap," he mused to Quill. "The Buddhist way allows 17 possessions—I had too many." The experience, perhaps, would have its main effect as a new stimulus to the songwriting of one of roots music's most imaginative and prolific creators.

kind). The song was later covered by U.S. folk singer Dar Williams. *Lipstick Lies & Gasoline* was released on the large independent Razor & Tie label and rose to the top five on the new Americana chart published by *Billboard* magazine. The album contained another dark Eaglesmith standard, "Spookin' the Horses" (You're spookin' the horses/And you're scarin' me). Eaglesmith kept up the momentum with 1999's *50-Odd Dollars* and 2002's *Falling Stars and Broken Hearts.*

Touring and performing up to 300 shows a year, Eaglesmith gained a strong following in the United States, Europe, and Australia. In August of 2002 he performed at a large festival devoted to Canadian songwriting held at New York's Lincoln Center, but ironically he remained less popular in Canada than in the United States. Eaglesmith moved into a house and recording studio in a converted bait shop in Port Dover, Ontario, on Lake Erie. He continued to visit and work his family's farm but lived away from his wife and children.

With his fan base expanding, Eaglesmith might have chosen to solidify his position in the roster of new country rockers who mining the vein in which he was already successfully working. Instead, the resolutely independent-minded performer changed course several times in the early 2000s. He turned to bluegrass with 2003's *Balin,* and *Dusty,* released the following year, was an entirely original departure, using the styles of the 1960s blue-eyed soul vocalist Dusty Springfield and the grandiose, romantic country-pop songwriter Jimmy Webb in the service of a bleak portrait of the rural poor during the time of an unpopular

## Selected discography

*Fred J. Eaglesmith,* Sweetwater, 1980.
*The Boy That Just Went Wrong,* New Woodshed, 1983.
*Indiana Road,* Sweetwater, 1987.
*There Ain't No Easy Road,* Sweetwater, 1991
*Things Is Changin',* Sweetwater, 1993.
*From the Paradise Motel,* Barbed Wire, 1994 (live).
*Drive-In Movie,* Vertical, 1995.
*Lipstick Lies & Gasoline,* Razor & Tie, 1997.
*50-Odd Dollars,* Razor & Tie, 1999.
*Ralph's Last Show: Live in Santa Cruz,* Signature, 2000.
*Falling Stars and Broken Hearts,* MAPL, 2002.
*Balin,* AML, 2003.
*The Official Fred Eaglesmith Bootleg, Vol. 1,* 2003.
*Dusty,* AML, 2004.
*The Official Fred Eaglesmith Bootleg, Vol. 2,* 2005.
*Milly's Café,* AML, 2006.

## Sources

### Periodicals

*Globe and Mail* (Toronto, Canada), August 17, 2002, p. R9.
*Ottawa Citizen* (Ottawa, Ontario, Canada), December 3, 1992, p. G1; November 30, 1995, p. E1; November 29, 1997, p. H1.
*Sacramento Bee,* March 16, 2003, p. TK8.
*Toronto Star,* January 30, 1993, p. H2; July 28, 2002, p. D1; November 25, 2004, p. J4; February 23, 2006, p. A18.
*Toronto Sun,* September 29, 2003, p. 38.

## Online

"Fred Eaglesmith," Fred Eaglesmith Official Website, http://www.fredeaglesmith.com (November 16, 2006).

"Fred Eaglesmith returns home," Jam! Music, http://jam.canoe.ca (November 16, 2006).

—*James M. Manheim*

# Sara Evans

---

**Singer, songwriter**

Frederick M. Brown/Getty Images

Throughout her life, Sara Evans held one dream: to sing and compose country songs. Moreover, she wanted to succeed by returning to the traditional country songs brought to life by such legendary stars as Patsy Cline, Hank Snow, Tammy Wynette, George Jones, and Patty Loveless, musicians she described as her greatest influences. During the late 1990s, an era when many aspiring country musicians turned to contemporary, pop radio-friendly tunes, Evans made her initial mark by performing country songs that looked to the past, exemplified by her 1997 debut, *True Lies.* But despite critical acceptance and a nomination by the Academy of Country Music in 1998 for best new female vocalist, *True Lies* made little impact. Thus, for her follow-up release, 1999's *No Place That Far,* Evans bowed to producers, who persuaded the artist to update her repertoire, and she finally earned the popular recognition she had longed for since her childhood.

Sara Evans was born February 5, 1971, in Columbia, Missouri. She spent her early years, along with her six brothers and sisters, on a farm outside Franklin, Missouri, where her family raised corn, beans, tobacco, and livestock for a living. Although the family remained poor, Evans nevertheless enjoyed a happy upbringing, recalling fond memories of the stories her grandfather used to tell her about the Grand Ole Opry in Nashville, Tennessee. The tales of the stars who graced the stage at the Grand Ole Opry struck a chord with the Evans children, and by the age of four, Evans, along with her two older brothers, had started traveling on weekends and during the summer as the Evans Family Band, performing gospel and bluegrass music at festivals and church revivals. Before long, word spread of the young girl's talent, leading the band to rename itself the Sara Evans Show. As the band's popularity grew, the Sara Evans Show eventually brought in about fifty dollars for each performance.

### Went to Nashville

Evans had longed to see Nashville since first hearing of the Grand Ole Opry, and she made her first trip to the city at age eleven, accompanied by her father. She recorded a single, "What Does a Nice Girl Do in the Meantime," with the song "I'm Going to Be the Only Female Fiddle Player in Charlie Daniels' Band" on the record's flip side, but the recording went unnoticed. After graduating from high school and briefly attending college, Evans returned to Nashville with serious plans for breaking into country music. "I skipped college, and had no other aspirations but to sing," Evans told John Meroney of *American Enterprise.* "So I came here with my older brother, started waiting tables at the Holiday Inn on Briley Parkway, and tried to meet whomever I could."

The person who inspired Evans the most was Craig Schelske, a musician from Oregon, whom she would later marry. "He was a room service waiter trying to do the same thing," the singer revealed to Meroney. "We started dating, fell in love, and he asked me to go to Oregon with him and sing in his band." Evans accepted her companion's offer and spent the next three years performing with Schelske's band throughout the Pacific Northwest. Evans met some of the biggest names in country music, as the band opened for such renowned performers as Willie Nelson, Tim McGraw, and Clay Walker. Evans earned decent money as well, usually performing six nights a week. Nevertheless, she felt that returning to Nashville would provide her with a more certain chance at success.

Upon her return to Nashville, Evans soon realized that most artists had turned away from traditional country and toward a style that appealed to a wider, mainstream audience, a trend accelerated by country superstar "hat acts" such as Garth Brooks, Clint Black, and Alan Jackson in the early 1990s. Thus, traditional country, with its use of fiddles, mandolins, and acoustic rhythm instruments, was often replaced by a more neutral pop sound recorded with rock and roll production elements. Progressive country revealed more complexity as well, often abandoning the use of just three chords per song in favor of more adventurous guitar work. By the mid-1990s, country music—fueled by contemporary artists—had surpassed both pop and urban contemporary formats as the number one music choice of music, behind rock.

## Traditional Debut

Although excited by such changes, Evans had always felt partial to the traditional style and sought out entertainment lawyer Brenner Van Meter. Impressed by Evans's gifted singing and songwriting ability, as well as by the singer's preference to perform traditional country, Van Meter arranged for Evans to meet her husband, John Van Meter, an executive at Sony Tree Publishing Company. Evans accepted a job at Sony recording songs for writers to submit to major artists as potential album tracks.

Eventually, Evans met well-known songwriter Harlan Howard, who wanted to sell his 1964 classic "I've Got a Tiger By the Tail." Believing that Evans's voice would help to promote the song, the Van Meters invited Howard to sit in during the recording session. According to Meroney, Howard said, "Are you that little girl in there singing? You're great. I've been looking for you for years to sing my music. I can't believe how country you are." With Howard's help and encouragement, Evans and her management felt confident enough to approach RCA Records about her own singing career. To Evans's amazement, RCA's chairman, Joe Galante, offered the singer a contract the same day of her audition.

Evans released her debut for RCA, *Three Chords and the Truth,* in the fall of 1997. Produced by Pete Anderson, her first full-length album included the Howard Owens single, in addition to the understated ballad "Unopened," the Patsy Cline-inspired "Imagine That," and her own co-written "The Week the River Raged." Although the album failed to bring in substantial revenues, critics were impressed. Chuck Eddy of *Rolling Stone* called *Three Chords and the Truth* "Nashville's most unjustly ignored debut." "Sara Evans is so good she's scary," wrote Paul Verna in *Billboard* magazine, who added, "At once a preserver of the best of country's history and a progressive writer and singer forging a timeless contemporary country sound, she invites favorable comparisons to the best country divas." The impressive debut also led the Academy of Country Music (ACM) to nominate Evans in 1998 as the year's best new female vocalist.

## Progressive Follow-up

Despite sluggish sales, critical recognition helped Evans forge ahead, and in 1998 she released a follow-up album, *No Place that Far.* For the project, RCA hired Nashville-based producers Norro Wilson and Buddy Cannon. Her label also encouraged the singer to collaborate with Nashville songwriters such as Tom Shapiro, Tony Martin, Billy Yates, and Mantraca Berg. "It was a difficult process," Evans told Chet Flippo in *Billboard,* "but I feel we did it without being too contemporary."

The album's title track and second radio single, written by Evans along with Shapiro and Martin, and featuring the vocals of Vince Gill, travels through uplifting gospel territory as well as into darker rural harmonies reminiscent of the Carter Family. The song became Evans's first hit, climbing to the number one position on *Billboard's* Hot Country Singles and Tracks chart in March of 1999. Evans's favorite song, though, was one written by Howard and Beth Nielson Chapman, titled "Time Won't Tell." "Garth [Brooks] and Trisha [Yearwood] wanted it for their duet project, but Harlan gave it to us," she revealed to Flipp. "He's always been very big about helping new artists."

*No Place that Far,* with its stylistically varied songs, also fared well with critics. And country music fans approved of Evans's effort as well. The release rose to the top of the *Billboard* country album chart in early 1999. That same year, the musician earned additional honors when the Country Music Association (CMA) nominated her for two awards: video event of the year and the CMA's Horizon award, both for her work in 1998. After marrying Schelske, Evans made her home in Springfield, Tennessee. The couple had one son, Jack Avery, born August 21, 1999, followed by daughters Olivia in 2003 and Audrey Elizabeth in 2004.

Following the release of *Born to Fly,* Evans's stardom skyrocketed, bolstered by the success of the title song and its accompanying video, which was a clever homage to the 1939 film classic *The Wizard of Oz. Restless,* released in 2004, yielded another mega-smash single with "Suds in the Bucket," a song very much in the tradition of "Wide Open Spaces" by the Dixie Chicks and "She's in Love with the Boy" by Trisha Yearwood. The following year witnessed the release of *Real Fine Place,* another polished effort that combined contemporary sounds with traditional country instrumentation and themes.

In 2006 Evans's concert tours and singles from the album *Real Fine Place* helped her net a 2006 Top

Female Vocalist award at the 41st Annual Academy of Country Music Awards. She was also introduced to a much wider audience of fans when she appeared as a contestant on the reality television series *Dancing with the Stars.* She resigned from the show, however, when her marriage dissolved. Despite her personal travails, Evans continues to be one of country music's most cherished singers and performers.

## Selected discography

*Three Chords and the Truth,* RCA, 1997.
*No Place that Far,* RCA, 1998.
*Born to Fly,* RCA, 2000.
*Restless,* RCA, 2004.
*Real Fine Place,* RCA, 2005.

## Sources

### Periodicals

*American Enterprise,* March/April 1998, pp. 52-57.
*Billboard,* October 11, 1997, p. 83; September 26, 1998, p. 32; March 6, 1999, p. 114.
*Country Music,,* June/July 1999, p. 44.
*Rolling Stone,* December 1, 1998, p. 128.

### Online

"Country Singer Sara Evans Gives Birth," *CDNOW,* http://www.cdnow.com/cgi-bin/mserver/redirect/leaf=allstararticle/fid=16030 (October 24, 1999).
*Today: theEnews,* http://www.theenews.com/bms/tdn-slug82499_saraevans.html (October 24, 1999).

—Laura Hightower and Bruce Walker

# The
# Exploited

## Rock group

Loud, brash, rude, crude, obscene, and unpolished, with loads of attitude to spare, The Exploited were Scotland's entry into the punk foray of the late 1970s. The genre sprang up in the middle of the decade when New York three-chord rockers The Ramones visited the United Kingdom, inspiring such like-minded groups as the Sex Pistols, the Clash, the Adverts, and the Damned. By the end of the 1970s other groups had emerged, including the Jam, the Vibrators, and the Buzzcocks. These groups were distinctly anti-establishment, and eschewed middle-class values, refined musicianship, manners, and recording production values in favor of the DIY (do-it-yourself) aesthetic, impassioned vocal deliveries, and a total lack of reverence for almost everything previously held in high regard, including the Royal Family, politicians, and celebrities. Punk performers channeled the anger and "no-future" perceptions of a once-great empire currently suffering economic depression and rampant unemployment. The Exploited rode the crest of this wave and beyond. While most punk groups disbanded, imploded, or lost members to drug overdoses by the early 1980s, The Exploited instituted a revolving-door policy that rotated around leader Walter David "Wattie" Buchan, and have continued to record and perform under the band's brand name.

The earliest lineup of The Exploited to actually record consisted of Wattie on vocals, "Big John" Duncan on guitar, Dru Stix (real name: Glen Campbell) on drums, and Gary McCormick on bass. Wattie joined the band after his discharge from military service. Some sources reported that Wattie's brother Terry formed the band originally, but left shortly after Wattie's military discharge, thus beginning a chronic lineup change that continued well past the band's celebration of its twenty-fifth anniversary. The group members hailed from East Kilbride outside of Edinburgh, Scotland. Their energetic performances and punk attitude led to an extensive touring schedule, including serving as an opening act for such groups as U.K. Subs and the Cockney Rejects. Wattie, for example, took to wearing a Nazi swastika on stage, generating a skinhead, fascist following for the group, which eventually hampered a wider acceptance beyond Scotland punk audiences. The group, however, consistently maintained that the swastikas were nothing more than an accessory meant to tweak bourgeois complacency rather than display a racist point of view.

The Exploited released the first of several highly regarded singles in the 1980s. "Army Life" and its flipside, "F–k a Mod," captured Wattie's attitude about military service and the reemergence of the Mod subculture championed by such bands as The Jam. The group followed up their debut single with "Barmy Army" and "Dogs of War," which continued the band's diatribes against military service. The following year, Oi! Records included two songs by The Exploited, "Daily News" and "I Still Believe in Anarchy," on a record company compilation album. Secret Records signed the group to a recording contract, and released the live set *On Stage* and the follow-up studio debut album *Punk's Not Dead.* Recorded in three days, *Punk's Not Dead* reinvigorated the flagging punk scene, which had mostly evolved into power pop and New Wave music. According to *The Rough Guide to Punk, Punk's Not Dead* "was the rallying cry the rump end of punk had been waiting for. Blasts of polemic were spattered around in all directions as Wattie's sawn-off shotgun vocals took out chunks of the establishment." The album established the band as proponents of pacifism—ironic, considering the band members' propensity for inciting violence from the stage; in fact, riot police frequently were called to break up melees at the group's performances.

After releasing *Punk's Not Dead,* The Exploited embarked on a tour with the groups Discharge, Anti-Pasti, Chron Gen, and The Anti Nowhere League. The Exploited's next move served them well financially, but was problematic strategically. The three-song extended play single *Dead Cities* proved enormously successful, resulting in an offer to appear on the BBC music series *Top of the Pops.* Appearing on the program, however, caused the band's hardcore fans to write them off as commercial sell-outs. The single allegedly sold 20,000 copies before their appearance, but sold only 50 copies the day following their television appearance. *The Rough Guide to Punk,* however, labeled the performance "incendiary" and "the perfect backing track to the long summer of 1981, when the cities of the UK were intermittently aflame and riots were the order of the day."

**For the Record . . .**

Members include **Walter "Wattie" Buchan,** vocals; **William "Wullie" Buchan** (joined band in 1980s), drums; **"Big John" Duncan** (left band in 1982), guitar; **Dru Stix** (left band in 1980s), drums; **Danny Heatley** (joined band in latter incarnation), drums; **Steve Roberts** (joined band in latter incarnation), drums.

Formed in East Kilbride, Scotland, 1979; released *Punk's Not Dead,* 1981; released *Troops of Tomorrow,* 1982; Big John leaves band, 1982; released *Let's Start a War (Said Maggie One Day), 1983; released Horror Epics,* 1985; released *Beat the Bastards,* 1996; released documentary, *Rock & Roll Outlaws/Sexual Favours,* 2001.

Addresses: *Website*—The Exploited Official Website: http://www.the-exploited.net.

After releasing *Dead Cities,* The Exploited experienced extensive lineup changes. Drummer Dru Stix was sentenced to seven years in prison for armed robbery. Following the release of the albums *Troops of Tomorrow* and *Let's Start a War (Maggie Said One Day),* the group left Secret Records, and "Big John" Duncan and Gary McCormick quit the band, with Duncan going on to form the group Blood Uncles and eventually to play briefly with Seattle grunge pioneers Nirvana. The Exploited consisted now of only Wattie and whatever group of musicians played behind him. As described by Al Spicer in *Rock: The Rough Guide,* "Since then The Exploited has essentially been Wattie—still raging at the moon and kicking against the pricks—plus whoever he can draft in and keep upright." *The Rough Guide to Punk* concurred: "By this point, Wattie was the only member of the band who actually remembered when they started and where their roots lay. He kept an immoveable hand on the tiller, refusing any musical compromise and sneering at the idea of changing course lyrically through to the end of the decade and beyond."

In 1985 Wattie released *Horror Epics,* which marked a gravitation toward metal music. In 1989 Wattie and his musical backing group released *Death Before Dishonour,* followed by 1991's *The Massacre.* The last two albums prompted Spicer to assess that the recordings "are pretty peripheral unless you've decided to devote yourself to late-period punk rock and need to brush up on Scottish rage." Wattie and the boys reemerged in 1996 for *Beat the Bastards,* a recording of new songs about old rage. Various anthologies and reissues followed, as well as numerous live appearances and full-scale European tours.

## Selected discography

*Punk's Not Dead,* Secret, 1981; reissued on Snapper Classics, 2004.
*Troops of Tomorrow,* Secret, 1982.
*Totally Exploited,* Dojo, 1984.
*Let's Start a War (Said Maggie One Day),* MNW, 1983.
*Horror Epics,* Sub Pop, 1985.
*Live at the White House,* Suck, 1987.
*Death Before Dishonour,* Rough Justice, 1987.
*Live Lewd Lust,* Step-1, 1989.
*The Massacre,* Rough Justice, 1990.
*The Singles Collection,* Cleopatra, 1993.
*Beat the Bastards,* Rough Justice, 1996.
*Live in Japan,* Rough Justice, 1996.
*Live on Stage,* Harry May Records, 2000.
*F–k the System,* Spitfire, 2003.
*The Singles Collection,* Snapper Classics, 2005.

## Sources

### Books

*Rock: The Rough Guide,* Rough Guides, Ltd., London, 1999.
*The Rough Guide to Punk,* Rough Guides, Ltd., London, 2006.

### Online

*All Music Guide,* http://www.allmusic.com (Nov. 14, 2006).
The Exploited Official Website, http://www.the-exploited.net/history.htm (June 4, 2004).
*Passagen Hemsidor,* http://www.hem.passagen.se/strebers/exploited.htm (Nov. 16, 2006).

—Bruce Walker

# John Fogerty

**Singer, songwriter, guitarist**

© Ken Settle

John Fogerty is "a great American songwriter, with the clean-cut narrative gifts of [rock pioneer] Chuck Berry, the honesty of [country star] Hank Williams and the rave-up musical skills of a perfesser in a Saturday night juke joint," declared Jay Cocks of *Time*. Perhaps best known as the driving force behind what Jim Miller of *Newsweek* labeled "the best American rock band of its era," Creedence Clearwater Revival, Fogerty, with his writing, lead guitar, and vocals, led the group to prominence during the late 1960s and early 1970s. With the other members of Creedence, he is responsible for rock classics such as "Proud Mary," "Bad Moon Rising," and "Who'll Stop the Rain." After Creedence disbanded in 1972, Fogerty's first attempt at making a solo career for himself was only moderately successful. During the mid-1970s he became embroiled in legal battles with Fantasy, Creedence's record label, and an accounting firm that had allegedly mishandled his funds. Embittered, he dropped out of the music scene for approximately nine years. In 1985, however, Fogerty resurfaced with a new album, *Centerfield*. In addition to the smash title track paean to baseball, it included the hits "The Old Man down the Road" and "Rock and Roll Girls." Hailed by critics and fans alike, the album established him as a popular artist in his own right.

## Found Fame with Creedence

The multi talented Fogerty began his musical career while still in junior high in El Cerrito, California. He joined with fellow students Stu Cook and Doug Clifford to form a group called the Blue Velvets. They were later joined by Fogerty's older brother, Tom, and performed in the San Francisco Bay area. The young men also made a few recordings on small local labels such as Kristy and Orchestra, but these efforts did not sell. In 1964, however, the Blue Velvets landed a contract with Fantasy Records in nearby Berkeley. A year later the group had changed its name to the Golliwogs, but they were still unable to craft a hit record. Fantasy lost interest in them, and the band recorded a few singles for the local Scorpio label. Eventually, label honcho Saul Zaentz encouraged the Golliwogs to re-sign, though he suggested the group find itself a better name. Thus, in 1968 they were re-christened Creedence Clearwater Revival.

Creedence's first hit single was a 1968 revision of Dale Hawkins's 1957 hit "Suzie Q.," with John Fogerty singing the lead. Subsequently, the band primarily kept to recording Fogerty's original compositions. In 1969 Creedence scored with several chart hits, including "Proud Mary," "Bad Moon Rising," "Lodi," "Green River," and "Commotion." They followed these up with 1970's "Who'll Stop the Rain," "Looking Out My Back Door," and "Run through the Jungle," which Cocks

Born John Cameron Fogerty on May 28, 1945, in Berkeley, CA; son of Gaylord Robert (a printer) and Lucille (a teacher) Fogerty; married; first wife, Martha Piaz, second wife, Julie Lebiedzinski; four children.

Singer, songwriter, guitarist, 1959–; played with the Blue Velvets beginning 1959, name changed to the Golliwogs, c. 1965, and then Creedence Clearwater Revival, 1968-72; joined the Army Reserve and served six months of active duty, 1966; solo artist, 1972-76; dropped out of music business, c. 1976-85; solo recording artist and concert performer, 1985–; has recorded for Fantasy, Asylum, Warner Bros., and Geffen.

Awards: Inducted into Rock and Roll Hall of Fame as member of Creedence Clearwater Revival, 1993; Grammy Award for Best Rock Album, for *Blue Moon Swamp*, 1997; Recipient of the Orville H. Gibson Lifetime Achievement Award, 1998; inducted into the Songwriters Hall of Fame, 2005.

Addresses: *Record company*—Fantasy / Concord Music Group, 270 North Canon Dr., 1212, Beverly Hills, CA 90210, label website: http://www.concordmusicgroup. com. *Booking*—Creative Artists Agency, 9830 Wilshire Blvd., Beverly Hills, CA 90212-1825. *Website*—Official John Fogerty Website: http://www.johnfogerty.com.

called one of "the first songs about Viet Nam that sounded as if [it] could have been sung by the soldiers as well as peace marchers." In 1971, however, tensions arising from John Fogerty's artistic domination of the group led older brother Tom to quit the band. Though John Fogerty subsequently shared the songwriting tasks with the remaining members, and completed a successful European tour with them, Creedence finally broke up in 1972.

## Went Solo in 1973

After Fogerty became a solo artist, he released the country-flavored *Blue Ridge Rangers* in 1973. Through the use of overdubbing different tracks during the recording process, he played all the instruments and sang all the vocals himself. Fogerty's efforts were re-

warded with borderline hit status for the album's single "Hearts of Stone."

Fogerty stopped recording in the mid-1970s, when legal disputes with Fantasy and his accounting firm began to take up much of his time. An album of disco-oriented material titled *Hoodoo* was planned in 1976 for Asylum, but the label's president convinced the artist to withdraw the mediocre disc and get to work on whatever was blocking his creative process. "There was an anvil over my head," Fogerty told Cocks. "Writing, the music, my understanding of 'arrange' and 'produce' were gone." But he planned to make a comeback when the legal battles were over, and he continued to practice daily.

Finally, during the early 1980s, Fogerty began to write songs again. He composed what would become *Centerfield* in roughly five and a half months, and took the results to Warner Brothers Records. According to Cocks, Fogerty asked Lenny Waronker, the president of the company, "How does a 39-year-old has-been rock singer get you to listen to his records?" But Waronker listened, and *Centerfield* was on its way.

Most critics raved about the 1985 release, on which Fogerty again played all the instruments himself; most of them also noted its relationship to the swampy-sounding Creedence repertoire. "Fogerty's new music [is] like rediscovering a long-lost friend," Miller observed, and Kurt Loder of *Rolling Stone* proclaimed it "a near-seamless extension of the Creedence sound and a record that's likely to convert a whole new generation of true believers." *Centerfield* rose quickly on the album charts, hitting the Top Ten in only three weeks. "The Old Man down the Road," the first single from the album, "sounds like nothing else on the radio," applauded Cocks, "a swampy, spooky piece of backcountry funk about a mojo man who becomes a figure of mystery, and of death." The album's title song, in which Fogerty uses his love of baseball as a metaphor for his joy in making music, became not only a hit record but a standard anthem played in baseball stadiums across the United States. Other interesting cuts from *Centerfield* included "Big Train," a tribute to the old rockabilly sound of Sun Records, and "Zanz Kant Danz," which Loder speculated might be an attack on the former head of Fantasy Records, Saul Zaentz. Indeed, to circumvent litigation, Warner changed the title of the tune to "Vanz Kant Danz" on later releases of the album.

Cocks declared that Fogerty's music seems "timeless ... torn out of some imaginary territory in rock's persistent past." Miller concluded that "Fogerty's sensibility has an enduring popular appeal," and hailed him as "the once and future poet laureate of the pop single."

### Re-embraced His Classic Songs

Fogerty quickly followed up with 1985's *Eye of the Zombie,* a less gimmicky, harder rocking album that sported darker overtones. The apocalyptic sentiments expressed in such songs such as "Violence is Golden," "Headlines," and "Eye of the Zombie" sat well with critics. Anthony DeCurtis of *Rolling Stone* praised Fogerty's "ability to dramatize sociopolitical realities in unpretentious flesh and blood terms."

Fogerty's recording career has endured notorious fits and starts. Some of the gaps between albums were due to his long and costly involvement in lawsuits, while others were caused by his slow, methodical working method. After a rash of creativity during the mid-1980s, he simply didn't release another album for eleven years. During that time away from the recording studio, he began playing live shows and benefits, eventually warming to the idea of performing some of his best-loved CCR material again.

This change in attitude crystalized after the 1997 release of *Blue Moon Swamp.* A simple, roots-music-drenched set boasting fine hook songs and heartfelt performance, the album featured smartly crafted rockers that echoed early CCR, ala "Hot Rod Heart," "Rambunctious Boy," and "Swamp River." While touring behind the disc, Fogerty caused a stir by performing several old classics along with his new material. Buoyed by the positive reaction to his old CCR tunes, Fogerty released the live concert set *Premonition* in 1998.

The inclusion of his classic CCR material in his live set made Fogerty a major concert draw again. Artistically, his early Vietnam protest anthems provided a sense of continuity for his 2004 release *Deja Vu All Over Again.* The album was a grab bag collection of neatly crafted rockers, swamp blues, and country, and the title track caused a stir by comparing the circumstances in Vietnam to the war in Iraq. Overnight, Fogerty was considered relevant again.

Fogerty surprised longtime fans by returning to the label where it all started for him, Fantasy Records. By then Saul Zaentz had sold the label to the Concord Music Group, and famed TV producer Norman Lear, an investor with the group, convinced the singer-songwriter to return to Fantasy in 2005. His first project there was a dual CD/DVD release that highlighted live renditions of his best-known songs from every phase of his career, titled *The Long Road Home—The Concert.* Sounding surprisingly young and commanding the stage with impressive energy and verve, the 60-year-old Fogerty used the disc to pay his respects to the fans who had remained loyal through all the legal battles and lengthy hiatuses. "God bless you for being fans. All that love that's coming up this way? Well, right back at you!. … Thank you for sticking with me all these years."

## Selected discography

### Singles

"Jambalaya (On the Bayou)," Fantasy, 1973.
"Hearts of Stone," Fantasy, 1973.
"Rockin' All Over the World," Asylum, 1975.
"Almost Saturday Night," Asylum, 1975.
"The Old Man Down the Road," Warner, 1985.
"Rock and Roll Girls," Warner, 1985.
"Centerfield," Warner, 1985.
"Working in a Hurricane," Warner, 1997.
"Premonition," Warner, 1997.

## Albums With Creedence Clearwater Revival

*Creedence Clearwater Revival,* Fantasy, 1968; reissued, 2005.
*Bayou Country,* Fantasy, 1969; reissued, 2005.
*Green River,* Fantasy, 1969; reissued, 2005.
*Willy and the Poor Boys,* Fantasy, 1969; reissued, 2005.
*Cosmo's Factory,* Fantasy, 1970; reissued, 2005.
*Pendulum,* Fantasy, 1970; reissued, 2005.
*Mardi Gras,* Fantasy, 1972; reissued, 2005.
*Live in Europe,* Fantasy, 1973; reissued, 2005.
*Live in Germany,* Fantasy, 1973; reissued, 2005.
*The Concert [Live]* Fantasy, 1980.
*Mardi Gras,* Fantasy, 1972; reissued, 2005.
*Creedence Clearwater Revival,* (Box Set), Fantasy, 2001.
*The Ultimate Creedence Clearwater Revival,* Fantasy, 2005.
*26 Greatest Hits,* Fantasy, 2006.

## Solo Albums

*Blue Ridge Rangers,* Fantasy, 1973; reissued, 1994.
*John Fogerty,* Asylum, 1975; reissued, Fantasy, 2002.
*Centerfield,* Warner Brothers, 1985; reissued, Dreamworks, 2005.
*Eye of the Zombie,* Warner Brothers, 1986; reissued, Dreamworks, 2001.
*Blue Moon Swamp,* Warner Brothers, 1997.
*Premonition [Live],* Warner Brothers, 1998; reissued, Geffen, 2004.
*Deja Vu All Over Again,* Geffen, 2004.
*The Long Road Home—In Concert,* Fantasy, 2006.

## Videos

*Premonition [Live],* Warner Brothers, 1998.
*The Long Road Home,* Fantasy/Concord Music Group, 2005.

## Sources

### Books

Bordowitz, Hank, *Bad Moon Rising—The Unofficial History of Creedence Clearwater Revival,* Schirmer, 1998.
Rees, Dafydd and Luke Crampton, *VH1 Music First—Rock Stars Encyclopedia,* Dorling Kindersly, 1999.

## Periodicals

*Newsweek,* February 18, 1985.
*Rolling Stone,* January 31, 1985; March 14, 1985.
*Time,* January 28, 1985.

## Online

"John Fogerty," *All Music Guide, http://www.allmusic.com* (November 2, 2006).

"John Fogerty," *Internet Movie Database,* http://www.imdb.com. (November 2, 2006).

"John Fogerty," *Rolling Stone.com,* http://www.rollingstone.com. (November 2, 2006).

"John Fogerty Embraces His Past," *CMT.com,* http://www.cmy.com/news/articles/1518067/20051213/fogerty_john.jhtml?headlines=t. (November 2, 2006)

—*Elizabeth Thomas and Ken Burke*

# David Foster

Keyboardist, songwriter, composer, producer, music arranger, recording executive

Frederick M. Brown/Getty Images

David Foster started his music career at the age of five in Victoria, British Columbia, Canada. He began with piano lessons, and his talent quickly distinguished him from other children his age. When he turned 13, Foster enrolled at the University of Washington to study music. He launched his professional career three years later when he joined the backup band of rock and roll legend Chuck Berry.

Foster moved to Los Angeles in 1971 with his band Skylark. In 1973 Skylark's song "Wildflower" reached number nine on the *Billboard* charts. Foster parlayed that milestone into a career as a session keyboard player. When Skylark disbanded and its members decided to return to Canada, Foster remained in Los Angeles. "I had this overwhelming desire to meet all the great musicians and play with them. I was young and hungry, and a very positive thinker," Foster told *Keyboard.*

He played keyboards in the orchestra pit for the Roxy Theatre's production of *The Rocky Horror Picture Show* for a year and eventually became the show's co-director. *Rocky Horror* garnered considerable recognition, and many producers and musicians noticed Foster's talents when they attended performances. The orchestra would play whatever the conductor chose for half an hour before the show. When people in the music industry heard Foster play keyboards, they began calling him to participate in their recording sessions during the day.

Foster built a strong reputation as a talented session keyboard player, working with such stars as John Lennon, George Harrison, Barbra Streisand, and Rod Stewart. He added his input to songwriting and arrangement in sessions, and eventually worked his way into producing and writing his own songs. His early production clients included Alice Cooper, the Average White Band, Boz Scaggs, and Carole Bayer Sager.

The turning point in Foster's production career came after a life-changing conversation with fellow producer Quincy Jones, when Foster realized that he needed to demand the best from the artists with whom he worked in order to make the best albums he could.

Foster earned his first big-name producing credit with two albums by Daryl Hall and John Oates. He not only proved he could recognize good songs, he confirmed he could write them as well. In 1979 he won his first Grammy Award, for best rhythm and blues song, for co-writing Earth, Wind and Fire's "After the Love Has Gone" with Jay Graydon and Bill Champlin.

Three years later he received his second Grammy, for Producer of the Year, for the cast album of the Tony Award-winning Broadway musical *Dreamgirls.* The album climbed to number eleven on the *Billboard* charts, the highest-charting cast recording since *Hair* in 1969.

Born November 1, 1950, in Victoria, British Columbia, Canada; immigrated to U.S., 1971. First wife named Rebecca; married Linda Thompson (a songwriter), divorced, July 11, 2005; children: (first marriage) four daughters, (second marriage) two stepsons. *Education:* Studied music at University of Washington.

Began playing piano with singer-guitarist Chuck Berry at 16; member of band Skylark; worked as session keyboard player; became producer, early 1970s; released first solo recording on Sound Design Records, 1982; released album *David Foster,* Atlantic, 1986; established David Foster Foundation, 1986; became senior vice president of A&R, Atlantic Records, 1994; produced music for films, including *The Secret of My Success, St. Elmo's Fire, Urban Cowboy, Summer Lovers, One Good Cop, If Looks Could Kill,* and *Karate Kid Part II*; produced songs and albums for numerous pop artists, including Whitney Houston, All-4-One, Celine Dion, Barbra Streisand, Color Me Badd, and Natalie Cole.

Awards: Grammy Awards (with Jay Graydon and Bill Champlin), for Best Rhythm and Blues Song, for "After the Love Has Gone," 1979; Producer of the Year, for *Dreamgirls,* 1982; Producer of the Year, for *Chicago 17* and Best Instrumental Arrangement Accompanying Vocals, for "Hard Habit to Break," both 1984; Producer of the Year, for "Somewhere," 1985; Producer of the Year, Song of the Year, and Record of the Year, all for *Unforgettable,* 1992; Record of the Year, for "I Will Always Love You"; Album of the Year, for "The Bodyguard"; Best Instrumental Arrangement Accompanying Vocals, for "When I Fall in Love," and Producer of the Year, Non-Classical, all 1994; Album of the Year, for "Falling Into You"; Best Instrumental Arrangement Accompanying Vocals, for "When I Fall in Love," both 1997; *Billboard* magazine, named top singles producer and top R&B singles producer of 1993; Order of Canada.

Addresses: *Record company*—Atlantic Records, 75 Rockefeller Plaza, New York, NY 10019.

Foster gained further accolades when Chicago's "Hard to Say I'm Sorry" from *Chicago 16,* which he cowrote and produced, reached number one on the *Billboard* charts.

Foster released his first solo album, *Best of Me,* on a Japanese label, and Sound Design Records released it in the United States in 1982. The following year, Foster produced Lionel Richie's album *Can't Slow Down,* which sold a whopping ten million copies. By that time, he had cemented his place as one of popular music's top producers. Yet he refused to rest on his laurels, relishing the variety his prominence allowed him. "I know I've done a little too much jumping around already in my career," Foster told Paul Green of *Billboard.* "Someone once described me as a person who couldn't keep a job. But I love the fact that I can produce the Tubes and get a big AOR [album-oriented rock] hit and turn around and do a solo album that sounds like 'Love Story' 83' and then also work with the R&B acts."

Foster continued producing and writing virtually nonstop, earning two more Grammy Awards in 1984: for Chicago's *Chicago 17,* he received Producer of the Year, and for the song "Hard Habit to Break" he was recognized for Best Instrumental Arrangement Accompanying Vocals.

But his nonstop work pace started to take its toll. After a lifetime of 16-hour days, Foster reached a point of such mental and physical exhaustion that he thought he'd lost his magical musical touch. He decided to return to Canada with his wife, Rebecca, and take a break. Just as he settled in, Quincy Jones asked him to write and produce a Canadian version of the English Band-Aid project and the American "We Are the World" effort that raised money for hunger relief in Africa. He rose to the occasion, composing and producing Northern Lights' "Tears Are Not Enough." When a video about the production hit Canadian TV, Foster gained the recognition that had previously eluded him in his homeland. Indeed, though many Canadians knew Foster's work, they did not realize that he was Canadian.

Giving up on his hiatus, he went back to Los Angeles. Shortly thereafter, the magic touch clearly still with him, he produced the hit single "Somewhere" for Barbra Streisand's *Broadway* album, for which he won his fifth Grammy.

Beginning on May 5, 1984, after "Stay the Night"—the first single from *Chicago 17*—debuted at number 49, Foster had at least one single on *Billboard*'s Hot 100 chart every week until April of 1986. During most weeks of that two-year period, he had two or more records on the charts simultaneously. And in August of 1985 he had a remarkable five singles on the charts at the same time.

Foster released a self-titled album on Atlantic Records in 1986, which included a duet with Olivia Newton-John. Also that year he established the David Foster Foundation to assist families of children who need organ transplants, and started the David Foster Celebrity Softball Game in Victoria, British Columbia, to raise funds for his foundation.

His next solo album, *The Symphony Sessions* (1988), featured Foster performing his compositions with the Vancouver Symphony Orchestra. This included "Winter Games," the song he wrote for the 1988 Calgary Winter Olympics. A one-hour TV special, "David Foster: The Symphony Sessions," aired on CBC-TV in Toronto to promote the album, and was released as a 36-minute home video. Also that year, Foster received the Order of Canada for his humanitarian efforts.

Foster released *River of Love* in 1990, which included the single "Grown-Up Christmas," sung by Natalie Cole. Brian Wilson, Bryan Adams, Bruce Hornsby, Mike Reno, and others contributed both songs and performances to the album. The following year, Foster released *Rechordings,* which featured instrumental versions of Foster's best-loved compositions. He also wrote music to second wife Linda Thompson's lyrics for "Voices That Care," the entertainment industry's salute to U.S. troops in the Persian Gulf War. The project raised more than $500,000 for the Red Cross and USO of America.

Foster received three more Grammy Awards in 1992 for Natalie Cole's hit album *Unforgettable,* and he also co-produced Streisand's album *Back to Broadway,* which entered the *Billboard* charts at number one in 1993. As if this weren't enough, at the end of the year he released *The Christmas Album,* which featured some of his favorite vocalists singing their best-loved Christmas songs backed by an 80-piece orchestra. *Billboard* named Foster top singles producer and top R&B singles producer in their 1993 year-end wrap-up.

*Time* reporter Charles P. Alexander noted in 1994, "Over the past two years, Foster productions have held the No. 1 spot on *Billboard* magazine's Hot 100 more than 25% of the time." The pop guru's domination of the charts was secured throughout 1993 and 1994 by Whitney Houston's "I Will Always Love You," Canadian pop singer Celine Dion's "The Power of Love," and newcomer All-4-One's "I Swear," each of which spent several weeks in the number one position.

Foster took his career in yet another direction in 1994 when he joined Atlantic Records as senior vice president of A&R (artists and repertoire), with a three-year production contract. Though his contract allowed him to work with artists on other labels, the position gave him an outlet to develop new artists. Between 1994 and 1997, four songs he produced reached the top of *Billboard's* Hot 100 and stayed there for 42 weeks. While at Atlantic, Foster also produced albums for country singer Kevin Sharp, Irish singers the Corrs, and classical singer Josh Groban.

In 2005 Foster began filming a reality series about his own life, "The Princes of Malibu." However, the show began to reveal stresses in his marriage to Linda Thompson, and the couple divorced later in 2005.

With a lifetime of writing, producing, and sometimes performing hit music, the 12-time Grammy-winning Foster summed up the purpose and theory of his career in one sentence of his Atlantic Records press biography, allowing, "I gravitate toward tugging at heartstrings—and I treat every day in the studio as life or death."

## Selective Works

*Best of Me,* Sound Design, 1982.
*David Foster,* Atlantic, 1986.
*The Symphony Sessions,* Atlantic, 1988.
*River of Love,* Atlantic, 1990.
*Rechordings,* Atlantic, 1991.
*David Foster: The Christmas Album,* Interscope, 1993.

## Sources

*Billboard,* July 30, 1983; October 26, 1985; May 24, 1986; July 26, 1986; April 23, 1988; October 5, 1991; March 14, 1992; October 9, 1993; December 4, 1993; December 25, 1993; February 5, 2005, p. 48.
*Hollywood Reporter,* August 31, 2006, p. 16.
*Keyboard,* February 1986; September 1986; March 1988; January 1992.
*Maclean's,* July 18, 2005, p. 50.
*New York Times,* December 10, 1993.
*People,* August 8, 2005, p. 26.
*Time,* August 29, 1994.
*Time International,* March 24, 2005, p.50.
*Variety,* May 21, 1986; May 11, 1988; July 8, 2005, p. 8.

Additional information for this profile was obtained from Atlantic Records press material, 1994.

—*Sonya Shelton and Kelly Winters*

# French Kicks

## Rock group

With three-part harmonies and an incomparable pop-rock sound, Brooklyn band the French Kicks have created an impressive and variant collection of albums since their creation in 1998. In the early 2000s, in terms of music and popular culture press, Detroit and New York City, especially Brooklyn, were the most talked about cities being credited for the "rebirth" of rock 'n' roll music. Along with a bevy of bands that included The Strokes and dozens of others, at their onslaught, the French Kicks thrived outside of the city and the a buzz, making their names known on the independent scene for their music merit and not just because they were from Brooklyn. "French Kicks are not a traditional rock 'n' roll band. Although they have elements of snarly garage rock, slick new wave, and giddy classic mod-pop, they remain completely unique," stated music video channel MuchMusic's website.

At six feet six inches tall, musician Nick Stumpf grew up in Washington, D.C., playing the piano at his mother's request. Although he now thanks his mother for forcing him to learn the piano, at the time, Stumpf wanted nothing more than to play the drums. In high school, once he was able to pay for them on his own, Stumpf finally bought his own drum set and started playing in bands with his friend and guitarist Matt Stinchcomb. After they set off to study at Oberlin College, a prestigious music and arts university in Ohio, the pair was joined by bassist Jamie Krents. When the trio picked up and moved to Brooklyn, New York, in 1998, they met Alabama-born guitarist/keyboardist Josh Wise at a party and soon the French Kicks were born.

Taking influences from the art-rock music scenes in D.C. and Oberlin, the quartet mixed sharp and angular guitar lines with savory three-part harmonies and just-catchy-enough pop choruses to make a distinctive and uncategorical new style of rock music. Stumpf was manning the drums, but also singing most of the lead vocals as well; a sight rarely seen in contemporary rock bands. Stinchcomb and Wise played guitars and harmonized with Stumpf while he buoyantly bounced up and down on his drum stool while singing his heart out. The band quickly scrounged up a self-titled, four-song demolike EP, and released it via independent Chicago label My Pal God Records in the fall of 1999.

Although the French Kicks' EP got some press, it was apparent that the band needed a record label that was as fresh as they were. In 2001, the quartet signed to StarTime International, a new label started by Isaac Green in Brooklyn. The French Kicks' next release would be the label's premiere artist. To record their new EP for StarTime, the French Kicks retreated to a farm in West Virginia for the summer. In the middle of nowhere, with producer Greg Talenfield (known for his work with Beck and Pavement), the French Kicks captured the guttural sound of the new blood of NYC bands juxtaposed with immaculate sunny harmonies. In 2001, StarTime released the *Young Lawyer* EP and sent the band on a tour of small clubs in the United States. *The Portland Mercury*'s Bradley Steinbacher called *Young Lawyer* "about as perfect as indie rock can be. Brief, packed-yet-simple, each song sheds the girth of what much of indie rock has become, and instead, leaves behind what you want and expect—a smart, catchy, and ridiculously creative recording."

Near the end of the year, the band and producer Talenfield embarked on a journey to make the French Kicks debut full-length album. Recorded in New York, and released in 2002, *One Time Bells* was a jump from *Young Lawyer*—cleaner and more streamlined, a mature album. Muchmusic.com called the record "a perfect crystallization of French Kicks' taut, clipped, frequently beautiful sound." In an interview with Mike Tiernan of *Boston's Weekly Dig,* Stumpf talked about the making of *One Time Bells,* recalling that there wasn't a concrete plan to have the album sound so different from *Young Lawyer.* "One of the rules that we go by is that we do whatever we feel like doing and go by what we like," he told Tiernan about the new record. "It doesn't have to sound like anything in particular." Tiernan described the effort as "a subtle gem that displays a unique concoction of rough harmony, tumbling drums, ringing keyboard, jolty guitar, and bouncing bass."

After touring exhaustively for *One Time Bells,* lead singer Stumpf made the decision to focus on his vocals and hire a drummer to fill out the band to a five-piece. In 2003, drummer Aaron Thurston joined the French Kicks pushing the band into new terrain. Without limitations of sitting behind the drum kit, Stumpf was able

## For the Record . . .

**M**embers include **Kush El Amin** (joined group, 2006), guitar, keyboards, percussion; **Matt Stinchcomb** (left group, 2005), guitar, vocals; **Lawrence Stumpf** (replaced Jamie Krents, 2001), bass; **Nick Stumpf**, lead vocals, keyboards; **Aaron Thurston** (joined band, 2003), drums; **Josh Wise**, guitar, vocals.

Group formed in Brooklyn, NY, 1998; released four-song self-titled EP, 1999; signed to new Brooklyn label StarTime International, released *Young Lawyer* EP, 2001; released debut full-length CD *One Time Bells*, 2002; released *The Trial of the Century*, 2004, and *Two Thousand*, 2006.

Addresses: *Record company*—StarTime International Records, 328 Flatbush Ave., PMB #297, Brooklyn, NY 11238; Vagrant Records, 2118 Wilshire Blvd. #361, Santa Monica, CA 90403. *Website*—French Kicks Official Website: http://www.frenchkicks.com.

to focus more on his vocals and keyboards, while moving about the stage, giving the band more vigor. The band tested out their new lineup in February of 2003 in a week-long residency at New York's Mercury Lounge.

In 2004, the band teamed with producer Doug Boehm for *The Trial of the Century*, an album miles away from their first recordings. "I think we've managed to capture something that is potentially difficult to do: just having a somewhat clean sound yet at the same time something that doesn't sound gutless," Stumpf told the website Straight.com. "It's got some balls in some way. It's not raw; that's not what we're doing." The critics began to judge the band on their musical merits and not just their zip code. *Billboard*'s Brian Garrity praised *The Trial of the Century*, labeling it "a fully realized work of sweet, sophisticated hipster rock that floats on atmospheric layers of keyboards and guitars."

After touring for the record, Stumpf and Wise spent a large part of 2005 writing and working on songs for what would be their third album. In an interview with website Skratchmagazine.com, Stumpf admitted that he and Wise stayed inside a lot that year, keeping themselves almost isolated from outside influences. "We were pretty insular about this one; we worked on

it on our own," he said. "We were interested in writing the best songs that we could and just structuring them and making them sound cool. So, we kind of had our head in the sand. We had blinders on." Before the band left for Los Angeles to begin recording their new album, founding member Stinchcomb left the group. As a four-piece yet once again, the French Kicks ventured out to Los Angeles for an intense one-month recording session with producer Boehm.

Bringing back some of the unrefined energy from their early days, the group's 2006 release, *Two Thousand*, was a continued wave of the atmospheric pop and sticky guitars heard on *The Trial of the Century*. "Though they've been around for eights years, Brooklyn's French Kicks always manage to seem young, playing their tender post-punk that's so pristined it *sounds* fresh-scrubbed … on every new effort," wrote Tristan Staddon in *Alternative Press*. To round out the band's live sound and help to play the myriad new sounds and instruments explored on *Two Thousand*, multi-instrumentalist Kush El Amin joined the French Kicks on guitar, keyboards, and percussion for the band's 2006 tour.

## Selected discography

*French Kicks* (EP), My Pal God Records, 1999.
*Young Lawyer* (EP), StarTime International, 2001.
*One Time Bells*, StarTime International, 2002.
*The Trial of the Century*, StarTime International, 2004.
*Two Thousand*, StarTime International/Vagrant Records, 2006.

## Sources

### Periodicals

*Alternative Press*, October 4, 2006.
*Billboard*, June 5, 2004, p. 31.
*Boston's Weekly Dig*, December 4, 2002.
*The Georgia Straight*, May 13, 2004.
*The Portland Mercury* (Portland, OR), January 31–February 6, 2002.

### Online

"French Kicks," *MuchMusic*, http://www.muchmusic.com/music/artists/index.asp?artist=301 (October 30, 2006).
"French Kicks," StarTime International Records, http://www.startimerecords.com/frenchkicks.html (October 30, 2006).
"French Kicks Interview," *Skratch Magazine*, http://www.skratchmagazine.com/interviews/interviews.php?id=192 (October 30, 2006).

—*Shannon McCarthy*

# David Gilmour

**Guitar player, singer, songwriter**

© Peter Andrews/Corbis

One of the most-recognized guitarists of the rock era for his distinctive blues-rock phrasings with the progressive British band Pink Floyd, David Gilmour consistently appears on magazine readers' polls of influential rock musicians. His turbulent relationship with Pink Floyd's bassist and chief lyricist, Roger Waters, however, led him to establish a solo career during the period of the band's peak success in the late 1970s. When the band went on hiatus in 1984 after the release of *The Final Cut,* Gilmour released his second solo album with help from the Who's principal songwriter, Pete Townshend. A subsequent solo tour failed to generate widespread excitement, due to the general public's failure to recognize Gilmour as one of the architects of Pink Floyd's distinctive sound, which resulted in his re-forming the band without Waters. The subsequent studio and live albums and tours proved that a Gilmour-led Floyd could be a financial if not a critical success in the same vein as the Waters-era group. Gilmour spent the next several years playing as a guest guitarist on albums by other artists, and recording tracks for his third solo album. Prior to the album's release, however, Gilmour and Waters put aside their longstanding differences long enough to reunite Pink Floyd with original members Nick Mason and Richard Wright for a one-off charity performance at Live 8 in 2005. Gilmour released *On an Island* on his sixtieth birthday in 2006.

Gilmour was one of four children born to Doug Gilmour, a professor of genetics, and his wife, Sylvia, a schoolteacher and film editor. The first recording the youngster purchased was Bill Haley and the Comets' "Rock Around the Clock" in 1954. He got his first guitar when he was 13, and taught himself to play using Pete Seeger instructional books and records. In 1962 he entered Cambridge Technical College, where he studied modern languages. While enrolled at Cambridge, he met Roger "Syd" Barrett. The pair became close friends, and Gilmour taught Barrett several guitar progressions from Rolling Stones records. The two attended performances by the Rolling Stones and Bob Dylan, listened to Beatles records, and performed together. While Barrett leaned more toward blues in his bands Those Without and The Hollerin' Blues, Gilmour focused more on pop music in his groups The Newcomers and The Ramblers. In 1965 the pair traveled as itinerant musicians through the south of France.

The two friends parted ways when Barrett was accepted at Camberwell College of Arts in London. Gilmour, in the meantime, stayed at Cambridge, where he formed the band Jokers Wild with drummer Clive Welham. Jokers Wild played U.S. military bases and established a residency at the Victoria Ballroom, where they opened for such internationally successful acts as the Animals. The steady income served him well, as his parents moved to New York City and left their son to fend for himself.

## For the Record . . .

**B**orn David Gilmour on March 6, 1946, in Grantchester Meadows, England; son of Doug (a professor) and Sylvia (a teacher and film editor) Gilmour; married Ginger (divorced); married journalist Polly Samson, 1994.

Guitarist with group Jokers Wild, 1960s; joined Pink Floyd, 1968; recorded first solo album, *David Gilmour*, 1978; released second solo effort, *About Face*, 1984; re-formed band Pink Floyd with Nick Mason, 1986; reunited with all three members of post-Syd Barrett Pink Floyd for an appearance at Live 8, 2005; released third solo album, *On an Island*, 2006.

Addresses: *Record company*—Sony BMG Entertainment, 550 Madison Ave., New York, NY 10022-3211.

In October of 1965, Jokers Wild played a bill with Barrett's new band, Pink Floyd, and Paul Simon. Pink Floyd, under Barrett's leadership, went on to become the darlings of London's psychedelic drug-fueled underground. They released their critically acclaimed debut album, *The Piper at the Gates of Dawn,* in 1967. Gilmour spent 1967 in France with bassist Rick Wills and drummer John "Willie" Wilson. Billing themselves as Flowers and, later, Bullitt, the group endured such hardships as the theft of all their equipment before a concert in Paris. The trio returned to England penniless, the rhythm section returning to Cambridge while Gilmour went to London, where he attended a Pink Floyd concert. By this time Barrett had become a victim of mental illness, most likely exacerbated by ingesting copious amounts of the drug LSD. Barrett's bandmates asked Gilmour to join as a fifth member, and shortly thereafter they fired Barrett.

The next ten years was a rollercoaster of artistic struggles and successes, including the 1973 release of the group's masterpiece, *Dark Side of the Moon,*1975's *Wish You Were Here,* and 1977's *Animals.* Personality clashes within the band resulted from Waters's reputed autocratic drive to create the concepts and lyrics for the group's albums subsequent to *Wish You Were Here.* By the time Pink Floyd recorded *Animals,* Waters had assumed nearly total creative control of the band. Gilmour's trademark guitar and plaintive vocals were still very much part of the album's song cycle, but his participation in the project's creation was minimal. He later disparaged the album, and refused to play any *Animals* material in either solo or latter day Pink Floyd concerts. During the 1970s he focused on producing

such bands as Unicorn, Sutherland Brothers and Quiver, worked with vocalist Roy Harper, and helped launch the musical career of Kate Bush, introducing her to EMI Records.

Following the release of *Animals* and its subsequent tour, Gilmour recorded his first solo album, *David Gilmour.* He enlisted help from his old bandmates from Bullitt, Rick Wills and Willie Wilson, for the effort, which consisted mainly of atmospheric guitar-based instrumentals composed by Gilmour. Gilmour returned to the Pink Floyd fold to record *The Wall* (1979) and *The Final Cut* (1983). By the time these albums were recorded, Waters had been instrumental in firing keyboardist Richard Wright from the band, and had become increasingly estranged from Gilmour and Nick Mason.

Following the release of *The Final Cut,* Gilmour recorded his second solo effort. In *About Face* (1984), Pete Townshend contributed lyrics to two of the album's songs, but the remainder were written by Gilmour. The funky "Blue Light" was released as a single and video, with modest success. Gilmour became the first Floyd member to mount a solo tour, with help from Mott the Hoople and Bad Company lead guitarist Mick Ralphs. The shows from that tour featured songs from both *David Gilmour* and *About Face,* as well as a healthy sampling of Floyd classics, including "Money" and "Comfortably Numb." Ticket sales were far below the level of Pink Floyd concerts, however, and Gilmour spent the next two years working as a hired gun for such artists as Townshend and Roxy Music's Bryan Ferry.

Gilmour's relationship with Waters grew into a full-blown feud in the mid-1980s, when Gilmour announced his plans to record his next album as a Pink Floyd project without Waters's help. From 1987 to 1994, Gilmour led the remaining members of Pink Floyd and a cadre of hired musicians and backup singers through two studio albums, two massively successful concert tours, and two live albums. He also recorded and performed with former Beatle Paul McCartney. Then, perhaps with nothing left to prove to his arch-rival Waters, he reunited with Waters, Mason, and Wright for a one-off performance at Live 8 in 2005. The performers seemed cordial with one another, and the old Pink Floyd magic from the mid-1970s was recaptured for a brief moment before the four members once again went their separate ways.

Gilmour turned 60 years old on March 6, 2006, the same day he released his third solo album, *On an Island.* The album marked a more organically relaxed approach to creating music for Gilmour, who had seemingly come to terms with his strained relationship with Waters, found domestic happiness with his second wife, journalist and lyricist Polly Samson, and gained purpose in political and social activism. Guest musicians on the album included Robert Wyatt, Roxy

Music guitarist Phil Manzanera, Gerogie Fame, Richard Wright, and vocalists David Crosby and Graham Nash. In between sporadic live appearances to support the critically lauded release, Gilmour donated the proceeds from the sale of his house to a homeless charity, and participated in protests intended to raise political awareness of global climate change.

## Selected discography

### With Pink Floyd

*Saucerful of Secrets,* Columbia, 1968.
*More,* Columbia, 1969.
*Ummagumma,* Columbia, 1969.
*Atom Heart Mother,* Columbia, 1970.
*Meddle,* Columbia, 1971.
*Obscured by Clouds,* Columbia, 1972.
*Dark Side of the Moon,* Columbia, 1973.
*Wish You Were Here,* Columbia, 1975.
*Animals,* Columbia, 1977.
*The Wall,* Columbia, 1979.
*The Final Cut,* Columbia, 1983.
*A Momentary Lapse of Reason,* Columbia, 1987.
*Delicate Sound of Thunder,* Columbia, 1988.

*The Division Bell,* Columbia, 1994.
*Pulse,* Columbia, 1995.

### Solo albums

*David Gilmour,* Harvest, 1978.
*About Face,* Harvest, 1984.
*On an Island,* EMI, 2006.

## Sources

### Books

Manning, Toby, *The Rough Guide to Pink Floyd,* Rough Guides, Ltd., London, 2006.
Mason, Nick, *Inside Out: A Personal History of Pink Floyd,* Chronicle Books, San Francisco, 2003.

### Online

*All Music Guide,* http://www.allmusic.com (Nov. 12, 2006).
David Gilmour Official Website, http://www.davidgilmour.com (June 28, 2006).

—*Bruce Walker*

# Golden Smog

Rock group

Golden Smog was a roots rock and alternative country super group before either genre was even named. Featuring moonlighting members from such groups as Uncle Tupelo, The Jayhawks, The Replacements, Big Star, Soul Asylum, The Honeydogs, and Wilco, Golden Smog became a side project for the members to alternately follow their individual muses and let their hair down to perform covers of songs by their favorite artists. Categorizing the results, however, is difficult, due to the ever-changing lineups of the band and the continuous musical exploration of core members Dan Murphy from Soul Asylum and Gary Louris from The Jayhawks. The music produced has ranged from loose adaptations of Eagles, Kinks, the Faces, and Rolling Stones' songs to highly refined original collaborations between Louris and Uncle Tupelo and Wilco founder Jeff Tweedy.

Golden Smog first formed in the heady Minneapolis/St. Paul, Minnesota, music scene of the late 1980s. The so-called Twin Cities had been put on the map musically by such post-punk bands as The Replacements and Hüsker Dü, and had become a draw for music talent from throughout the Midwest, including members of the Jayhawks. The latter group featured members formerly associated with area rockabilly bands Mark

AP Images

## For the Record . . .

Members include **Kraig Johnson**, vocals; **Noah Levy**, drums; **Gary Louris**, guitar, vocals; **Chris Mars**, drums; **Dan Murphy**, guitar; **Marc Perlman**, bass; **Dave Pirner**, vocals; **Jody Stephens**, drums; **Bill Sullivan**, vocals; **Jeff Tweedy**, guitar, vocals.

Formed in Minneapolis, Minnesota, late 1980s; released extended play single *On Golden Smog*, 1992; released first full-length album, *Down by the Old Mainstream*, 1996; released *Weird Tales*, 1998; released *Another Fine Day*, 2006.

Addresses: Record Company—Lost Highway, Universal Music Group, 54 Music Square East, Nashville, TN 37203.

Olson and Gary Louris. The Jayhawks earned national attention with the release of their Twin/Tone debut, *Blue Earth.* Louris formed the Golden Smog side project at around the same time, with vocalist Kraig Johnson of the Twin Cities' band Run Westy Run and Soul Asylum guitarist Dan Murphy. The group played shows based on such themes as covering songs by the Eagles and the Rolling Stones. The Stones-based show was cheekily titled "Her Satanic Majesty's Paycheck," after the Rolling Stones' late 1960s foray into psychedelia, *Her Satanic Majesty's Request.*

Louris, Johnson, and Murphy entered the studio to cut the 1992 extended play release *On Golden Smog,* which featured reworked versions of songs by such groups as Bad Company, Thin Lizzy, obscure 1960s band Michelangelo, and the Rolling Stones, as well as a cover of "Easy to Be Hard" from the musical *Hair,* which had previously been a hit for the pop band Three Dog Night. Soul Asylum member Dave Pirner provided vocals for the remake of Bad Company's "Shooting Star," and Soul Asylum roadie Bill Sullivan contributed vocals to the remake of Thin Lizzy's "Cowboy Song." Replacements' drummer Chris Mars contributed drums and created the album art work; and bass guitar was performed by Jayhawks' member Marc Perlman.

For the group's first full-length album, 1996's *Down by the Old Mainstream,* Louris, Murphy, Perlman, and Johnson were joined by Uncle Tupelo veteran and Wilco frontman Jeff Tweedy and by Honeydogs' drummer Noah Levy. A parody of typical rock band press releases appeared on the website of the Rykodisc record label, inventing pseudonyms and fictional histories for the group members. Since the group's individual members were under contract with other record labels, they decided to adopt aliases. Like fellow "supergroup" The Traveling Wilburys (featuring Beatle George Harrison, Tom Petty, Roy Orbison, Bob Dylan, and Electric Light Orchestra leader Jeff Lynne disguised as the fictitious Wilbury family), Golden Smog members took license with creating fictional personal biographies. The group premiered some of the songs on *Down by the Old Mainstream* at the South by Southwest Music Conference in Austin, Texas, building buzz for the band among alt-country and roots rock critics and fans. Among the original songs on the album are "He's a Dick," which takes to task the archetypal so-called friend who borrows albums and never returns them. Reviewing the album for *All Music Guide,* critic Stephen Thomas Erlewine wrote: "Unlike most supergroups, the members of Golden Smog improve on their regular bands…. The musicians are relaxed and loose, giving the songs a raw, rootsy kick."

In 1998 Golden Smog released their second full-length release, *Weird Tales.* The lineup this time around consisted of Louris, Tweedy, Perlman, Murphy, former Big Star drummer Jody Stephens and violinist and singer Jessy Greene. Guests on the album included Dave Pirner, who provided backup vocals on "Keys," and Memphis musical and production wizard Jim Dickinson, who contributed Wurlitzer organ accompaniment on "Until You Came Along."

After an extended recording hiatus, Golden Smog entered the studio to produce the 2006 album *Another Fine Day.* Tweedy returned to the fold to contribute co-writing credits on two songs with Louris, but the Wilco leader appeared on only six of the album's 15 songs. The impetus for the group's reunion was an offer from General Motors to write and record a song for a new Corvette commercial, which was to be directed by Guy Ritchie and premiered during the Super Bowl broadcast. The song, "Corvette." was rejected by General Motors and advertising agency Campbell-Ewald, but became the first song written for *Another Fine Day.* The album was recorded at Louris's vacation home in Puerto Santa Maria in Spain. The band experienced several hardships, however, despite the idyllic surroundings. "Their gear and luggage failed to arrive, rains delayed the promised studio upgrades and Tweedy was called home, so the musicians slogged through the early sessions grumpy and frustrated," according to *Paste* reporter Bud Scoppa. "About ten days into it," Louris told Scoppa, "we … decided to listen to what we'd done from start to finish. We were just blown away—the songs were cool, the sounds were not standard, and it was not something we could've ever planned, which is what's so great about it." The group returned to Minneapolis to finish the album with Tweedy back onboard, and released it on the Lost Highways label. The album consisted of original songs by the band members, with the exception of "Strangers," the Dave Davies song written and performed with the Kinks. Summing up the advantage of recording a side project with other musicians, Louris told Scoppa: "For us, it's almost a relief to become part of an ensemble, as opposed to leading the charge. … It works with the Smog; it's hard to do outside of that. There's more of a letting go – that's why there's a danger of ever taking it to the next level."

## Selected discography

*On Golden Smog,* Crackpot, 1992; reissued, Rykodisc, 1996.
*Down by the Old Mainstream,* Rykodisc, 1996.
*Weird Tales,* Rykodisc, 1998. (Acadia, 2000s).
*Another Fine Day,* Lost Highway, 2006.

# Sources

### Books

*The Rolling Stone Encyclopedia of Rock,* Rolling Stone Press, 2001.

### Periodicals

*Paste,* August 2006.

### Online

*All Music Guide,* http://www.allmusic.com (Nov. 20, 2006).
*Lost Highway Records Website,* http://www.losthigh wway records.com (Nov. 20, 2006).
*Rykodisc Website,* http://www.rykodisc.com/RykoInternal/ Features/209/gsbio.html (Nov. 20, 2006).

—*Bruce Walker*

# Kevin Gordon

## Singer, songwriter

Louisiana singer/songwriter Kevin Gordon writes country songs that combine poetic lyrics and heavy rhythms. His music reveals a blend of what Bob Mehr in the *Chicago Reader* called "economical but finely etched narratives" with "an earthy mix of backwoods country, big-city blues, and febrile Cajun sounds." In *Playback,* Bryan A. Hollerbach wrote that Gordon "makes music thrilling in its multifarious resonance—believe it."

### "It Hit Me Hard"

Gordon was born in Shreveport, Louisiana, and grew up in the town of Monroe, in a family that loved music. His parents frequently had parties where they played lively records, including Jerry Lee Lewis and Ray Charles. Gordon wrote on his website, "That music—it hit me hard. I loved it so much—that's what drove me to want to sing, play, and write."

He began teaching himself to play guitar, and evolved through a variety of styles, including punk, rockabilly, and blues. At the same time, he went through college and graduate school, studying poetry at the prestigious University of Iowa Writers Workshop. While he was in college, he played at an open mic jam in Iowa City, where singer Bo Ramsey heard him and offered him a spot in his band. Gordon played with Ramsey for two years.

In an interview in *On Milwaukee,* Gordon told Jeff Bentoff that it was not easy to choose between poetry and music. "It almost feels like the battle of the personalities at times," he said. "For me personally, [poetry and songwriting are] two entirely different things." He also commented that he avoids "calling great songwriters poets and all that … Let's face it—poets probably don't have nearly as much fun as I do, getting to play songs in front of people, playing in a band. Poetry is a much lonelier enterprise."

He also noted that once out of the Iowa Workshop he did not miss his "wonderful little aesthete sort of existence," as he described it to Bill Friskics-Warren on the *No Depression* website. "You go to the bookstore, you go to the bar and you drink, and you talk about writing and you get up in the morning with a hangover and you write your poems. Part of that's really wonderful, in that people are so passionate about ideas, but part of it's just silly to me now."

Gordon's first album, *Cadillac Jack's #1 Son,* was made as a result of a conversation he had with coproducer and guitarist Joe McMahan. "I called Joe and said, 'Let's make a record—next week,'" he reported on his website. In a *Popmatters.com* review, Sarah Zupko wrote that the artist's songs told "vivid narratives" of life along the Mississippi River, and that it was "great story-telling country music."

*Down to the Well* was coproduced by Bo Ramsey, who played or sang on seven of the tracks. The title song is a duet with Lucinda Williams that, according to a reviewer in *Puremusic,* "sets the bar high and it never comes down." The reviewer also added that there was "not a weak song on the disc."

### *O Come Look at the Burning*

In 2000 Gordon made another album, *O Come Look at the Burning.* It was done with the same spontaneity as his first record. He commented on his website that he wanted to record while he still felt his creative fires burning. The album was recorded in a home studio in a rented house in East Nashville, using 15 tracks of an old 16-track machine. Unlike many contemporary albums, which are recorded one track at a time, usually starting with the rhythm track and building up from there, this one was recorded live. Gordon noted on his website that "for this record, we wanted the sound of the band playing together—a performance of the song, with everybody playing and interacting as it went down. Nothing felt as good as the vocals that were cut with the band—so we stuck with them." The songs on the album feature Gordon's trademark of intensely poetic lyrics delivered in a down-to-earth style. Ten are original, written by Gordon, but he also does covers of Willie Dixon's "Crazy Mixed-Up World" and Eddie Hinton's "Something Heavy." Mehr praised these two cover songs, but noted that the original songs are what "truly show his mastery of American vernacular music."

Frank Goodman wrote in *Puremusic.com* that on this album, "The music jumps less and digs deeper. It's

Born Kevin Gordon in Shreveport, LA; married; two children. *Education:* University of Iowa Writers Workshop, master of fine arts degree in poetry.

Released *Cadillac Jack's #1 Son,* 1998; released *Down to the Well,* 2000; released *O Come Look at the Burning,* 2005.

Addresses: *Record company*—Shanachie Records, 37 E. Clinton St., Newton, NJ 07860.

a side of Gerard Manley Hopkins; it leads you to some interesting places."

## Selected discography

*Illinois 5 A.M.* (EP), Orchard, 1997.
*Cadillac Jack's #1 Son,* Shanachie, 1998.
*Down to the Well,* Shanachie, 2000.
*O Come Look at the Burning,* Crowville Collective, 2005.

## Sources

### Periodicals

*Chicago Reader,* October 21, 2005.
*Playback,* St. Louis, June, 2006.

### Online

"Gordon Brings Inspired Louisiana Rock to Milwaukee," *On Milwaukee,* October 13, 2005; http://www.onmilwaukee.com/music/articles/kevgordon.html?7639 (November 8, 2006).
"Kevin Gordon: Cadillac Jack's #1 Son," *Popmatters.com,* http://www.popmatters.com/music/reviews/g/gordonkevin-cadillac.shtml ; (November 10, 2006).
"Kevin Gordon," *No Depression,* http://www.nodepression.net/issues/nd11/tc.html (November 8, 2006).
"Kevin Gordon: O Come Look at the Burning," *Popmatters.com,* http://www.popmatters.com/music/reviews/g/gordonkevin-ocome.shtml (November 10, 2006).
Kevin Gordon Official Website, http://www.myspace.com/kevingordonmusic (November 7, 2006).
"Kevin Gordon,"*Puremusic.com,* http://www.puremusic.com/kevin/html (November 8, 2006).
"O Come Look at the Burning: Kevin Gordon," *Puremusic.com,* December 15, 2003, http://www.puremusic.com/54kevin.html (November 8, 2006).

—Kelly Winters

more trancelike, more hypnotic, but in a bluesy way." He added that the album "has a visceral live sound reminiscent of the electrifying show Gordon throws down." In *Popmatters.com* Steven Horowitz commented, "The ability to craft songs that combine the real and surreal has always been one of Gordon's strengths." He added that "Gordon's gift comes from a deeper place. Maybe his Louisiana upbringing is responsible. Gordon's guitar playing seems like it came out of the swamp. His strings seem to go chuggin' and chompin' like an alligator chasing after a shifty water rat."

In the blog on his website Gordon wrote that he is tired of this type of description of his music and his background: "Please, no more Cajun food metaphors, okay? You know, 'swampy gumbo of sound' and all that crap. I'm not a Cajun; I grew up in northern Louisiana, which is about as generically redneck a place [as anyone could find]." About his style, he commented on his website, "I'm a self-taught guitar player who studied poetry in grad school—I take my John Lee Hooker with

# Matt Haimovitz

**Cellist**

He has been called the coolest cellist of our times, and the performer who brought classical music to the masses. Israeli-born cellist Matt Haimovitz has performed Bach in bars, and contemporary classical music in nightclubs. When Haimovitz started performing, he appeared in conventional concert venues, and he has never given up his traditional classical career. "I've never forsaken the concert hall," Haimovitz explained to Channing Gray of the *Providence Journal*. "But I wouldn't give up the more intimate settings and a chance to play for new audiences. … I'm bringing back the heart of what we do as performers."

Matt Haimovitz was born in suburban Tel Aviv, Israel, on December 3, 1970. His mother was a pianist, and the cellist who would later perform the music of Jimi Hendrix and Led Zeppelin on his instrument was raised on classical music exclusively. Haimovitz's father was an engineer who sought his fortune in Palo Alto, in California's booming Silicon Valley in 1975. When Haimovitz was seven, he heard a cello for the first time and showed an immediate liking for the instrument. He soon started lessons with a local teacher, Irene Sharp, and then moved on to study with a Hungarian-born teacher, Gabor Rejto, who had been a student of the great Spanish cellist Pablo Casals. Both teachers

## For the Record . . .

Born December 3, 1970, in Tel Aviv, Israel; moved to U.S. with family at age five; married Luna Pearl Woolf (a composer). *Education:* Attended Princeton University and Harvard University; studied cello with Irene Sharp, Gabor Rejto, Leonard Rose, and Ron Leonard.

Made debut, with Israel Philharmonic Orchestra, 1984; performed with top orchestras in U.S. and Europe, 1990s; recorded for Deutsche Grammophon label, 1989-99; formed Oxingale Records and began recording for label, 1999; began performing in pop venues such as bars and clubs, 1999; professor of cello, University of Massachusetts at Amherst, 1999-2004; professor of cello, McGill University, Montreal, Quebec, Canada, 2004–.

Awards: Avery Fisher Career Grant, 1986; Grand Prix du Disque and Diapason d'Or (France), 1991; Harvard University, Louis Sudler Prize, 1996; Premio Internazionale "Accademia Musicale Chigiana," 1999.

Addresses: *Office*—Schulich School of Music, Room E203, Strathcona Music Building, 555 Sherbrooke St. West, Montreal, QC H3A 1I3, Canada. *Record company*—Oxingale Records, P.O. Box 161 Montreal, QC H2X 4A4, Canada, website: http://www.oxingale.com.

stressed musical expression over technical drills.

When Haimovitz was eleven he went to New York's Juilliard School to audition for Leonard Rose, one of the top cellists in the United States. Rose agreed to take him on as a student, and encouraged the entire Haimovitz family to move to New York. Adding a strong grasp of basic cello technique to his already unusually expressive style, Haimovitz quickly developed into a teenage prodigy. Rose was diagnosed with cancer and died in 1984, and shortly before his death Haimovitz was tapped to fill in for his teacher in a Carnegie Hall performance of Franz Schubert's String Quintet in C major, with all four of the other players being giants of the classical music world.

Soon after that, Haimovitz was invited by conductor Zubin Mehta to appear with the Israel Philharmonic Orchestra, and his international career grew steadily. As a student at Princeton University, Haimovitz was introduced to contemporary classical music, but mostly he played a group of durable classical cello favorites like the Cello Concerto No. 1 in A minor by French composer Camille Saint-Saëns and Franz Joseph Haydn's Cello Concerto in C major. The pattern continued when Haimovitz was signed to the Deutsche Grammophon label in 1989; he recorded some new music, and even participated in an improvisation project, *Trios with Rob Wasserman* (1993), but mostly he stuck to established classical repertoire.

In the 1990s, various factors worked together to slow Haimovitz's career and increase his frustration. Together with other musicians who came of age during a boom in classical music that accompanied the rise of the compact-disc medium, he faced the problem of making the transition to a career as an adult. Deutsche Grammophon hit hard times as sales declined, and Haimovitz worked with a revolving-door sequence of executives. Most of all, he was disturbed by the impersonal quality of classical concerts. Once he performed at the prestigious Alte Oper hall in Frankfurt, Germany. "I remember finishing the recital—there was nobody backstage—and leaving the hall without any feedback from the audience or anyone," he explained to Graham Rockingham of Canada's *Hamilton Spectator.* "It left me feeling very cold."

Haimovitz shelved a finished Deutsche Grammophon recording because he was dissatisfied with his performance, and the label responded by dropping him from its roster. He enrolled for graduate study at Harvard University and supported the career of his wife, composer Luna Pearl Woolf. In 1999 the two took a radical step in what was then a centrally controlled classical world: they formed their own label, Oxingale Records. For his debut release on the label, Haimovitz recorded one of the cornerstones of the cello repertoire, the six suites for unaccompanied cello of Johann Sebastian Bach.

Making inquiries with his agent about the possibility of touring in support of the album, Haimovitz was turned down flat. But the cellist and his wife, who served as producer, decided that the album at least deserved a release party. By that time Haimovitz was teaching cello at the University of Massachusetts at Amherst, and he made inquiries about performing at the Iron Horse, a durable folk music club in nearby Northampton. The club agreed to book Haimovitz if he would assume some of the financial risk. As it happened, hundreds of people were turned away from the 250-seat club.

Playing in a situation so different from what he was used to, Haimovitz was disconcerted at first but quickly found positive aspects to the experience. "It was quite a shock to play in a venue like that," he told Tim Janof of the Internet Cello Society. "I remember playing the first Suite and becoming fixated on some uneaten

French fries in front of me, and it wasn't until the Courante or Sarabande [movements or sections of the piece] that I got over it. But people really responded in a very honest and open way to the music, and something clicked. Perhaps the classical music world has become too stuffy and has scared people away."

That concert grew into a unique tour of about 80 venues, mostly folk and rock clubs, that Haimovitz called the Bach Listening Room Tour. He found that the concerts drew a wide mix of listeners, from traditional classical enthusiasts in suits to punk-rock fans in T-shirts. Haimovitz stopped in to the venerable New York rock club CBGB to record his next Oxingale album, *Anthem,* which sent him off on a second, longer tour of nontraditional venues. On both the album and the tour, Haimovitz introduced one of his trademarks: an arrangement for cello of the "Star-Spangled Banner" solo played by rock guitarist Jimi Hendrix at the Woodstock festival in 1969. His tours did not constitute an easy way to make a living. At one performance in a Los Angeles club, Haimovitz had to stop playing and break up a brawl between two drunken patrons. His fee for an evening of music in a bar was much less than he might get for traditional symphony concerts (which he continued to perform), but he told Gray that "I'm able to pay the bills, and that's what I've been after, to show that this kind of music can stand on its own two feet, that there's a loyal audience for it."

Stimulated creatively by the freedom that came with running his own label rather than answering to an artists-and-repertoire executive, Haimovitz delved into new music for the cello with *Anthem* and its successor, *Goulash* (2005). That album used a general focus on the music of Eastern Europe (the ancestral home of Haimovitz's own family) to perform a wide range of music: the Hungarian-folk-influenced pieces of composer Béla Bartók, Led Zeppelin's "Kashmir," music by contemporary Romanian composer Adrian Pop, a work for cello and guitar by Argentine-Israeli-American composer Osvaldo Golijov called *Oración Lucumí,* and improvisations by Haimovitz and ambient electronic musician DJ Olive. The disc was Haimovitz's biggest seller up to that point, and he told Gray that he expected it to turn a profit in "a year or so."

By that time, Haimovitz had landed a new teaching job that provided him with a stable base of operations for his performance experiments. In 2004 he became professor of cello at McGill University in Montreal. The university encouraged him to tour, and presenters trying to attract new audiences for classical music were keenly interested in what he might do next. For his part, Haimovitz seemed intent on nurturing the new bond he had formed with rock and pop audiences. "Even if a

handful show up" to one of his concerts, he told Andrew Druckenbrod of the *Pittsburgh Post-Gazette,* "the magic between us can bring out my best."

## Selected discography

*Saint-Saëns, Lalo: Cello Concertos: Bruch, Kol Nidrei,* Deutsche Grammophon, 1989.
*Haydn, C.P.E. Bach, Boccherini,* Deutsche Grammophon, 1990.
*Suites and Sonatas for Solo Cello* (Britten, Crumb, Ligeti, Reger), Deutsche Grammophon, 1991.
(With Joan Jeanrenaud and Rob Wasserman, also featuring other musicians) *Trios with Rob Wasserman,* GRP, 1993.
*Kodaly: Sonata, Op. 8, Britten, Suite No. 3, Berio, "Les mots sont allés,"* Deutsche Grammophon, 1995.
*The 20th-Century Cello, Volume 2,* Deutsche Grammophon, 1997.
*Portes Ouvertes: The 20th-Century Cello, Volume 3,* Deutsche Grammophon, 1999.
*UnderTree* (Luna Pearl Woolf: *The Orange and the UnderTree*), Oxingale, 1999.
*J.S. Bach: Six Suites for Solo Cello,* Oxingale, 2000.
*Lemons Descending,* Oxingale, 2001.
*The Rose Album,* Oxingale, 2002.
*Haydn/Mozart* (concertos for cello and orchestra), Transart Live, 2003..
*Anthem,* Oxingale, 2003.
*Epilogue* (Mendelssohn, String Quartet in F minor, Op. 80, Schubert, String Quintet in C major, D. 956), Oxingale, 2004.
*Goulash,* Oxingale, 2005.

## Sources

### Periodicals

*Detroit Free Press,* February 8, 2006.
*Hamilton Spectator* (Hamilton, Ontario, Canada), August 31, 2006, p. G11.
*Pittsburgh Post-Gazette,* October 6, 2005, p. W15.
*Providence Journal,* February 2, 2006, p. L16.
*Santa Fe New Mexican,* February 11, 2005, p. PA28.

### Online

Briggs, Newt, "Music: Taking back Bach," *Las Vegas Mercury,* http://www.lasvegasmercury.com (November 18, 2006).
Janof, Tim, "Conversation with Matt Haimovitz," Internet Cello Society, http://www.cello.org/Newsletter/Articles/haimovitz/haimovitz.htm (November 18, 2006).
"Matt Haimovitz," Oxingale Records, http://www.oxingale.com (November 18, 2006).

—*James M. Manheim*

# Roy Hargrove

**Jazz musician, trumpet player**

AP Images

After recording his highly acclaimed first album at age 20, trumpet and flugelhorn player Roy Hargrove became a charter member of a precocious group of jazz prodigies known as "The Young Lions." Hargrove, along with fellow trumpeters Nicholas Peyton and Marlon Jordan, saxophonists Antonio Hart and Joshua Redman, bassist Christian McBride, and a host of other young players, ignited a global resurgence in the popularity of jazz. Intelligent, well-educated, and articulate, with a strong sense of jazz's rich history, these musicians were signed by major recording labels and supported by the kind of publicity formerly reserved for pop stars.

In an astonishingly brief time, Hargrove became one of the most influential artists of this young generation. He developed an extremely personal style that tempered brilliant virtuosity with grace and passion. Tom Masland of *Newsweek* remarked of Hargrove, "He plays with a sweetness that speaks of a world of hurt." Even early in his career, Hargrove's work showed a sense of order that many players take decades to achieve. As *New York Times* writer Richard B. Woodward put it, his solos are a "string of sentences that read as paragraphs."

## Introduction to Jazz

Hargrove was surrounded by music from an early age, but it was his elementary and high school band director, Dean Hill, who sparked his interest in a performing career. Hill not only guided Hargrove's development as an improviser, but introduced him to a variety of great jazz musicians, including David "Fathead" Newman, a legendary sax player who many years later joined Hargrove on his eighth album, *Family.*

While working with Hill, Hargrove discovered the music of Clifford Brown, a brilliant trumpeter who recorded extensively in the 1950s and who died at age 25. It was Brown's example, Hargrove told *Rocky Mountain News* writer Norman Provizer, that gave the young trumpeter confidence in his own musical gifts. "That was the key that opened the door for me," he recalled. "There have always been musicians who could play no matter what age they were. If you love it, you will search it out regardless of your age."

Like many jazz musicians of his generation, Hargrove also owed an important debt to trumpeter Wynton Marsalis. After hearing Hargrove perform at Dallas's Arts Magnet High School, Marsalis invited him to sit in with his group at the Caravan of Dreams Performing Arts Center in Fort Worth, Texas. The performance effectively launched Hargrove's career, and though some writers later tried to promote competition between Hargrove and his mentor, the younger musician has demonstrated nothing but respect and admiration for Marsalis. "I really dig Wynton's place in society," he told Woodward. "He's a tremendously dedicated person." In 1995 Hargrove put all rumors of a feud to rest by inviting Marsalis to join him on his *Family* album.

Hargrove's debut at the Caravan of Dreams led to extensive tours of the United States and Europe. In 1990, after two years at Boston's prestigious Berklee School of Music, he moved to New York City, formed his first quintet, and released his debut album, *Diamond in the Rough.* This album, and the three succeeding recordings Hargrove made for the Novus label, were among the most commercially successful jazz recordings of the early 1990s, and made the young trumpeter one of the music's hottest properties. Unimpressed by stardom, Hargrove continued to develop his craft by performing with jazz giants such as saxophonist Sonny Rollins and trumpeter Dizzy Gillespie.

As Hargrove's talents as a soloist matured, so did his strength as a bandleader. During the early 1990s Hargrove experimented with a variety of personnel, trying to build a tightly focused ensemble. As he told Provizer, "No matter how many people you have in a group, you need to think as one." In 1992 he laid the foundation for future groups by hiring bassist Rodney Whitaker and drummer Gregory Hutchinson, who together comprised one of the finest rhythm units in modern jazz. By the release of 1993's *Of Kindred Souls,* Hargrove's exacting taste and hard work had paid off. In the words of *San Francisco Chronicle* writer Derk Richardson, he had found "the kind of unified group feeling that has distinguished the most fondly remembered acoustic jazz units, from the Max Roach-Clifford Brown Quintet, through the classic Miles Davis bands of the 1960s."

In 1994 Hargrove made a widely publicized move to Verve Records and released *The Roy Hargrove Quintet with the Tenors of Our Time.* The concept for the recording was unique: Hargrove's own quintet, featuring sax player Ron Blake and pianist Cyrus Chestnut, in addition to Whitaker and Hutchinson, was joined by some of jazz's greatest tenor sax players, including veterans such as Joe Henderson and Stanley Turrentine, and relative newcomers like Branford Marsalis (Wynton's brother) and Joshua Redman. But unlike other "all-star" jam recordings, the album presented each guest soloist individually, in repertory especially chosen to illustrate his talents. The recording, dubbed "a jazz classic" by Star-Ledger critic George Kanzler, was one of the best-selling jazz albums of 1994.

In June of 1995 Hargrove released *Family,* his second recording for Verve. As the title suggests, the album paid tribute to the musicians and relatives who played a significant role in the trumpeter's life. Like *The Tenors of Our Time, Family* featured a variety of guest artists. "Young Lions" such as Christian McBride and sax player Jesse Davis, as well as established figures like pianist John Hicks and drummer Jimmy Cobb once again joined Hargrove's quintet. The result was an exciting and heartfelt look at jazz's past, present, and future.

*Family* also showcased several of Hargrove's own works. "The Trial" was a dark and intense movement from his extended composition "The Love Suite in Mahogany," which had premiered at New York City's Lincoln Center in September of 1993. The piece featured an imaginative duet for bowed bass and soprano sax. The Latin-tinged "Another Level" placed the innovative solos of Hargrove, Blake, and pianist Stephen Scott against a complex background of shifting rhythmic patterns. And "Trilogy" painted brief portraits of three of Hargrove's family members: the lush, tender "Velera" paid homage to Hargrove's mother; "Roy Allan" evoked the sousaphone playing of Hargrove's father with an infectious, driving bass line; and the looping melody of the blues number "Brian's Bounce" was inspired by Hargrove's energetic brother.

## Jazz "Makes a Difference"

As Hargrove's star continued to ascend, he also dedicated himself to spreading jazz's affirmative message to a new generation of musicians. Following Wynton Marsalis's lead, he began giving workshops for jazz musicians in high schools throughout the United States. "There is a positive aspect to playing music, and it makes a difference when you can reach young people around the country and tell them about jazz," he told *Down Beat* columnist June Lehman. "You may inspire a young person to do great things just by having music in their life."

Later in 1995 Hargrove released *Parker's Mood.* The album was recorded to commemorate the 75th birthday of saxophone legend Charlie Parker—nicknamed "Bird"—with Christian McBride on bass and Stephen Scott on piano. According to *The Penguin Guide to Jazz on CD,* the album was "a delightful meeting of three young masters, improvising on sixteen themes from Bird's repertoire. Hargrove's luminous treatment of 'Laura' provides further evidence that he may be turning into one of the music's pre-eminent ballad players, but it's the inventive interplay among the three men that takes the session to its high level."

For his next musical endeavor, Hargrove abandoned bop for Afro-Cuban. *Habana,* released in 1997, was inspired by jam sessions between the trumpeter and the Cuban dance band Los Van Van. The chemistry between the performers culminated in the formation of a ten-piece group named Cristol, which also included Cuban piano sensation and jazz legend Chucho Valdes and guitarist Russell Malone.

Hargrove's musical restlessness led him from Afro-Cuban and borderline progressive jazz to orchestral jazz on his 1999 follow-up, *Moment to Moment.* On this disc, Hargrove was joined by drummer Willie Jones III, alto sax player Sherman Irby, pianist and arranger Larry Willis, and bass player Gerald Cannon. Gild Goldstein and Cedar Walton also contributed string arrangements. In 2003 Hargrove released an all-star collaboration, *Hard Groove,* which featured such guests as Erykah Badu, Common, D'Angelo, Marc Cary, Q-Tip, Me'Shell NdegeOcello, Cornell Dupree, and Karl Denson. *All Music Guide* critic Paula Edelstein wrote: "Overall, Roy Hargrove has evolved as a hipper version of himself and given his listeners an entirely new musical direction than that heard on his Grammy-winning *Habana* or his sensuous ballad recording *Moment to Moment.*"

In 2006 Hargrove released two albums, *Distractions* and *Nothing Serious.* The former album featured electric instrumentation, and the latter is an acoustic bop album. *All Music Guide* critic Thom Jurek declared *Distractions* a "deeply gratifying, fun, and in-the-pocket album. It's perfect for a steamy summertime." Featur-ing guest appearances by David "Fathead" Newman and D'Angelo, the album's tracks veer into the funk territory established in the 1970s by such horn-based bands as the Ohio Players and George Clinton's Parliament Funkadelic. *Nothing Serious,* on the other hand, was an acoustic outing that found Hargrove once again flirting with Afro-Cuban sounds, swing, and, of course, bop.

# Selected Discography

*Diamond in the Rough,* Novus, 1990.
*Public Eye,* Novus, 1991.
(Contributor) Antonio Hart, *For the First Time,* Novus, 1991.
(Contributor) Sonny Rollins, *Here's to the People,* Milestone, 1991.
(Contributor) Stephen Scott, *Something to Consider,* Verve, 1991.
(Contributor) *New York Stories,* Capitol, 1992.
*The Vibe,* Novus, 1992.
*Roy Hargrove and Antonio Hart: The Tokyo Sessions,* Novus, 1992.
*Of Kindred Souls,* Novus, 1993.
*Approaching Standards,* Novus, 1994.
*Roy Hargrove Quintet with the Tenors of Our Time,* Verve, 1994.
(Contributor) Johnny Griffin, *Chicago, New York, Paris,* Verve, 1995.
(Contributor) Christian McBride, *Gettin' to It,* Verve, 1995.
(Contributor) Teodross Avery, *In Other Words,* GRP, 1995.
(Contributor) David Sanchez, *Sketches of Dreams,* Columbia, 1995.
*Family,* Verve, 1995.
*Parker's Mood,* Verve, 1995.
*Habana,* Verve, 1997.
*Moment to Moment,* Verve, 1999.
*Hard Groove,* Verve, 2003.
*Distractions,* Verve, 2006.
*Nothing Serious,* Verve, 2006.

# Compositions

"The Love Suite in Mahogany," 1993.
"Trilogy," 1995.

# Sources

### Books

*The Penguin Guide to Jazz on CD,* The Penguin Group, 1996.

### Periodicals

*Billboard,* April 2, 1994; July 8, 1995.
*Chicago Sun-Times,* June 12, 1994.
*Detroit Free Press,* Sept. 24, 1993.
*Down Beat,* July 1994; August 1994; September 1994; August 1995.

*Essence,* December 1991.
*Los Angeles Times,* January 19, 1995.
*Metro Times* (Detroit, MI), September 2, 1992.
*Newsweek,* December 12, 1994.
*New York Post,* April 4, 1994.
*New York Times,* June 23, 1994; September 7, 1994.
*Rocky Mountain News* (Denver, CO), February 16, 1994.
*San Francisco Chronicle,* May 14, 1994.
*Star-Ledger,* June 5, 1994.
*Washington Post,* March 4, 1995.

## Online

*All Music Guide,* http://www.allmusic.com (November 12, 2006).

Additional information for this profile was obtained from Verve Records, 1995.

—*Jeffrey Taylor and Bruce Walker*

# Harvey Danger

Rock group

When Seattle band Harvey Danger first started out, none of its members actually knew how to play their instruments very well, if at all. A mere two years later, the band was recording songs for what would become their debut album, *Where Have All The Merrymakers Gone?* With the album's infectious geek-chic alternative single "Flagpole Sitta," before they knew it, come the summer of 1998, Harvey Danger were MTV darlings and road warriors. The album eventually sold more than half a million copies, a heroic effort considering it cost $3,000 to make it. An album later the band failed to reach half the success of their debut and ended up disbanding for a few years before reuniting for their 2005 album *Little by Little....*

Students at the University of Washington in Seattle in 1992, friends Jeff Lin and Aaron Huffman decided they wanted to start a band; it didn't matter that neither one knew how to play an instrument. Lack of experience didn't stop Lin from picking up the electric guitar and Huffman, the bass. The new rock duo saw a piece of graffiti labeled "Harvey Danger" on a wall near the student newspaper office and thought that would be a good name for a band. A year or two in, Lin and Huffman asked their friends Evan Sult and Sean Nelson—who also had no previous musical experi-

### For the Record . . .

**M**embers include **Aaron Huffman**, bass; **Rob Knop**, keyboards; **Jeff Lin**, guitar; **Sean Nelson**, lead vocals; **Michael Welke** (replaced Evan Sult, 2004), drums.

Group formed in Seattle, WA, c. 1994; released *Where Have All The Merrymakers Gone?*, Arena Rock Recording Company, 1997; signed to London/Slash Records, reissued debut, 1998; released *King James Version*, London/Sire, 2000; disbanded, 2001–04; reunited for *Little By Little...*, released on the band's label Phonographic Records, 2005; signed to Kill Rock Stars, reissued *Little By Little...*, 2006.

Addresses: *Record company*—Kill Rock Stars, 120 NE State Ave., PMB 418, Olympia, WA 98501. *Website*—Harvey Danger Official Website: http://www. harveydanger.com.

ence—to join Harvey Danger. Sult began to bang away at the drums and Nelson discovered a brawny singing voice. Harvey Danger played their first show as a quartet on April 21, 1994, in a Seattle bar. Nelson and Sult weren't yet legal drinking age and were forced to wait outside the venue before and after the band's set.

In the wake of grunge, Harvey Danger developed a style of '90s wiry alternative rock that was intelligent, sardonic, and overflowing with showmanship. A year after their first show, Harvey Danger recorded a set of rough songs and sold them as a six-song cassette tape at their shows. In 1996, the quartet befriended sought after local producer John Goodmanson and worked with him to record a collection of impressive demos. London Records intern Greg Glover heard the demos and signed the band to his own independent label, Arena Rock Recording Co. He sent the band back into the studio to record another handful of songs to add to the previous ones to put together for a full-length album.

Recorded for $3,000 Arena Rock released Harvey Danger's debut album, *Where Have All the Merrymakers Gone?*, in the summer of 1997. A few months later, Seattle radio station KNDD put the album's lead single, "Flagpole Sitta," in regular rotation. By January of 1998, "Flagpole Sitta" was KNDD's number one most-requested song. Influential LA station KROQ picked up on the buzz and added Harvey Danger to their play list.

Major labels began to wine and dine the band, who eventually signed with London/Slash Records (where Glover had worked). Slash re-released their debut in 1998. *Where Have All the Merrymakers Gone?* ended up selling over half a million copies, but the album's second single, "Private Helicopter," failed to make a dent in radio. The band's newfound notoriety and whirlwind lifestyles created a bit of uncertainty in the band as they weren't quite ready for that kind of success. In an interview with *Chart Magazine,* Nelson admitted that they didn't really know what they were doing when they initially signed to London; they just needed more albums pressed. "And they said 'we'll meet the need,' and there was need," Nelson said. "And we were selling tons of records and all the doors were opening for us and we just went through them. But it was pretty clear right away that they weren't doors that were going to stay open, and in a lot of cases, they weren't doors that I was even interested in being in the rooms they led to."

Toward the end of 1998, Harvey Danger was more than ready to begin work on a new album. In March of 1999, the band went to Bearsville Studios near Woodstock, New York, to record the bulk of their sophomore album. Although London Records gave the band $200,000 to record, Harvey Danger heard little to nothing from their record label during the recording process. After finishing things up back in Seattle, the band was set to release the new album. After the major label shake-ups that affected hundreds of bands that year, by the summer of 1999, the band still had no release date from London. Finally in September, London, now London-Sire, released the band's second and impressive album, *King James Version.* With the cool single "Sad Sweetheart of the Rodeo," and album guests like The Posies' Ken Stringfellow and Grant Lee Phillips, *King James Version* was set to take off. David Wild of *Rolling Stone* regarded the album as "... a step forward in both ambition and accomplishment—it's barbed but exceptionally tuneful postmodern pop...." Unfortunately, no one really paid attention to the album's release. "By the time [the label] got sorted out no one even remembered us at that point," Nelson confessed to MTV.com's Rodrigo Perez. After a show in April of 2001, due to low record sales and frustrated members, the band decided to put Harvey Danger on hold.

After the band's breakup (that turned out to be a hiatus), its member stayed busy. Nelson had been writing for Seattle alternative weekly *The Stranger* for years, and now that he was in one place, his freelance features picked up. While Lin went back to school, Huffman returned to the stage with the band Love Hotel. In 2002, Sult moved to Chicago where he joined the rock band Bound Stems. From 2002 to 2003, Nelson added keyboards and vocals to the John Roderick project The Long Winters. Nelson also became a partner in the independent label Barsuk and helped launch the career of Seattle friends Death Cab for Cutie, whom Harvey Danger had taken on tour. In addition to a gig as a part-time DJ on Seattle radio station KEXP, Nelson also added vocals to a number of successful indie albums over the years, including ones for Death Cab for Cutie and The Decemberists.

In early 2004, Nelson was itching to record again. After recruiting Lin, Huffman, and Nada Surf drummer Ira Elliott to lay down new tracks, the former Harvey Danger bandmates thought it was about time to put Harvey Danger back together. With Sult in Chicago, drummer Michael Welke joined the band, along with keyboardist Rob Knop, for a succession of inspiring shows that year. In the following February, Harvey Danger entered Robert Lang Studios in Seattle with longtime producer Goodmanson and Steve Fisk (known for his work with Nirvana and Screaming Trees) to record a collection of songs that were just as smart as the band's early work, but with age came maturity and mellowness. With loads of piano, the new record, *Little By Little...*, took cues from some of Nelson's favorite singer-songwriters like Paul McCartney and Harry Nilsson. In September of 2005, Harvey Danger released *Little By Little...* on their own label, Phonographic Records. At the same time, the band also put the album, in its entirety, available for free download on their website. The following year, famed Seattle label Kill Rock Stars reissued the album.

## Selected discography

*Where Have All The Merrymakers Gone?* Arena Rock Recording Co., 1997; reissued, London/Slash, 1998.
*King James Version,* London/Sire, 2000.
*Little By Little...,* Phonographic Records, 2005; reissued, Kill Rock Stars, 2006.

## Sources

### Periodicals

*Rolling Stone,* October 2000.

### Online

"Harvey Danger," *All Music Guide,* http://www.allmusic.com (November 4, 2006).
Harvey Danger Official Website, http://harveydanger.com; http://www.myspace.com/hdanger (November 6, 2006).
"Harvey Danger Return on their Terms, Little by Little," *Chart Magazine,* http://www.chartattack.com/damn/2006/09/2909.cfm (November 4, 2006).
"Remember 'Flagpole Sitta'? Harvey Danger Return," MTV.com, http://www.mtv.com/news/articles/1509358/09122005/harvey_danger.jhtml (November 4, 2006).

*—Shannon McCarthy*

# Robyn Hitchcock

## Singer, songwriter, guitarist

"I wished for the impossible when I was a kid," British rocker Robyn Hitchcock once told *Rolling Stone.* "When I couldn't realize it, I retreated into fantasy." Thirty-some years and eleven albums later, the eccentric Hitchcock has yet to fully emerge. With his witty lyrics and surrealist imagery, the singer/songwriter has created an elaborate fantasyscape populated by bizarre life forms—slimy amphibians, antennaed insects, and creepy crustaceans. And behind the artist's psychedelic inventions is a devoted cult following; Hitchcock's fans have developed quite a taste for his peculiar brand of primordial soup.

Born in London in 1953, Hitchcock developed an "intense contempt for normalcy in all its forms" at an early age, he told the *San Francisco Chronicle.* Inspired by Bob Dylan's "Like a Rolling Stone," he gravitated toward music as a means of expressing that contempt. At 16, Hitchcock discovered William Shakespeare and avant-garde rock figure Captain Beefheart, the two influences that would establish the foundation for his unique musical perspective. In the early 1970s his interest in Shakespeare led him to study English at Cambridge University, while the allure of Beefheart propelled Hitchcock to the coffeehouse folk scene, where he explored his burgeoning musical style as a solo guitarist.

On the coffeehouse circuit Hitchcock developed the distinctive right-hand picking style that *Guitar Player* called "a kind of finicky folk that's not sentimental enough for the coffeehouses, and too acerbic and sharply poetic for most rock audiences."

Following the demise of his short-lived acoustic quartet, Maureen and the Meatpackers, Hitchcock formed his first recording group with bassist and keyboardist Andy Metcalf and drummer Morris Windsor in 1976. Dubbed the Soft Boys, the art-punk rock band derived its title from two William Burroughs novels, *The Soft Machine* and *The Wild Boys.* Its mission: to "avoid cliche whenever possible." That was the group's "manifesto," Hitchcock told the *Chronicle.*

It was with the Soft Boys that Hitchcock perfected his signature surrealist style, characterized by a psychedelic quality that was typical of the musicians of his generation. Although the Soft Boys developed a consistent following after the release of the band's first recordings in 1977 and 1978, their irreverent pop sound was ultimately drowned out by angrier young men like the Sex Pistols; unable to withstand the punk rock tide, the group disbanded in 1981.

Three years later the Soft Boys were reborn as the Egyptians; in addition to Hitchcock, Metcalf, and Windsor, the group counted two new members, Otis Horns Fletcher and Roger Jackson. The band fared well in the United States in its new incarnation. The albums *Fegmania!, Gotta Let This Hen Out!,* and *Elements of Light,* released on the alternative Slash and Relativity labels, rated high on college radio playlists. The band's reputation was enhanced by the enthusiastic endorsement of R.E.M. guitarist Peter Buck, with whom they began a lasting musical collaboration. In 1988 the Egyptians recorded *Globe of Frogs,* their first album on the major label A&M. *Queen Elvis* and *Perspex Island* followed in 1989 and 1991, respectively.

*Perspex Island,* Hitchcock's first recording with an outside producer, Paul Fox, was "mixed on a car stereo in L.A. because it's designed to be listened to in traffic," reported the *Chicago Tribune.* The album showed a different aspect of Hitchcock's talent. "There's a side of me I've been hesitant to reveal in the past," he told *Pitch* magazine. "I've always avoided being too vulnerable, too open, afraid of coming off maudlin."

The emotional openness reflected on *Perspex Island* seemed to reflect Hitchcock's new-found contentment, which may have had something to do with contributions from Peter Buck and R.E.M. vocalist Michael Stipe. Buck played guitar and mandolin on eight of the album's 11 tracks, and Stipe contributed vocals to the cut "She Doesn't Exist."

Despite its sincerity, *Perspex Island* did not sacrifice the surreal imagery so dear to Hitchcock's die-hard fans. The album's title, in fact, was inspired by an acrylic material that's used to make souvenir paperweights; trinkets are suspended in the substance, creating a fossilized Jello effect. "Birds in Perspex," one of the singles off the album, "is basically about wanting something that's dead or frozen to suddenly reani-

## For the Record . . .

Born in London, England, in 1953. *Education:* Attended Cambridge University.

Member of acoustic quartet Maureen and the Meatpackers, early 1970s; with bassist-keyboardist Andy Metcalf and drummer Morris Windsor, formed band the Soft Boys, 1976; group disbanded, 1981; group re-formed as the Egyptians, 1984; signed with A&M Records, and released *Globe of Frogs,* 1988; released *Respect,* 1993; signed with Warner Brothers and released *Moss Elixir,* 1996; released soundtrack to Jonathan Demme-directed Hitchcock film *Storefront Hitchcock,* 1998.

*Addresses: Record company*—Yep Roc Records, P.O. Box 4821, Chapel Hill, NC 27515-4821. *Publicist*—Yep Roc, Nic Brown, phone: (336) 395-1141, e-mail: nic@yeproc.com, or Tresa Redburn, Dept. 56, phone: (818) 702-6253, e-mail: tmumba@aol.com.

*Elixir.* In 1998 director Jonathan Demme filmed Hitchcock's solo live performances in the concert film *Storefront Hitchcock,* and a soundtrack album was released. His last album for the label was 1999's *Jewels for Sophia.* Subsequent releases on independent labels have yielded positive results. Of *Luxor,* released in 2003, *All Music Guide* critic Brian Downing wrote: "There is not only a strong sense of his own musical past evident, but also the past of pop music in general; sort of like a musical tea party with the ghosts of Syd Barrett, John Lennon, and Bob Dylan as the special guests."

*Spooked,* released in 2004, and *Ole! Tarantula,* released in 2006, featured guest appearances by Gillian Welch and David Rawlings on the former and Peter Buck, Ian McLagan, and Kimberley Rew, recording as the Venus 3, on the latter. *Ole! Tarantula* was notable for Hitchcock's songwriting collaboration with XTC mainstay Andy Partridge, "'Cause It's Love (Saint Parallelogram)." According to *All Music Guide* critic James Christopher Monger: "His greatest strength has always been his ability to toss a clear nugget of profundity into his most surrealist rants. … It's that perfect balance of sadness, vitriol, and absurdity that makes Hitchcock (when he's on) such a legendary social commentator. He's the jester, the king, the convict, and the executioner all wrapped up into one."

mate," Hitchcock explained in an A&M Records press release. In fact, that "something" does come alive on the album's cover, a creature-filled composition of Hitchcock's own making.

Critics were overwhelmingly positive about *Perspex Island's* accessible love songs, assuring Hitchcock that his fear of "coming off maudlin" was unfounded. Quickly becoming a college favorite, the album was praised not only for its exacting rhythms and three-part harmonies but also for its disarming candor. The first single, "So You Think You're in Love," rose to the top of the CMJ Album Network, Gavin Report, and Radio and Records Alternative charts.

Fittingly, *Perspex Island's* popularity mirrored Hitchcock's feelings about his shift in musical style. He told *Spin,* "It's taken about half my life to actually stagger into accepting being Robyn Hitchcock. My aim now is to write songs that have emotion."

Hitchcock followed up *Perspex Island* with 1993's *Respect,* which he dedicated to his late father. He earned critical praise for such songs as "The Yip Song," "When I Was Dead," and "Wafflehead." The album also featured Hitchcock's guitar mastery on the solo instrumental "Serpent at the Gates of Wisdom." Reviewing the album for *Rock: The Rough Guide,* Iain Smith wrote that the album was "Robyn Hitchcock & the Egyptians most finely crafted work to date."

*Respect* was Hitchcock's final album for A&M. He signed to Warner Brothers for his 1996 release *Moss*

## Selected Discography

(With the Soft Boys) *Underwater Moonlight* (import), Armageddon, 1980.
(With the Egyptians) *Fegmania!,* Slash, 1985.
*Gotta Let This Hen Out!,* Relativity, 1985.
*Element of Light,* Relativity, 1986.
*Globe of Frogs,* A&M, 1988.
*Queen Elvis,* A&M, 1989.
*Perspex Island,* A&M, 1991.
*Respect,* A&M, 1993.
Solo releases *I Often Dream of Trains,* Relativity, 1984.
*Eye,* Twin/Tone, 1990.
*Moss Elixir,* Warner Bros., 1996.
*Storefront Hitchcock,* Warner Bros, 1998.
*Live at the Cambridge Folk Festival,* Varese, 1998.
*Jewels for Sophia,* Warner Bros., 1999.
*A Star for Bram,* Editions PAF!, 2000.
*Robyn Sings,* Editions PAF!, 2002.
*Luxor,* Editions PAF!, 2003.
*Spooked,* Yep Roc, 2004.
*Obliteration Pie,* 3rd Japan, 2006.
*Ole! Tarantuala,* Yep Roc, 2006.
*This Is the BBC,* Hux, 2006.

## Sources

### Books

*Rock: The Rough Guide,* Rough Guides, Ltd., 1999.

## Periodicals

*Chicago Tribune,* February 23, 1992.
*Guitar Player,* April 1992.
*High Fidelity,* May 1988.
*Lincoln Journal* (Lincoln, NE), September 1991.
*Los Angeles Reader,* September 13, 1991.
*Musician,* September 1991; April 1992.
*Pitch* (Kansas City, MO), August 21, 1991.
*Pulse!,* September 1991.
*Rolling Stone,* January 29, 1987; November 4, 1991.
*San Antonio Light,* August 18, 1991.

*San Francisco Chronicle,* September 22, 1991.
*Spin,* September 1991; October 1991.
*Washington Post,* January 31, 1992.

## Online

*All Music Guide,* http://www.allmusic.com (Nov. 14, 2006).

Additional information for this profile was obtained from an A&M Records press release, 1991.

—Marcia Militello and Bruce Walker

# Fred Ho

## Composer, saxophonist, author

Jazz musician and composer Fred Ho has combined revolutionary ideology, modern jazz experiments, and popular forms in an accessible fusion that has won him a growing audience among jazz and theater devotees in the United States and around the world. Ho, a bass saxophonist and composer, has performed in conventional jazz ensembles. But he has also become well known for stage works such as *Voice of the Dragon: Once Upon a Time in Chinese America,* which employ jazz, popular music, Chinese opera, and martial arts in multimedia theater fusions. Ho is a professed Marxist-Leninist, and his aims are explicitly political. "I've never separated music from the activism of social change and the struggle to liberate oppressed people," he told Eunnie Park of New Jersey's Bergen County *Record.* "So my musical-political life has been about finding all forms of liberation."

Ho was born Fred Wei-han Houn in Palo Alto, California, in 1957. He adopted the name Ho in the 1980s, in the early stages of his musical career. Ho's father was a Chinese-born political science professor in the early stages of his career, and the family had to move several times when he got jobs at different institutions. Finally, when Ho was six, they settled in Amherst, Massachusetts. Even in that cosmopolitan college town, Ho experienced discrimination from teachers and classmates no matter how hard he tried to fit in. Ho's father also dealt with discrimination, but took it out on his family in the form of physical abuse. "One of my first insurrections," Ho told Nell Porter Brown of *Harvard Magazine,* "was to defend my mother against his physical beatings and give him two black eyes."

One positive force in Ho's life was the baritone saxophone, which he initially took up because it was one of the few instruments left unselected by the other members of his high school music class. With classmates like the sons of jazz musicians Archie Shepp and Max Roach, both of whom lived in Amherst at the time, Ho quickly learned to produce edgy, exciting sounds. With revolutionary ideas in the air on nearby college campuses, Ho abandoned his efforts to fit in and began to develop a radical Chinese-American identity. He also joined the Nation of Islam. Still unsure of what he wanted to do, he enlisted in the U.S. Marine Corps. He was trained as a hand-to-hand combat specialist but suffered a dishonorable discharge after an altercation with a superior officer, brought on by the officer's use of racial slurs. Ho later successfully contested the dishonorable discharge.

Enrolling at Harvard University, Ho studied sociology and joined the school's jazz band as well as a host of activist student organizations. The school "taught me by negative example and changed me by convincing me of what I didn't want to become: a functionary or manager in the system. … part of the elite," he told Brown. "And I developed a disdain for the mainstream culture I considered to be a polluted pond, a pond of racism, sexism, homophobia, and capitalist commodified culture—so I can imagine an ocean of possibilities and not have to settle for any stream." Ho joined I Wor Kuen, an Asian-American group modeled on the radical Black Panthers, but later left the organization.

Two years after receiving his degree from Harvard in 1979, Ho moved to Brooklyn, New York. His life involved a rejection of American commercial culture on various levels. He has never owned a car, and he has even designed and made the clothing he wears. The most important focus in his life became music, which he had partly set aside during his Harvard years. Ho performed with Shepp, Dizzy Gillespie, and other jazz musicians (although he rejected the use of the term "jazz," believing that it had roots in derogatory white usage), but soon he had ambitions of leading a group that played his own compositions. A key influence was bassist Charles Mingus, who like Ho realized an original musical vision both through composition and through innovative use of a bass instrument. The boundary-breaking jazz of saxophonist John Coltrane was another major influence, as were the large ensemble tapestries of ethnic experience penned by bandleader Duke Ellington. Ho formed the Asian American Art Ensemble and then, in 1982, the Afro Asian Music Ensemble.

As the name of the latter group implied, Ho sought to fuse African-American musical techniques with Asian ideas and political themes. Several albums released by the group in the late 1980s and early 1990s won widespread acclaim: two of them, *Tomorrow Is Now!* (1986) and *We Refuse to Be Used and Abused* (1989), were later selected by New York's influential *Village*

*Voice* for its list of 1980s Choice Albums of the Decade, and *Bamboo That Snaps Back* was named Critics' Choice Album of the Year by *Coda* magazine in 1987.

In 1990 Ho formed another group, the Monkey Ensemble. This group was connected with a *Monkey Trilogy* he wrote for the stage, featuring a trickster-like monkey and based on a sixteenth-century Chinese novel. Ho's interest in theatrical works began with a 1986 score he wrote for a work by Asian-American playwright Genny Lim. His bilingual *A Chinaman's Chance: An Afro Asian Opera* (1989) has been called the first contemporary Chinese-American opera; it had its premiere at the Brooklyn Academy of Music. His

1991 multimedia piece *Turn Pain into Power!* also combined Chinese and English texts. But the work that did most to broaden Ho's name recognition beyond New York and the West Coast was *Voice of the Dragon: Once Upon a Time in Chinese America* (1995), which he described on the website of his Big Red Media company as a "Martial Arts Ballet and Music/Theater Epic." Ho hired a scriptwriter, a director, a choreographer, lighting and costume designers, and a multiethnic cast for a production that appeared around the United States over the next decade and spawned two sequels. *Voice of the Dragon* attracted fans from beyond political and contemporary music circles, including young viewers drawn by the martial arts element. The show's 2002-03 tour was booked by Columbia Artists Management, a major force in classical music. The work, Ho told Fred Crafts of the Eugene (Oregon) *Register-Guard,* "reflects my influences both from the vast 20th-century tradition of African American music, with composers like Ellington, Basie, Coltrane, Mingus, along with some popular musical influences and, of course, Chinese folk and theater music as well."

Even a widely circulated production like *Voice of the Dragon* did not turn profits in the amount required to support even Ho's modest lifestyle. Instead, Ho turned to a combination of fellowships (including six from the Rockefeller Foundation and two from the National Endowment for the Arts), scholarly residencies and research posts, and lectures delivered at colleges and universities, meetings of arts organizations, and stores. Ho also wrote articles about his own music and that of other creative figures, and one article, published in the *Movement Research Journal* in 1996, was called "How to Sell But Not Sell Out: Some Personal Lessons from Making a Career as a Subversive and Radical Performing Artist." Profits he realized were often plowed back into his production and publishing enterprises. Ho edited several books of writings about revolutionary music, one of which, *Sounding Off! Music as Subversion/Resistance/Revolution,* won an American Book Award in 1996. A collection of Ho's articles, *Wicked Theory, Naked Practice,* was issued by the University of Minnesota Press in 2006.

By that time Ho had become a well-established creative figure with several more major productions under his belt—but with no mellowing in his attitude. He continued to record, both on his own and as part of the Brooklyn Sax Quartet, which he co-founded in 1997. Sometimes Ho was criticized as heavy-handed in his politics. Ho's 2000 opera, *Warrior Sisters,* was set during China's Boxer Rebellion but featured action encompassing the oppression of women on several continents. "All in all," wrote Jon Pareles of the *New York Times,* "the opera seems to come out of some alternative reality: an America with cultural commissars stipulating politically correct fables."

However, Ho's reputation was steadily on the rise. Over time he broadened his work to include feminist and Latino-oriented themes, and in 2005 he formed a new group, Caliente! Circle Around the Sun, with poets Magdalena Gomez and Raul Salinas. He was the subject of studies in several books, including Bill Mullen's *Afro-Orientalism* and Deborah Wong's *Speak It Louder: Asian Americans Making Music.* As of late 2006, new projects on Ho's schedule included the *Struggle for a New World Suite,* to be performed at Temple University in Philadelphia. Continuing to blaze a path of his own, Fred Ho was an artist who challenged the status quo. Art, he told *Harvard Magazine,* "is about risk-taking on a maximum level where everything is put on the table—your reputation, your career, your credibility, and your own personal money." A collection of Fred Ho materials is housed in the library at the University of Connecticut.

## Selected discography

*Tomorrow Is Now!,* Soul Note, 1986.
*Bamboo That Snaps Back,* Finnadar/Atlantic, 1987.
*A Song for Mamong,* AsianImprov, 1988.
*We Refuse to Be Used and Abused,* Soul Note, 1989.
*The Underground Railroad to My Heart,* Soul Note, 1994.
*Monkey: Part One,* Koch Jazz, 1996.
*Monkey: Part Two,* Koch Jazz, 1997.
*Turn Pain into Power!,* O.O. Discs, 1997.
*Yes Means Yes,, No Means No, Whatever She Says, Wherever She Goes!,* Koch Jazz, 1998.
*Warrior Sisters: The New Adventures of African and Asian Womyn Warriors,* Koch Jazz, 1999.
*Night Vision: A Third to First World Vampyre Opera* (book with double CD), Autonomedia and Big Red Media, Inc., 1999.
*The Way of the Saxophone,* Innova and Big Red Media, 2000.
*Voice of the Dragon: Once Upon a Time in Chinese America,* Innova and Big Red Media, 2001.
*The Black Panther Suite: All Power to the People!* (DVD), Innova/Big Red Media, 2003.
(With Raul Salinas) *Red Arc: A Call for Liberacion,* Wings Press, 2005.
*Voice of the Dragon 2: Shaolin Secret Stories,* forthcoming.

## Selected stage presentations

*A Chinaman's Chance: An Afro Asian Opera,* 1989.
*Turn Pain into Power!,* 1991.
*The White Peril: Too Wrong for Too Long!,* 1994.
*The Journey Beyond the West: The New Adventures of Monkey!,* 1995, 1997.
*Once Upon a Time in Chinese America,* 1995.
*Warrior Sisters: The New Adventures of African and Asian Womyn Warriors,* 2000.
*Voice of the Dragon 2: Shaolin Secret Stories,* 2002.
*Deadly She-Wolf at Armageddon!,* 2005.
*Dragon Versus Eagle! (Enter the White Barbarians: Voice of the Dragon 3),* 2005 (premiere slated for 2008).

## Selected writings

(co-editor, with Ron Sakolsky) *Sounding Off! Music as Subversion/Resistance/Revolution,* Autonomedia/Semiotext, 1995.
*Legacy to Liberation: Politics and Culture of Revolutionary Asian Pacific America,* AK Press, 2000.
(co-editor, with Bill V. Mullen) *AFRO-ASIA: Revolutionary Political and Cultural Connections between African and Asian Americans,* Duke University Press, 2006.
*Wicked Theory, Naked Practice: Collected Political, Cultural and Creative Writings by Fred Ho,* University of Minnesota Press, 2007.

## Sources

### Periodicals

*Albuquerque Journal,* April 1, 2005, p. 13.
*New York Times,* November 28, 1997; December 2, 2000, p. A25; January 10, 2004, p. B21.
*Record* (Bergen County, NJ), January 17, 2003, p. 33.
*Register-Guard* (Eugene, OR), February 9, 2003, p. L3.
*Star-Ledger* (Newark, NJ), March 24, 2001, p. 21.

### Online

"Biography," Fred Ho papers collection, University of Connecticut, http://www.lib.uconn.edu/online/research/speclib/ASC/findaids/HO/MSS19990036.html (November 28, 2006).
Brown, Nell Porter, "Chords of Revolution: A Jazz Musician Thrives in Brooklyn," *Harvard Magazine,* http://www.harvardmagazine.com/on-line/050562.html (November 28, 2006).
"Fred Ho," http://www.kalvos.org/hofred.html (November 28, 2006).
"Fred Ho resumé," Big Red Media, Inc., http://www.bigredmedia.com/FredHoResume.html (November 28, 2006).

—James M. Manheim

# The (International) Noise Conspiracy

**Rock group**

The (International) Noise Conspiracy is a Swedish rock band influenced by the political activity of influential leaders Che Guevara and Karl Marx as much as they are by '70s punk, garage-rock, and '60s soul music. Lead by singer Dennis Lyxzén (who once fronted the seminal Swedish hardcore band Refused), the INC (as they are commonly referred), have based their vibrant careers on spreading their revolutionary political mantras to their audiences while at the same time demanding their bodies to dance along. *Eye Weekly*'s Stuart Berman described the INC as, "... Karl Marx as soundtracked by the Kinks." With matching outfits, on stage and in press photos, the INC knock listeners' feet off the ground dancing while putting social issues in their heads—even if they don't notice at first. The *Los Angeles Times* called the INC, "... rock's most politically radical band." But making socialism sexy may be the band's primary agenda.

With brash sounds that no one could ignore, Dennis Lyxzén's hardcore group Refused was heavy in style and content. After the band called it quits in 1998, Lyxzén and former Separation guitarist Lars Strömberg wanted to start a new band that had some of the political notion of Refused but with a more danceable style of music played behind it. What resulted was a

Dave Benett/Getty Images

## For the Record . . .

Members include **Sara Almgren** (left group, 2004), organ; **Ludwig Dahlberg**, drums; **Inge Johansson** (born on May 10, 1977, in Sweden), bass; **Dennis Lyxzén** (born on June 19, 1972, in Sweden), lead vocals; **Lars Strömberg** (born on March 21, 1978, in Sweden), guitar, vocals.

Group formed in Umeå, Sweden, c. 1998; released debut album *The First Conspiracy, G-7 Welcoming Committee,* 1999; reissued, Burning Heart Records, 2002; signed with Burning Heart/Epitaph Records, released *Survival Sickness,* 2000; *A New Morning, Changing Weather,* 2001; *Bigger Cages, Longer Chains* EP, 2003; released *Armed Love,* Burning Heart, 2004; signed to American Recordings/Warner Bros., reissued *Armed Love,* 2005.

Addresses: *Record company*—American Recordings/Warner Bros. Records, 3300 Warner Blvd., Burbank, CA 91505. *Website*—The (International) Noise Conspiracy Official Website: http://www.internationalnoise.com.

mélange of '60s garage-rock, soul ideas, and punk aesthetics. Lyxzén and Strömberg were joined by bassist Inge Johansson, organist Sara Almgren, and drummer Ludwig Dahlberg. "We wanted to be a soul band originally, but we realized we were all too white and living in the north of Sweden, so that won't work," Lyxzén told Berman. "We aren't interested in the avant-garde, we just want to play music that could appeal to a lot of people, widening the spectrum of who could get into the ideas that we're saying."

Shortly after forming, the group recorded a dozen songs that were then released as a series of 7 inch records on four different independent record labels. Many of those same songs then appeared on the band's first full-length album, *The First Conspiracy,* released via independent label G-7 Welcoming Committee. In true militant fashion, the INC decided that their first tour outside of Sweden would be to spend a month playing shows in the People's Republic of China.

Not long after the band's first tour, the five-piece went back into the studio to record a more substantial col-

lection of songs. After signing a deal with Burning Heart Records in Sweden and U.S. punk label Epitaph in 2000, the INC released *Survival Sickness.* With the lead single, "Smash It Up," roaring out of the cages like a lion, the album did well and the band spent most of their year touring all over the United States and Europe with bands like The Hives, At the Drive-In, and Rocket From the Crypt. "Blending punk with the influence of 1960s British Invasion bands like the Kinks and the Who, the Conspiracy remind us how captivating simple, basic, groove-oriented rock & roll can be," wrote *All Music Guide*'s Alex Henderson. "You don't have to agree with the band's politics to find *Survival Sickness* hard to resist," he concluded.

Led by the raging single "Capitalism Stole My Virginity," in 2001 came the album *A New Morning, Changing Weather.* Produced by Jari Haapalainen, the record came at a time when Sweden was burgeoning as a hotbed of fresh rock 'n' roll and most especially, garage-rock. With, "… beefier rhythms, psychedelic textures and *Funhouse*-style sax jams—the album also marks an ideological evolution for INC, building upon the 'Smash It Up' fervour of *Sickness* to explore deeper levels of Marxist philosophy," wrote Berman. "In a lot of interviews, we talk about political issues, and people are like, 'These guys don't seem to be a lot of fun,'" Lyxzén told Berman. "But this band is such a great mix of politics, music and aesthetics, and we're fascinated by books, records and pop culture," Lyxzén said. "Whenever we play music, it actually is a lot of fun, and when we play live, we hope people will see we're not boring-stiff people that just want to talk about politics all day long, because that's not what we do when we're at home."

Touring exhaustively for *A New Morning,* the band played all over the world, capturing one of their finest moments at the Oslo Jazz Festival in 2002. The following year, the band released a recording of that show as the album *Live at Oslo Jazz Festival.* The six-song EP *Bigger Cages, Long Chains* also came out that year and contained a tad less vocal socialism and even an unusual cover of N.E.R.D.'s "Baby Doll." Bradley Torreano of *All Music Guide* noted the EP's bursting energy when he wrote that, "… sheer passion … rings out of every tense baseline and raging chorus…."

Known for his work with some of the finest hip-hop and metal albums of all time, record producer Rick Rubin had been a fan of the INC for a number of years. The legendary hit-maker had seen the band play on their first U.S. tour, and in 2003, emailed Lyxzén to say that he would like to produce the INC's next record. A big fan of the Rubin-produced metal album *Reign in Blood* by Slayer, Lyxzén immediately wrote Rubin an email back and said "yes," before even asking the rest of the band. "A lot of times it seems that Rick knows more about who you are than you do," Lyxzén admitted to *Rolling Stone's* Andrew Dansby.

The INC's new recordings with Rubin were made without bassist Almgren who left the band to join The Vicious. The new album was shaping up to be slicker, with catchier choruses, and, lyrically, a bit of a different outlook since the September 11 tragedy. "When we wrote the last record, the whole anti-globalization movement was happening," Lyxzén told Corey Moss of VH1.com. "There was protests everywhere, we traveled the world, we played protests and you could kind of feel like something was happening and revolution was in the air. Then 9/11 happened, and it was like a huge backlash on all the political movements that we were a part of. It's hard to wake up one morning and be like, 'Yeah, the revolution didn't happen.' Like, what to do now? And that inspired a lot of the new record, kind of finding the strength to carry on, and this is what we need to do."

*Armed Love* was released via longtime label Burning Heart in Sweden in 2004 and set to be released in the United States at the same time. After some record company trouble, Rubin helped the INC out by signing the band to his own label, American Recordings. A division of Warner Bros., Rubin's eclectic label released *Armed Love* in the States in 2005. *London Free Press's* Darryl Sterdan called the new album, "... their most polished and poised production to date, with a dozen fist-pumping counterculture anthems fueled by hip-shaking soul grooves...." In Lyxzén's interview with Dansby, the musician explained the slight differences of the band's lyrics, post-September 11. "The way things are today, it *is* easy to find things to write about, but you must be careful not to wear yourself down," he said. "I've been singing songs about these issues for a long time. But if you compare the lyrics with the last few records, there is a different approach. They're very political, but they talk about politics from a personal standpoint."

## Selected discography

*The First Conspiracy,* G-7 Welcoming Committee, 1999; reissued, Burning Heart Records, 2002.
*Survival Sickness,* Burning Heart/Epitaph, 2000.
*A New Morning, Changing Weather,* Burning Heart/Epitaph, 2001.
*Bigger Cages, Longer Chains,* Burning Heart, 2003.
*Live at Oslo Jazz Festival,* Moserobi, 2003.
*Armed Love,* Burning Heart, 2004; reissued, American Recordings, 2005.

## Sources

### Periodicals

*Eye Weekly* (Toronto, Ontario), October 19, 2000; November 8, 2001.
*London Free Press,* October 11, 2005.

### Online

"(International) Noise Conspiracy Prefer *Armed Love* to Hippie Love," VH1.com, http://www.vh1.com/artists/news/1508663/0802005/international_noise_conspiracy.jhtml (November 1, 2006).
"Noise Conspiracy Get 'Armed,'" *Rolling Stone,* http://www.rollingstone.com/news/story/5937215/noise_conspiracy_get_armed (November 1, 2006).
"The (International) Noise Conspiracy," *All Music Guide,* http://www.allmusic.com (November 1, 2006).
"The International Noise Conspiracy," Epitaph Records, http://www.epitaph.com/artists/artist/70 (November 1, 2006).
The (International) Noise Conspiracy Official Website, http://www.internationalnoise.com/presskit_biography.asp (November 1, 2006).

—*Shannon McCarthy*

# Wyclef Jean

## Rap musician, guitarist

Amy Sussman/Getty Images

Multi-talented hip-hop guitarist Nel Wyclef Jean, one-third of the renowned band The Fugees, released a platinum-selling solo debut album titled *The Carnival* in 1998 to positive and often gushing reviews. Jean drew upon Creole folk music, Afro-Cuban, reggae, rhythm and blues, funk, and rap music to forge a refreshing brand of hip-hop, and this variety of musical styles was also evident in the music of The Fugees. In addition to artfully fusing a myriad of musical styles, Jean is one of the few hip-hop artists to play the guitar and still be accepted as a rapper by hardcore hip-hop fans. In this respect, he combined an appreciative alternative music fan base with his hip-hop and rap fans and achieved a rare feat. *Time* magazine's Christopher John Farley wrote, "The Carnival puts Wyclef up there with Billy Corgan, Trent Reznor and Tricky as one of the most creative people working in pop music."

Jean was born in Haiti in 1971, and moved to Brooklyn near Coney Island in New York City with his parents at the age of nine, before eventually moving to Newark, New Jersey, to attend high school. His father, Gesner Jean, was pastor of Newark's Good Shepherd Church of the Nazarene. Jean studied at Newark's Vailsburg High School, learning as much as he could about music and the music business. His cousin, Prakazrel 'Pras' Michel of the Fugees, lived in South Orange, New Jersey, and Jean began experimenting with hip-hop along with Michel and Lauryn Hill of The Fugees while still in high school. Jean told *Rolling Stone*'s David Sprague, "When I'd come back from the studio, I'd get a whipping from my dad, 'cause I was playing devil's music." While Jean was still underage, a recording contract fell through because his father refused to condone it.

In 1988 the Vailsburg High School Swing Choir included Jean on bass and Michel on vocals; they sang for the Young Americans National Invitational Performance Choir Festival in Hollywood, where the choir won an award for costumes and Jean was honored for an original composition. Jean wrote songs on the choir's bus while traveling from one event to the next. Back in Newark, Jean and Michel formed a rap group called Exact Change, which was distinguished by the fact that they wore tuxedoes, rapped in six languages, and had a positive message. Then the two Haitian cousins and Lauryn Hill began rapping together under the name Tranzlator Crew, and by 1993 they were signed to Ruff House/Columbia Records and working on their first full-length release.

The group changed their name due to a legal objection by a new wave group named Translator, and chose The Fugees as a shortened version of refugees—since they sought refuge in their music. Their first release, *Blunted on Reality,* was released to positive reviews in late 1993. After producing their second release, *The Score,* in their own studio in East Orange, free of the constricting terms of their original production contract, the group saw their sophomore effort attain instant success. *The Score* was more focused and strident, and drew from the band's myriad musical influences—everything from Caribbean music to Roberta Flack, and early 1980s new wave musicians like Tears for Fears and the Pet Shop Boys. *The Score* topped the charts for weeks, sold more than 15 million copies worldwide, and was followed by an extensive tour that ended in Port-au-Prince, Haiti. *The Score's* "Killing Me Softly," a remake of Roberta Flack's early 1970s single, graced the R&B singles chart for seven months and the pop chart for six months. When the Fugees returned to the group's native homeland for a concert at the Bicentenaire in Port-au-Prince, an estimated 80,000 jubilant fans greeted them.

While The Fugees were touring, Jean continued recording; he initially intended to release a solo album of songs in Creole, but he expanded his reach. He also did remixes for Cypress Hill, Sublime, Simply Red, Whitney Houston, TLC, Michael Jackson, and Bounty Killer while the band was on the road. The prolific Jean was the primary writer, producer, and performer on *The Carnival,* but he enlisted an impressive array of international talent for his debut solo release. Lauryn Hill and Michel assisted his effort, as did the Latin supernova salsa singer Celia Cruz on "Guantanamera," the New Orleans-based Neville Brothers on "Mona Lisa,"

members of the New York Philharmonic Orchestra, conducted by Jean, on "Gone 'Til November," and reggae's I Threes on "Gunpowder." Pablo Diablo was featured on "Crazy Sam" and "Talent." "Yele" featured the Creole folk music of Jean's Haitian homeland, as did "Sang Fezi," "Jaspora," and the calypso-infused "Carnival." The French-Creole songs on *The Carnival* topped the charts in Haiti.

Jean's father died in an accident in September of 2001. In that same year his wife, Marie Claudinette, lost her mother and an uncle. Jean told Steve Dougherty and Mark Dagostino in *People,* "We went through a death spell, losing three people back-to-back. Then, after a year of mourning, I finally understood. To conquer death, you have to celebrate life."

In 2002 Jean released *Masquerade.* He followed this with *Greatest Hits* and *The Preacher's Son* in 2003.

In 2005 he branched out into acting. He appeared in four episodes of NBC's "Third Watch" and appeared in two independent films, *One Last Thing* and *Dirty.* He also signed a deal with HBO to produce and star in a comedy series based loosely on his own life. Jean told *People,* "I love performing. It's time for that right now—to celebrate life and give people hope."

## Selected discography

(With the Fugees) *Blunted on Reality,* Ruff House/Columbia Records, 1993.
(With the Fugees) *The Score,* Ruff House/Columbia Records, 1996.
*Presents The Carnival,* Ruff House/Columbia Records, 1997.
*Ecleftic: 2 Sides II a Book,* Columbia Records, 2000.
*Masquerade,* Ruff House/Columbia Records, 2002.
*Greatest Hits,* Ruff House/Columbia Records, 2003.
*The Preacher's Son* J-Records, 2003.
*Welcome to Haiti: Creole 101,* Koch, 2004.

## Sources

### Periodicals

*Billboard,* June 14, 1997.
*Ebony,* November 1996.
*Entertainment Weekly,* December 26, 1997.
*Guitar Player,* January 1998.
*Harper's Bazaar,* June 1996.
*Interview,* May 1996.
*Newsweek,* October 6, 1997.
*People,* July 7, 1997.
*Rolling Stone,* September 5, 1996.
*Time,* July 28, 1997.
*Us,* August 1996.

—*B. Kimberly Taylor and Kelly Winters*

# Johnny Jenkins

## Singer

While Johnny Jenkins's name never reached the heights of his contemporaries, his flamboyant guitar style backed the earliest recordings of Otis Redding and influenced Jimi Hendrix's technical flourish. Jenkins fronted the Pinetoppers in the late 1950s, had brief chart success with "Love Twist" in 1961, and recorded *Ton-Ton Macoute!* with members of the All-man Brothers Band in 1970 (released 1972). After 1970 Jenkins, bitter over what he considered ill-treatment by his manager, retired from the music business for the next 25 years. In 1996, however, he returned with *Blessed Blues,* another winning album featuring his heartfelt blues style. "I thought my entire world rotated around Johnny Jenkins' guitar," Phil Walden told the London *Independent* in 1996. "I was convinced he could have been the greatest thing in rock 'n' roll."

Jenkins was born in Macon, Georgia, on March 5, 1939, and grew up in rural Swift Creek. He listened to R&B, hillbilly, and blues on a small battery-powered radio, and built his first guitar by combining a cigar box and rubber bands when he was nine. Left handed, he played the guitar upside down, a method he stuck with after his sister bought him a real guitar. Jenkins absorbed the music of his day, from Bill Doggett to Chuck Berry, and played at a local gas station for tips.

Jenkins formed the Pinetoppers in the late 1950s, a band that eventually included rhythm guitarist Samuel Davis, drummer Willie Bowden, saxophonist Ish Mosley, and singer Otis Redding. When Phil Walden heard the Pinetoppers on a local radio show, he began working as the band's agent, booking the group at fraternity and high school parties. In 1961 the Pinetoppers had a regional hit with "Love Twist" on Tifco Records, selling 25,000 copies. The recording was eventually distributed by Atlantic Records.

When Jenkins and the Pinetoppers returned to the studio for a follow-up session in 1962, nothing went well. The band recorded two tracks, "Spunky" and "Bashful Guitar," but still had 40 minutes of studio time to fill ("Spunky" and "Bashful Guitar" were released by Vox in 1964). During that 40 minutes, Otis Redding recorded "These Arms of Mine," with Jenkins on guitar and Steve Cropper on piano. This single helped launch Redding's career, and he received a recording contract. Jenkins, left out of the deal, was asked to form part of Redding's backing band, but he refused, primarily because of his fear of flying, but also because he believed the plane they planned to use was unsafe. His fears would later seem like a powerful portent when Redding's plane crashed, killing the singer, on December 10, 1967.

After parting with Redding, Jenkins returned home and worked a number of jobs to support his family, restricting his music to local venues. In 1969 Jenkins was invited to play with Jimi Hendrix at The Scene, a New York club owned by Steve Paul. Hendrix had seen Jenkins play while visiting relatives in Macon, and many commentators later noted the influence. "Jimi Hendrix admitted to having sat at his feet, copying everything he played," Phil Walden told Fred Shuster in the Los Angeles *Daily News.* "They both played the same way: upside down and left-handed. Johnny was playing the guitar behind his head and with his teeth back in 1958."

Walden asked Jenkins to record an album in 1970 to be issued on his fledgling Capricorn Records. Jenkins received the backing of several members of the Allman Brothers Band, including slide guitarist Duane Allman. *Ton-Ton Macoute!* was well received, and many cited Jenkins's exemplary version of Dr. John's "I Walk on Guilded Splinters" (also cited as the template for Beck's "Loser"). "What a fine bowl of Southern gumbo this Johnny Jenkins disc is," noted James Chrispell in *All Music Guide.* Other standout tracks included "Sick and Tired" and "Voodoo in You." But the album was held back until 1972 and did little to advance Jenkins's career, and he later complained that Walden, distracted by his work with the Allman Brothers, failed to promote the album. Ultimately, Jenkins' experience with the recording left him bitter. Jenkins told Shuster, "I was so hurt because of what happened to me during and after that album. There were a lot of bad feelings. They kept me in the dark about a lot of things. I was just a poor country boy with no education."

Other misunderstandings also marred Jenkins and Walden's relationship. In 1970 Jenkins was scheduled

## For the Record . . .

Born Johnny Jenkins on March 5, 1939, in Macon, GA; died on June 26, 2006.

Formed the Pinetoppers, late 1950s; Pinetoppers' "Love Twist" became a regional hit, 1961; backed Otis Redding on "These Arms of Mine," 1962; performed with Jimi Hendrix at The Scene in New York City, 1969; issued *Ton Ton Macoute!*, 1972; released *Blessed Blues*, 1996, *Handle With Care*, 2001, and *All in Good Time*, 2005.

to play the Atlantic Pop Festival before 200,000 people. "We rehearsed for weeks," Walden told Shuster, "and then Johnny got up there and abandoned everything we had worked on and began to play songs. I was a little startled and confused to say the least."

Following the recording, Jenkins dropped out of the music business for the next 25 years. He stayed at home with his wife and children, and while he was frequently invited to perform, he refused. Jenkins strongly disapproved of drug use, and avoided old musician friends who were involved with them.

When Jenkins returned to recording in the mid-1990s, it surprised many that he was working, once again, with Walden. "I was always willing to forgive and forget because holding grudges never paid off for anyone," he told Shuster. After reaching an agreement concerning money, Jenkins felt confident about going forward with the project. Walden gave the green light for Jenkins to choose his own players and own material, allowing him full artistic control. The results, *Blessed Blues*, revealed the singer-guitarist still at the top of his form, delivering rough and ready renditions of "Statesboro Blues," "Don't Start Me Talkin'," and a new version of his own "Miss Thing."

Following his 1996 comeback album, Jenkins recorded *Handle With Care* in 2001 and *All in Good Time* in 2005, both on Mean Old World Records and featuring many originals. He died of a stroke on June 26, 2006. "Guitarist, singer and songwriter Johnny Jenkins may have had a long pause between records," noted Richard Skelly in *All Music Guide,* "but his heart, ears and mind were always close to blues music."

## Selected discography

*Ton Ton Macoute!,* Capricorn, 1972.
*Blessed Blues,* Capricorn, 1996.
*Handle With Care,* Mean Old World, 2001.
*All in Good Time,* Mean Old World, 2005.

## Sources

### Periodicals

*Daily News* (Los Angeles, CA), August 28, 1996.
*Independent* (London, England), July 1, 2006.

### Online

"Johnny Jenkins," *All Music Guide,* http://www.allmusic.com/ (June 9, 2006).

—*Ronnie D. Lankford, Jr.*

# Big Jack Johnson

**Guitarist, singer**

© Jack Vartoogian/FrontRowPhotos

Blues singer and guitarist Big Jack Johnson is known for his Delta Blues style, and he has been compared to Muddy Waters and John Lee Hooker. Unlike other blues singers, Johnson has remained in the Delta, retaining a classic style and a down-to-earth vibe.

In an article posted on the PBS Network's website, a reviewer noted that Johnson's music "has a raw, country feel that city bands somehow can never capture," and praised Johnson's "earthy, knowing" vocal style. In the *Arkansas Leader* Garrick Feldman commented, "Jack Johnson is surely one of the region's greatest living bluesmen and is as good as any of those blues giants from the past." Feldman also wrote, "His blues rocks and swings and moves you like a thunderstorm blasting through the night."

### "Country—That's About All I Heard"

Johnson's father was a guitarist and fiddler who played at weddings, picnics, and parties in his home town of Clarksdale, Mississippi. However, the family music was not blues but, unexpectedly, country. Johnson told Mark Jordon in *Weekly Wire,* "My favorite artists growing up were guys like Hank Williams, Roy Acuff. Yeah, man. Country—that's about all I heard." His family listened to the Grand Ole Opry country music show on the radio. He was not allowed to hear blues; there was no blues music on the television at that time, and none on the radio. To hear blues, people had to go to juke joints, and he was not allowed to go to them. So, he told Jordon, "On summer nights we'd take the radio outside and you could hear [country singer] Grandpa Jones hollering all over the neighborhood, 'Howww-deee.'"

By the time he was 13, Johnson had begun sitting in with his father's band, playing acoustic guitar. When he was 18, his love of B.B. King's music inspired him to make the switch to electric guitar. In 1966 Johnson joined with drummer Sam Carr and multi-instrumentalist Frank Frost to play at the Savoy Theatre in Clarksdale. Johnson told Jordon, "It was just like we were meant for each other when we met. We've got something together that's a lot bigger than when we're apart." They played first as Frank Frost and the Nighthawks and then as Sam Carr and the Blues Kings, a collaboration that continues on and off to this day.

In 1979 Johnson recorded with Frost and Carr again, this time calling themselves the Jelly Roll Kings; this was the first time Johnson's vocals were recorded. The Jelly Roll Kings were one of the hottest bands in the Delta region, playing at juke joints and making the area justifiably famous for its unique style. On the PBS website, a reviewer described a Jelly Roll Kings gig: "As Carr and Frost hold down a grinding, boiling beat, Johnson plays electric slide with the dirty, greasy feel of Elmore James and shouts verses that sound as old as

## For the Record . . .

**B**orn July 30, 1940, in Clarksdale, MS.

Performed with Sam Carr and Frank Frost as Frank Frost and the Nighthawks, Sam Carr and the Blues Kings, and the Jelly Roll Kings, 1966–; began solo career with *The Oil Man,* 1988; released *Daddy, When Is Mama Comin Home?,* 1989; released *We Got to Stop This Killin',* 1996; released *The Memphis Barbecue Sessions,* 2002.

Awards: Living Blues Best Live Performer, 1994; Living Blues Most Outstanding Blues Musician, 1995.

Addresses: *Record company*—M.C. Records, P.O. Box 1788, Huntington Station, New York, NY 11746.

the land, telling stories about roosters that creep into the wrong henhouse and lovers walking down long, lonesome roads."

### Solo Career

In 1988 Johnson finally recorded an album, *The Oil Man,* under his own name, with the Earwig label; the title came from his nickname, earned on the job as an oil company truck driver. This album showed Johnson's juke-joint roots. His next album, *Daddy, When Is Mama Comin Home?,* was more experimental and did not sell as well as *The Oil Man*; it featured backing horns and a style similar to that of B.B. King.

In 1992 Johnson released *The Memphis Barbecue Sessions* on the M.C. label. The album included 13 tracks, mingling original songs with traditional blues favorites. In the *Austin Chronicle,* Margaret Moser wrote that although the music on the album was not new, "real blues fans don't go looking for new frontiers, they're satisfied with the lowdown."

In 1996 Johnson recorded *We Got to Stop This Killin'* with backing by the Oilers (Rodger Montgomery on guitar, Maury Saslaff on bass, and Chet Woodward on drums). Until this album came out, Johnson had made ends meet by driving for an oil company, but after this release, he had enough success with his music to stop driving and play full time.

Although Johnson's music has a traditional feel, many of his lyrics discuss contemporary social issues. For

example, on *Mama, When Is Daddy Comin' Home* he talked about AIDS and domestic abuse, and on *We Got to Stop This Killin'* he lamented the senseless violence that seems to be increasing in many communities—topics that other blues musicians had seldom explored.

Johnson told Jordan that he was aware that other blues musicians did not discuss these contemporary issues. He said, "I just got off on another track. I'm just trying to be a different guy…I always keep my roots in the blues and stuff, but I'm just trying to be myself, come up with something new so people can relate to what I'm doing."

Meanwhile, Johnson, Frost, and Carr continued to perform together occasionally, while also pursuing their solo careers. In 1987 and 1991 they reunited for the Chicago Blues Festival, and in 1996 they joined together again for the Jelly Roll Kings' CD *Off Yonder Wall,* released on the Fat Possum label.

In 2002 Johnson released *Big Jack Johnson With Kim Wilson: The Memphis Barbecue Sessions.* Also featured on the album was piano player Joe Willie "Pine Top" Perkins. On the album, the three presented classic acoustic blues, the kind of songs Johnson played in juke joints as a young man.

Johnson has been recognized for his musical achievements. In 1994 he was named Best Live Performer by *Living Blues* magazine, and in 1995 the magazine named him the Most Outstanding Blues Musician. He has been nominated for two Handy Awards for *We Got to Stop This Killin'.* Unlike many blues players, Johnson stayed in the Delta region, where he can still be found playing in local clubs. He has traveled to Japan, Germany, the Netherlands, and other countries, as well as all over the United States, but always returns home. A *Deltaboogie.com* reviewer declared, "Big Jack spends a lot of time on the road with his band but occasionally during a lull you can catch him at home in one of the jukes around Clarksdale, Mississippi. That's Blues at its best."

## Selected discography

*The Oil Man,* Earwig, 1988.
*Daddy, When Is Mama Comin Home?,* Earwig, 1989.
*We Got to Stop This Killin',* MC Records, 1996.
*The Memphis Barbecue Sessions,* M.C., 2002.

## Sources

### Periodicals

*Billboard Bulletin,* January 22, 2003, p. 2.
*Guitar Player,* January 1995, p. 74.
*Sing Out,* Summer 2002, p. 140.

## Online

"Big Jack Johnson," *Austin Chronicle,* March 15, 2002, http://www.austinchronicle.com/gyroase/Issue/review?oid=oid%A85150 (November 6, 2006).

"Big Jack Johnson," *Deltaboogie.com,* http://www.deltaboogie.com/deltamusicians/johnsoja/ (November 6, 2006).

"Big Jack Johnson: Great Bluesman," *Arkansas Leader,* August 29, 2006, http://www.arkansasleader.com/BLUES/2006/08/big-jack-johnson-great-bluesman.html (November 6, 2006).

"Jack Johnson," *PBS.org,* http://www.pbs.org/riverofsong/artists/e3-jack.html (November 6, 2006).

"A Slick Guitarist," *Weekly Wire,* August 25, 1997, http://www.weeklywire.com/ww/08/25/97/memphis_mus.html (November 6, 2006).

*—Kelly Winters*

# Beyoncé Knowles

**Singer, actor**

Gareth Cattermole/Getty Images

Beyoncé Knowles has become such a force in popular music that she is known by just her first name. After launching her singing career at the age of 10, Beyoncé helped Destiny's Child become one of the most successful female vocal groups of all time. The group's first three R&B/pop albums sold 33 million copies before Beyoncé embarked on a solo career. With her two solo albums, and a multitude of Grammy Awards, Beyoncé has become a worldwide superstar able to ease from pop to hip-hop radio in a heartbeat. Collaborations with boyfriend Jay-Z and the best producers in the game, has earned Beyoncé comparisons to the some of the greatest female singers of all time, foreshadowing an extensive and successful career.

Born on September 4, 1981 in Houston, Texas, like many future singing stars, Beyoncé began singing in the church choir at seven years old. Born to be on a stage, she was taking dancing lessons as well when her father, Matthew Knowles, acting as manager, put together a singing group consisting of Beyoncé, her cousin Kelly Rowland, Latavia Roberson, and Letoya Luckett. Dubbed Destiny's Child, the group began performing in public as early as 1990. Beyoncé's mother, Tina Knowles, made the girls' costumes and Matthew kept the singing group on a very tight rehearsal schedule. Homeschooled until the eighth grade, Beyoncé and her friends would practice nearly every day on a stage her father built in the back yard. When she was a teen, Beyoncé attended the High School for the Performing and Visual Arts in Houston.

Seventeen years old, and already writing songs, Beyoncé and Destiny's Child signed a deal with Columbia records to release their self-titled debut album in 1998. The following year, Destiny's Child released *The Writing's on the Wall*. With the hit singles "Bills, Bills, Bills," "Say My Name," and "Jumpin' Jumpin,'" *The Writing's on the Wall* went to sell more than six million copies and earned the group two Grammy Awards in 2000 (Best R&B Performance by a Duo or Group with Vocal for "Say My Name" and Best R&B Song "Say My Name"). Soon after their success, the group would go through changes, adding and losing members over the next few years. The first Destiny's Child change up was the replacement of Luckett and Roberson by Michelle Williams and Farrah Franklin (who left shortly after).

With millions of album sales under their belts, Destiny's Child was on their way to becoming one of the most successful female singing groups of all time. Now a trio, in 2001 Destiny's Child delivered the Grammy-winning album *Survivor*. With sales of over 4.3 million copies, *Survivor* issued a string of hugely popular singles, including "Independent Women Part I," "Survivor," and "Bootylicious." Although the group seemed tight knit, it was always clear from the beginning that with her voice, looks, and songwriting talent, Beyoncé was the star of the group. Beyoncé's first venture outside the group was with a starring role in the MTV made-for-TV movie *Carmen: A Hip Hopera*. In 2002,

## For the Record . . .

Born Beyoncé Giselle Knowles on September 4, 1981 in Houston, Texas; daughter of Matthew and Tina Knowles.

With group Destiny's Child, signed to Columbia, released debut *Destiny's Child,* 1998, *The Writing's on the Wall,* 1999; won two Grammy Awards, 2000; released *Survivor,* won Grammy Award, 2001; as a solo artist signed to Columbia, released *Dangerously in Love,* won five Grammy Awards, 2003; (With Destiny's Child) released *Destiny Fulfilled,* 2004; released sophomore solo album *B'Day,* 2006. Actress in films, including MTV's *Carmen: A Hip Hopera,* 2001, *Austin Powers in Goldmember,* 2002, *The Fighting Temptations,* 2003, *The Pink Panther,* 2006, *Dreamgirls,* 2006.

Awards: (With Destiny's Child) Grammy Awards, Best R&B Performance By a Duo or Group with Vocal for "Say My Name" and Best R&B Song for "Say My Name," 2000; Grammy Award, Best R&B Performance By a Duo or Group with Vocal for "Survivor," 2001; ASCAP Pop Songwriter of the Year, 2002; (Solo) Grammy Awards, (With Jay-Z) Best Rap/Sung Collaboration for "Crazy in Love," Best Contemporary R&B album for *Dangerously in Love,* Best R&B Song for "Crazy in Love," Best Female R&B Vocal Performance for "Dangerously in Love 2," and (With Luther Vandross) Best R&B Performance By a Duo or Group with Vocals for "The Closer I Get To You," 2003; Grammy Award, (With Stevie Wonder), Best R&B Performance By a Duo or Group with Vocals for "So Amazing," 2005.

Addresses: *Record company*—Columbia Records, 2100 Colorado Ave., Santa Monica, CA 90404; 550 Madison Ave., 24th Fl., New York, NY 10022, website: http://www.columbiarecords.com. *Website*—Beyoncé Official Website: http://www.beyonceonline.com.

Beyoncé broke more ground as the second woman ever to win the ASCAP Pop Songwriter of the Year award.

Beyoncé's dominating beauty was a clear force on the big screen and after co-starring with Mike Myers in 2002's *Austin Powers in Goldmember,* offers came left and right for the singer/actress. It had been rumored that Beyoncé had a romantic relationship with hip-hop mega star Jay-Z and with her appearance on Jay-Z's 2002 single "'03 Bonnie & Clyde," it was obvious that the couple also had chemistry.

With Destiny's Child on hiatus, Beyoncé set time to write and record a solo album. In June of 2003, Columbia produced the multiplatinum album *Dangerously in Love.* Entering the Billboard 200 chart at number one, Beyoncé blew up radio airwaves with the singles "Crazy in Love" (featuring Jay-Z), "Me, Myself and I," "Baby Boy" (with Sean Paul), and "Naughty Girl." Beyoncé took home an incredible five Grammy Awards that year, including awards for Best Rap/Sung Collaboration, Best Contemporary R&B album, Best R&B Song, Best Female R&B Vocal Performance, and with Luther Vandross, Best R&B Performance By a Duo or Group with Vocals for the duet "The Closer I Get To You." That spring, Beyoncé embarked on a solo summer tour with Alicia Keys and Missy Elliott.

With Beyoncé's success as a solo artist, many forgot about Destiny's Child. The group came out of hiding for their final album of new recordings with 2004's *Destiny Fulfilled.* Later issuing the hits package *#1's,* the trio announced that after their final tour, Destiny's Child would be no more. A much in demand solo performer, in 2005, Beyoncé and Stevie Wonder took home a Grammy for Best R&B Performance by a Duo or Group with Vocals for their duet "So Amazing" (a track from the Luther Vandross Tribute album *So Amazing: An All-Star Tribute to Luther Vandross*). The singer also filmed the movie *The Pink Panther* with Steve Martin, which was released in early 2006 along with her the new single "Check on It."

When it came time for Beyoncé to work on her sophomore solo album, she wanted to do it on her own accord, without a deadline. So without telling Columbia Records or even her father, Beyoncé recorded her second album on her own dime. Wanting to step up her music a notch and break out, Beyoncé co-produced tracks with The Neptunes, Jay-Z, and Swizz Beatz. During writing and recording, Beyoncé used a method she had learned from Jay-Z in which she put all of her producers in three separate rooms in the studio at the same time. She would go back and forth between them, sharing ideas. "My ear for beats has changed," she explained to *Blender.* "I used to pick beats for big pop records, but that's not what I want now. My taste is more interesting since Jay."

Beyoncé's second solo album, *B'Day,* was released on September 5, 2006, one day after her 25th birthday. *B'Day,*, like *Dangerously in Love,* debuted at number one. "On … *B'Day,* the songs arrive in huge gusts of rhythm and emotion, with Beyoncé's voice rippling over clattery beats; you'd have to search far and wide— perhaps in the halls of the Metropolitan Opera—to find a vocalist who sings with more sheer force," wrote Judy Rosen in *Entertainment Weekly*. With guest vocals by Jay-Z, *B'Day*'s first single "Deja Vu," instantly topped the charts. "I think he's one of the best rappers; he thinks I'm one of the best singers," Beyoncé told *Blender* about featuring Jay-Z yet again on her first single. "If you've got Jay-Z's phone number, why would you get anyone else?" Eclectic producer Swizz Beats helped to create the album's second single, "Ring the Alarm." The siren-blasting song was heated and confrontational, offering a harder edge to Beyoncé, confirming her ingenuity. "I didn't want to write some 'angry' song," Beyoncé stated on her website about the explosive "Ring the Alarm." "Swizz's track had that tough vibe, like the guy had cheated, and I wanted to write something honest. If you're in a relationship, even if the man's cheating and you end up not wanting him, the thought of another woman benefiting from the lessons you taught him. That's gonna kill you!" *People*'s Chuck Arnold noticed the difference when he wrote that the album contained "beat-driven tracks boasting more soul, more sass and more sex appeal."

# Selected discography

(With Destiny's Child) *Destiny's Child,* Columbia, 1998.
(With Destiny's Child) *The Writing's on the Wall,* Columbia, 1999.
(With Destiny's Child) *Survivor,* Columbia, 2001.
(Contributor) *Carmen: A Hip Hopera* (soundtrack), Columbia, 2001.
(Contributor) *Austin Powers in Goldmember* (soundtrack), Maverick, 2002.
(Contributor) *The Fighting Temptations* (soundtrack), Sony, 2003.
*Dangerously in Love,* Columbia, 2003.
(With Destiny's Child) *Destiny Fulfilled,* Columbia, 2004.
*B'Day,* Columbia, 2006.
(Contributor) *Dreamgirls: Music from the Motion Picture* (soundtrack) Columbia, 2006.

# Sources

## Periodicals

*Blender,* October 2006.
*Essence,* September 2006.
*People,* September 11, 2006, p. 47.

## Online

"Beyoncé," "Destiny's Child," *All Music Guide,* http://www.allmusic.com (November 10, 2006).
Beyoncé Official Website, http://www.beyonceonline.com (November 10, 2006).
"B'Day," *Entertainment Weekly,* http://www.ew.com/ew/article/review/music/0,6115,1516025_4_0_,00.html (November 10, 2006).

—Shannon McCarthy

# Ladysmith Black Mambazo

## A capella group

"Humanity's first instrument was the human voice." This is the basic philosophy behind much of post-modern experimental performance. It is also the truth behind the music that a Zulu choir brought out of South Africa into recording and concert prominence in the United States. The ten members of Ladysmith Black Mambazo were the best-selling group in the Union of South Africa. After their participation in Paul Simon's 1986 *Graceland* album and tour, they became popular recording artists in the United States and worldwide.

The group, led by Joseph Shabalala, present a Zulu harmonic and variation style known as *mbube.* Stefan Grossman, distributor of the group's albums on Shanachie Records and a major influence on the rise of knowledgeable audiences for African music in America, described their style as "a timeless beauty that transcends culture, language and all other artificial barriers dividing humanity." American audiences, attracted by the beat and the shifting harmonies, have purchased Ladysmith Black Mambazo's own four albums, *Induku Zethu, Umthombo Wamanzi, Ulwande Olungwele,* and *Inala,* in greater and greater numbers.

The group began in 1964, when Joseph Shabalala dreamed of pure vocal harmonies in the style known as

Paul Natkin/Photo Reserve, Inc.

## For the Record . . .

**M**embers include founding member **Joseph Shabalala**, the mainstay of the group; early members included his brothers **Headman Shabalala** and **Enoch Shabalala**, cousins **Albert Mazibuko, Milton Mazibuko, Funokwakhe Mazibuko, Abednego Mazibuko,** and **Joseph Mazibuko**; and friends **Matovati Msimanga** and **Walter Malinga**. Other members have included **Geophrey Mdletshe; Russel Methembu; Jabulane Mwelase; Inos Phungula; Ben Shabalala** (died 2004); and **Jockey Shabalala** (died 2006). Current members include **Joseph Shabalala, Msizi Shabalala, Russel Mthembu, Albert Mazibuko, Thulani Shabalala, Sibongiseni Shabalala,** and **Abednego Mazibuko.**

Over thirty different men have sung with the group over the more than four decades it has been in existence; some have stayed only long enough to record an album in the studio, and others have been with the group since its inception. Very popular in South Africa, the group came to prominence in the United States after performing on the Paul Simon album *Graceland,* 1986; toured with Simon, 1987, and appeared on his television special; have also toured the United States independently and appeared on television series *Saturday Night Live;* released *Raise Your Spirit Higher,* 2004; released *No Boundaries,* 2004; released *Long Walk to Freedom,* 2006; have performed at numerous international occasions, including inaugurations of South African presidents and at performances for the Pope and the Queen of England; their music has been featured in many films and commercials.

Awards: Sarie Award, Best Choral Group on Disc, 1981; Grammy Award, Best Traditional Folk Recording, 1988; Drama Desk Award, Best Original Music Score, 1996; S.A.M.A. Award, Best Zulu Music Album and Best Duo or Group Award, 1998; S.A.M.A. Award, Best Zulu Music Album, 2001; S.A.M.A. Award, Best Traditional World Music Album, 2005.

Addresses: *Record company*—c/o Shanachie Record Corp., P.O. Box 208, Newton, NJ 07860. *Agent*—Triad, 10100 Santa Monica Blvd., 16th Fl., Los Angeles, CA 90067.

*isicathamiya,* originated by black workers in the South African mines. Impoverished and far from their families, they entertained themselves after six-day work weeks by singing. When they returned to their homes, they brought this music with them, and the fierce vocal and musical competitions among groups became a much-loved feature of local life. When Shabalala returned to his home town of Ladysmith after working in a factory in Durban, he founded his own singing group. In 1964, after hearing the music in his dream, he taught it to the members of his group, and after they incorporated it, they won almost every singing competition they entered. He named his group Ladysmith Black Mambazo after his hometown; "black" is a reference to a black ox, considered to be the strongest kind; and "mambazo" means "axe" symbolizing the group's skill in "chopping down" their musical competitors. They were so good at winning, in fact, that they were eventually banned from competing, but they were welcome to perform at any competition.

In 1970 they won their first record contract after a radio performance. In 1975, Shabalala converted to Christianity, and the group released their first Christian album, *Ukukhanya Kwelanga.* After this, the group's music was based largely on Methodist hymns, and their 1976 album, *Ukusindiswa,* became a popular religious album in South Africa. The group first traveled outside South Africa in 1981, when the government of South Africa allowed them to go to Germany to perform.

## World Recognition

However, it was not until the release of the *Graceland* album in 1986, with its subsequent tour and television special, that most North Americans got to know Ladysmith Black Mambazo. Paul Simon heard the group when he was considering which of many African musical ensembles to include in his 1986 album (which was recorded in London). He selected the group, along with Tao Ea Matsekha, the Boyoyo Boys and others, as examples of the "mbaqanga" sound (roughly translatable as "township jive"). The sound had political connotations within Africa and, as Simon recognized, the music had an attractive beat with international appeal. The group's cuts on the *Graceland* album, "Diamonds on the Soles of her Shoes" and "Homeless" (by Simon and Shabalala), were tremendously successful, as were Ladysmith's promotional performances with Simon on NBC's "Saturday Night Live" and their participation in the Graceland concerts.

New York critics were fervent in their praise. Commenting on the first set of Graceland performances at Radio City Music Hall in April of 1987, David Hinckley wrote in the *New York Daily News* that Ladysmith "won the crowd most easily with amazingly rich 10-part harmony whose elements ranged from call-and-response gospel to rhythm and blues and human beat box." Don Aquilante wrote in the *New York Post* that "the real show-stoppers of the evening were Ladysmith Black Mambazo. ... I have no idea what [Shabalala] called out in Zulu or what the gentlemen in his band responded, but it was fantastic, joyous, heartfelt, and big." Their call-and-response mode also caught the attention of Jon Pareles, writing in the *New York Times*: "In a tradition of competitive singing called *iscanthamiya*, Zulu choruses do dance routines while they harmonize, and Ladysmith Black Mambazo, led by Joseph Shabalala, has great moves."

Critical and audience acclaim was just as positive when the *Graceland* tour returned to New York in July for appearances at Madison Square Garden, and the group's rapport was also evident in the television special "Graceland: The African Concert," taped in Zimbabwe for Showtime Entertainment and broadcast on the cable network in May of 1987. Vince Aletti in the *Village Voice* described Ladysmith as "a 10-man a capella choir that fills the stage with concentrated energy [and] begins to pivot, kick and bounce in unison."

*Graceland* was awarded the Grammy Award for Record of the Year in 1986, and the album helped to bring New African popular music out of the boycott/embargo that apartheid had erected around it. In the years since, the musical forms, as represented by Ladysmith Black Mambazo, have quickly become popular for both listening and dancing, with a growing audience throughout the world.

After *Graceland*, Simon was producer of three of the group's records: *Shaka Zulu* (1987), *Journey of Dreams* (1988), and *Two Worlds, One Heart* (1990). This busy and productive time came to an end in 1991, when Shabalala's brother, Headman Shabalala, who sang bass with the group, was shot and killed by Sean Nicholas, an off-duty security guard. Nicholas was white, and Simon, who viewed the killing as racially motivated, led the court proceedings against him. Shabalala, grieving, stopped singing, but eventually his Christian beliefs helped him get through this dark time. After three members retired in 1993, he added four of his sons to the group.

South African politics played a part in the group's career in the early 1990s. The apartheid system that separated racial groups was abolished in 1991, and Nelson Mandela was released after 27 years in prison. The group's first post-apartheid release, *Liph' Iqiniso*, included a song that celebrated the demise of the repressive system. In 1994, when Mandela was inaugurated as president of South Africa, the group sang at his inauguration.

## Music and Television

In 1998, the group's song "Inkanyezi Nezazi" (The Star and the Wiseman) was featured in a series of television commercials for Heinz in the United Kingdom. The advertisements were so popular that the group released the song as a single, then followed it with *The Best of Ladysmith Black Mambazo: The Star and the Wiseman*. Helped by the popularity of the commercials, the album sold a million copies in the UK alone and the single reached #2 in the British pop charts. In the United States, the group was featured in two well-known commercials for Lifesavers candy and for 7-Up.

Ladysmith Black Mambazo was also featured in film productions, including the Michael Jackson video "Moonwalker" and Spike Lee's *Do It A Cappella*. Their songs have appeared on soundtracks for Disney's *The Lion King Part II*, Eddie Murphy's *Coming to America*, Marlon Brando's *A Dry White Season*, James Earl Jones's *Cry the Beloved Country*, and Sean Connery's *League of Extraordinary Gentlemen*.

In 1992, the group was featured in a play about the apartheid era, *The Song of Jacob Zulu*, first performed by the Steppenwolf Theater Company of Chicago. The play opened on Broadway in the spring of 1993 and was nominated for six Tony Awards. The group won the Drama Desk Award for Best Original Score for the music used in the play.

Over the years, the group has performed at many prestigious events, including a performance for the Queen of England and the Royal Family at the Royal Albert Hall in London. They have also sung at two Nobel Peace Prize ceremonies; for Pope John Paul II in Rome; for South African presidential inaugurations; for the 1996 Summer Olympics; and at music award ceremonies around the world. They also represented South Africa at the celebration of Queen Elizabeth II's 50th anniversary as monarch of the United Kingdom.

In 2001, *On Tip Toe: Gentle Steps to Freedom,* a documentary film about Shabalala and the group, was released. It was nominated for an Academy Award for Best Short Documentary and was also nominated for an Emmy Award for Best Cultural Documentary on American television.

In 2005 the group won the Grammy Award for Best Traditional World Music album, for *Raise Your Spirit Higher*. According to the group's website, South African president Thako Mbeki said of the award, "The Grammy Award that has been so spectacularly won by the isicaphamiya group Ladysmith Black Mambazo makes us all proud to be South Africans ... the people and government salute this remarkable group." In that same year, they released *No Boundaries,* a collaboration with the English Chamber Orchestra. This album was less well received, and many critics felt that the group's sound was tentative and watered-down in this collaboration. Jennifer Byrne summed up this assessment in *Sing Out!,* commenting, "The main failing with this collaboration comes down not to the fact that both [the Chamber Orchestra and Ladysmith Black Mambzo] are outside their usual perimeter, but rather that neither is allowed to be expressive in their truest and greatest sense."

*Long Walk to Freedom* was released in 2006 to celebrate the twentieth anniversary of *Graceland*. The album was a collection of past favorites, including two from *Graceland*. The album, which was nominated for a Grammy award, also included many guest performers, including Emmylou Harris, Melissa Etheridge, Sarah McLaughlin, and guitarist Taj Mahal.

As his group has achieved worldwide recognition, Joseph Shabalala has broadened his ambitions for the future, and dreams of establishing an academy for the teaching and preservation of indigenous South African music and culture. He is currently an associate professor of ethnomusicology at the University of Natal in South Africa, and has also been appointed to a teaching position at the University of California in Los Angeles. On the group's Web page, Shabalala commented on teaching, "It's just like performing. You work all day, correcting the mistakes, encouraging the young ones to be confident in their action. And if they do not succeed I always criticize myself. I am their teacher. They are willing to learn. But it is up to me to see they learn correctly." Throughout his singing and teaching, he remains aware of his original intention and the message he strives to impart; as he told an interviewer from *Jet*, the group's music is about "encouraging people—don't forget who you are. Love yourself. It has that message in harmony without words. It soothes the mind."

# Selected discography

*Unkanka Odla Amacembe*, S.A.B.C., 1966.
*Amabutho*, Gallo, 1973.
*Imbongi*, Gallo, 1973.
*Ufakazi Yibheshu*, Gallo, 1973.
*Umamu Lo!*, Gallo, 1974.
*Isitimela*, Gallo, 1974.
*Ukhukanya Kwelanga*, Gallo, 1975.
*Amaqhawe*, Gallo, 1976.
*Ukusindiswa* Gallo, 1977.
*Shintsha Sithothobala*, Gallo, 1977.
*Phezulu Emafini*, Gallo, 1977.
*Ushaka*, Gallo, 1978.
Indlela Yase Zulwini, Gallo, 1978.
*Ezinkulu*, Gallo, 1979.
*Intokozo* Gallo, 1980.
*Nqonqotha Mfana*, Gallo, 1980.
*Ulwandle Olungcwele*, Gallo, 1981; Shanachie, 1987.
*Cologne Zulu Festival*, Gallo, 1981.
*Phansi Emgodini*, Gallo, 1981.
*Umthombo Wamanzi*, Gallo, 1982; Shanachie, 1987.
*Induku Zethu*, Gallo, 1983; Shanachie, 1987.
*Ibhayibheli Liyindlela*, Gallo, 1984.
*Inkazimulo*, Gallo, 1985.

*Inala*, Gallo, 1985: Shanachie, 1987.
*Ezulwini Siyakhona*, Gallo, 1985.
(With Paul Simon) *Graceland*, Warner Brothers, 1986.
*Kuyakhanya Madoda*, Gallo, 1986.
*Mabahambe Abathakathi*, Gallo, 1986.
*Shaka Zulu*, Warner Brothers, 1987.
*Thandani*, Gallo, 1987.
*Zibuyinhlazane* Gallo, 1988.
*Journey of Dreams*, Warner Brothers, 1988.
*Isigai Zendoda*, Gallo, 1990.
*Two Worlds, One Heart*, Gallo, 1990.
*Zulu Traditional*, JVC World Sounds, 1990.
*Favourites*, Gallo, 1992.
*Classic Tracks*, Shanachie, 1992.
*The Best of Ladysmith Black Mambazo, Vol. 1*, Shanachie, 1992.
*Liph' Iqiniso*, Gallo, 1993.
*Gift of the Tortoise*, Gallo, 1994.
*Zulu Hits Vol. 1*, Gallo, 1995.
*Gospel Hits Vol. 2*, Gallo, 1995.
(With Shosholoza) *Shosholoza*, Gallo, 1995.
(With the Mahubo Nesigekle Ladies Choir) *Thuthukani Ngoxolo*, Gallo, 1996.
*Heavenly*, Gallo, 1997.
*Best of—The Star and the Wiseman*, Gallo, 1998.
*Live at the Royal Albert Hall*, Shanachie, 1999.
*Lihl' Ixhibia Likagogo*, Gallo, 2000.
*Thandani/Umthombo Wamanzi*, Gallo, 2001.
*Friends in Concert*, Gallo, 2002.
*Wenyukela*, Gallo, 2003.
*Raise Your Spirit Higher*, Gallo, 2004.
(With English Chamber Orchestra) *No Boundaries*, Gallo, 2004.
*Live at Montreaux*, Gallo, 2005.
*Long Walk to Freedom*, Gallo, 2006.

# Sources

### Periodicals

*African Business*, May 2005, p. 66.
*Billboard*, January 22, 2005, p. 32; January 21, 2006, p. 56.
*Booklist*, November 1, 2004, p. 499.
*Jet*, May 2, 2005, p. 36.
*Mother Jones*, March-April 2006, p. 82.
*National Geographic Traveler*, October, 2003, p. 126.
*New York Daily News*, April 27, 1987.
*New York Post*, April 27, 1987; July 4, 1987.
*New York Times*, April 27, 1987.
*Sing Out!*, Summer 2005, p. 134; Fall 2006, p. 134.
*Sojourners*, April 2004, p. 42.
*Times* (London), July 30, 2004, p. 30.
*Vanity Fair*, November 2004, p. 366.
*Village Voice*, May 12, 1987.

### Online

Ladysmith Black Mambazo's Official Web Site, http://www.mambazo.com/ (January 5, 2006).

*—Barbara Stratyner and Kelly Winters*

# Eddie Lang

## Musician, guitarist

In the early 1920s popular music, and jazz in particular, was in transition. Players like Eddie Lang had started out playing banjo, an instrument that worked well with the tuba, but were now switching to guitar. The change arrived, certain critics argued, because guitar blended better with the new string bass. Others believed that the invention of the electric microphone, making it easier to record acoustic guitar, augmented the change. But James Sallis, writing in *The Guitar Players,* offered another, more succinct reason for the transition. "More than anything else the change resulted from the playing of Eddie Lang."

Lang's life was tragically short, but within the span of ten years, he revolutionized jazz guitar and inspired a generation of players. "If Eddie had lived longer than his short 30 years," *Guitar Player* quoted George Van Eps, "he would have been as modern as tomorrow." During that time period Lang worked continually, traveling with a number of bands and recording prolifically. He attended sessions with the era's greatest musicians, including Joe Venuti, Louis Armstrong, Red Nichols, Lonnie Johnson, and Bix Beiderbecke. Lang's reputation as an accompanist also led to invitations from vocalists, including Bing Crosby and Ruth Etting. In 1929 he appeared briefly in the feature film *The King of Jazz* and accompanied Crosby in *The Big Broadcast of 1932.* In 1933, however, Lang died unexpectedly, following a botched operation for a tonsillectomy.

Lang was born Salvatore Massaro on October 25, 1902, in South Philadelphia, the son of an Italian banjo and guitar maker. Massaro borrowed the name Lang from a favorite baseball player. As a young man he learned to play violin and loved classical music; later, he would learn to play both the guitar and banjo. He also admired the Spanish classical guitarist Segovia, and would later translate Rachmaninoff's "Prelude in C# Minor" to solo guitar. Lang befriended violinist Joe Venuti, and later the two learned to improvise while playing duets with one another. "I'd slip something in," Venuti told Sallis, "Eddie would pick it up with a variation. Then I'd come back with a variation. We'd just sit there and knock each other out."

In 1921 Lang began his professional career, switching between banjo, violin, and a hybrid six banjo-guitar. He played violin with Bert Estlow's quintet at a restaurant in Atlantic City, his first professional job, and also played banjo with Charlie Kerr's orchestra and Russs Morgan. By 1923 Lang had settled on the guitar as his instrument of choice, though he never completely abandoned the banjo. Lang's first success came in 1924 when he joined the Mound City Blue Blowers at the Beaux Arts Café in Atlantic City. He continued to play with the group throughout most of 1925, while also performing separately with Venuti in Atlantic City.

Lang quickly gained a reputation as a studio musician due to his distinct style and ability to complement vocalists. He worked with singers Cliff Edwards (Ukulele Ike) and Al Jolson (later to star in the *The Jazz Singer,* the first "talkie" motion picture). Lang, along with Venuti, began an ongoing association with the Goodkette orchestra, a 14-piece band. The orchestra also completed several sessions with cornet player Bix Beiderbecke. Lang and Beiderbecke recorded impressive versions of "Singin' the Blues," "Clementine," and "I'm Coming Virginia" in 1927. In 1926-27, Lang also recorded with Red Nichols and the Five Pennies, and continued an enduring series of recordings with violinist Venuti that began in 1926.

In November of 1928, Lang joined another guitarist at the Okeh studios for a series of legendary recordings. Because guitarist Lonnie Johnson was African American and Lang was white, however, certain facts about the recording session at Okeh had to be concealed: jazz, like most American music of the time, remained largely segregated. Since Lang was already well known, he called himself Blind Willie Dunn for the session. Over the next 11 months, the two guitarists cut ten duets. "Historical importance aside," wrote Tony Russell in *Masters of Jazz Guitar,* "this is also music of enormous charm, whose power to excite the listener has scarcely dimmed in the seven decades since it was made."

During the sessions, Lang supported Johnson with complex chord patterns, allowing Johnson the freedom to construct tantalizing solos. The duo covered "Hot Fingers," "A Handful of Riffs," and "Bull Frog Moan." "He was the finest guitarist I had ever heard in 1928

## For the Record . . .

Born on October 25, 1902, in Philadelphia, PA; died March 26, 1933, in New York City.

Played violin with Bert Estlow's quintet, 1921; played banjo with Charlie Kerr's orchestra and Russs Morgan, early 1920s; joined Mound City Blue Blowers, 1924; performed with singers Cliff Edwards (Ukulele Ike) and Al Jolson; recorded series of duets with violinist Joe Venuti; worked with cornet player Bix Beiderbecke, 1927; performed series of guitar duets with Lonnie Johnson, 1928-29; appeared with Bing Crosby in *The Big Broadcast of 1932*.

Addresses: *Record company*—Yazoo Records Corp., 37 East Clinton St., Newton, NJ 07860, website: http://www.yazoorecords.com/.

and 1929," Johnson told Sallis. "I think he could play anything he felt like."

During the late 1920s, Lang also performed as a soloist with the Paul Whiteman Orchestra, one of the most popular bands of its day. Whiteman distanced himself from hot jazz, co-opting a popular style that included vocalists like Mildred Bailey and Bing Crosby. It was during his residency with Whiteman that Lang met Crosby, leading to a close friendship and, later, a working relationship. Lang's second wife, Kitty Lang, was a friend of Crosby's wife Dixie Lee.

Both Lang and Crosby left Whiteman's orchestra in 1930, and in 1931 Lang accompanied Crosby full-time. The pair worked as many as four theater shows a day, and when Crosby went to Hollywood for a five-film contract, Lang followed. In 1932 Lang made a brief appearance with Crosby in *The Big Broadcast of 1932*. When time allowed, Lang participated in other recording sessions, including cutting two duets with guitarist Karl Kress in 1932, "Pickin' My Way" and "Feelin' My Way." He also recorded with the Boswell Sisters, a vocal trio, and recorded four sides with the Venuti-Lang All-Star Orchestra. "The four sides cut by this band are generally considered classics," wrote Sallis, "a fair summation of the past decade's achievements and a preview of music soon to come."

Lang's death at the age of 30 was both unexpected and tragic. In this short time, however, George Van Eps was still willing to bestow on Lang the title "father of jazz guitar." While Django Reinhardt would expand the guitar's palette in the Cafés of Paris during the 1930s, and Charlie Christian would popularize the electric guitar in the early 1940s, it was Lang who opened the field for these and many other players.

Lang decided, perhaps at the suggestion of Crosby, to have an operation on his throat. "Lang's chronic sore throat had worsened and begun to affect his general health." Complications during what should have been a routine operation caused excessive hemorrhaging. Lang never regained consciousness, and died on March 26, 1933. "The first jazz guitar virtuoso, Eddie Lang was everywhere in the late '20s," wrote Scott Yanow in the *All Music Guide to Jazz*. "All of his fellow musicians knew that he was the best."

## Selected discography

*Jazz Guitar*, Yazoo, 1989.
*A Handful of Riffs*, AVA/ Living Era, 1992.
*Pioneers of Jazz Guitar, 1927-1938*, Challenge, 1998.
*Blue Guitars, Vol. 1-2*, BGO, 1998.
*The New York Sessions, 1926-1935*, JSP, 2003.

## Sources

### Books

Erlewine, Michael, editor, *All Music Guide To Jazz*, Miller Freeman Books, 1998.
Russell, Tony, *Masters of Jazz Guitar: The Story of the Players and Their Music*, Balafon Books, 1999.
Sallis, James, *The Guitar Players: One Instrument and Its Masters in American Music*, William Morrow and Company, 1982.

### Periodicals

*Guitar Player*, March 1998.

—Ronnie D. Lankford, Jr.

# Jerry Lee Lewis

---

**Singer, songwriter, pianist**

---

Kicking his piano stool back before leaping on top of his piano, Jerry Lee Lewis burst onto the emerging rock scene in 1957 with "Whole Lotta Shakin' Goin' On." At his early peak, his action-packed live shows and follow-up hits "Great Balls of Fire" and "Breathless" soon put him in a position to rival Elvis Presley for the title of "King of Rock and Roll." Dubbed "the Killer" because of his pulverizing affect on live audiences, he has been known to bang his piano with fists, feet, head, and buttocks during concerts. According to legend, he even once doused his instrument with gasoline and set it on fire. The hottest musical performer not named Elvis of his time, Lewis drew huge audiences wherever he performed, until public disapproval of his marriage to a 13-year-old third cousin sent his career into decline. Unofficially blacklisted from most northern radio playlists, he continued performing in small clubs for far less money until 1968, when his switch to country music yielded a string of major genre hits ranging from "What Made Milwaukee Famous" and "Middle Age Crazy" to "Over the Rainbow" and "Thirty Nine and Holding." Despite a career marred by controversy, alcoholism, and drugs, he has remained an international concert attraction. Of his contemporaries, only Johnny

AP Images

Born September 29, 1935, in Ferriday, LA.; son of Elmo (a carpenter, contractor, and farmer) and Mamie Ethel; married Dorothy Barton, c. 1951 (marriage ended); married Jane Mitcham, c. 1952 (marriage ended); married Myra Gale Brown, December, 1957 (divorced, c. 1970); married Jaren Gunn Pate, 1971 (deceased, 1982); married Shawn Michelle Stephens (a cocktail waitress), June, 1983 (deceased, 1983); married Kerrie Lee McCarver Mann (a country singer), 1984 (divorced, 2004); children: (second marriage) Jerry Lee, Jr. (died in a jeep accident); (third marriage), Steve Allen (drowned in backyard pool accident), Phoebe Allen; (fourth marriage) Lori Leigh, (sixth marriage) Jerry Lee Lewis III. *Education:* Attended Bible Institute (Waxhatchie, Texas), c. 1953.

Solo vocalist and pianist, 1956– rock and country performer, 1956– appeared in motion pictures, including *High School Confidential, American Hot Wax,* and *Disc Jockey Jamboree,* and as Iago in a rock version of Shakespeare's *Othello,* retitled *Catch My Soul,* staged at the Los Angeles Music Center, 1968; appeared on numerous network television programs, 1957– provided soundtrack to the movie based on his life, *Great Balls of Fire,* 1989; autobiography, *Killer! The Baddest Rock Memoir Ever,* dictated to author Charles White, 1995; recorded for various labels including Sun, Smash, Mercury, Elektra, MCA, SCR, Bellaphon, Sire, and Artists First, 1956-2006.

Awards: Inducted into Rock and Roll Hall of Fame, 1986; Grammy Award for Best Spoken Word or Non-Musical Album, Interviews from the *Class of '55* Recordings Sessions, 1986; awarded star on Hollywood Walk of Fame, 1989; inducted into Rockabilly Hall of Fame, 1997; inducted into the Mississippi Musicians Hall of Fame, 2001; inducted into Delta Music Hall of Fame, 2002; Grammy Award for Lifetime Achievement, 2005.

Addresses: *Booking*—Steven Green, Artists International Management, 9850 Sandalfoot Blvd., Ste. 458, Boca Raton, FL 33428, website: http://www.airocks.com., e-mail: booking@jerryleelewis.com. *Website*—Official Jerry Lee Lewis Website: http://www.jerryleelewis.com.

Cash and Elvis Presley have enjoyed a more enduringly loyal fan base.

## Sun Records Made Him a Star

When he was only eight years old, Lewis's parents observed him attempting to play "Silent Night" on a relative's piano using only the black keys. Impressed by his natural ability, they mortgaged the family farm to buy their son his first piano. Born into a Pentecostal family in Ferriday, Louisiana, young Jerry Lee, along with Mickey Gilley and Jerry Lee's cousin Jimmy Swaggert, gathered around the piano to sing and play hymns while their parents were present, but would sneak off to hear the forbidden, rousing music of black rhythm and blues players in juke joints like Haney's Big House, which often featured the likes of Albert and B.B. King. (Lewis's cousins achieved their own measures of fame, Swaggert as a piano playing televangelist, Gilley as a Jerry Lee sound-a-like country star.) Lewis also heard country artists such as Jimmie Rodgers and Hank Williams from his father's collection of 78 rpm records, along with popular country boogie singer/pianist Moon Mullican.

Although radio broadcasts of the *Grand Ole Opry* and *Louisiana Hayride* fed his growing repertoire of country, folk, gospel, blues, and boogie, Lewis cited vaudeville superstar Al Jolson as the artist who made the biggest impression on him. In an interview for Arnold Shaw's *The Rockin' 50s* he explained, "When I was about twelve, I walked into a theater. … Before the picture went on, they played a record. I never stayed for the picture. That record hit me so hard I rushed out, ran all the way home, sat down at the piano, and tried to sing 'Down Among the Sheltering Pines' exactly as Al Jolson had done it." Lewis also admired famed singing cowboy Gene Autry, whose ability to sing and play a guitar while riding a horse mystified him until he made his own very first film appearance.

Lewis told *Rolling Stone* that his first public appearance was made at a local Ford dealership when he was 13, where his father passed the hat and collected $13. After that, Lewis turned pro. Playing whenever and wherever he could, the youngster briefly hosted his own radio show on WNAT in Natchez, Mississippi, and cut his first demos, which clearly demonstrated that the youngster played rock 'n' roll long before the music derived its official name.

Sexually precocious, the teenaged Lewis had two brief teenage marriages; the second, to Jane Mitcham, produced a son, Jerry Lee Jr., who died at the age of 19 in a car accident. While married to Mitcham, Lewis's strong Pentecostal upbringing led him to enter the Bible Institute in Waxahachie, Texas, in hopes of becoming a preacher. He was expelled within a year, however, when he was caught playing "My God is Real" with an improvised rhythm and blues beat. By his own admission, Lewis has always been torn between the righteousness of Pentecostalism and his wild secular life, replete with women, drugs, and alcohol.

Lewis had unsuccessfully auditioned for labels in Nashville, and had returned to playing clubs in Louisiana and Mississippi when he heard "That's Alright (Mama)" by Elvis Presley. Reading that Sam Phillips of Sun Records had discovered Presley, he and his father sold 33 dozen eggs, and set off for Memphis. Phillips was away on business, but recently hired producer Jack Clement was intrigued by Lewis's claim that he could play piano like Chet Atkins played the guitar. Quickly, he recorded a demo of Ray Price's hit "Crazy Arms" that eventually became Lewis's first Sun single.

Although "Crazy Arms" was a modest regional success, Lewis found it necessary to work as a session pianist behind other artists to support himself. During a Carl Perkins session that yielded "Matchbox" and "Put Your Cat Clothes On," Elvis Presley—by then a superstar for RCA—dropped in and jammed with Lewis and Perkins. When Johnny Cash arrived, the four had their pictures taken together and were promptly dubbed "The Million Dollar Quartet."

During a tour of Canada with Carl Perkins and Johnny Cash, Lewis discovered the gimmick that made him a show-stealing star. After a less than stellar audience response, the piano player bemoaned the fact that he wasn't connecting with live audiences the way his guitar playing contemporaries did. According to Michael Lydon's book *Rock Folk,* Perkins advised, "Turn around so they can see you; make a fuss." The next night he stood up, kicked the piano stool back and the crowd roared with approval. "And we regretted it because he damn near stole the show," recalled Perkins. "Four nights later he was top of the bill."

The piano-pumper's cover of Big Maybelle's "Whole Lotta Shakin' Goin' On" was initially banned by most radio stations, but when Lewis performed it on NBC's *The Steve Allen Show,* he became a rock and roll star overnight. He almost didn't record "Great Balls of Fire," a song sent to Sun by black artist and songwriter Otis Blackwell, because he felt it was too sinful. However, the hit garnered Lewis a gold record, and the collective sales of the two hit singles were over eleven million copies, as reported by Mark Humphrey in *Esquire.*

Lewis recorded prolifically at Sun, partly due to his compulsive need to show off and partly because he enjoyed it. Working primarily with drummer J.M. Van Eaton and guitarist Roland Janes, the body of work he crafted at the 706 Union Avenue studio represents some of the finest examples of personal interpretation in the history of American popular music. Lewis refined a style that garnered airplay on pop, country, and R&B stations nationwide. Only Elvis Presley was more successful with this model of tri-market success.

By 1958 Lewis enjoyed a solid Top Ten pop hit with "Breathless," and set out to tour Great Britain. In England, reporters noticed the young wife who accompanied him; though Lewis claimed the former Myra Gale Brown—the daughter of his bass player/personal manager Jay W. Brown—was 15, investigation revealed that she was not only 13, but was his third cousin, and that he had married her before his divorce from Mitcham was final. Though in the South women often married young, and marriage between distant cousins was not uncommon, the British papers cried scandal, and there was talk of deporting Lewis. He returned from England early to find many of his concert bookings in the United States cancelled as well. As a result, the single "High School Confidential," one of the hot teen rockers of the 1950s, stalled out at number 21 on the charts and Lewis's career plummeted.

## Made a Comeback in Country Music

Initially banned by many important radio stations, Lewis felt things easing up by 1960, when he recorded a version of Ray Charles's "What's I Say." The record hit the Top 30 on the national pop, country, and R&B charts. However, Sun records was losing ground to better organized and financed major labels, and the piano pounding singer's recording career stayed in decline despite several well-reviewed recordings and an increasingly popular live show.

In late 1963 Lewis began recording for Smash Records, a division of Mercury, where for four years he recorded prolifically without much success. On one of his best albums, *The Greatest Live Show on Earth,* his performance of Buck Owens's "Together Again" brought cheers from the predominantly rock crowd. Out of desperation, Smash had Lewis record an album of pop-coated cover songs, titled *Country Songs For City Folks.* Welsh belter Tom Jones took "Green Green Grass of Home" from it and turned it into a major pop hit, but few others were buying.

Convinced by producer Eddie Kilroy to give a true country session a try before he left the label for good, Lewis cut "Another Place, Another Time" in mid-1968. By the fall of that year, it was a bona fide hit. Kenny Lovelace, Lewis's guitarist and fiddle player since 1967, played on that first full country session.

Taking up where the departing Kilroy had left off, producer Jerry Kennedy had the magic touch with Lewis. He chose songs such as "Once More With Feeling" and "Touching Home," that fit the singer's persona as well as his unique interpretive gifts. After a decade of struggle, Jerry Lee Lewis was once again a hot record act. By the time his run in this genre was over, he would rack up nearly four dozen Top 40 country hits.

Lewis's career benefitted from both his fresh blast of country hits and the rising rock 'n' roll revival of the late

1960s and early 1970s. After hitting number one with a Grammy-nominated version of the Big Bopper's "Chantilly Lace," Lewis's comeback had reached its zenith. He returned to the rock 'n' roll charts in 1973 with the all-star double LP *London Sessions* and worked out an album deal with Mercury with the intention of cutting as much rock as country. That's when things started to crumble.

### Dogged by Personal Tragedy

Touring for months without end, Lewis began to burn out his voice. Once a regular studio workhorse, Mercury began to have trouble getting him in to record. The switch to Elektra records in 1979 gave his country career its final chart boost. However, before he could build on the momentum of "Over The Rainbow" and "Thirty Nine and Holding," his stomach lining tore open and he nearly died. As he recuperated, his label dropped him. And health issues were among many problems that the singer had to endure.

Lewis's marriage to Myra Gale lasted for 13 years, seeing him through years in small clubs and his return as a popular country performer. They had two children, daughter Phoebe and son Steve Allen, but the boy drowned in a swimming pool accident at the age of three. After Myra Gale divorced him, his mother died of cancer, and his son Jerry Lee Jr. died in a jeep accident. Fourth wife Jaren Gunn, a.k.a. Jaren Pate, then estranged from him and seeking divorce, was found drowned in a swimming pool in June of 1982. In June of 1983 Lewis married Shawn Stephens; approximately two and a half months later, she was found dead in their home of a drug overdose. The media reported what seemed to be suspicious circumstances surrounding the deaths of both Gunn and Stephens, and in a *People* article, Jane Sanderson reported that Stephens's family had asked the FBI to investigate her death. Eventually, Lewis was completely exonerated of any wrongdoing in the two deaths, but the accusations derailed the last phase of his career as a country hit maker. Tax problems forced him to flee to Ireland during the 1990s; he returned only after a deal had been struck. In the meantime, the lone bright spot in his tempestuous sixth marriage, to Kerrie McCarver Mann, was the arrival of a son, Jerry Lee Lewis III.

### The Last Man Standing

Lewis did not fare well at MCA, where two spotty albums did little to resurrect his chart momentum, although occasionally Lewis's prodigious talent seemed to prevail. His work on the soundtrack from the semi-autobiographical movie *Great Balls of Fire,* was the best aspect of an otherwise poorly acted film, and his eponymous album for Sire in 1995 was a brilliantly distilled cornucopia of roots and rock that drew enthusiastic reviews, but relatively few sales.

Serious health problems continued to affect his output and performance into the 2000s. By that time, contemporaries Elvis Presley, Carl Perkins, and Johnny Cash had all died. Physicians restricted his time on stage, and Lewis began taking gigs opening for his rivals Little Richard and Chuck Berry. Further, an album of rock and country songs cut at Sam Phillips's studio in 2003 couldn't find a home. Initially, it was scheduled to be released by Columbia and called "The Pilgrim," then on Sony as "Old Glory," but the project was temporarily dropped by the labels without comment.

Manager/guitarist Jimmy Ripp helped make the project more attractive by calling in high-powered guest stars such as Mick Jagger, Eric Clapton, B.B. King, Bruce Springsteen, Neil Young, Rod Stewart, Toby Keith, and John Fogerty. Surprisingly, the beleaguered rock pioneer attacked the mix of blues, rock, and country with the flair and abandon of the old days, showing up most of the younger musicians with his dazzling keyboard pyrotechnics.

Appropriately titled *Last Man Standing,* the 21-song album was released in 2006 on the little known Artists First label. Benefitting from numerous television appearances and glowing reviews, the 71 year-old Lewis enjoyed the highest charting album of his career. Moreover, he sang what might prove to be his final epitaph. Empathizing with Kris Kristofferson's ballad of a rounder fallen on hard times ("The Pilgrim Chapter 33"), he channeled a character who offers no apologies for the life he's led, singing with resignation tempered by pride, "the going up was worth the coming down."

## Selected discography

### Singles

"Crazy Arms," Sun, 1956.
"Whole Lotta Shakin' Goin' On," Sun, 1957.
"Great Balls of Fire," Sun, 1957.
"You Win Again," Sun, 1958.
"Breathless," Sun, 1958.
"High School Confidential," Sun, 1958.
"I'll Make It All Up to You," Sun, 1958.
"Break-Up," Sun, 1958.
"I'll Sail My Ship Alone," Sun, 1959.
"What'd I Say," Sun, 1961.
"Sweet Little Sixteen," Sun, 1962.
"Cold Cold Heart," Sun, 1962.
"Pen And Paper," Smash, 1964.
"Another Place Another Time," Smash, 1968.
"What's Made Milwaukee Famous (Has Made a Loser Out of Me," Smash, 1968.
"She Still Comes Around (To Love What's Left of Me)," Smash, 1968.
"To Make Love Sweeter For You," Smash, 1969.
"One Has My Name (The Other Has My Heart)," Smash, 1969.
(With Linda Gail Lewis) "Don't Let Me Cross Over," Smash, 1969.

"Invitation to Your Party," Sun International, 1969.
"She Even Woke Me Up To Say Goodbye," Smash, 1969.
"One Minute Past Eternity," Sun International, 1969.
"Once More with Feeling," Smash, 1970.
"I Can't Seem to Say Goodby," Sun International, 1970.
"There Must Be More to Love Than This," Mercury, 1970.
"Waiting For A Train (All Around the Watertank)," Sun International, 1970.
"Touching Home," Mercury, 1971.
"Love On Broadway," Sun International, 1971.
"When He Walks On You (Like You Have Walked On Me)," Mercury, 1971.
"Would You Take Another Chance On Me," Mercury, 1971.
"Me and Bobby McGee," Mercury, 1971.
"Chantilly Lace," Mercury, 1972.
"Think About It Darlin'," Mercury, 1972.
"Lonely Weekends" Mercury, 1972.
"Whose Gonna Play This Old Piano," Mercury, 1972.
"No More Hanging On," Mercury, 1973.
"Drinking Wine Spo-Dee O'Dee," Mercury, 1973.
"Sometimes a Memory Ain't Enough," Mercury, 1973.
"I'm Left, You're Right, She's Gone," Mercury, 1974.
"Tell Tale Signs," Mercury, 1974.
"He Can't Fill My Shoes," Mercury, 1974.
"I Can Still Hear the Music in the Restroom," Mercury, 1975.
"Boogie Woogie Country Man," Mercury, 1975.
"Let's Put it Back Together Again," Mercury, 1976.
"The Closest Thing to You," Mercury, 1977.
"Middle Age Crazy," Mercury, 1977.
"Come On In," Mercury, 1978.
"I'll Find It Where I Can," Mercury, 1978.
(With Jimmy Ellis, a.k.a. Orion) "Save the Last Dance For Me," Sun International, 1979.
"Rockin' My Life Away," Elektra, 1979.
"I Wish I Were Eighteen Again," Elektra, 1979.
"Who Will the Next Fool Be," Elektra, 1979.
"When Two Worlds Collide," Elektra, 1980.
"Honky Tonk Stuff," Elektra, 1980.
"Over the Rainbow," Elektra, 1980.
"Thirty Nine and Holding," Elektra, 1981.

## Albums

Jerry Lee Lewis, Sun, 1958.
Jerry Lee's Greatest, Sun, 1961.
Golden Hits, Smash, 1964.
Greatest Live Show On Earth, Smash, 1964.
Country Songs for City Folks, Smash, 1965; reissued as All Country, Smash, 1969.
Return of Rock, Smash, 1967.
By Request, Smash, 1967.
Soul My Way, Smash, 1967.
Another Place, Another Time, Smash, 1968.
She Still Comes Around, Smash, 1969.
Ole Tyme Cuntry Music, Sun International, 1969.
Country Music Hall of Fame, Vol. 1, Smash, 1969.
Country Music Hall of Fame, Vol. 2, Smash, 1969.
Rockin' Rhythm & Blues, Sun International, 1969.
She Even Woke Me Up to Say Goodbye, Smash, 1970.
Taste of Country, Sun International, 1970.
(With Linda Gail Lewis) Together, Smash, 1970.
Best of Jerry Lee Lewis, Smash, 1970.
Live at the International Hotel, Mercury, 1970.
Original Golden Hits, Sun, 1970.
Original Golden Hits Volume 2, Sun, 1970.
Monsters, Sun International, 1971.

The Golden Cream of Country, Sun International, 1971.
There Must Be More to Love, Mercury, 1971.
In Loving Memories, Mercury, 1971.
Touching Home, Mercury, 1971.
Original Golden Hits, Volume 3, Sun, 1972.
The Killer Rocks On, Mercury, 1972.
Would You Take Another Chance, Mercury, 1972.
Who's Gonna Play This Old Piano, Mercury, 1973.
Sometimes A Memory Ain't Enough, Mercury, 1973.
London Session, Mercury, 1973; reissued, Lemon Recordings, 2003.
I-40 Country, Mercury, 1973.
Southern Roots, Mercury, 1974.
Boogie Woogie Country Man, Mercury, 1975.
Odd Man In, Mercury, 1975.
Country Class, Mercury, 1976.
Country Memories, Mercury, 1977.
Best of Jerry Lee Lewis, Volume 2, Mercury, 1978.
Keeps On Rockin', Mercury, 1978.
(With Jimmy Ellis, a.k.a Orion) Duets, Sun International, 1979.
Jerry Lee Lewis, Elektra, 1979.
When Two Worlds Collide, Elektra, 1980.
Killer Country, Elektra, 1980.
(With Johnny Cash and Carl Perkins) The Survivors, Columbia, 1982; reissued, Razor & Tie, 1995.
My Fingers Do the Talking, MCA, 1983.
Live at the Star Club Hamburg, London, 1964; reissued, Rhino, 1983, 1992.
I Am What I Am, MCA, 1984.
Silver Eagle Presents Jerry Lee Lewis Live, Silver Eagle, 1984; reissued, 1997.
Get Out Your Big Roll Daddy, SCR, 1984.
(With Carl Perkins & Elvis Presley) The Complete Million Dollar Session, Charly, 1985; reissued, BMG, 2006.
Live at the Vapors Club, SCR, 1985; reissued, Ace, 1993.
(With Mel Tillis, Webb Pierce, and Fraon Young) Four Legends, Plantation, 1985.
Six of One Half A Dozen of the Other, SCR, 1985.
(With Johnny Cash, Carl Perkins, and Roy Orbison) Class of '55, America/Smash/Mercury, 1986.
Rocket, Bellaphon, 1988.
Rocket 88, Tomato, 1989.
Heartbreak, Tomato, 1989.
Rockin' My Life Away, Tomato, 1989; reissued, 1992.
Rare Tracks: Wild One, Rhino, 1989.
Killer: The Mercury Years, Volume One, 1963-1968, Mercury, 1989.
Killer: The Mercury Years, Volume Two, 1969-1972, Mercury, 1989.
Killer: The Mercury Years, Volume Three, 1973-1977, Mercury, 1989.
Classic Jerry Lee Lewis (1956-1963) (8 CD set of Sun material), Bear Family, 1989; reissued, 1992.
Great Balls of Fire!, (original motion picture soundtrack), Polydor, 1989.
Rockin' My Life Away: The Jerry Lee Lewis Collection (Elektra recordings), Warner Bros., 1991.
Live in Italy, Magnum, 1991.
The Killer's Private Stash, Electrovert, 1991.
Jerry Lee Lewis Jokes and Sings Mona Lisa, Flash, 1991.
That Breathless Cat, Stomper Time, 1992.
Honky Tonk Rock'n'Roll Piano Man, Ace, 1992.
Pretty Much Country, Ace, 1992.
Great Balls of Fire Live!, Pilz, 1993.
Whole Lotta Shakin' Goin' On Live!, Pilz, 1993.

*Locust Years…And the Return to the Promised Land* (8 CD set), Bear Family, 1994.
*Young Blood,* Sire, 1995.
*At Hank Cochran's,* Stomper Time, 1995.
*Killer Country,* Mercury, 1995.
*Old-Time Rock'n'Roll,* Killer, 1997.
*Mercury & Smash Recordings,* Collectables, 1997.
*Whole Lotta Shakin; Goin' On—he Very Best of Jerry Lee Lewis, Vol. 1,* Collectables, 1999.
*Invitation to Your Party—The Best of Jerry Lee Lewis, Vol. 2,* Collectables, 1999.
*Live at Gilleys,* Atlantic, 1999.
*Mercury Smashes and Rockin' Sessions* (10 CD set), Bear Family, 2000.
*Rockin' the Blues—25 Great Sun Recordings: Rare and Unreleased Classics,* Varese Sarabande, 2002.
*Alabama Show [Live],* Universal International, 2004.
*Jerry Lee Rocks,* Bear Family, 2006.
*The Definitive Collection,* Hip-O, 2006.
*A Half Century of Hits,* Time Life, 2006.
*Platinum Collection,* Warner Bros., 2006.
*Last Man Standing,* Artist First, 2006.

## Videos

*America's Music—Country & Western 2,* Century Home Video, 1981.
*Jerry Lee Lewis Live!,* CBS Fox, 1983.
*Fats Domino & Friends (features Jerry Lee Lewis, Ray Charles, and Ron Wood),* HBO Video, 1986.
*The Legends of Rock & Roll (features Lewis, James Brown, Ray Charles, Bo Diddley, Fats Domino, B.B. King, and Little Richard,* HBO Video, 1989; reissued, 2004.
*Jerry Lee Lewis—The Story of Rock and Roll,* Pioneer, 1991; reissued, 2005.
*Jerry Lee Lewis and Friends (with Dave Edmunds, Van Morrison, and Brian May),* MCA, 1991.
*Shindig! Presents: Jerry Lee Lewis,* Rhino, 1992.
*I Am What I Am* [documentary], J2 Communications, 1995; reissued, White Star, 2002.
*High School Confidential,* Republic, 1993; reissued, 2004.
*The Jerry Lee Lewis Show (from 1969, features guests Carl Perkins and Jackie Wilson),* Magnum, 2002.
*The London Rock & Roll Show (features concert footage from 1972 with co-stars Lewis, Bill Haley, Little Richard, Chuck Berry & Bo Diddley),* St. Clair Vision, 2003.
*Jamboree [1957],* Warner Bros, 2005.

# Sources

## Books

Balfour, Victoria, *Rock Wives (contains chapter on Myra Gale Lewis),* Beech Tree Books, 1986.
Cain, Robert, *Whole Lotta Shakin' Goin' On: Jerry Lee Lewis,* Dial Press, 1981.
Fong-Torres, Ben, editor, *The Rolling Stone Rock 'n' Roll Reader,* Bantam Books, 1974.
Guterman, Jimmy, *Rockin' My Life Away—Listening to Jerry Lee Lewis,* Rutledge Hill Press, 1991.
Lewis, Jerry Lee, and Charles White, *Killer! The Baddest Rock Memoir Ever,* Arrow Books, 1996.
Lewis, Linda Gail, and Les Pendleton, *The Devil, Me and Jerry Lee,* Longstreet Press, 1998.
Lewis, Myra, with Murray Silver, *Great Balls of Fire! The Uncensored Story of Jerry Lee Lewis,* St. Martin's Press, 1982.
Lydon, Michael, *Rock Folk,* First Citadel Underground Edition, 1990.
Palmer, Robert, *Jerry Lee Lewis Rocks!,* Omnibus Press, 1981.
Shaw, Arnold, *The Rockin' 50s,* Hawthorn, 1974.
Tosches, Nick, *Hellfire: The Jerry Lee Lewis Story,* Dell, 1982.

## Periodicals

*Esquire,* June 1982.
*People,* April 24, 1978; September 12, 1983; May 14, 1984; October 27, 1986.
*Rolling Stone,* March 1, 1984; November 21, 1985.
*Time,* March 14, 1983.

## Online

"Jerry Lee Lewis," *All Music Guide,* http://www.allmusic.com (October 18, 2006).
"Jerry Lee Lewis," *Internet Movie Database,* http://www.imdb.com. (October 18, 2006).
Official Jerry Lee Lewis Website, http://www.jerryleelewis.com. (October 19, 2006).

—*Elizabeth Thomas and Ken Burke*

# Kenny Loggins

**Pop singer, songwriter**

© Reuters/CORBIS

Michael Jackson may be the king of pop, but the media have often crowned Kenny Loggins the king of the movie soundtrack. It would be difficult to remember the Tom Cruise smash hit *Top Gun* without humming "Danger Zone" at the same time. However, Loggins's movie music career actually accounts for only a small portion of his pop-rock past. Beginning with a $100 per week job writing music for others, and peaking with platinum albums and Grammy Awards, Loggins has continued to write and perform music that people like to hum.

Loggins was born January 7, 1948, in Everett, Washington. His love of music became evident when he began playing the guitar at age 12. His father was a salesman, and the family also lived in Seattle and Detroit before moving to California. Loggins knew by the time he was in high school that he wanted a career in music. He even had trouble studying for final exams in his senior year because he was busy writing the song "House at Pooh Corner." Twenty-eight years later, *Return to Pooh Corner*—a children's album—became one of his best-selling records.

When Loggins was attending Pasadena City College, he was a member of a folk group, and later joined a rock group called Gator Creek. Gator Creek did some recording for Mercury, but Loggins later joined another band called Second Helping. By 1969, when Loggins was 21, he quit Second Helping to take a steady job in Los Angeles, writing music for a publishing company called Milk Money. The job proved to be a launching pad for his very successful career. While working as a writer, he toured with members of the Electric Prunes, and then met the Nitty Gritty Dirt Band. Later, a family friend who was an employee of Columbia thought that Loggins might be good enough to record a solo album. That friend, Don Ellis, introduced Loggins to Jim Messina. Loggins's pop-rock career success began after that introduction.

Jim Messina was a guitarist for the band Poco and then the band Buffalo Springfield. He never intended to become a part of a musical duo; he just wanted to produce a few acts for Columbia. He liked the songs Loggins wrote for the Nitty Gritty Dirt Band, and in 1971, decided to take on Loggins as his first project. After Loggins signed for Columbia, Messina began working with him on a new album. The two decided that the songs sounded best when they played together, and they decided to record the album as a duo. Thus, "Loggins and Messina" was born.

Their first album in 1972 was appropriately called *Kenny Loggins with Jim Messina Sittin' In*–what Messina assumed he was doing. They didn't break up until 1976, seven albums later. Three of the albums went platinum, the other four were gold. The duo produced several hits. The first album went platinum with hits like "Danny's Song" and "Vahevala." The platinum

## For the Record . . .

Born Kenneth Clarke Loggins, January 7, 1948, in Everett, WA; son of Robert George (in sales) and Lina (Massie) Loggins; married Eva Ein (marriage ended); married Julia Cooper, 1992; children: Crosby, Cody, Isabella, Lukas, Hana. *Education:* Attended Pasadena City College.

Started playing guitar and writing songs in seventh grade; joined folk group while attending Pasadena City College; joined Gator Creek and Second Helping rock bands, 1969; quit Second Helping to write music for Milk Money Publishing, 1969; met Jim Messina after writing several Nitty Gritty Dirt Band songs, 1970; formed duo group called Loggins and Messina, 1972; Loggins and Messina yielded seven albums—three platinum, four gold—including songs "Vahevala," "Danny's Song," and "Your Mama Don't Dance," 1972-76; went solo, 1976; eleven solo albums yielded hits like "Whenever I Call You Friend," "This Is It," "Celebrate Me Home," and "Return to Pooh Corner," 1976– solo hit singles on several movie soundtracks including "I'm Alright" from *Caddyshack,* 1980, "Footloose," 1984, "Danger Zone" from *Top Gun,* 1986, "For the First Time" from *One Fine Day,* 1996; composed Disney Channel Special "This Island Earth," 1993; wrote book and album with wife Julia called *The Unimaginable Life,* 1997; released *December,* 1998, *More Songs From Pooh Corner,* 2000, and *It's About Time,* 2003; reunion with Jim Messina, 2005; issued *Live: Sittin' in Again at Santa Barbara Bowl* with Messina, 2005; initiated Christmas tour, 2006.

Awards: Rock 'n Roll Sports Classic Gold Medal; Grammy Award, Song of the Year, for "What a Fool Believes" (cowritten with the Doobie Brothers), 1980; Grammy Award, Best Pop Vocal, for "This Is It," 1981; Cable Ace Award and Emmy Awards for Outstanding Original Song and Outstanding Achievement in Writing, for "This Island Earth," 1993.

Addresses: *Record company*—Columbia Records, 550 Madison Ave., 24th Fl., New York, NY, 10022, phone: (212)-833-4000, website: www.columbiarecords.com. *Office*—c/o William Morris Agency, 151 South El Camino Dr., Beverly Hills, CA, 90212- 2704.

follow-up album, *Loggins and Messina,* (no more "sittin' in"), yielded the songs "Your Mama Don't Dance" and "Thinking of You." The next album, *Full Sail,* also went platinum in 1973. The next four albums went gold, but were discouraging. After they broke up in 1976, two more albums were released, a greatest hits, called *Best of Friends,* and a live album, called *Finale.*

Loggins did not wait long to release his first solo effort, *Celebrate Me Home.* The album sold over a million copies in 1977, as did the follow-up album *Nightwatch.* The popular song from *Nightwatch* was "Whenever I Call You Friend," sung with Stevie Nicks. That song reached number five on the pop charts and sealed Loggins's reputation for being optimistic, even cheerful, in his songwriting. *Keep the Fire* went platinum in 1979 and included a favorite sports anthem, "This Is It." In 1981 Loggins won a Grammy Award for Best Pop Vocal for "This Is It." Loggins had already won his first Grammy in 1980 for cowriting the Song of the Year, "What a Fool Believes," with the Doobie Brothers.

In 1985 Loggins tried his hand at producing his own album, *Vox Humana.* Ralph Novak of *People* commented, "Loggins is as polished as they come in the pop-rock business, with a precision and versatility that save him from ever being bad." Loggins's wife at the time, Eva Ein, helped to write some of the songs on the album. *Vox Humana* sold poorly and Loggins waited three years before releasing *Back to Avalon* in 1988.

Loggins's next album, Leap of Faith, was released in 1991. About this time, his music had shifted from Pop-Rock to New Age to Adult Contemporary. A *Stereo Review* critic remarked, "With little more than his positive, spiritual attitude and supple falsetto to lead the way, it may take a leap of faith, indeed, for his audience, New Age or otherwise, to follow." *Leap of Faith* was a very personal album for Loggins, with songs about his children and about his divorce with wife Eva. It also contained a song about the planet, "Conviction of the Heart," which marked the beginning of Loggins's public concern for the environment.

Loggins followed *Leap of Faith* with a live album called *Outside: From the Redwoods.* That album yielded a concert video tape with the same name, aired by the Public Broadcast Network in 1993. Loggins was not new to television. The previous year he had a TV special called "This Island Earth" for the Disney Channel. That special earned him a Cable Ace Award and two Emmy Awards for Outstanding Original Song and Outstanding Achievement in Writing. In 1994 Loggins released *Return to Pooh Corner* with a concert videotape that included interview segments. Loggins explained to *Billboard* why he made the children's record. He said, "I wanted to create an atmosphere for bedtime that was also listenable to me as a dad."

Loggins started making songs for movie soundtracks in the early 1980s. The first, "I'm Alright," was for the movie *Caddyshack*. "I'm Alright" made it to number seven on the pop charts. Next came songs for the *Footloose* soundtrack: "I'm Free (Heaven Help the Man)" and "Footloose," which topped the pop chart in 1984. "Forever" from *Vox Humana* was written for a short film called *Access All Areas*. His next big movie hit was "Danger Zone" from *Top Gun*. "Danger Zone" made it to number two in 1986. The movie *Over the Top*, with Sylvester Stallone, yielded the top 20 hit "Meet Me Halfway." "Nobody's Fool" from the movie *Caddyshack II* reached the top ten in 1988. In 1996 Loggins earned rave reviews, an Oscar nomination, and a live appearance on the Academy Award show for his song "For the First Time" from the *One Fine Day* soundtrack.

In March of 1997 Loggins released *Yesterday, Today, Tomorrow—The Greatest Hits of Kenny Loggins.* Along with all of Loggins's chart topping hits, there was a new song on the album called "The Rest of Your Life." In the liner notes, Loggins wrote, "This song is a centerpiece from the upcoming album *The Unimaginable Life.* I consider this project to be the most ambitious, artistic undertaking of my career." Loggins and his second wife Julia wrote a book called *The Unimaginable Life,* and the album *The Unimaginable Life* is "a soundtrack for the book," to quote Loggins's words. The book and the album were released simultaneously in July of 1997. Loggins recorded the album at his home studio in Santa Barbara, California, so he could be with his wife and four children.

Loggins released *December* in 1998, a holiday album covering classics like Irvin Berlin's "White Christmas" and originals like the title cut. He was joined by David Crosby and Graham Nash on the traditional "Coventry Carol." Next, Loggins issued *More Songs From Pooh Corner,* a children's album. The album's eclectic selection featured Randy Newman's "That'll Do" from *Babe, Pig in the City,* and Paul McCartney and John Lennon's "Good Night." In 2001 Columbia Records issued *The Essential Kenny Loggins,* a career retrospective featuring over 35 songs, including his best-known hits, followed in 2003 by *It's About Time,* an album that included a collaboration between Loggins and country music singer Clint Black on "Alive 'N' Kickin'."

Following the release of the compilation *The Best of Loggins and Messina: Sittin' In Again* in 2005, Loggins re-teamed with ex-partner Jim Messina for a number of concert dates. The same year, the duo released *Live: Sittin' in Again at Santa Barbara Bowl,* documenting one of the early shows. "It's a warm, friendly show, with just the right amount of slickness," wrote Stephen Thomas Erlewine in *All Music Guide.* While Loggins enjoyed the shows and a chance to revisit old material, he soon felt constricted by the format. "I found myself playing 30-year-old music night after night," he told Gary Budzak in the *Columbus Dispatch,* "and was dying to put new material into the show."

In 2006 Loggins added a fresh element to his songs, performing with the Columbus Symphony Orchestra in Ohio. "It's a nice change of pace," he told Budzak, "and the audience loves it. And I've got so much material that lends itself to the symphonic approach that it's really fun to do."

Loggins is well known for his environmental efforts and applauds the environmental groups who try to make a difference. Loggins lectures informally on the joy of spiritual growth and relationships. One line from "The Rest of Your Life" is "Oh I believe there's a god watching over me." He must believe that someone up there likes him, but his success has proved that he also appeals to many down here. Loggins continues to inspire a large audience and he created enough music to please them all.

# Selected discography

## With Jim Messina on Columbia Records

*Loggins and Messina,* 1972.
*Full Sail,* 1973.
*On Stage (Live),* 1974.
*Mother Lode* 1974.
*So Fine,* 1975.
*Native Sons,* 1976.
*Best of Friends (Collection),* 1977.
*Finale (Live),* 1977.
*The Best of Loggins and Messina: Sittin' In Again,* Rhino, 2005.

## Solo albums; on Columbia Records, except where noted

*Celebrate Me Home,* 1977.
*Nightwatch,* 1978.
*Keep the Fire,* 1979.
*Kenny Loggins Alive (Live),* 1980.
*High Adventure,* 1982.
*Vox Humana,* 1985.
*Back to Avalon,* 1988.
*Leap of Faith,* 1991.
*Outside: From the Redwoods,* 1993.
*Return to Pooh Corner,* Sony Wonder, 1994.
*Yesterday, Today, Tomorrow—The Greatest Hits of Kenny Loggins,* Sony, 1997.
*The Unimaginable Life,* Sony, 1997.
*December,* Sony, 1998.
*More Songs From Pooh Corner,* Columbia, 2000.
*It's About Time,* All the Best, 2003.

## Soundtracks

*Caddyshack* (includes "I'm Alright"), 1980.
*Footloose,* 1984.
*Top Gun,* CBS, 1986.
*Over the Top,* 1987.
*Caddyshack II ,* 1988.
*One Fine Day,* 1996.

## Albums with the Nitty Gritty Dirt Band

*Make a Little Magic,* 1980.
*Jealousy,* 1981.
*Let's Go,* 1982.

## With Others

*Gator Creek,* Mercury, 1970.
(With Sanford & Townsend) *Sanford & Townsend Band,* 1976.
(With Sanford & Townsend) *Smoke from a Distant Fire,* 1976.
(With Phoebe Snow) *Never Letting Go,* 1977.
(With Pages) *Future Street,* 1979.
(With Max Gronenthal) *Whistling in the Dark,* 1979.
(With Bill Champlin) *Runaway,* 1981.
(With Michael McDonald) *If That's What It Takes,* 1982.
(With Donna Summer) *Donna Summer,* 1982.
(With Don Felder) *Airborne,* 1983.
(With Graham Nash) *Innocent Eyes,* 1986.
*Child's Celebration of Song,* 1992.
(With the Winans) *All Out,* 1993.
(With Benoit Freeman Project) *Benoit Freeman Project,* 1994.

# Sources

## Books

*The New Rolling Stone Encyclopedia of Rock & Roll,* edited by Patricia Romanowski, Fireside, 1995.

## Periodicals

*Billboard,* December 21, 1996; February 22, 1997.
*Columbus Dispatch,* July 22, 2006.
*Entertainment Weekly,* August 20, 1993.
*People,* May 6, 1985; September 26, 1988.
*Publishers Weekly,* May 16, 1994; July 15, 1996.
*Rolling Stone,* November 3, 1988.
*Stereo Review,* January, 1992.

## Online

"Kenny Loggins," *All Music Guide,* http://www.allmusic.com/ (November 9, 2006).

Additional information for this profile was obtained from Columbia Media Department press material, 1997, and liner notes by Kenny Loggins to *Yesterday, Today, Tomorrow— The Greatest Hits of Kenny Loggins,* 1997. Information for this profile was also provided by the Internet website www.kennyloggins.com.

—*Christine Morrison and Ronnie Lankford*

# Lindsay Lohan

## Singer, actor

AP Images

With red hair and freckles galore, as a child Lindsay Lohan was a fresh face in the modeling and acting world. As Lohan matured, her films did as well, and after 2004's *Mean Girls* and 2006's *Bobby,* Lohan proved herself to be a sought-after actress capable of both comedy and dramatic roles. Lohan's music career, unfortunately, was often overshadowed by her films as well as her perpetual appearance in tabloid magazines. With her vibrant acting roles and now two solo albums, Lohan's well-rounded career has helped her standout from the "teen queen" set. "I feel blessed to be able to do this," Lohan said about her music career in an AOL online interview. "And I'm not trying to put something out there that is not real or me."

Born on July 2, 1986 in New York City, Lohan grew up in Long Island with three younger siblings and her parents Dina (a former Rockette) and Michael (a former Wall Street trader). At five years old, with endless freckles and red hair, Lohan was a standout in a sea of blondes as a Ford Model. Appearing in some 60 commercials, Lohan's acting career took off with a role on the television soap opera *Another World,* and later with the lead role in Disney's 1998 remake of *The Parent Trap.*

Lohan wasn't just acting by the time she was six, she was also taking voice lessons. "I've been singing since I was a little kid," Lohan said in an interview with MSNBC.com. "I used to put on shows for my Barbie dolls singing Madonna or Paula Abdul. But I started acting first, so it made more sense to just go with that, and I was young when I started." *The Parent Trap* was just the beginning of a slew of Disney films Lohan would make, including another remake with 2003's *Freaky Friday.* Lohan co-stars with Jamie Lee Curtis in a role in which mother and daughter switch bodies. In the film, the daughter happens to play in a rock band, and subsequently, Lohan sang the film's theme song "Ultimate," which also appeared on the popular soundtrack. Now fully a maturing teenager, the success of *Freaky Friday* was the beginning of Lohan's perpetual appearance in the celebrity gossip realm. Rumors abounded when the media propelled an alleged conflict between Lohan and actress/singer Hilary Duff over a mutual ex-boyfriend, pop singer Aaron Carter.

In Lohan's next tween film, 2004's *Confessions of a Teenage Drama Queen,* she got to show off her singing voice in the starring role. Four songs from the film were included on the album's soundtrack. The movie and its soundtrack failed; however, these were eclipsed by the spring release of *Mean Girls,* Lohan's first PG-13 role. *Mean Girls,* a film written by *Saturday Night Live* alumni Tina Fey, brought in a remarkable $112 million at the box office alone. As Lohan's fame rose, so did her tabloid coverage. Speculating on everything from her underage drinking in nightclubs to rumored plastic surgery, after *Mean Girls,* Lohan was officially more than famous.

Born Lindsay Lohan on July 2, 1986, in New York City, New York; daughter of Dina and Michael Lohan.

A child model and actress, Lindsay Lohan began her music career singing pop songs for her film soundtracks' including *Freaky Friday*, 2003; *Confessions of a Teenage Drama Queen*, 2004; signed to Casablanca Records/Universal, released *Speak*, 2004; *A Little More Personal (Raw)*, 2005. Actress in feature films including *The Parent Trap*, 1998, *Freaky Friday*, 2003, *Confessions of a Teenage Drama Queen*, 2004, *Mean Girls*, 2004, *Herbie Fully Loaded*, 2005, *A Prairie Home Companion*, 2006, *Just My Luck*, 2006, *Bobby*, 2006.

Addresses: *Record company*—Casablanca Records/ Universal Motown Records, 2220 Colorado Ave., Santa Monica, CA 90404; 1755 Broadway, New York, NY 10019. *Website*—Lindsay Lohan Official Website: http://www.lindsaylohanmusic.com.

---

In July of 2004, Lohan turned 18 and the following month appeared on the cover of *Rolling Stone* magazine. Now a legal adult, Lohan went public with her relationship with the then 24-year-old actor Wilmer Valderrama from *That '70s Show*. Lohan's year was made complete when she signed to Tommy Mottola's reemerged label Casablanca Records for her solo album debut.

With a handful of top-notch producers who previously made hits for Britney Spears, Destiny's Child, and Ashlee Simpson on her team, Lohan began working on her debut album at the same time she was filming Disney's *Herbie Fully Loaded*. Her schedule was so tight that she recorded much of the album in her trailer on the *Herbie* set. Lohan got so overworked during this period that she was hospitalized for exhaustion, and subsequently began to lose weight.

Released in December of 2004, Lohan's album *Speak* was teased by the single "Rumors." The song, which was actually a bonus track tacked on the end of the album, was a slickly produced pop song set for the dance clubs. The song and its glossy video spoke of something Lohan knew about personally: gossip magazine rumors and the endless paparazzi. "You can't really complain [about the gossip] because it's what you have to accept is going to happen when you're in the spotlight. And you want this. And I understand that," Lohan told MSBN about the song. "At the same time, it's hard when you're just waking up and you're going out to get your mail and there are people there. It bugs me sometimes, of course." The provocative video earned a nomination for Best Pop Video at MTV's 2005 awards show. In Lohan's interview with AOL, she explained the message behind the album title, stating "... it was titled *Speak* encouraging people to know that it is always okay ... to speak your mind. In terms of speaking about ... love, hate, fear, anger, truth, lies ... everything. Just to be open to what's out there. It's very therapeutic."

Even when Lohan wasn't busy filming her next slew of movies in 2005, her name and face were constant gossip material. Lohan's parents had separated and her father was sent to prison in 2005 for aggravated assault and a handful of other charges. When Lohan was a preteen, Michael Lohan had served a four-year prison sentence for stock fraud. The Lohan family was boiling over in 2005, which only fueled the tabloid fire. Ironically, Lohan's public family troubles added some validity and emotion to Lohan's music. A year after *Speak*, Lohan released *A Little More Personal (Raw)*, debuting it at number 4 on the Billboard 200. Contributing more of herself lyrically and emotionally to her second record, Lohan used her tumultuous relationship with her father as the subject of the album's first single. Lohan co-wrote the jarring "Confessions of a Broken Heart (Daughter to Father)" and directed the video in which she and her look-alike younger sister appear. "This album has been so therapeutic for me," Lindsay stated on her website. "But at the same time I think it captures the kind of collective hyper-existence a lot of young people find themselves in these days. I'm just thankful music has provided me with a forum to break out and express the kind of emotions that often get pushed aside."

With the work of writers/producers including Butch Walker (Avril Lavigne, The Donnas), Greg Wells (Michelle Branch), and former Evanescence guitarist Ben Moody, Lohan was able to work more directly on each song's lyrics and feeling than she had on *Speak*. Many critics compared the album with Ashlee Simpson's sophomore album, and like *All Music Guide's* Stephen Thomas Erlewine, agreed that Lohan's had more heart and artistic vision. "She really means it ... when she sings about her father, or when she sings about alienation and heartbreak, and this emotional investment when married to the duly professional, straight-ahead songcraft of her collaborators makes for interesting listening."

Before and after recording her sophomore album, Lohan was almost continually filming movies. Released in

2006 alone, Lohan had roles in *Just My Luck, A Prairie Home Companion,* and *Bobby.* In Robert Altman's *A Prairie Home Companion,* Lohan not only sang a song during the film, but appeared on the soundtrack as well.

## Selected discography

(Contributor) *Freaky Friday* (soundtrack), Hollywood, 2003.
(Contributor) *Confessions of a Teenage Drama Queen* (soundtrack), Hollywood, 2004.
(Contributor) *The Princess Diaries 2: Royal Engagement* (soundtrack), Disney, 2004.
*Speak,* Casablanca Records, 2004.
(Contributor) *Herbie: Full Loaded* (soundtrack), Hollywood, 2005.
*A Little More Personal (Raw),* Casablanca Records, 2005.
(Contributor) *A Prairie Home Companion* (soundtrack), New Line, 2006.

## Sources

### Periodicals

*Rolling Stone,* August 19, 2004.

### Online

"Lindsay Lohan," *All Music Guide,* http://www.allmusic.com (November 9, 2006).
Lindsay Lohan Official Website, http://www.lindsaylohanmusic.com/ (November 6, 2006).
"Lindsay Lohan on Breasts, Break-Up," MSNBC.com, http://msnbc.msn.com/id/6680479 (November 6, 2006).
"Lindsay Lohan Speaks!," AOL Music, http://music.aol.com/aiminterview/chat_lindsay_lohan (November 9, 2006).

—*Shannon McCarthy*

# Guy Lombardo

**Bandleader, violinist**

Ray Fisher/Time Life Pictures/Getty Images

Canadian-born bandleader Guy Lombardo contributed to North American culture a New Year's Eve tradition that has become practically universal: the singing of the old Scottish song "Auld Lang Syne" on New Year's Eve. In their heyday, however, Lombardo and his band, the Royal Canadians, were popular year-round, and not just during their annual New Year's Eve radio and television broadcasts from New York City. Guy Lombardo and His Royal Canadians reportedly sold more recordings than any other group among the big bands popular in the middle decades of the twentieth century, with total sales estimated at between 100 million and 300 million discs.

Guy Lombardo was born Gaetano Alberto Lombardo to Italian-Canadian immigrants in London, Ontario, Canada, on June 19, 1902. His father, Gaetano Sr., worked as a tailor but loved music and had a fine baritone voice. All of the seven Lombardo children were given the chance to take music lessons, and five would eventually pursue music professionally. Guy also inherited a love for boating from his father, who owned a rowboat that Guy would paddle along the city's Thames River. As the oldest child, Guy studied the orchestra leader's instrument—the violin. His early lessons from an Italian teacher named Pasquale Venuta were strictly limited to classical music, and once, when his father caught him improvising, he broke a small violin over his son's head.

This conflict did not discourage young Lombardo, who made his performing debut along with his brother Carmen at a local women's club in 1914. With another brother, Lebert, and pianist friend Freddie Kreitzer on board, the group started playing for local dances. The area around London was heavily populated with Canadians of Scottish descent, and the young Italian group quickly learned that a sing-along to "Auld Lang Syne" provided the perfect way to wind things down with the crowd after an evening of partying. "Auld Lang Syne," originally written (or adapted from earlier folk songs) by Scottish poet Robert Burns, was not in itself a song of New Year's celebration but a meditation on loss and the passage of time—the words "auld lang syne" mean "old long since," or "in times long gone by" in Scots dialect. By the early 1920s the Lombardo Brothers Orchestra had graduated to choice performing dates, playing at the resort hotels that lined the shores of lakes Erie and Huron.

In 1923, realizing that their talents were outstripping what southwestern Ontario had to offer, the group headed for Cleveland, Ohio, the nearest large American city. Their first gig, at an Elks Club, was modest, and at one early show they occupied a slot on the bill below a trained seal. But playing up their unusual Canadian background helped set them apart from the crowd. Their agent, Mike Shea, suggested dressing the musicians in Canadian Mountie uniforms, but the name "Royal Canadians" was agreed upon as a more dignified compromise. In 1924 Guy Lombardo and His

## For the Record . . .

**B**orn June 19, 1902, in London, Ontario, Canada; married Lilliebell Glenn, 1926; became U.S. citizen, 1938; died November 5, 1977, in Houston, TX. *Education:* Attended schools in London, Ontario, Canada.

Began performing with siblings in London, Ontario, Canada, area, 1914; moved group to Cleveland, OH, 1923; leader, Lombardo Brothers Orchestra and Concert Company, renamed Guy Lombardo and His Royal Canadians, ca. 1924; performed at Claremont Tent Club, Cleveland, 1924-26; began recording (for Gennett label, Richmond, IN), 1924; performed at Granada Café and made broadcasts on radio station WBBM, Chicago, IL, 1927-29; performed at Roosevelt Grill, New York, 1929-62; annual New Year's Eve performances at Roosevelt Grill (and later at Waldorf-Astoria Hotel) featured song "Auld Lang Syne," beginning 1929; won numerous hydroplane racing championships, beginning 1940; produced musical theater presentations at Jones Beach Marine Theater, Long Island, NY; toured U.S. and Canada, 1962-75.

Royal Canadians settled in for what would become a two-year stint at the Claremont Tent nightclub.

The band also made its first recordings that year, for the Richmond label in Gennett, Indiana. Early Lombardo discs showed the band members experimenting with the hot new jazz rhythms and improvisations that were sweeping the country, but soon the band took another step that set them apart. Partly at the urging of Claremont Tent owner Louis Bleet, the band toned down its volume levels and hot tempos. They began playing medleys of hits of the day, with all the tunes fitted to easily danceable schottisch or two-step rhythms. The saxophone section, led by Carmen Lombardo, perfected a seamless blend, inspiring critical praise that soon coalesced into the band's "Sweetest Music This Side of Heaven" tag line.

Some of the more jazz-oriented musicians, Lombardo was quoted as saying by documentary filmmaker Christopher Doty, "looked at me like I was an idiot. I was restricting their creative ability." Lombardo's instincts proved correct, however, as the band's popularity grew. Even though their music completely avoided the improvisational element of jazz and presented a song's melody in unadorned form, Lombardo

and His Royal Canadians numbered the fiery trumpeter Louis Armstrong and other jazz greats among their fans. They once had a successful engagement at the citadel of African-American jazz, the Savoy Ballroom in New York's Harlem neighborhood. With his fortunes on the rise, Lombardo married Lilliebelle Glenn in 1926.

In 1927 the band moved to Chicago and began performing at the Granada Café. Lombardo was quick to sense the power of the emerging radio medium, and steered the band toward unpaid appearances on Cleveland radio station WTAM. After establishing himself in Chicago, Lombardo persuaded a ballroom owner to permit the broadcast of the Royal Canadians' evening show on the city's mighty clear-channel radio station WBBM. Heard all over the Midwest, the program vaulted the Royal Canadians to national popularity. "At 5 p.m. in the afternoon we were absolutely unknown," Lombardo recalled in the *Cincinnati Post,* "and the next morning we were like the Beatles."

New York's swank Roosevelt Hotel on Madison Avenue booked the sensational new band with the sweet sound for the 1929 New Year's Eve show at its Roosevelt Grill restaurant, and the CBS radio network signed on to broadcast the show. As the countdown to the new year reached its end, Lombardo signaled the musicians for "Auld Lang Syne," a tune they had often included in shows before. But it had never before gone out to an audience of millions. From that day forward, its association with New Year's Eve was solid—as was that of Lombardo and the Royal Canadians. They remained America's all-but-official New Year's Eve band until Lombardo's death in 1977, moving to the Waldorf-Astoria hotel in 1962.

Lombardo parlayed this exposure into a steady stream of hits that lasted well into the 1950s, placing a record on the pop charts every year between 1929 and 1952. After recording for Columbia and Brunswick, they signed with the Decca label in 1934 and remained there until 1957. The Royal Canadians continued to record hits of the day like "Stars Fell on Alabama" and "The Last Round-Up," but they also introduced originals penned by Carmen Lombardo: such songs as "Coquette" and "Sweethearts on Parade" (often performed and recorded by Louis Armstrong) became integral to the jazz repertory, even as jazz hipsters derided Lombardo as "Gooey Lumbago." Younger sister Rose Marie Lombardo joined the band as a female vocalist in 1942, helping the group adapt to the new vocal-centered styles that grew after World War II. Lombardo appeared in the films *Many Happy Returns* (1934), *Stage Door Canteen* (1943), and *No Leave, No Love* (1946). On the side, he was an avid hydroplane racer who won numerous U.S. championships and was inducted into the Canadian Motorsport Hall of Fame.

The rise of rock and roll in the mid-1950s finally relegated Lombardo and His Royal Canadians to the status of nostalgia act, but Lombardo chose new projects wisely in later life. At the invitation of New York State Parks Commissioner Robert Moses, he began producing musical shows at the Jones Beach Theater on Long Island (near his home in Freeport, New York), an activity he continued until the end of his life. He also renewed his ties with audiences in London, where he had rarely appeared during his years of stardom.

The Royal Canadians' band survived Lombardo's death from coronary problems on November 5, 1977, in Houston, Texas. A long tradition of Royal Canadians performances at U.S. presidential inaugurations was revived at the beginning of President Ronald Reagan's second term in 1985. In 1990 Cleveland musician Al Pierson was selected by surviving members of the Lombardo family to assume the directorship of the band, which continued to tour. A small museum honoring Lombardo and containing memorabilia related to his career stands in a park in London, near the Thames River. And subsequent generations of rock-oriented New Year's Eve shows on television have done nothing to break the American habit of singing "Auld Lang Syne" to mark the turning of the calendar.

## Selected discography

*Your Guy Lombardo Medley,* 1957.
*Berlin by Lombardo,* 1958.
*The Sweetest Music This Side of Heaven* (4 vols.), Decca, 1961-65.
*Sing the Songs of Christmas,* 1967.
*Golden Medleys,* MCA, 1976.
*Uncollected Guy Lombardo & His Royal Canadians,* Hindsight, 1982.
*Greatest Hits,* MCA, 1983.
*Dancing in the Dark,* MCA 1985.
*16 Most Requested Songs,* Columbia/Legacy, 1989.

*Best of Guy Lombardo,* Capitol, 1990.
*Auld Lang Syne,* Pro Arte, 1993.
*Enjoy Yourself: The Hits of Guy Lombardo,* MCA, 1996.
*The V-Disc Recordings,* Collectors' Choice, 1998.
*Take It Easy,* Vocalion, 2001.
*The Band Played On: 25 Number One Hits,* Living Era, 2002.
*Best of Guy Lombardo: The Early Years,* Collectors' Choice, 2003.
*20th Century Masters: The Millennium Collection,* Universal, 2005.
*Live Jazz from Club 15,* Request, 2006.
*Lombardo Goes Latin/Bells Are Ringing,* Dutton, 2006.
*Drifting and Dreaming/Dancing Room Only,* Dutton, 2006.

## Sources

### Books

*Encyclopedia of World Biography Supplement,* Vol. 23, Gale, 2003.

### Periodicals

*Beaver: Exploring Canadian History,* December 2002, p. 49.
*Cincinnati Post,* December 27, 2001, p. C6.
*New York Times,* December 29, 1998.

### Online

"Guy Lombardo," *All Music Guide,* http://www.allmusic.com (November 10, 2006).
"Guy Lombardo," The Canadian Encyclopedia, http://www.thecanadianencyclopedia.com (November 10, 2006).
"Guy Lombardo," Canadian Motorsport Hall of Fame, http://www.cmhf.ca (November 10, 2006).
"The Guy Lombardo Story," http://www.dotydocs.com/lombardo.htm (November 10, 2006).

—*James M. Manheim*

# Shelby Lynne

---

**Singer, songwriter**

---

AP Images

Shelby Lynne, like musicians such as Lyle Lovett and k.d. lang who preceded her, was destined to become an exceptionally gifted singer and songwriter whose talent proved too broad for the confines of country music. "Unlike many more popular artists," noted Miriam Longino in the *Atlanta Journal-Constitution,* "whose pleasant voices tend to sound interchangeable on radio, Lynne can wrap her pipes around a song to squeeze every choke, growl and he-done-me-wrong out of it. She has the guts and delivery of Patsy Cline laid over the choo-choo boogie of Asleep at the Wheel." Though she walked away with the Academy of Country Music Award for best new female artist in 1991 and was hawked as a mainstream country singer early in her career, Lynne's roots are nonetheless firmly planted in history, beckoning back to Dusty Springfield's Memphis-era recordings, as well as the nearly-forgotten western swing, big-band sound of Bob Wills. At the same time, however, Lynne has mined the past sparingly, most notably on her acclaimed 2000 release *I Am Shelby Lynne,* enabling her own identity to filter through.

A teen phenomenon in the 1980s who was signed the day she arrived in Nashville, Lynne, a small girl with a grand, soulful voice, seemed poised for stardom. However, after three record deals, none of which yielded significant radio hits, Nashville's Music Row had given up hopes of making Lynne the next Patty Loveless or Tanya Tucker. Not only could she belt out torch songs and country standards on a par with the best, Lynne could also sing in other tones: "a drooping twang, a bluesy moan, conversational asides or the confiding delicacy of a jazz singer," wrote John Parles in a *New York Times* review. A notorious Nashville rebel to boot, Lynne failed to fit into the country music industry's cookie-cutter ideal. Nonetheless, Lynne never held any doubts about her talent or her career choice. "I was born a star," she added. "That's not the issue."

Born on October 22, 1968, in Quantico, Virginia, Shelby Lynne Moorer was raised in the south Alabama swamp town of Jackson in the even smaller settlement of Frankville, population 150. Lynne discovered her love for music and performing at the tender age of four, when her father, a high school English teacher, lifted the youngster onto a table at Shakey's Pizza in Mobile and she sang "You Are My Sunshine" for all the other patrons. "I've always been serious about my music, since I picked up the guitar when I was 8 and taught myself to play," Lynne told Longino. "Anything I do musically is natural, and I sing it the way I feel at the time. Each song usually takes me somewhere, and I go."

## Found Comfort in Her Music

Lynne was a self-described tomboy and outcast at school. By the age of ten she preferred listening to old Elvis Presley records and singing and playing guitar

## For the Record . . .

Born Shelby Lynne Moorer on October 22, 1968, in Quantico, VA; daughter of a high school English teacher and a legal secretary; married and divorced.

Started singing at age four and playing guitar at age eight; with her mother and sister, recorded a cover of the Four Knights' song "Couldn't Stay Away From You" at the age of 15; moved to Nashville at the age of 18; appeared on TNN's *Nashville Now,* 1987; released three albums for Epic Records, 1989-91; released Western swing album *Temptation,* 1993; released her most celebrated album, *I Am Shelby Lynne,* on Island Records, 2000; released *Love, Shelby,* 2001, *Identity Crisis,* 2003, and *Suit Yourself,* 2005; appeared as Carrie Cash in the feature film *Walk the Line,* 2005.

Awards: Grammy Award, for Best New Artist, 2000.

Addresses: *Record company*—Capitol Records, 1750 N. Vine St., Los Angeles, CA 90028-5209, phone: (323)-462-6252, website: http://www.capitolrecords.com/.

over making friends and studying, and found comfort from an unhappy childhood in her music. She grew up listening to her father's Willie Nelson and Waylon Jennings albums, as well as to rock and roll music from the 1950s and 1960s, compliments of her mother, a legal secretary. At home, the young singer also discovered her grandmother's 78 rpm records, memorizing songs by Bob Wills, Jimmie Rodgers, and the Mills Brothers.

With her records spinning, Lynne would practice singing, using a hairbrush for a microphone and dreaming of one day becoming a star herself. Her mother, along with sister Allison, would occasionally join in, and when Lynne was 15, the harmonizing trio cut a single, a cover of the Four Knights' song "Couldn't Stay Away From You." Lynne's father also contributed to the project, the flip side of the single being one of his own originals. But the record went nowhere.

However, Lynne's father, a heavy drinker who abused his wife, didn't live to see whether the record would spark his career. In 1985 her mother fled with the two girls to nearby Mobile, but her father soon discovered their whereabouts. In 1986, in front of 17-year-old Lynne and her younger sister, he shot his wife to death before taking his own life.

Lynne refused to discuss the details of her parents' deaths with the media, but later described the impact of the tragic event on her life and career. Critics repeatedly made the narrow assumption that her pain caused her talent and artistry to surface, a connection that Lynne always detested. She told Hilburn, "Everyone says, 'She's so good [a singer] because this happened' or 'She's so difficult because...'" Lynne, known for her own drinking and rebellious nature, told Hilburn, "Maybe so, but only partially. I was just as damn difficult when I was 7 years old as I was when I was 18."

## Nashville Bound

After the tragedy the girls moved in with their grandmother, who broadened Lynne's musical interests to include rhythm and blues and jazz singers. However, Lynne wanted to be on her own, and at 18 she married and moved to Nashville. The marriage lasted less than two years, but Lynne had already made important strides with her career. In the wake of a buzz generated by demo tapes as well as a chance appearance in October of 1987 singing on the TNN network's *Nashville Now,* she found herself recording a duet with George Jones titled "If I Could Bottle This Up," and working with Billy Sherrill, one of the most influential producers in country music. The hit-making artists he worked with included, among others, Tammy Wynette, Charlie Rich, Tanya Tucker, David Houston, and Barbara Mandrell.

"Isn't she something?" Sherrill said to Hilburn, recollecting his days of working with Lynne. "I thought she was the best thing I ever heard in my life, countrywise." Country superstar Willie Nelson, who shared a label, manager, and eventually a stage with the young singer, expressed a similar sentiment to Mark Schone of *Spin*: "To me, she's as good as Billie Holiday, but I knew she was going to have trouble being commercially successful in Nashville. They don't know what to do with someone that talented."

Thus, Lynne's five Nashville albums for various labels revealed only occasional moments of interest. Signing with Epic Records, Lynne released three country-pop albums, the Sherrill-produced *Sunrise* in 1989, *Tough All Over* in 1990; and the tepid *Soft Talk,* released in 1991.

By 1992 Lynne had begun to chafe at the style of music Epic pushed her to record. Frustrated with her label's demands, Lynne left Epic: "That was when I started taking control of how I wanted to make records. I had at that point decided I'm not gonna be able to do this until I do it for me."

## Disillusioned with Music Row

Striking out on her own, Lynne remained without a label for two years. During this time the singer focused on writing songs. Those originals ended up on her acclaimed 1993 album for the short-lived Morgan Creek label, titled *Temptation,* an album that sought to recreate the big-band Western swing era and demonstrated Lynne's versatility. After Morgan Creek folded, Lynne moved to Nashville's independent label, Magnatone Records, to record 1995's *Restless.* Here, she mixed country, bluegrass, big band, and blues into an electrifying concoction, but she would later disavow her stab at another mainstream country album.

Tired of Nashville, Lynne put her singing career on hold in 1997 and moved to Mobile Bay. Soon thereafter, she found hope in Bill Bottrell, whose roots-tinged production on Sheryl Crow's 1995 debut *Tuesday Night Music Club* she greatly admired. From the onset, Bottrell encouraged Lynne to drop the pretense of her upbeat songs and face the tragedies in her life through her writing, including what her father had done. "I don't know if she'd want me saying this," Bottrell ventured to Schone, "but I kind of forced her to do that, and we spent months on it. The song [about the death of Lynne's parents] is called 'The Sky Is Purple,' and it's not on the album. But that's sort of how she learned to do confessional songwriting."

A creative breakthrough, the painful song helped the developing songwriter to further explore her own feelings about ruined relationships and self-doubt. Other songs that explored the darker side included "Why Can't You Be?," and "Life Is Bad," a song full of images of blood, tombs, and sinking ships that she wrote in ten minutes one morning. Lynne also returned to some of her musical roots, aside from country, spending hours reexamining the songs of Springfield, Nina Simone, Aretha Franklin, and The Band, all of which influenced the music for her personal lyrics.

### Won Acclaim and Validation

When Lynne and Bottrell took the album to label executives, *I Am Shelby Lynne* was met with enthusiasm. "We were knocked out," recalled Island Records executive Jim Caparro to Hilburn. "We all felt she made a brilliant record." Island took time to put together a special marketing plan, which included releasing *I Am Shelby Lynne* in England first, hoping to attract attention across Europe before bringing it to the United States. The plan worked, and reviews and sales in England skyrocketed. "When the reviews started coming in from Europe, she finally felt validated," noted Bottrell.

In 1999, while patiently awaiting the album's release in America, Lynne moved to Palm Springs, California, well outside the orbit of the major music cities. "The sun is out all the time, and nobody's here," she explained to Weingarten, adding, "the only way to make a change is to do it radically." Reveling in a solitary lifestyle, Lynne spent most of her time writing songs, reading, or cruising the desert highways in a black 1960s Cadillac.

In 2000 Lynne won a Grammy for Best New Artist, a prestigious but nonetheless ironic award for someone who had been recording since 1989. In 2001 Lynne quickly followed *I Am Shelby Lynne* with *Love, Shelby,* produced by Glen Ballard. While Ballard was noted for his work with Alanis Morissette on *Jagged Little Pill,* critics complained that *Love, Shelby* was overly slick, working against the singer's earthy vocals. "In all honesty," Zac Johnson wrote in *All Music Guide,* "this would actually be a more successful album if her previous work hadn't been so strong." Lynne recorded her next album, *Identity Crisis* (2003), at her home studio in Palm Springs, determined to maintain complete artistic control. "She didn't show that album to record labels until it was finished," wrote Lawrence Specker in the Syracuse, New York, *Post-Standard.* "Capitol took her 'take it or leave it' offer, and released the disc in 2003 to widespread critical acclaim."

In the summer of 2005 Lynne reminded her fans of her country roots when she appeared as Johnny Cash's mother, Carrie, in *Walk the Line,* her first role in a feature film. Lynne was deeply moved by Cash's death in 2005, leading her to pen "Johnny Met June" for her next album, *Suit Yourself.* The album, released in May of 2005, was Lynn's ninth release. Relying on a number of demos recorded at home and other tracks recorded live in the studio with a band, *Suit Yourself* was her most down-to-earth recording. "*Suit Yourself* is aptly named," wrote Thom Jurek in *All Music Guide,* "Lynne dressed herself this time out with great players and finely wrought songs, and put it all together on her own. This is her finest moment."

With Lynne's genre-crossing music embracing soul, country, and rock, it is difficult to predict what direction her career will take next. Even Lynne no longer tries to predict the future. "I don't make many plans," she told Daniel Durchholz in the *St. Louis Post-Dispatch.* "Just go with the moment, that's my motto in life. The music that I make is the music I feel has to be made at that moment."

## Selected discography

*Sunrise,* Epic, 1989.
*Tough All Over,* Epic, 1990.
*Soft Talk,* Epic, 1991.
*Temptation,* Morgan Creek, 1993.
*Restless,* Magnatone, 1995.
*I Am Shelby Lynne,* Island, 2000.
*Love, Shelby,* Universal, 2001.
*Identity Crisis,* Capitol, 2003.
*Suit Yourself,* Capitol, 2005.
*The Definitive Collection,* Hip-O, 2006.

# Sources

## Periodicals

*Atlanta Journal-Constitution,* June 9, 1995; April 20, 2000.
*Billboard,* March 23, 1996.
*Fortune,* February 21, 2000.
*Los Angeles Times,* February 13, 2000.
*New York Times,* April 15, 2000.
*People,* November 22, 1993; February 26, 1996.
*Post-Standard,* (Syracuse, NY), May 29, 2005.
*Rolling Stone,* September 30, 1993; February 17, 2000.

*Sarasota Herald Tribune,* November 18, 2005.
*Spin,* March 2000, pp. 109-10.
*St. Louis Post-Dispatch,* August 25, 2005.
*Village Voice,* April 11, 2000.
*Washington Post,* March 12, 2000; April 14, 2000.

## Online

"Shelby Lynne," *All Music Guide,* http://www.allmusic.com/ (October 9, 2006).

*—Laura Hightower and Ronnie Lankford*

# Paul Mauriat

## Orchestra leader, composer

In early 1968, with rock music of all kinds pushing new experimental boundaries, an entirely different kind of song rose to the number-one position on music sales charts in the United States and remained there. "Love Is Blue," recorded by French orchestra leader Paul Mauriat, was an easy listening instrumental, instantly recognizable many decades later even for listeners who were unable to identify the name of the artist who had recorded it. Yet Mauriat's contribution to popular music did not begin or end with "Love Is Blue." By the end of the 20th century he was largely forgotten except among chroniclers of pop trivia, but his influence was greater than the size of his reputation would suggest.

Paul Mauriat (More-ee-AH) was born in the southeastern French city of Marseille on March 4, 1925. His father was a postal inspector who played classical piano on the side. When Mauriat was three or four, his father spotted his ability to play tunes straight through on the piano, and, Mauriat told Emmanuel Legrand of *Billboard,* "had the wisdom not to show me around like one of those brilliant young puppets." Mauriat took lessons from his father, and then, when he was ten, enrolled at the Marseille Conservatory of Music, studying violin as well as piano.

By the time he was 15, Mauriat had earned the school's top prize. At that point family finances interrupted his budding classical career; he had to take a job as a postman. He had also begun to get interested in popular music and in American jazz that had acquired a strong French following. In 1942, with the ranks of French musicians depleted by World War II, Mauriat was offered a job as a band conductor at a salary higher than his father was making. With his father's blessing, he embarked on a musical career.

For many years, Mauriat was based in Marseille and worked behind the scenes in the French music industry. He honed his skills as an arranger, and in the 1950s he toured with and worked as music director for Charles Aznavour and Maurice Chevalier, two of France's top male vocalists. He was particularly closely associated with Aznavour, for whom he eventually made a total of some 135 arrangements. In 1958, with help from bandleader and fellow Marseille native Franck Pourcel, Mauriat moved to Paris. Beginning around that time, he made occasional recordings for small French labels. Depending on the flavor of or intended market for the song he was recording, he used one of a variety of pseudonyms that included Willy Twist, Eduardo Ruo, Nico Papadopoulos, and Richard Audrey.

Among the other young arrangers working in Paris at the time was future American pop giant Quincy Jones, who was studying with French music teacher Nadia Boulanger. Jones encouraged Mauriat's efforts, which by this time had branched out into composition as well as arranging. In 1963 he scored his first major hit as a writer (under the pseudonym Del Roma, and with Pourcel and others as co-writers) with a song called "Chariot," recorded (in French) by British pop star Petula Clark. Retitled "I Will Follow Him," given new English lyrics, and recorded in the United States by teen pop singer Little Peggy March, the song topped *Billboard* magazine's Hot 100 chart. Like "Love Is Blue," "I Will Follow Him" had a long life as a pop standard, appearing in a spoof choral arrangement in the 1992 film comedy *Sister Act.*

In 1965 the easy listening genre was selling strongly worldwide, and the recordings of Mauriat's associate Pourcel, many of which resemble Mauriat's own, were hitting a peak of popularity. Mauriat, at the request of the Philips label, formed Le Grand Orchestre de Paul Mauriat in order to compete with Pourcel and began a busy recording schedule that often included three albums a year. No systematic discography of Mauriat's work exists, and he himself eventually lost track of the total number of his album releases, but he estimated in his interview with Legrand that he had recorded more than 1,000 individual songs. Mauriat's albums were released in the United States, but, facing strong competition from those by homegrown orchestra leaders such as Ray Conniff, they notched modest sales totals of around 25,000 copies.

In 1967 Mauriat was given a minor-key song called "L'amour est bleu" ("Love Is Blue"), written by André Popp and Pierre Cour. In a version sung by pop star Vicky Leandros, it had nearly won the 1967 Eurovision Song Contest as an entry from Luxembourg, but was

**For the Record . . .**

Born Paul Mauriat on March 4, 1925, in Marseille, France; died on November 3, 2006, in Perpignan, France. *Education:* Attended the Marseille Conservatory of Music, Marseille, France.

Worked as conductor, arranger, and bandleader, Marseille, France, 1942–58; moved to Paris, 1958; (with Franck Pourcel and others) wrote "Chariot," recorded in English as "I Will Follow Him," by Little Peggy March, 1963; formed Le Grand Orchestre de Paul Mauriat, signed to Philips label, 1965; recorded "L'amour est bleu" ("Love Is Blue"), 1967; U.S. and world tours, late 1960s–1980s; signed to Pony Canyon label (Japan), 1994; gave farewell concert, Osaka, Japan, 1998; recorded more than 1,000 songs and instrumental pieces.

Awards: First Prize in piano, Marseille Conservatory of Music; Grand Prix du Disque; Midem Trophy (French recording industry awards).

Addresses: *Record company*—Pony Canyon International, 2-5-10, Toranomon, Minato-Ku, Tokyo, Japan, 105-8487.

edged out by Pourcel's French entry. "To be honest, I wasn't very fond of the song," Mauriat told Legrand, but since it had been issued by Philips' publishing arm he agreed to cover it. In France, Mauriat's record stalled after sales of 30,000 copies, but Minneapolis disc jockey Alan Mitchell aired the song and asked listeners to comment on it. Flooded with calls, he passed on news of his success to other radio personnel, and on February 10, 1968, the song settled in for a five-week run at the top of the charts. The album containing "Love Is Blue," entitled *Blooming Hits,* also rose to the number-one spot. "Love Is Blue" was the first instrumental to hit *Billboard's* top spot since the Tornados' "Telstar" in 1962, and it remains the only French release ever to have accomplished the feat.

Mauriat had a few other small American hits, including "Love in Every Room" and the theme song for the film *Chitty Chitty Bang Bang.* He never duplicated the massive success of that single song, but "Love Is Blue" cemented his international fan base, and as late as 1996 Mauriat estimated his worldwide sales at 800,000 recordings a year. In the late 1960s and early 1970s, Mauriat applied his arranging skills to the careers of a new generation of French singers, serving for several years as musical director for vocalist Mireille Mathieu. He and his orchestra toured the United States, Mexico, and the Far East.

Japanese (and Taiwanese) audiences had special affection for Mauriat's sentimental but very precise music, and he eventually performed over 1,000 concerts in Japan. Mauriat claimed to be the first Western performer to announce all his songs in Japanese while performing there, and in 1994, after his nearly three-decade association with Philips (and its successors) ended, he signed with a Japanese label, Pony Canyon. Mauriat chose Osaka, Japan, as the site of his final concert, in 1998. His orchestra continued to tour under the conductorship of his protégés. In 2002 a French-language biography of Mauriat, *Un vie en bleu* (*A Life in Blue*), was issued by author Serge Elhaik. Mauriat's compositional legacy lived on in the song "Guilty Conscience," modeled by rapper Eminem partly on "I Will Follow Him," but above all in the immortal melody of "Love Is Blue." Mauriat died in Perpignan, France, on November 3, 2006.

## Selected discography

*Blooming Hits,* Philips, 1968.
*Mauriat Magic,* Philips, 1968.
*More Mauriat,* Philips, 1968.
*Prevailing Airs,* Philips, 1968.
*Doing My Thing,* Philips, 1969.
*The Soul of Paul Mauriat,* Philips, 1969.
*The Christmas Album,* Philips, 1970.
*Gone Is Love,* Philips, 1970.
*El Condor Pasa,* Philips, 1971.
*Classics in the Air,* Philips, 1974.
*Love Is Blue,* Philips, 1987.
*A Paul Mauriat Christmas,* PSM, 1994.
*Love Is Blue: The Best of Paul Mauriat,* Polygram International, 2000.
*Sayonara Concert,* Blue Moon, 2000; reissued, Import, 2003.
*Best of Paul Mauriat,* Universal, 2003.

## Sources

### Periodicals

*Billboard,* January 20, 1996, p. P3.
*Time,* March 22, 1968.

### Online

"Artist Profile: Paul Mauriat," The Breeze: Easy Listening Music, http://www.radioentertainment.com/artistProfiles/pMauriat.html (November 1, 2006).
"Paul Mauriat," *All Music Guide,* http://www.allmusic.com (November 1, 2006).
"Paul Mauriat," Space Age Pop Music, http://www.spaceagepop.com/mauriat.htm (November 1, 2006).

—*James M. Manheim*

# Jesse McCartney

**Singer, songwriter, actor**

Singer and actor Jesse McCartney has the pop idol good looks, winning smile, and personality to make him a star, but he was not an overnight success. A Broadway vet and a Daytime Emmy-nominated soap opera actor before he could drive, McCartney began his career in entertainment at an early age. With the children's vocal group Sugar Beats to his days in boy band Dream Street, it was really with McCartney's 2004 solo debut *Beautiful Soul,* and a starring role on the TV show *Summerland,* that by 2005 made McCartney the new teen dream. With a more mature sound on his sophomore album and more daring acting roles in his future, McCartney (known to many of his fans as Jesse Mac), aims to mature with each project he does. Often called a new Justin Timberlake for the younger generation, like the former *NSYNC star, McCartney never shied away from classic pop music. "Pop is always gonna be ragged on," McCartney told *Entertainment Weekly,* "but pop will never die."

Born on April 9, 1987, McCartney grew up in Westchester, a suburb of New York. After singing, acting, and dancing in local musicals, at 10 years old, McCartney was performing in the Broadway production of *The King and I* and later *A Christmas Carol* (with The Who's Roger Daltry). "I thrived on getting the loudest applause that I could get," McCartney admitted to *Teen People* about his earliest inclinations of stardom. "Since I was seven, it's been all about making people happy." McCartney excelled at both singing and acting, and pursued both avenues. From 1997 through 2000, with a handful of other children singers, McCartney recorded a number of albums under the moniker Sugar Beats. The Sugar Beats' album collections contained classic rock and pop songs of the '60s and '70s sung by groups of kids. Sugar Beats' 1998 record, *How Sweet It Is,* earned a Grammy nomination for Best Children's album.

McCartney's next venture was with the grueling soap opera filming schedule. From 1998 through 2001, McCartney played the role of Adam Chandler, Jr., on the ABC long-running soap opera *All My Children.* McCartney was nominated for a Daytime Emmy for Outstanding Younger Actor in a Drama Series at both the 2001 and 2002 awards. In 1999, McCartney was chosen to be part of the new boy band Dream Street. The quintet released their self-titled debut in 2000 and their follow-up, *The Biggest Fan,* in 2002, before splitting up. "It was a great stepping stone for me. But that situation [Dream Street] just showed me how much I wanted to have creative input and go the solo artist route," he stated on his website. The singer was more than ready to begin his own career and write his own songs. "I grew up in a very musical household," he told *Scholastic News.* "My parents were both musicians and singer-songwriters, and we listened to a lot of legendary musicians, from the Beatles to James Taylor to Carole King to Ray Charles. That was engrained in my head early on and built a foundation of music and a taste in music. Eventually I found people I idolized on

## For the Record . . .

Born Jesse McCartney on April 9, 1987, in New York, NY; son of Ginger and Scot McCartney.

Joined the children's singing group Sugar Beats, 1998; featured on four albums, 1998–2000; joined boy band Dream Street, 1999; released *Dream Street,* Atlantic, 2000; *The Biggest Fan,* Sony, 2002; Dream Street disbanded, 2000; released solo debut *Beautiful Soul,* Hollywood, 2004; released sophomore album *Right Where You Want Me,* Hollywood, 2006.

Awards: Teen Choice Awards, Best Crossover Artist, Choice Music Breakout Artist Male, and Choice Music Male Artist, 2005; Nickelodeon Kid's Choice Award, Favorite Male Singer, 2006.

Addresses: *Record company*—Hollywood Records, 500 S. Buena Vista St., Burbank, CA 91521, website: http://www.hollywoodrecords.go.com. *Website*—Jesse McCartney Official Website: http://www.jesse mccartney.com.

my own, people like Daniel Bedingfield, Craig David and Sting. They've all inspired me to make music."

The ground for a solo career began in a slew of songs for film soundtracks. In 2004, McCartney's songs could be found on the soundtrack albums to *A Cinderella Story, Stuck in the Suburbs,* and *Ella Enchanted.* In the meantime, he was finishing up his solo debut when he got a role on a new WB drama. Just months before his debut album was released, McCartney was reintroduced as Bradin Westerly, a bad boy surfer in the new TV show *Summerland.* The show only lasted one season, but coupled with the September release of his album, *Beautiful Soul,* 2004 was the year McCartney had dreamed of. With almost two years of work into his debut, *Beautiful Soul* topped the Billboard chart at number 15, with sales of over 1.5 million. "It took us two years to make this album," he stated on his website. "Part of that time was spent focusing where I wanted to go musically. In the process, I discovered my voice and the sound I wanted." With the sunny ballads "Beautiful Soul" and "She's No You," the latter which McCartney co-wrote, the teen was soon the new heartthrob on the block, a staple on MTV's TRL program. "...It's light and cheerful, but it has the sleek, sultry grooves that made *Justified,* [Justin Timberlake] a blockbuster...," wrote *All Music Guide's* Stephen Thomas Erlewine.

In 2005, McCartney won Teen Choice Awards for Best Crossover Artist, Choice Music Breakout Artist Male,

and Choice Music Male Artist, and the video for "Beautiful Soul" was nominated for Best Pop Video at the MTV Video Music Awards. The cancellation of *Summerland* didn't stop McCartney from keeping up his popularity. After a big Australian fall tour in 2005 with the Backstreet Boys and the following spring, McCartney won the award for Favorite Male Singer at the 2006 Nickelodeon Kid's Choice Awards.

For McCartney's sophomore solo record, the singer wanted to demonstrate that he had matured as a person and as a songwriter. Co-writing nearly every song, in September 2006, McCartney released *Right Where You Want Me.* The title track served as the record's first single and with its edgier subject matter and heavier beats, McCartney displayed the voice of a young adult who had experienced more in life. He was careful, however, not to alienate his younger fans. With a production team that included John Shanks (Kelly Clarkson, Ashlee Simpson), Marti Frederiksen (Pink), and others, McCartney used *Right Where You Want Me* as a way to express himself artistically and emotionally, something he was never able to do in his earlier work. Touring around the world and back, McCartney experienced the ups and downs of the entertainment business, learning everywhere he went. "After being on the road … traveling the world, being inspired by different cultures and taking it all in, the songs just started flowing out of me," he said on his website. "I became more aware of people, the world and how it works. It was a challenge and ultimately satisfying to put that to a melody."

In addition to McCartney's music, he plans to take more mature acting roles. In 2006, he filmed the independent film *Keith.* In his first feature length film role, McCartney took on a darker character, something his young fans might not expect, or should even possibly see. The actor hopes to take on more serious roles, and maybe someday move into directing, while keeping his music going.

# Selected discography

(With Dream Street) *Dream Street,* Atlantic, 2000.
(With Dream Street) *The Biggest Fan,* Sony, 2002.
(Contributor) *A Cinderella Story* (soundtrack), Hollywood, 2004.
(Contributor) *Ella Enchanted* (soundtrack), Hollywood, 2004.
(Contributor) *Stuck in the Suburbs* (soundtrack), Disney, 2004.
*Beautiful Soul,* Hollywood, 2004.
*Right Where You Want Me,* Hollywood, 2006.

# Sources

### Periodicals

*Entertainment Weekly,* March 11, 2005, p. 91.
*Teen People,* May 1, 2005, p. 106.

## Online

Hollywood Records' Jesse McCartney Official Website, http://hollywoodrecords.go.com/jessemccartney/ (November 10, 2006).

"Jesse McCartney," *All Music Guide,* http://www.allmusic.com (November 10, 2006).

"Jesse McCartney: All in a Day's Work," *Scholastic News,* http://content.scholastic.com/browse/article.jsp?id=7488 (November 10, 2006).

Jesse McCartney Official Website, http://www.jessemac.com (November 10, 2006).

*—Shannon McCarthy*

# Modest Mouse

## Rock group

Seattle's Modest Mouse is considered to be one of the few American post-punk guitar rock bands to produce music that sounds new and can stand next to the canonical albums of the 1980s by bands like Sonic Youth, Hüsker Dü, the Meat Puppets, and the Minutemen. The group's first two albums, 1996's *This Is a Long Drive for Someone with Nothing to Think About* and 1997's *The Lonesome Crowded West,* became instant indie classics, firmly establishing Modest Mouse as a leading emotional guitar rock band. And although many worried when the group signed to Epic Records for the release of 2000's *The Moon and Antarctica,* Modest Mouse laid the fears of fans and critics to rest with their major label debut. The album won accolades as the most ambitious major label alternative release since the Flaming Lips' celebrated 1999 album *The Soft Bulletin.*

Unusual among many indie rock/alternative bands of today, Modest Mouse has embedded its trippy and spacey music—part tangled guitar, part modern boogie—with what feels like a fully developed worldview, envisioning suburban and rural isolation through the eyes of a man at odds with the world around him. "Listening to Modest Mouse is a bit like looking at one of those warped mirrors in a boardwalk arcade," wrote

Frazer Harrison/Getty Images

## For the Record . . .

**M**embers include **Isaac Brock** (born c. 1976), vocals, guitar; **Eric Judy** (born c. 1976), bass; **Jeremiah Green** (born c. 1978), drums; **Johnny Marr** (born c. 1963), guitar.

Formed band in 1992 in Issaquah, WA; released debut album, *This Is a Long Drive for Someone with Nothing to Think About,* Seattle's Up Records, 1996; released *The Lonesome Crowded West,* 1997; Up released *Building Nothing Out of Something,* Modest Mouse signed to Epic Records, 1999; released*The Moon and Antarctica,* 2000; issued EP *Everywhere and His Nasty Parlor Tricks* and *Sad Sappy Sucker* (originally recorded in 1994), 2001; joined Unlimited Sunshine Tour, 2002; issued *Good News for People Who Love Bad News,* 2004.

Addresses: *Record company*—Epic Records, 550 Madison Ave., New York, NY 10022, phone: (212) 833-7442, website: http://www.epicrecords.com/. *Website*—Official Modest Mouse Website: http://www.modestmousemusic.com. Label *Website*—http://www.epicrecords.com/epiccenter/custom/1204/begcontent-nf.html.

*Salon* online magazine contributor Joe Heim. "The sound is both familiar and perplexing, filled with pleasing hooks and dissonant, disorienting distortion. The most experimental of Modest Mouse songs often sound as if they were recorded in slow motion. … It is the woozy intensity created by these musical ebbs and flows that has become the band's signature formula."

### Artistic Integrity or Commercial Success?

But amid all the acclaim and growing popularity, vocalist Isaac Brock, who plays guitar and serves as the trio's primary songwriter/lyricist, and his fellow mice, who feel more comfortable staying in their lead vocalist's shadow, remain most interested in maintaining their artistic integrity and are less concerned about achieving commercial success. "More than anything," Brock told *Pandemonium*'s Claude Iosso, "I don't want to lose it and dry up." Moreover, the band has stayed true to the working class ethic of their roots, preferring a frugal lifestyle over one of excess. The group accepted a bare-bones recording budget with Epic, but no signing bonus. And for their tour during the summer

and fall of 2000, the trio turned down a bus in order to save money. Instead, Modest Mouse loaded up an old Dodge van that had been their traveling vehicle for years.

Deciding between austerity versus opulence was never a difficult choice for the members of Modest Mouse, all of whom emerged on the indie rock scene from humble beginnings. "You should totally feel proud about earning your own keep," Brock told R.J. Smith in *Spin,* "about not having had anything … handed to you." Born around 1976, Brock spent a year of his early childhood living on a hippie commune in Oregon. Then, after his mother and stepfather turned to religion, joining the Grace Gospel Church, the family relocated to a small town in Montana. Living in relative isolation, Brock said he developed few social skills and rarely played with other kids.

At age 11, he and his family moved to the quiet, suburban logging town of Issaquah, Washington, located some 15 miles east of Seattle, where Brock spent much of his time in a shed next to his parents' house. It was in Issaquah that Brock, by now a fan of the Tree People, Talking Heads, the Beatles, and the Pixies, met the other members of Modest Mouse. In 1992 Brock met Eric Judy, and the two 17-year-olds immediately hit if off. Soon thereafter, they met Jeremiah Green, at the time around 15, who was on his way to a free meal sponsored by a group of Hari Krishnas hoping to recruit young members.

From the onset, the three teenagers dedicated themselves entirely to music, practicing in Brock's shed. Brock, who wrote and sang all the songs, named the trio Modest Mouse, after a reference he once came across labeling America's working classes as "modest, mouselike people." Judy, at the time struggling with personal problems, left the group early on, but Brock continued to write songs and record with Green and various other friends.

These casual sessions resulted in three tapes of 40 songs. A short time later Judy rejoined Brock and Green. The trio has remained a stable unit ever since, with Brock taking on duties as the showman and songwriter, while his cohorts are content to play backing roles both on stage and off. Judy and Green are skilled musicians, providing Modest Mouse with their lush sound. "They're the talent, I'm the personality," Brock claimed, as quoted by Iosso.

### Debut Album

After releasing a handful of singles, Modest Mouse released its debut album, *This Is a Long Drive for Someone with Nothing to Think About* (1996), on Seattle's Up Records, an independent "anti-grunge" label. Standout tracks of the gallivanting, off-funky set included the reflective yet furious "Exit Does Not Exist," the expansive and flowing "Make Everyone Happy/ Mechanical Birds," and the glorious closing song "Talking Sh** About a Pretty Sunset." "Few bands, from any region, can make such a range of beautiful yet intense sounds move forward so relentlessly," concluded Sam Jeffries for the online magazine *Netspace.* That same year the trio released the *Interstate 8* EP, a collection of surreal suburban snapshots, followed by the witty *The Fruit that Ate Itself* EP in 1997.

With the group's next album, 1997's *The Lonesome Crowded West,* Modest Mouse came to the attention of the mainstream music press. "At a time when American guitar rock is so desperately lacking imagination," wrote Jason Fine in *Rolling Stone,* "the feisty songs of *The Lonesome Crowded West* are a sign that some real vitality can still be squeezed from the post-punk mold." Eclectic without feeling showy, the album featured anxious guitars and loping drum beats as a backdrop for Modest Mouse's rich, sprawling sound, incorporating everything from aggressive punk to country-inspired guitar lines.

In terms of lyrical content, Brock further explored the concept of suburbia creeping into the remaining rustic regions of the western frontier, each song featuring seedy characters living on the fringes of the American West. In the tune "Teeth Like God's Shoeshine," the singer forecasts the day when nature will take back her lost land, while in "Trailer Trash" Brock contemplates the lives of people who survive by "eating snowflakes with plastic forks and a paper plate of course."

By now Modest Mouse had amassed a sizable following on the college charts, and in 1999 they signed with Epic Records. Late that year, Up released *Building Nothing Out of Something,* a collection of early seven-inch singles and three songs from *Interstate 8.* Understandably, many fans wondered whether recording for a major label would compromise Modest Mouse's experimental bent and creativity. However, *The Moon and Antarctica,* released in June of 2000 and produced by former Red Red Meat member Brian Deck, won approval from longtime fans and critics alike.

"The result was powerful enough that anyone looking for a straight-ahead re-creation of the band's fine, melodic new album could have found themselves overwhelmed by volume, but hardly disappointed," insisted *Los Angeles Times* contributor Steve Appleford.

In 2001 Modest Mouse issued the EP *Everywhere and His Nasty Parlor Tricks,* a collection of songs originating from the *The Moon and Antarctica* sessions. The band followed with *Sad Sappy Sucker,* known as the lost Modest Mouse album. Originally, *Sad Sappy Sucker* was slated as the band's first release in 1994, but was set aside and presumably lost. In 2002 Modest

Mouse joined the Unlimited Sunshine Tour, an American musical festival fronted by Cake and featuring a number of other bands, including De La Soul and the Flaming Lips.

In 2004 Modest Mouse issued *Good News for People Who Love Bad News,* relying on a more aggressive rock sound to deliver its ruminations on life and mortality. "By drawing an even sharper contrast between the harsh and beautiful things about their music, as well as life," wrote Heather Phares in *All Music Guide,* "Modest Mouse have made an album that's moving and relevant without being pretentious about it." The album proved to be a commercial breakthrough for the group, reaching number 18 on the Billboard 200 chart, and scoring two Modern Rock hits with "Float On" and "Oceans Breath Salty." "The new album has made Modest Mouse palatable to an entirely new audience," noted Mikel Jolet at *All Things Considered* on National Public Radio. In 2005 the band's track "The View" appeared on the compilation *Music From the O.C.: Mix 4.*

In the summer of 2006 Modest Mouse decided to postpone touring in order to concentrate on finishing a new album produced by Dennis Herring. The album was to be titled *We Were Dead Before the Ship Even Sank,* for release by Epic at the beginning of 2007. Ex-Smiths' guitarist Johnny Marr also became a full-member of the band in 2006. Modest Mouse returned to touring in the fall of 2006 and slated a number of dates in New York, Los Angeles, and London.

# Selected discography

## Singles

*Do You Connect?* (EP), K, 1994.
"Broke," SubPop, 1996.
*Interstate 8* (EP), Up, 1996.
"Life of Arctic Sounds," Suicide Squeeze, 1997.
"Birds vs. Worms," Hit or Miss, 1997.
*The Fruit that Ate Itself* (EP), K, 1997.
"Other People's Lives," Up, 1998.
"Neverending Math Equation," SubPop, 1998.
*Night on the Sun* (EP), Rebel Beat Factory, 1999.
*Night on the Sun* (EP), *Everywhere and His Nasty Parlor Tricks,* Sony, 2001.

## Albums

*This Is a Long Drive for Someone with Nothing to Think About,* Up, 1996.
*The Lonesome Crowded West,* Up, 1997.
*Building Nothing Out of Something,* Up, 1999.
*The Moon and Antarctica,* Epic, 2000.
*Sad Sappy Sucker,* K, 2001.
*Good News for People Who Love Bad News,* Epic, 2004.

# Sources

## Periodicals

*Boston Phoenix,* August 22, 1996.
*Los Angeles Times,* February 25, 1998; May 23, 1998; June 10, 2000.
*Rolling Stone,* February 5, 1998; July 6-20, 2000.
*Spin,* July 2000.
*Village Voice,* November 4, 1997; January 27, 1998; February 1, 2000; May 23, 2000.
*Washington Post,* May 19, 2000; June 21, 2000.

## Online

"Modest Mouse," *All Music Guide,* http://www.allmusic.com/ (November 9, 2006).

Modest Mouse (unofficial site), http://www.crystal-night.com/~bwillen/MMWelcome.htm (August 9, 2000).
Netspace, http://www.netspace.org (August 9, 2000).
Pandemonium Online, http://www.seattlesquare.com/pandemonium (August 9, 2000).
Pitchforkmedia, http://www.pitchforkmedia.com (August 9, 2000).
Salon, http://www.salon.com (August 9, 2000).
*Seattle Times,* http://www.seattletimes.com (August 9, 2000).
Wall of Sound, http://www.wallofsound.go.com (August 9, 2000).

Further information for this profile was obtained from *All Things Considered,* National Public Radio, May 3, 2004.

—Laura Hightower and Ronnie Lankford

# Monica

**Singer**

AP Images

The young chanteuse named Monica needed no last name to distinguish her, as word of her talent emerged in the music press during the mid-1990s. Her first recording, released when she was only 14 years old, sealed her reputation as a talented singing sensation. Despite her youth and the rapid rise of her career, Monica amazed the music world with the strength of her voice. Even as a young teenager she drew praise from critics, who compared her powerful voice to R&B legends such as Aretha Franklin, Whitney Houston, and Anita Baker.

With "Don't Take It Personal (Just One Of Dem Days)" in 1996, Monica became the youngest artist ever to top the *Billboard* R&B singles chart. Her first album, *Miss Thang,* appeared shortly after the hit single, and by the time she turned 16 the recording had gone double platinum. When she released her second album, *The Boy Is Mine,* in 1997, the title song was already a chart-topping hit. In the early 2000s, after enduring a sequence of personal problems, Monica successfully made the transition from teenage sensation to adult star.

Monica Arnold was in born in October of 1980 in College Park, Georgia. Her father, M.C. Arnold Jr., left the family when Monica was only four years old. Monica's mother, Marilyn, an airline employee, supported the family on her own until 1993, when she married the Rev. Edward Best. Monica first sang in her church choir as a very young child. Stories hold that she made her singing debut at age two when her mother, a member of the church choir, allowed the toddler to join the group.

At any rate, by the age of four, Monica was a bona fide member of the choir at Jones Chapel United Methodist Church in Newman, Georgia. Outside of church, Monica was too shy to perform in front of anyone, including her friends. Yet she was completely enamored of singing, and sang in her room, turning everyday objects into microphone props. She lived all of her young life in College Park until she was discovered as a preteen in a talent contest.

Monica was only ten years old when she first entered a talent contest, after years of singing in the choir and alone in her room. Two years later she took first prize in a contest, winning $1,000 for her rendition of the Whitney Houston hit "The Greatest Love of All." Her performance solicited a standing ovation from the crowd, including record producer Dallas Austin. An associate of superstar singers including Madonna and TLC, Austin was impressed when he heard the youngster. He signed Monica to a recording contract with Rowdy Records in 1992.

Monica's life assumed a whirlwind pace as she attended high school at Atlanta Country Day School and fulfilled her agreement under Austin's contract with

Rowdy Records. Despite her extreme youth, Monica immediately began work on her *Miss Thang* album, which was two years in production. At 14 she completed her first chart-topping hit, "Don't Take It Personal (Just One of Dem Days)." She graduated from high school at age 16 with a solid 4.0 grade point average, despite the demands of her recording schedule, public appearances, and touring engagements. These included a ten-week concert tour in the spring and summer of 1996.

In October of 1997, after the demise of Rowdy Records, Monica signed with Arista Records. Her tall, striking appearance garnered her further work in modeling and acting assignments, all before she turned 17 years old. Along with her manager, rap singer Queen Latifah, Monica appeared on the Fox sitcom *Living Single,* as well as on the *Tonight Show.* She cultivated an image of tough glamor, acquiring (against medical advice) a set of diamond implants in her front teeth.

Monica's second album with Austin, 1998's *The Boy Is Mine,* held the number one spot on the *Billboard* charts for two months. The album included the hit single "The Boy Is Mine," a duet with fellow teenaged R&B star

Brandy that debuted at number one and stayed there for six uninterrupted weeks. Hitmaker Rodney "Darkchild" Jerkins served as producer of the song, which was inspired by the earlier Michael Jackson/Paul McCartney collaboration "The Girl Is Mine." The two young singers performed the duet to a live audience for the first time at the 1998 MTV Awards in Los Angeles, amid rumors of an embittered rivalry between the superstars. The words of the duet, which imply that there is a love triangle going on between the two singers, were misconstrued by fans, who believed that the song told a personal story about Monica and Brandy. Although rumors persisted, both women asserted a sense of individual confidence and denied that there was anything other than mutual respect between the two.

After becoming famous, Monica continued to live with her mother and stepfather, her younger brother Montez, and her grandmother in College Park. In music, Monica found an escape from the painful circumstances surrounding her father's absence. She developed an extremely close bond with her mother, and in time developed an acute sensitivity to her mother's burden of raising five children alone. As word of Monica's fame spread, she reconciled with her father.

More personal trials were on the way, however, and they forced a temporary halt to the singer's career. First, while Monica was still basking in the glow of the Grammy Award for best R&B duo that she received (with Brandy) for "The Boy Is Mine," she received word that her 25-year-old cousin Selena Glenn had died suddenly of a brain aneurysm. Monica became romantically involved with a drug dealer, Jarvis Weems, and moved from the upscale Buckhead neighborhood in north Atlanta to the Leila Valley housing project. In 2000 Weems called Monica in a state of intense depression, and she arrived at his home just in time to see him shoot himself.

The resulting glare of publicity only made things worse. "Everywhere I went, people took my picture," Monica told Aliya S. King of *Essence.* "My only rest was on my knees and in my mother's arms." Then another boyfriend, rapper C-Murder (Corey Miller) was sentenced to life in prison on a murder charge. Slowly, after a period of time, Monica returned to work. She recorded an album called *All Eyez on Me,* whose title seemed to refer to her experiences in the media spotlight. The album was released in Japan, but the appetite for new Monica material in the United States was so strong that bootleg copies of the songs on the album began to circulate in great numbers. Monica returned to the studio to rework the music with the help of her friend Missy "Misdemeanor" Elliott, who served as executive producer.

When the new album appeared as *After the Storm* in 2003, it proved to be worth the wait. The album made its debut at number one on *Billboard*'s chart of top-selling albums, thanks to collaborations with many of the top names of the day: singer Tyrese, rapper DMX, and rapper-composer Kanye West, among others. Things became more stable on the romantic front for Monica, as she and her boyfriend, label executive Rodney Hill, had a son, Rodney Ramone Hill III, in 2005. In 2006 Monica released her fourth album, *The Makings of Me*. A sample of Curtis Mayfield's hit "The Makings of You" on the song "A Dozen Roses (You Remind Me)" was one of several touches that helped the album to another top ten *Billboard* appearance. Ryan Dombal of *Entertainment Weekly* called the album "a solid addition to her quietly consistent career," and Monica seemed to have surmounted the dangers of both teenage stardom and gangster life to become a steady presence on the pop and R&B charts.

## Selected discography

*Miss Thang,* Rowdy, 1995.
"Don't Take It Personal (Just One of Dem Days)," 1996.
(With Brandy) "The Boy Is Mine," 1997.
(Contributor) *Space Jam* (soundtrack), 1997.
*The Boy Is Mine,* Arista, 1998.

*All Eyez on Me,* J, 2002 (released only in Japan).
*After the Storm,* J, 2003.
*The Makings of Me,* J, 2006.

## Sources

### Books

*Newsmakers,* Issue 2, Gale, 2004.

### Periodicals

*Ebony,* September 1998.
*Entertainment Weekly,* October 2006, p. 41.
*Essence,* October 1998, November 2006, p. 67.
*Jet,* October 5, 1998.
*Newsweek,* July 27, 1998.
*Rolling Stone,* December 24, 1998.
*People,* April 22, 1996; August 3, 1998.

### Online

"Bio," Monica Official Website, http://www.monica.com (November 20, 2006).
"Monica," *All Music Guide,* http://www.allmusic.com (November 20, 2006).

—*Gloria Cooksey and James M. Manheim*

# The Northern Pikes

**Rock group**

The Northern Pikes emerged as one of Canada's hottest bands of the 1980s, touring North America along with such names as Duran Duran, David Bowie, and The Fixx. Before vaulting onto the big stage, they established themselves as an exciting live act through their relentless touring of the bar circuit across Canada's prairie lands in the mid-1980s, and with two indie releases, before attracting the attention of executives at Virgin Records Canada in 1985. After completing a multi-album contract with Virgin, the group disbanded in 1993. Individual band members pursued solo projects for several years, but reunited again in late 1999 to release a collection of old songs as well as embark into new territory in the 2000s.

The band formed smack dab in the middle of North America in Saskatoon, Saskatchewan, Canada, in 1983. Prior to the band's final quartet incarnation in 1986 that included Bryon Potvin on lead guitar, Jay Semko on bass, Merl Bryck on guitar, and Don Schmid on drums, the group had included drummers Rob Esch (1983-84) and Glenn Hollingshead (1984-85). The band's genesis traced its roots to the prairies of central Canada, where the group evolved out of a changing roster of players from Saskatoon bands Doris Daye, The Idols, and Envelope 17. Despite hailing from the

windswept flatlands of Canada's interior, the band's sound, as it ultimately morphed into The Northern Pikes, was a bit more new wave than the country or pop their audience demanded. Potvin joked in a 1987 interview for the *Ottawa Citizen,* "We didn't get a lot of work. The music was pretty off the wall. We thought if we had been in a bigger centre that these groups might have turned out differently. But in the end it worked to our advantage. In the big city, you can get swept up by what's happening and lose yourself."

### Indie Route Led to Popular Success

The band's relentless touring schedule bolstered their recognition, and they were able to produce two self-funded independent albums, *The Northern Pikes* in 1984 and *Scene in North America* the following year. The band's indie releases caught the attention of Doug Chappell, who was president of Virgin Records, Canada. In late 1986 The Pikes signed a deal with Virgin, and by January of 1987 the band had assembled with producers Fraser Hill and Rick Hutt to record their major label debut, *Big Blue Sky,* which was released in June of 1987 and included the hit singles "Teenland" and "Things I Do for Money." The band hitched a ride on the star wagon, opening for David Bowie, Duran Duran, and The Fixx. The band's sophomore release, *Secrets of the Alibi,* came out in 1988, but did not have widespread appeal with critics, who seemed unwilling to accept the band's shift from a "buoyant pop" sound to what Montreal *Gazette* critic Mark Lepage called "the great Canadian angst band." Although Lepage applauded the album, noting that "Every song here is steeped in coming-of-age feelings of loneliness, post-adolescent introspection and questioning," he concluded, "The Northern Pikes may be too introspective for some. There's no levity whatsoever on this record," and suggested that the band members might be taking themselves too seriously. One artist who did take the band seriously was Robert Palmer, who asked The Pikes to open for him on his North American tour in 1989.

### Riding the Crest and Sinking to the Trough

*Snow in June,* The Pikes' third major label release, was passed over for distribution by Virgin in the United States, but was put out by Scotti Brothers Records in 1991 after its 1990 Canadian release. Virgin passed on what proved to be The Pikes' most successful commercial album, as it ultimately went double platinum and garnered a Juno nomination for The Northern Pikes as Best Group in 1991. Hit singles "She Ain't Pretty," "Girl with a Problem," and "Kiss Me You Fool" gave the Canadian quartet a following outside its home territory with heavy airplay.

The band could not sustain the popularity they had reached with *Snow in June* on their next release, *Neptune,* in 1992, nor with their fifth release, *Gig,* a live album of their final tour, released in 1993. By the time *Gig* was released, the band had already anticipated this album to be their swan song, as the members had grown frustrated with the lack of marketing put into their work outside of Canada. Potvin recalled in Toronto's *National Post,* "We were banging our heads against the wall in the States a little bit.... There was sort of this adrift-at-sea kind of feeling." The band officially broke up in 1993 when Semko quit to produce the solo album *Mouse* and write the music for the television show *Due South.* Potvin released a solo album of his own called *Heartbreakthrough* in 2000, and Schmid formed the indie band The NoN Happner's.

### Reunion Sparked New Music

After a six-year hiatus, the band regrouped again in December of 1999, after Schmid had contacted Virgin to release a best-of-album, *Hits and Assorted Secrets: 1984-1993.* On the heels of the buzz created by *Hits,* the rejuvenated Northern Pikes toured Canada, later releasing *Live* in 2000. Looking at the prospect of a reunion tour, Potvin noted in the Montreal *Gazette,* "It just seemed like a natural thing. Everyone's timetable was pretty open, so we thought maybe we should go out just for a laugh." Banking on the success of their tour and not wanting to become another heritage act, The Northern Pikes then returned to the studio and their indie roots to release two new CDs, *Truest Inspi-*

*ration* in 2001 and *It's a Good Life* in 2003. Glad to be making new music together again, the band planned to keep cranking out fresh sounds. In the *Ottawa Citizen* Schmid summarized the band's approach: "It's fun. That's the key to it. If it's not fun, why, at our age, would we be doing it? We play the old songs and we feel good about the fact that we're making new records."

# Selected discography

*The Northern Pikes,* Independent, 1984.
*Scene in North America,* Independent, 1985.
*Big Blue Sky,* Virgin Records, 1987.
*Secrets of the Alibi,* Virgin Records, 1988.
*Snow in June,* Virgin Records, 1990; reissued, Scotti Brothers Records, 1991.
*Neptune,* Virgin Records, 1992.
*Gig,* Virgin Records, 1993.
*Hits and Assorted Secrets 1984–1993,* Virgin Records, 1999.
*Live,* Northern Pike Songs, 2000.
*Truest Inspiration,* Northern Pike Songs, 2001.
*It's a Good Life,* EMI Canada, 2003; reissued, Northern Pike Songs, 2004.

# Sources

## Periodicals

*Chicago Tribune,* November 3, 1987.
*Gazette* (Montreal, Canada), September 1, 1988; July 29, 2000.
*Globe and Mail* (Toronto, Canada), August 25, 1988.
*National Post* (Toronto, Canada), February 19, 2000.
*Ottawa Citizen,* August 7, 1987; January 20, 1989; March 22, 1991; March 19, 2004.
*Toronto Star,* February 24, 2000.

## Online

"Northern Pikes," *JAM! Music: The Canadian Pop Encyclopedia,* http://www.jam.canoe.ca/Music/Pop_Encyclopedia/N/Northern_Pikes.html (November 15, 2006).
Northern Pikes Official Website, http://www.thepikes.com (November 15, 2006).

—*Elizabeth Henry*

# Maura O'Connell

## Singer

Just the sound of Maura O'Connell's name conjures sonic images of tin whistles, fiddles, accordions and mandolins. When she opens her mouth to speak with a County Clare brogue, those sonic images are reinforced with mental images of windswept countryside, thatched roofs and a handsome race with pale skin, ruddy cheeks and strong penchants for drink and romantic ballads. As a singer, however, O'Connell defies such easy categories. Although the Nashville-based singer got her start as an interpreter of standard Irish tunes in her native Ireland, she has evolved into a first-rate interpreter of contemporary songwriters from both sides of the pond.

O'Connell came to music naturally. Her mother was an acclaimed singer who earned her reputation in light opera. "My mother's music was mostly classical, but there is a musical osmosis—you can't help but be influenced by Irish music, which is how I found the lilt in my voice," she recalled in an interview.

O'Connell had no desire to pursue a career in music, however. "I was co-opted into the music biz," she explained. The young O'Connell was invited to perform with traditional Irish band De Danann, and shared vocals on the group's bestselling album, *Star Spangled Molly,* with Dolores Keane. "I was with De Danann for two years," she explained. "I toured all over Europe and did three U.S. tours. We were very popular, but I never intended to be a professional performer." The success of *Star Spangled Molly* led some fans to think of O'Connell as the song's title character, and many of them began calling her Molly, which did not go over well with O'Connell, she explained in the interview.

Despite the guarantee of a continued audience for traditional Irish music, O'Connell determined to buck the trend by recording more contemporary songs. In fact, she had already been exposed to a wide variety of music while still living in County Clare. She subsequently left De Danaan to travel to Dublin, where she lived for four years in order "to embrace the city." While performing in Dublin as a member of the duo Tumbleweed, she encountered New Grass Revival banjo player Bela Fleck and dobro maestro Jerry Douglas. "We were all very young people with a musical commonality," she explained. "It was a natural meeting of young minds and musicians who were constantly misrepresented. I'm not just a singer of traditional Irish songs, and Jerry and Bela were always introduced as bluegrass musicians, rather than what they really are, which are giants of acoustic music."

Douglas invited O'Connell to visit the United States. She relocated in the late 1980s, and proceeded to record a string of albums from her home base in Nashville, most of which were produced by Douglas. She enjoyed modest success, but noted that the difficulty of classifying her music made it difficult to market her music in an increasingly brand-oriented industry. "There is no mainstream American music," she declared. "You can call what I do Americana, but there's also a certain style I do that is contemporary, but not country. Genres keep changing to exclude me once a radio format is named for it."

Along with a Grammy nomination in 1989, O'Connell received many offers to sing backup with such performers as Van Morrison, Rosanne Cash, Peter Rowan, Nanci Griffith and Dolly Parton on the latter's acclaimed bluegrass albums *The Grass Is Blue* and *Little Sparrow.* During the same period, she endeavored to popularize the songwriting of such acclaimed tunesmiths as Patty Griffin, Hillary Lindsey, and Mindy Smith.

While her string of albums earned critical accolades, her live performances solidified her reputation as a singer of rare talent. "Maura O'Connell is so alarmingly good that it's enough to make one rethink one's notions of what comprises talent and artistry," gushed *Musician* writer Elizabeth Wurtzel in 1993. "At New York's Bottom Line in December, O'Connell's delivery was so impassioned and lively, her voice so warm and full, and her onstage persona such a funny and unpretentious pleasure that she proved that certain talents undervalued in popular music today—like the ability to carry a tune—can be the province of true artistry."

Asked about her favorite career moments, O'Connell fondly recalled her work with Martin Scorsese on his epic film of Irish Americans in nineteenth-century New York City, *Gangs of New York.* But she also recalled working with her musical idol: "One of my career highlights as far as I'm concerned is being asked to duet

## For the Record . . .

Born in September 1958 in County Clare, Ireland.

Member of traditional Irish music group De Danaan, early 1980s; released album of contemporary Irish songs, *Wandering Home,* 1997; signed with Sugar Hill Records, 2001; appeared in Martin Scorsese film *Gangs of New York,* 2001.

Addresses: *Home*—Maura O'Connell, P.O. Box 150312, Nashville, TN 37215. Publicist and *Media*— Ronna Rubin, Rubin Media, P.O. Box 158161, Nashville, TN 37215, phone: (615) 298-4400, e-mail: rubinmedia1@aol.com. Artist Management Mitchell Drosin, S.A.D. Management, 218 Sawyer Rd., Sherburne, NY 13460, phone: (607) 674-6473, e-mail: drosinm@aol.com.

with Bonnie Raitt on Angel from Montgomery. I also sang it with (song's author) John Prine," she said.

Wrapping up her interview, O'Connell said: "I'm 48 now. I can relax a little bit more. Singing's my hobby again—I can listen to a lot of music these days and maybe even see a show or two simply for the sheer enjoyment of the music rather than as research for my next album." For a 2006 mini-tour, O'Connell enlisted bass player Don Johnson and multi-instrumentalist phenomenon John Mock. "I adore being on stage in front of an audience," she said. "I really have a great time, and I get a great kick out of it. It is a drug, and I have to do it."

## Selected Discography With De Danaan

*Star Spangled Molly,* 1981.

## Solo

*Just in Time,* Philo,1988.
*Helpless Heart,* Warner Bros, 1989.
*Blue Is the Colour of Hope,* Warner Bros., 1992.
*Stories,* Hannibal, 1995.
*Wandering Home,* Hannibal, 1997.
*Walls and Windows,* Sugar Hill, 2001.
*Don't I Know,* Sugar Hill, 2004.

## Sources

### Periodicals

*Musician,* February 1993.

Additional information for this profile was obtained from a personal telephone interview conducted with Maura O'Connell on Sept. 21, 2006.

—Bruce Walker

# Paco Pena

**Flamenco guitarist**

Paco Pena's long career in flamenco began when he first picked up his brother's guitar around the age of six. Singing, dancing, and celebrating the ups and downs of life through musical expression were long a part of his life. Steeped in the experiences of his youth, Pena's dedication to the art and history of flamenco culture and music has guided him through more than thirty years of performance. He has won numerous awards for his guitar playing and presented audience-pleasing performances that have introduced people all over the world to the intricacies of flamenco singing, dancing, and guitar playing. In reviewing a 2000 show for the *Evening Mail* in Birmingham, England, Dave Freak wrote of Pena, "The … dexterity of his fingers was little short of breathtaking, his mastery of both his guitar and flamenco unquestionable."

Pena was born Francisco Pena Perez on June 1, 1946, in Cordoba, Spain. He was the youngest child of nine, which included seven sisters. His family was poor and lived in shared housing with nine other families. Pena described the house to Michael Church of the *Independent,* " [We] rented two rooms of an old house … sharing a toilet and tub with nine other families … we were like one very big family. Every birth, marriage or bereavement involved everyone. And we were surrounded by

© Jack Vartoogian/FrontRowPhotos

music—sung and played, not out of a radio." Growing up in those conditions, Pena was deeply influenced by the way music permeated daily life.

Shy as a young child, Pena found that by playing guitar he could connect with the people around him much easier. He also found that it enriched his life, giving it some meaning. He explained to Arminta Wallace of the *Irish Times,* "For me it was a pretty significant tool in my communication with people. So I took it really seriously. I just played and played and played." He described to Church the joy he found in performing, staying out late at night, playing his guitar in the street, happy to know that what he was doing was pleasing those who listened. By age 12, Pena was performing for money. Throughout his teens he played and toured with small flamenco groups. His goal eventually was to see the world and continue playing guitar. He told Annie Taylor of the *Guardian,* "My dreams were not focused in Cordoba. Playing guitar and moving on was my fascination."

## Found His Way to London

In the late 1960s, Pena found himself performing in England as accompanist for a group of dancers on tour. His solo debut in England came in 1968 when he played at London's Wigmore Hall. That same year he opened for Jimi Hendrix when he played at the Royal Festival Hall. In 1968, he also released his first album, *The Incredible Paco Pena.* Two years later he founded the Paco Pena Flamenco Dance Company. Through this collaborations with other flamenco performers Pena has created touring theater events that bring to light different aspects of flamenco culture.

Throughout the 1970s, Pena worked with his flamenco company while also releasing several albums, including *Paco Pena Presents the Art of Flamenco, Art of Flamenco Guitar,* and *Fabulous Flamenco.* Pena's goal has always been to bring the art and history of flamenco to the world. In fact, Pena is well versed in the historical events that fused together to create what he considers to be one of the most passionate forms of music. Mitch Potter related Pena's discussion of that history in the *Toronto Star,* "Flamenco at its purest ... emerged in the early 19th century from a poverty-stricken melting pot of Gypsies, Moors, Jews and Spaniards in southern Spain's Andalucia region. It was originally an expression of song and dance that poignantly mirrored the people's brutal persecution." Pena's most successful album was *Flamenco Guitar Music of Montoya and Ricardo.* Released in 1987, it was acclaimed by the critics, with sales that put it on the Billboard charts for 30 weeks. At one point the album was in the Top 10 chart for crossover artists.

## Flamenco's Past and Future

Pena made a home for himself in London while also maintaining ties to his birthplace of Cordoba. In 1981, Pena founded the Centro Flamenco Paco Pena in Cordoba, Spain, which became one of the leading schools of flamenco. He explained his motivation for opening the center on his website, "I wanted to build a bridge between the rest of the world and the region of my birth. For anyone wanting to learn flamenco, seeking to appreciate it to the full, there is no substitute for the potent atmosphere of Andalucía."

Pena often pulls performers for his flamenco company from the students who come to the flamenco center. It is with the flamenco company that Pena has created some of his most important and challenging works. Pena described on his website the importance of the collaborative effort that is part of his flamenco company, "The depth of feeling—and the tragedy of flamenco's history—is always there. We take flamenco very seriously, not least the singing. The singers are the greatest source of inspiration for all of us, whether dancers or guitarists." At first their performances were limited to London and small festivals throughout

Europe. Soon the company was touring and performing in Australia, Israel, and Hong Kong. Eventually, the company went on to create grander works.

In 1991, Pena created the work called *Misa Flamenca.* Based on the Catholic Mass, the performance integrated flamenco with a classical choir, thus bringing together two of the main ingredients that helped form Pena as a child—flamenco and Catholicism. The performance premiered in London at the Royal Festival Hall. *Misa Flamenca* was then taken on a world tour. Its North American debut was in 1993, in Vancouver, British Columbia. Other touring theatrical shows by Pena include *Musa Gitana,* which premiered in 1999, and *Voces y Ecos,* which was directed by Jude Kelly. His other touring shows include *A Compas!* and *Requiem Flamenco.*

Pena has also worked outside of his flamenco troupe, branching out for solo tours and performances at festivals around the world. He has also teamed up with composer John Williams and the formerly exiled Chilean music grouped called Inti-Illimani. In 1988, the collaboration produced the album *Fragments of a Dream.* They also released an album in 1990 called *Leyenda.* In 2000, this unlikely collaborative group went on tour together. As late as the mid-2000s, he was part of a trio of acts featured at the Hispanic and Latin-American Guitar Extravaganza in Daytona, Florida.

Pena's talent is not only evident in his guitar-playing ability, which garnered him *Guitar Player Magazine* awards numerous years in a row for best flamenco guitarist, but also in a number of other areas. He is a teacher and mentor to rising talents in flamenco. He has composed and produced critically acclaimed theater pieces. He is also one of traditional flamenco's most vocal and dedicated proponents.

## Selected discography

*The Incredible Paco Pena,* Fontana, 1968.
(With Los Maracuchos) *Carnival,* Fontana, 1969.
*Paco Pena Presents the Art of Flamenco,* CBS, 1970; reissued, Sony, 1995.
*Flamenco Puro Live,* Decca, 1971; reissued, 1997.
*Art of Flamenco Guitar,* Decca, 1972.
*Fabulous Flamenco!,* Decca, 1975; reissued 1991.
*Flamenco from Spain,* Decca, 1977.
*La Gitarra Flamenca,* Decca, 1977.
*The Flamenco World of Paco Pena,* Decca, 1978.
*Paco Pena Live in London,* Decca, 1979.
*Paco Pena Flamenco Company: Live at Sadler's Wells,* Decca, 1980.
*Flamenco Vivo: Live in Munich,* Aconcagua, 1981.
(With Paco Lucia) *Paco Doble,* Phillips, 1983.
*Flamenco Guitar Music of Ramon Montoya and Nino Ricardo,* Nimbus, 1987.
*Azahara,* Nimbus, 1988.
(With John Williams and Inti-Illimani) *Fragments of a Dream,* CBS, 1988.
(With Eduardo Falu) *Encuentro,* Nimbus, 1989.
(With John Williams and Inti-Illimani) *Leyenda,* CBS, 1990.
*Misa Flamenca,* Nimbus, 1991.
*The Art of Paco Pena,* Nimbus, 1993.
*Arte Y Pasion, Live in Concert* Nimbus, 1999.
(With The Losadas) *Paco Pena Flamenco Guitar,* Nimbus, 2000.
*Paco Pena Flamenco Master,* Manteca Records, 2003.

## Sources

### Periodical

*Birmingham Post* (Birmingham, UK), May 3, 2004, p 13.
*Evening Mail* (Birmingham, UK), July 12, 2000, p. 23.
*Guardian* (Manchester, UK), November 10, 1997, p. 2.
*Independent* (London), April 17, 2006, p. 41.
*Irish Times* (Dublin), July 3, 2006, p. 12.
*New York Times,* May 18, 1987, p. C.16.
*Times* (London), October 16, 2002, p. 19.
*Toronto Star,* April 14, 1989, p. D8; April 20, 1989, p. C2.
*Vancouver Sun* (Vancouver, BC), February 26, 2005, p. D5.

### Online

Paco Pena Official Website, http://www.pacopena.com/ (November 5, 2006).
"Paco Pena Flamenco Dance Company," A&L News Release, http://www.artsandlectures.ucsb.edu/archive/2003-2004/pr/pena.asp (November 5, 2006).

—Eve Hermann

# Asha Puthli

**Singer, songwriter, producer**

© Jack Vartoogian/FrontRowPhotos

Indian-born vocalist Asha Puthli (pronounced PUT-lee) anticipated several major developments in Western popular music with a series of recordings she made for the CBS label in Europe in the 1970s. Her sexy, slinky vocals, deployed against a pulsing background of electronic beats, pointed the way toward disco. Rediscovered in the late 1990s by hip-hop and electronic dance-music DJs, Puthli also seemed to be a forerunner of the East-West fusion dance styles that had become popular among clubgoers, especially in Britain. A boundary-crosser in music and life, Puthli returned to performing in 2006 and prepared to release a new album in the genre that had first attracted her to Western music:—jazz.

Puthli was born in Bombay (now Mumbai), India, into a family with the resources to give her a musical education. She has refused to discuss her age, telling Jon Pareles of the *New York Times* in 2006 that "I'm spiritually 6,000, I'm mentally 98, I'm emotionally 5, and chronologically in between." Although an adherent of Hinduism, she attended Catholic schools. She studied both Indian classical vocals (and dance) and Western opera as a young woman, but she was entranced by Western music she heard on the airwaves—jazz from the Voice of America, and the British pop of Dusty Springfield on Radio Ceylon, from the island of Sri Lanka. When she was 13 she started taking female-vocal slots with local bands. Her teachers told her that singing pop music could damage her technique, but she chose in favor of the pop world. "I'm like a wild horse," she told Pareles. "I decided, I have to give up opera if it's going to put any kind of restraint on me."

Puthli's first exposure to Western audiences came when she was still living in Bombay and singing in nightclubs there. *New Yorker* magazine contributor Ved Mehta, a blind writer whose vivid sketches of Indian life introduced many Western readers to the country's cultures, heard her singing and devoted part of a long article on "Jazz in Bombay" to Puthli; the article was reprinted in Mehta's book *Portrait of India.* At the same time, Puthli was breaking into films. She visited a house in Bombay where the duo of Ismail Merchant and James Ivory was filming *The Guru* (1969). "I was absolutely dying to be discovered," she told Pareles. Hearing a call for silence on the set, she gave a big, operatic stage laugh. Merchant entered the room and demanded to know who had laughed, and Puthli launched into a false apology routine. Her ploy worked: the director identified her as a performer who could project vocally, and cast her in a bit part.

Having already made one small recording and performed a unique jazz-Indian fusion piece at the Bombay Arts Festival, Puthli was determined to try to crack the American market. At first she applied for a job as a BOAC (British Airways) flight attendant in order to be able to travel internationally. Winning a dance scholarship from the company of choreographer Martha Graham, she came to New York and tracked down Mehta.

## For the Record . . .

Born in Bombay (now Mumbai), India; children: one son, Jannu. *Education:* Attended Catholic schools and a university in Bombay, India; studied traditional Indian and Western operatic singing in Bombay.

Appeared on EP with Indian band the Surfers, 1968; appeared in film *The Guru,* 1969; moved to New York on dance scholarship; featured female vocals on album *Science Fiction,* by Ornette Coleman, 1972; signed to CBS label; released album *Asha Puthli,* 1973; released *She Loves to Hear the Music,* 1974; released *The Devil Is Loose,* 1976; signed to TK label, released disco album *Asha L'Indiana,* 1979; signed to Autobahn label and released albums in Europe, 1980s; re-emerged after discovery by hip-hop and electronica artists, 2000s; appeared on album *Asana Vol. 3: Peaceful Heart,* by Bill Lasswell, 2003; appeared on recording "Hey Diwani, Hey Diwana," by the Dum Dum Project; performed in Central Park, New York, 2006.

Addresses: *Booking*—Superlatude Music Group, Inc., P.O. Box 578, Prince St. Station, New York, NY 10012. *Website*—Asha Puthli Official Website: http://www. ashaputhli.com.

The writer introduced her to the legendary Columbia Records executive John Hammond, discoverer of a sequence of innovative vocalists running from Billie Holiday through Bob Dylan to Bruce Springsteen. Hammond himself produced a Puthli single called "Asha's Thing," but it went unreleased. She recorded a cover of Marvin Gaye's "Ain't That Peculiar" with the Peter Ivers Blues Band, and then Hammond arranged her real breakthrough: a featured-vocalist slot on the 1972 *Science Fiction* album by avant-garde jazz saxophonist Ornette Coleman.

That album, considered a jazz classic, garnered Puthli a best female jazz vocalist award in the influential *Down Beat* magazine critics' poll and was reissued in 2000 with unreleased material as *The Complete Science Fiction Sessions.* At the time, however, experimental jazz was on the decline commercially. Seeking new opportunities, Puthli began working in Britain with Elton John producer Del Newman, focusing on pop rather than jazz. The result was the 1973 release *Asha Puthli,* which featured a wide mix of styles. Some tracks, such as "Right on Time," evoked later R&B and disco styles with its slinky bass and horns. "I Dig Love" was a cover of an Indian-influenced composition by Beatle George Harrison. Puthli turned the song's emphasis around. "The way the Beatles saw it was as a spiritual song," she explained to Pareles. "They did it like a bhajan, an Indian religious song. In 1973, when I did it, I felt I was already Indian, and the spirituality was inside me. I was trying to become Western, so I brought out the material aspect, the sexual aspect." Many of her songs had a calm, chilled-out feel that anticipated acid jazz and ambient dance styles that were still several decades in the future.

*Asha Puthli* and its successor, 1974's *She Loves to Hear the Music,* gained audiences in European clubs, and Puthli went to Germany to make her third album, *The Devil Is Loose* in 1976. The album saw Puthli moving into a full-fledged disco sound. The single "Space Talk" was later sampled in "The World Is Filled," a 1997 single by the Notorious B.I.G. (and miscredited on the cover). With a major presence in European disco and soul, Puthli also began to find new popularity in India, even though she had scandalized conservative audiences there by appearing partially nude in the 1972 Merchant-Ivory film *Savages.* In the 1970s, Puthli was a high-fashion icon, appearing in shoots by such photographers as Richard Avedon. In 1979 she released the album *Asha L'Indiana* on the disco-oriented TK label. As dance music's popularity declined, so did Puthli's along with it. She recorded music for film soundtracks and tried a straight rock album, *Only the Headaches Remain.* For much of the 1980s and 1990s she curtailed her performing activities to focus on raising her son, Jannu; occasionally she emerged to record in India.

The insatiable appetite of Western dance music DJs and producers for retro and exotic sounds revived Puthli's career in the late 1990s and early 2000s. Samples of her 1970s work began to appear on major hip-hop releases by the likes of Jay-Z (*The Blueprint Vol. 2: The Gift and the Curse*). Puthli realized the depth of interest in her music when her son told her that New York DJ Sean Dinsmore had paid $100 for a copy of one of her albums, and she subsequently sang on an Indian-flavored track called "Diwani Diwana" recorded by Dinsmore under the name the Dum Dum Project. During her heyday, Puthli had rarely sung in ways that drew fully on Indian styles, although her Indian classical training was audible in many small ways. Now, however, with electronic music incorporating a host of world music traditions, Puthli found herself in demand as a specifically Indian vocalist.

She appeared on two albums by electronic music experimentalist Bill Lasswell, *Asana Vol. 3: Peaceful Heart* (2003) and *Asana Ohm Shanti* (2006), on the successful electronica release *Fear of Magnetism* by

Stratus (2005), and on various other electronica and "chillout" releases. In 2006 she resumed live performances with a summer concert in New York's Central Park—but not in electronic dance genres. Instead, Puthli returned to jazz, the music she had learned from records and radio in Bombay.

## Selected discography

(With the Surfers) *Angel of the Morning,* EMI, 1968.
*Asha Puthli,* CBS, 1973.
*She Loves to Hear the Music,* CBS, 1974.
*The Devil Is Loose,* CBS, 1976.
*Asha L'Indiana,* TK, 1979.
*1001 Nights of Love,* Polygram/Worrell, 1980.
*I'm Going to Kill It Tonight,* Autobahn/Worrell, 1981.
*Only the Headaches Remain,* Autobahn/Polygram, 1982.
*Hari Om/Railway Bazaar,* CBS India, 1990 (not released).
*The New Beat of Nostalgia,* Top of the World, 1998.

## Selected guest appearances

Ornette Coleman, *Science Fiction,* Columbia, 1972.
Dum Dum Project, *Export Quality,* Times Square, 2001.
Bill Lasswell, *Asana Vol. 3: Peaceful Heart,* Meta, 2003.
Stratus, *Fear of Magnetism,* Klein, 2005.
Bill Lasswell, *Asana Ohm Shanti,* Meta, 2006.

## Sources

### Books

Mehta, Ved, *Portrait of India,* Farrar, Straus and Giroux, 1970.

### Periodicals

*New York Times,* August 12, 2006, p. B7.

### Online

"Bio," Asha Puthli Official Website, http:/www.ashaputhli.com (November 20, 2006).
"Recording Superstar Asha Puthli Stages Comeback," All About Jazz, http://www.allaboutjazz.com/php/news.php?id=10659 (November 20, 2006).
Sai, Vijay, "All That Jazz," *The Hindu,* http://www.thehindu.com/mag/2006/10/15/stories/2006101500120500.htm (November 20, 2006).

—*James M. Manheim*

# Dottie Rambo

## Singer, songwriter

As a solo artist and as a member of her family group the Rambos, Dottie Rambo has exerted a fundamental influence on the development of modern Southern Gospel music. Rambo has released award-winning recordings and appeared on numerous television programs and video recordings. Yet her greatest impact has been as a songwriter, with several major gospel classics among her more than 2,500 published compositions. According to her Kentucky Music Museum Hall of Fame biography, "Dottie ranks with the beloved Fanny Crosby [the nineteenth-century composer of "Blessed Assurance" and other standard hymns] among the women who have had the greatest impact in the field of gospel music."

Dottie Rambo was born Joyce Reba Lutrell in Madisonville, Kentucky, on March 2, 1934. Her family suffered hard times during the Great Depression, and moved several times between towns and failing farms. In her composition "Mama Always Had a Song to Sing," she wrote that "I've seen my daddy tracking swamp rabbit in our back holler/More than once that was all we had to eat," and whether or not the line was directly autobiographical, she certainly knew poverty at an early age. Her father sometimes worked as a prison guard.

When Rambo was eight, she composed, to her mother's disbelief, her first song. It was secular, and soon she had taken up the guitar and learned country songs that came over the radio from Nashville, Tennessee, like Ernest Tubb's "Walkin' the Floor Over You." Her performing debut came on a local radio

station. At age 11 or 12, Rambo had a conversion experience in a local Pentecostal church. "The Holy Spirit did a number on me," she told the *Tampa Tribune*. "Just washed over me and set everything on fire." From then on, despite various offers to sing secular music when she became famous, she performed gospel exclusively.

Rambo's father was not pleased. "He says he didn't want any Holy Roller in the house," she told the *Tribune*. "He was so mad, he went outside and destroyed a whole acre of corn. Just pulled it all up by the roots!" He hoped instead that she would become a country star who could appear on the Grand Ole Opry in Nashville. As Rambo's commitment to Christianity deepened, her father's anger grew into physical abuse of Rambo and her mother. In order to help her daughter, Rambo's mother altered her own favorite dress so that it would fit her daughter's body, and walked with her for seven miles to the nearest bus stop. Rambo, aged 12, departed on the bus for Indianapolis, where she had been invited to sing.

Abuse from older men continued to mark Rambo's life; living as a teenage Christian singer on the road, she found lodging mostly in the homes of preachers, doing housework in exchange for a room. But often, she told Waveney Ann Moore of the *St. Petersburg Times,* she had to hide in closets from preachers who tried to molest her. Music provided a positive aspect to her life, as she won applause from audiences at churches, Sunday schools, and revivals. It was at a revival where she was performing that she met Buck Rambo, who had come to hear her sing. The two were married when she was 16, and the couple's daughter, Reba, was born 18 months later.

Rambo's powerful alto voice, smoother than but evocative of country gospel star Martha Carson, gained her fans wherever she went. Dottie and Buck Rambo formed the Singing Echoes (later the Gospel Echoes) and spent $600 making an album, quickly recouping their investment by selling 1,000 copies out of the back of their car. They later began touring as the Singing Rambos, and when daughter Reba was 13 she joined them to form a trio. At first they performed in front of the same small religious groups that had hosted Rambo before her marriage. The group became known for its so-called inverted harmonies, in which members traded off lead vocals over the course of a song.

In the early 1960s Rambo's career as a writer saw a breakthrough: she was signed to a publishing company headed by Louisiana governor Jimmie Davis, who had gone through successful musical careers as a raunchy bluesman and singing cowboy movie star (the latter while serving as governor) and embarked on a gospel career of his own. Davis encountered Rambo's music

## For the Record . . .

Born March 2, 1934, in Madisonville, KY; married Buck Rambo, ca. 1950 (divorced); one daughter, Reba.

Left home at age 12 to tour as gospel singer; began performing with husband, Buck Rambo; performed as the Singing Echoes and the Gospel Echoes; performed with husband and daughter Reba as the Singing Rambos, early 1960s; group signed to Heart Warming label, 1964; toured Vietnam, 1967; recorded album *It's the Soul of Me* with African-American gospel choir, 1968; wrote widely recorded song "He Looked Beyond My Fault and Saw My Need," 1970; released more than 70 albums as soloist and with the Singing Rambos, later renamed the Rambos; composed more than 2,500 songs; underwent numerous surgeries for back problems, 1980s and 1990s; composed children's gospel musical *Down by the Creek Bank,* 1996; returned to performing; released *Stand by the River* album, 2003.

Awards: Grammy Award, Best Soul Gospel Performance (for *It's the Soul of Me*), 1968; *Billboard* magazine trendsetter of the year award, 1968; Dove Awards, Songwriter of the Year, Song of the Year, for "We Shall Behold Him," 1981; Gospel Music Hall of Fame, inducted 1991; Christian Country Music Association, Songwriter of the Century award, 1994, songwriter of the year award, 2003; ASCAP lifetime achievement award, 2000; Kentucky Music Hall of Fame, inducted 2006.

Addresses: *Office*—Dottie Rambo Ministries, P.O. Box 120039, Nashville, TN 37212.

because other performers had begun to sing her songs—he heard the gospel group Happy Goodman Family sing one of her songs, and asked who had written it. Rambo was subsequently invited to perform at the governor's mansion in Baton Rouge. The Singing Rambos scored a breakthrough of their own in 1964 when they were signed to the Heart Warming label, one of the two most successful gospel imprints (along with Canaan) of the day. They briefly recorded for Warner Brothers, which made an unsuccessful attempt to persuade Rambo to sing secular folk music.

She toured Vietnam in support of American troops in 1967.

It was the wide-open spirit of the late 1960s that propelled Rambo to stardom. In 1968 she recorded *It's the Soul of Me,* a groundbreaking collaboration with an African-American gospel choir that earned her a Grammy Award for Best Soul Gospel Performance, a *Billboard* magazine Trendsetter award, markedly broadening her commercial reach. The Rambos' albums of the late 1960s and early 1970s also had a strong soul flavor, replaced by an orientation toward country gospel music in the late 1970s. Almost alone among Southern Gospel artists and songwriters, Rambo gained a following in the African-American community. Her best-known song, "He Looked Beyond My Faults" (written in 1970 as her brother converted to Christianity on his deathbed) was recorded by major black gospel artists including Andraé Crouch and Vanessa Bell Armstrong.

Other Rambo compositions were hardly less famous. She could write with equal effectiveness in a variety of idioms, from bluegrass harmony, to soulful religious ballads with long, majestic lines that solo singers loved, to big-beat black-influenced pieces like "I Go to the Rock," sung by R&B star Whitney Houston on the soundtrack of the film *The Preacher's Wife.* The list of performers who have recorded Rambo's songs includes Barbara Mandrell ("I Will Glory in the Cross"), Jerry Lee Lewis ("He Looked Beyond My Faults"), Connie Smith ("Remind Me, Dear Lord" and others), the Oak Ridge Boys ("On the Sunny Banks"), and Bill Monroe ("It's Me Again, Lord"). A key backer and Rambo friend was Elvis Presley, who recorded "If That Isn't Love" in 1973; at the time of his death in 1977 he was planning to record an entire album of Rambo songs.

The Rambos remained a consistent presence on the gospel scene in the 1970s and 1980s, and Rambo appeared on numerous Christian television programs. She took home a Gospel Music Association Song of the Year award for "We Shall Behold Him" in 1982, and her children's Christmas album *Down by the Creek Bank* eventually reached million-seller status. But she began suffering from back problems due to a ruptured disc. For much of the 1990s she was sidelined as she underwent 12 surgical procedures to try to correct the problem. One of these left her partially paralyzed, and her marriage to Buck Rambo dissolved after 43 years. Honors came Rambo's way, including an award as Songwriter of the Century from the Christian Country Music Association in 1994 and a lifetime-achievement award from the ASCAP licensing agency in 2000.

Few would have expected Rambo to resume her performing career, but she did just that. "I decided that I would not go down the road of depression," Rambo told John Lanier of *Christian Voice.* "Physical pain is one thing, but there is no pain like that of a broken heart, and only God can heal that." Undergoing rehabilitation and learning to walk once again, Rambo welcomed Dolly Parton and other guest stars who appeared on her 2003 album *Stand by the River*. She conducted seminars for aspiring gospel songwriters, and kept writing songs with an eye to the future. In 2006 she was inducted into the Kentucky Music Museum Hall of Fame.

## Selected discography

*It's the Soul of Me,* Heart Warming, 1968.
*Makin' My Own Place,* Heart Warming, 1981.
*Down by the Creek Bank,* Impact, 1996.
*Stand by the River,* Spring Hill, 2003.
*Dottie Rambo with the Homecoming Friends,* Gaither Gospel, 2004.

## With the Rambos

*If That Isn't Love,* Vista, 1969.
*The Soul Singing Rambos,* Heart Warming, 1969.
*An Evening with the Singing Rambos,* Heart Warming, 1970.
*Nashville Gospel,* Heart Warming, 1970.
*Soul in the Family,* Heart Warming, 1972.
*Belief,* Vista, 1973.
*Too Much to Gain to Lose,* Vista, 1973.
*Alive and Live at Soul's Harbor,* Heart Warming, 1974.

*Rambo Country,* Heart Warming, 1976.
*Naturally,* Heart Warming, 1977.
*Silver Jubilee,* Heart Warming, 1979.
*Memories Made New,* Heart Warming, 1983.
*Rambos Collection,* Riversong, 1998.
*Very Best of the Rambos,* New Haven, 2003.
*Best of the Rambos,* Benson.

## Sources

### Periodicals

*Christian Reader,* November-December 2003, p. 14.
*Christian Voice,* November 2006, p. 14.
*PR Newswire,* January 5, 2006.
*St. Petersburg Times,* September 2, 2000, p. B6.
*Tampa Tribune,* September 2000, p. 7.

### Online

"Dottie Rambo," *All Music Guide,* http://www.allmusic.com (November 18, 2006).
"Dottie Rambo," Kentucky Music Museum, http://www.kentuckymusicmuseum.com/hall_of_fame.htm (November 18, 2006).
"Dottie Rambo Bio," Dottie Rambo Official Website, http://www.dottierambo.net (November 18, 2006).
"The Rambos," GMA Gospel Music Hall of Fame, http://www.gmahalloffame.org (November 18, 2006).

—*James M. Manheim*

# Lou Rawls

**Singer**

© Lynn Goldsmith/CORBIS

Lou Rawls was a rhythm-and-blues (R&B) singer with a career marked by extraordinary longevity and great generosity. His soulful singing career spanned more than 40 years, and his philanthropy helped raise over $200 million for the College Fund/United Negro College Fund (UNCF). His early roots were in gospel music, but his secular singing career began, ironically, after his life nearly ended in 1958 in a car accident.

Rawls was born on December 1, 1933, in Chicago, home to many great blues musicians. The son of a Baptist minister, he was raised on the city's South Side, where he started singing in church at age seven. In the mid-1950s he toured with his gospel group, the Pilgrim Travelers, until he joined the U.S. Army in 1956. He served with the 82nd Airborne Division in Fort Bragg, North Carolina, for two years. When he returned from military service, he toured again in 1958 with the Pilgrim Travelers. One rainy night, on the way to one of their concerts, they were in a car wreck, colliding with an 18-wheeler. Rawls was initially pronounced dead; Eddie Cunningham was killed; Cliff White broke his collarbone; Sam Cooke was hardly injured. Rawls lay in a coma for five days before waking and eventually recovering from the severe concussion.

## On His Own

In 1959 the Pilgrim Travelers broke up, and Rawls embarked on a solo career. The Pilgrim Travelers were based in Los Angeles, so Rawls stayed there after the breakup and toured small nightclubs and coffee shops. His location helped him earn a small acting role in the television series *77 Sunset Strip.* Rawls's big break came when he performed in a coffee shop called Pandora's Box. A producer from Capitol Records, Nick Benet, was in the coffee shop. To Rawls's surprise and delight, Benet asked him to record an audition tape. Capitol eventually signed Rawls to a contract in 1962. That same year, Rawls recorded the prominent background vocals for Sam Cooke's called "Bring It on Home to Me," now considered a classic.

Rawls's first recordings were fairly successful. His first album was *Stormy Monday.* His 1963 album *Black and Blue* made the pop charts, but it wasn't until the 1966 album *Lou Rawls Live* that he crossed over to major market success; *Lou Rawls Live* became the first of several gold or platinum albums for Rawls. In 1966 the song "Love Is a Hurtin' Thing" went to number 13 on the pop charts and hit number one on the R&B charts. Rawls began reaching white audiences with his smooth baritone, opening for the Beatles at their Crosley Field concert in Cincinnati, Ohio, in 1966. During the mid-1960s, Rawls liked to mix his songs with spoken monologues (perhaps derived from the spoken routines in his increasingly successful nightclub act). In 1967 one of those songs, "Dead End Street," reached number 29 on the pop charts and number 3 on the R&B charts. "Dead End Street" earned Rawls his first

## For the Record . . .

**B**orn Louis Allen Rawls, December 1, 1933, in Chicago, IL; son of Virgil (a Baptist minister) and Evelyn (a homemaker) Rawls; married Lana Jean, 1962 (marriage ended, 1972); married Nina Malek Inman, a flight attendant, 2004; children: Louanna, Lou Jr., Aiden.

Started singing gospel music in church at age seven; member of the gospel group Pilgrim Travelers, mid-1950s; solo career as rhythm and blues singer started, 1959; toured Los Angeles nightclubs until signed by Capitol, 1962; first album, *Stormy Monday,* released 1962; major market success began with first gold album *Lou Rawls Live,* 1966; starred in numerous television variety shows and Las Vegas shows, 1960s and 1970s; appeared in several films and in animated cartoons (including *Garfield* television specials), 1969-early 2000s; honorary chairman, College Fund/United Negro College Fund (UNCF), 1980; began hosting "Parade of Stars" televised telethon for The College Fund/UNCF, 1980; recorded for Epic, 1982-86; recorded *At Last* album for Blue Note, 1989; released gospel albums *I'm Blessed* (2001) and *Oh Happy Day* (2002); released *Rawls Sings Sinatra* on Savoy Jazz, 2003.

Awards: Grammy Awards, for "Dead End Street," 1967, *A Natural Man,* 1971, and *Unmistakably Lou,* 1977; American Music Award for "You'll Never Find Another Love Like Mine," 1976; street named after Rawls in Chicago, 1987.

Addresses: *Website*—Lou Rawls Official Website: http://www.lourawls.com.

Grammy Award. In the mid and late 1960s, Rawls guest-starred on many television variety shows and played the Las Vegas nightclub scene. In 1969 he even appeared in a movie, *Angel Angel Down We Go.*

In 1970 Rawls recorded a single called "Your Good Thing Is About to Come to an End," a title that belied the success he experienced in the 1970s. The song was nominated for a Grammy Award. Rawls changed record companies in 1971, signing with MGM Records and recording *A Natural Man,* which earned Rawls a second Grammy Award in 1972. The song reached number 17 on the pop and R&B charts. Rawls released only one more album with MGM before signing with Philadelphia International records.

The signing with Philadelphia International was memorable because it paired Rawls with legendary producers Kenny Gamble and Leon Huff. His first album with Gamble and Huff, *All Things in Time,* went platinum, with sales of over one million copies, and reached number three on the R&B charts. Rawls's most notable single was the first one he recorded with Gamble and Huff in 1976, called "You'll Never Find Another Love Like Mine." It reached number two on the pop charts and number one on the R&B charts, and was played in numerous discos across the United States. The song was Rawls's first gold single, and it won him an American Music Award and a Grammy nomination. "Groovy People," the next single recorded with Gamble and Huff, also earned a Grammy nomination. Other singles released with Gamble and Huff included "See You When I Git There," "Lady Love," and "Let Me Be Good to You."

## A Notable Career

In 1977 Rawls won his third Grammy Award. This time it was for Best Male Rhythm and Blues Performance, for the album *Unmistakably Lou.* Rawls was seen on television often in the 1970s on variety shows and as an actor, and he also represented Budweiser as a national spokesperson in the late 1970s.

Rawls's last notable single was "I Wish You Belonged to Me," which reached number 28 on the R&B chart. *At Last,* recorded in 1989, earned a Grammy nomination and included a variety of guest stars. When *Portrait of the Blues* was released in 1993, Phyl Garland of *Stereo Review* commented that "Central to [Rawls's] longevity have been the undeniable appeal of his deep baritone voice and his craftsmanship as a singer." Underscoring the singer's accomplishments, Garland also remarked, "In a pop world where the duration of fame seems to have been cut back from 15 to 10 minutes, Lou Rawls has maintained his popularity over more than thirty years."

Rawls continued to tour and record, and he appeared in many television shows and films, including the grim *Leaving Las Vegas* (1995). Throughout the 1980s and 1990s, however, he mainly established himself as a generous humanitarian. Through his efforts as honorary chairman, he raised over $200 million for The College Fund/UNCF. He accomplished this by hosting a telethon every January called the "Parade of Stars." Beginning in 1980, fellow performers appeared live on the show to raise money for the fund. These included: Marilyn McCoo, Gladys Knight, Ray Charles, Patti LaBelle, Luther Vandross, Anita Baker, Boyz II Men, and many others. Rawls was adamant in his opinion about the role of education in guiding today's youth. He told

*Jet,* "If you look around you, you see the adults constantly pointing the finger at the kids, saying, 'You're doing wrong.' But do you give them an option? I think the option should be education. Our future depends on it, man."

In 1989 Rawls's hometown of Chicago changed the name of South Wentworth Avenue, renaming it Lou Rawls Drive in his honor. In 1993 Rawls attended ceremonies for the groundbreaking of the Lou Rawls Theater and Cultural Center, which was to include a library, two cinemas, a restaurant, a 1,500-seat theater, and a roller skating rink. The center was built on the original site of the Regal Theater on the south side of Chicago, where the gospel and blues music played there in the 1950s had inspired a young Lou Rawls.

Reaching an age when he could have relaxed and accepted such awards, Rawls continued to release new music, often returning to the gospel and jazz sounds with which he had begun his career. His *I'm Blessed* and *Oh Happy Day* albums of 2003 were gospel releases. In 2003 Rawls also released *Rawls Sings Sinatra,* with arrangements by veteran jazz composed Benny Gholson. In January of 2004, Rawls married flight attendant Nina Malek Inman. A year later the couple had a son, Aiden; Rawls had two other children from earlier marriages. Soon, however, Rawls, a former smoker, began to suffer symptoms of lung cancer that eventually spread to his brain.

Though gravely ill, Rawls delivered an electrifying performance of "The Star-Spangled Banner" before game two of baseball's 2005 World Series in Chicago. He died in Los Angeles on January 6, 2006. The Rev. Jesse Jackson delivered the eulogy, telling the mourners (according to *Jet*) that Rawls "wasn't able to go to college, but he sent thousands." And Los Angeles County Supervisor Yvonne Brathwaite Burke declared, "People talked about his magnificent voice, but he had a magnificent soul."

## Selected discography

*Stormy Monday,* Blue Note, 1962.
*Black and Blue,* Capitol, 1963.
*Tobacco Road,* Capitol, 1963.
*For You My Love,* Capitol, 1964.
*Lou Rawls and Strings,* Capitol, 1965.
*Merry Christmas Ho! Ho! Ho!,* Capitol, 1965.
*Nobody but Lou,* Capitol, 1965.
*Lou Rawls Live,* Capitol, 1966.
*Lou Rawls Soulin',* Capitol, 1966.
*Lou Rawls Carryin' On,* Capitol, 1966.
*Soul Stirring Gospel Sounds of the Sixties,* Capitol, 1966.
*That's Lou,* Capitol, 1967.
*Too Much,* Capitol, 1967.
*You're Good for Me,* Capitol, 1968.

*Feelin' Good,* Capitol, 1968.
*Best from Lou Rawls,* Capitol, 1968.
*The Way It Was/The Way It Is,* Capitol, 1969.
*Your Good Thing,* Capitol, 1969.
*A Natural Man,* MGM, 1971.
*Silk and Soul,* MGM, 1972.
*All Things in Time,* Philadelphia International, 1976.
*Philly Years,* Philadelphia International, 1976.
*Unmistakably Lou,* Philadelphia International, 1977.
*When You Hear Lou, You've Heard It All,* Philadelphia International, 1977.
*Lou Rawls Live,* Philadelphia International, 1978.
*Let Me Be Good to You,* Philadelphia International, 1979.
*Sit Down and Talk to Me,* Philadelphia International, 1980.
*Shades of Blue,* Philadelphia International, 1981.
*When the Night Comes,* Epic, 1983.
*At Last,* Blue Note, 1989.
*Greatest Hits,* Curb, 1990.
*It's Supposed to Be Fun,* Blue Note, 1990.
*Portrait of the Blues,* Manhattan, 1993.
*Christmas is the Time,* Manhattan, 1993.
*Seasons 4 U,* Rawls & Brokaw, 1998.
*Anthology,* Capitol, 2000.
*I'm Blessed,* Malaco, 2001.
*Oh Happy Day,* 601, 2002.
*Finest Collection,* EMI, 2003.
*Rawls Sings Sinatra,* Savoy Jazz, 2003.
*Love Songs,* Right Stuff, 2005.
*Best of Lou Rawls: The Capitol Jazz & Blues Sessions,* Blue Note, 2006.
*Very Best of Lou Rawls: You'll Never Find Another Love Like Mine,* Capitol, 2006.

## Sources

### Books

Hawkins, Walter L., editor, *African American Biographies: Profiles of 558 Current Men and Women,* McFarland and Company, Inc., 1992.
Romanowski, Patricia, editor, *The New Rolling Stone Encyclopedia of Rock & Roll,* Fireside, 1995.

### Periodicals

*Down Beat,* January, 1990.
*Jet,* June 26, 1989; August 30, 1993; January 9, 1995; January 13, 1997; January 12, 2004; January 9, 2006; January 20, 2006.
*People,* January 23, 2006.
*Stereo Review,* July 1993.

### Online

"Biography," Lou Rawls Official Website, http://www.lourawls.com (November 22, 2006).
"Lou Rawls," *All Music Guide,* http://www.allmusic.com (November 22, 2006).

—*Christine Morrison and James M. Manheim*

# Paloma San Basilio

## Singer

AP Images

Among the biggest and most glamorous European-born stars in the Latin music field, Paloma San Basilio is also one of the genre's most versatile singers. While San Basilio gained an international reputation in the early 1980s with her starring role in the musical *Evita,* she has also recorded and performed pop music in both Spanish and English, and has held her own on stage with opera star Plácido Domingo. Following her own artistic instincts rather than trying to tailor her style to specific audiences, San Basilio has gained a growing audience among Hispanic and even non-Hispanic audiences in the United States. "For most of three decades," wrote David Cazares in South Florida's *Sun-Sentinel* newspaper, "Paloma San Basilio has built her reputation as one of Spain's classiest singers."

Paloma San Basilio was born in Madrid, Spain, on November 22, 1950—the feast day of Saint Cecilia, the patron saint of music in the Catholic liturgical calendar. She grew up partly in Seville. San Basilio's family was middle-class, and she was encouraged to pursue a university education. She studied philosophy, psychology, and literature, and continued to enjoy writing even after she became a vocal star, sometimes penning her own song lyrics. It was during her student years that San Basilio began her performing career—but as a stage actress, not as a singer. She appeared in university theatrical productions, and in 1969 she had a small part in a Spanish television production of Shakespeare's *Richard III.*

At this point, San Basilio sang only for friends. With an eye on an acting career, she dropped out of school and worked as an art book salesperson, then as a psychiatric nurse. In March of 1971 she landed a role as a presenter on a television magazine program called *Siempre en domingo* (Always on Sunday); despite her lack of experience, she became popular enough to become the subject of interview requests from romance magazines. In 1972 she married athlete Ignacio Gómez Pellico, and the following year she had a daughter, Vanessa. When the program was canceled in 1973, San Basilio found a less satisfying slot on a program where she had to lip-synch with recordings of famous Spanish zarzuela (operetta) performances. When a friend suggested that she make a demo tape and try to break into the music business, she was ready.

### Made Musical Theater Debut

San Basilio grew up hearing a variety of music in addition to local Spanish productions; she was fond of African-American music, and her demo contained three songs by 1970s R&B star Roberta Flack. Her first album, *Sombras* (Shadows), was released in 1975 and featured a diverse group of songs that included a cover of the Beatles' "The Long and Winding Road." San Basilio's 1977 release, *Dónde vas* (Where Are You Going) was her commercial breakthrough. The follow-

## For the Record . . .

Born Paloma San Basilio on November 22, 1950, in Madrid, Spain; grew up in Madrid and Seville; married Ignacio Gómez Pellico, an athlete, 1972; one daughter, Vanessa, born 1973. *Education:* Studied philosophy, literature, and psychology at a university in Spain.

Made first recording, *Sombras,* 1975; recorded for EMI label; began appearing as Evita Perón in musical *Evita,* 1980; performed at Eurovision Song Festival, 1985; "Paloma Flying High" tour of Spain, Latin America, and U.S., 1986; several million-selling albums in Spain, late 1980s; *Música* tour of Latin America and U.S., 1993; appeared as Dulcinea in Spanish version of musical *Man of La Mancha,* 1997; released *Clasicamente tuya* album, appeared with Miami City Ballet, 1998; recorded *Perlas* album of covers of English-language songs, 1999; toured Mexico and U.S. West Coast, 2001; released *Diva* album, 2006.

*Awards:* Latin Recording Academy, Lifetime Achievement Award, 2006.

*Addresses: Record company*—EMI Latin, 404 Washington Ave., Ste. 700, Miami Beach, FL 33139. *Website*—Paloma San Basilio Official Website: http://www.palomasanbasilio.net/.

then, I knew I would do well in theater."

After several years of performing in *Evita,* San Basilio proved her label wrong by resuming her pop career with a sequence of consistently successful albums in the late 1980s. These included 1986's *Vuela alto* (Flying High), which became the basis for a "Paloma Flying High" tour (the word "paloma" means "dove" in Spanish) that introduced San Basilio to U.S. audiences. She released *Grande* (The Great) in 1987, and *Vida* (Life) the following year. In 1991 she recorded *Por fin juntos* with operatic tenor Plácido Domingo. That album resulted in joint performances by the two, including a concert that drew 12,000 fans to the Miami Arena in Florida in 1991. Although *Miami Herald* critic James Roos felt that San Basilio "couldn't hold a candle to Domingo" in a duet from Franz Lehar's operetta *The Merry Widow,* he noted that the two "were potent collaborators, with a dashing sense of theater, and their voices stirred exuberant excitement that precipitated more and more encores. San Basilio can tell you what a lyric is all about and she knows all about using a microphone effectively, too, as the best popular singers do."

### Broadened Her Audience

San Basilio's next tour, in 1993, brought her back to the United States and saw her trying to broaden her English-speaking audience with a signature version of the jazz standard "Stormy Weather" and shows in locations like Atlantic City, New Jersey, that had only moderate-sized Latin populations. "I belong to a generation that basically grew up with Anglo-American music," she explained to John Lannert of the *Sun-Sentinel.* Her high-energy concerts mixed songs from several European countries with Spanish and American numbers, often reserving her Spanish-language version of "Don't Cry for Me, Argentina" ("No llores por mí, Argentina," from *Evita*) as a showstopper. San Basilio attracted large audiences along the U.S. eastern seaboard but found the West Coast, musically dominated by Mexican and Mexican-American stars, tougher to crack.

Whatever level of success she experienced, San Basilio remained true to her own artistic instincts. "It's an erroneous idea to think of two distinct markets with distinct tastes," she told the Los Angeles newspaper *La Opinión* (in Spanish), referring to Spanish and Latin American buyers. She had tried releasing separate albums for each market; 1989's *Quiéreme siempre* (Love Me Always) was aimed toward Spanish audiences, while *Nadie como tú,* made the following year, was marketed in Latin America. The albums did well, but San Basilio was dissatisfied. "I had two producers, and that created a terrible duality, because the artist becomes a kind of monster with two heads," she told *La Opinión.* "I've always defended my needs as an artist," she pointed out to Cobo-Hanlon. "And what

ing year she performed a concert with full orchestra at Madrid's giant Teatro Monumental, singing the Barbra Streisand hit "People" and the Broadway classic "Tea for Two" along with Spanish-language material. She was rapturously received, and her career as a full-blown star was on its way.

In 1980 San Basilio was offered the lead role in the Spanish production of *Evita,* a musical (equally popular in Spanish and English versions) that traced the life of the charismatic Argentine political figure Eva Perón. San Basilio's label, EMI, resisted the idea of interrupting her growing career, but she relished the new challenge and insisted on keeping control of her career. The role was a difficult one. "My mother was also dying at the time, and I felt very pressured," San Basilio recalled to Leila Cobo-Hanlon of the *Miami Herald.* "And I remember on opening night the theater was completely full, and that character helped me deal with my pain and channel my energy. And right there and

survives are those things that are faithful to what you want to be. I always say I have only one career, while they [my promoters and record executives] have more. I have to look out for what's mine." More changeable was San Basilio's visual image; like Madonna, another famous interpreter of the role of Evita, she was the subject of countless glamorous news photographs in which she rarely, if ever, looked the same twice.

### Released Classical-Inspired Album

Recordings such as *Paloma mediterranea* (Mediterranean Dove, 1993) and *Como un sueño* (Like a Dream, 1996) kept San Basilio in the minds of music buyers. In 1997 San Basilio returned to the musical stage in *Man of La Mancha,* and the following year she performed in a Miami City Ballet "Spanish Spectacular" with dancers and orchestral musicians. She returned to classical music with 1998's *Clasicamente tuya* (Classically Yours), which featured romantic ballads in full-scale symphonic arrangements, with tunes adapted from melodies by Beethoven and other classical composers. "San Basilio's vocals shine in this setting, and she reveals new facets of her musical personality, particularly in the way she can tackle these grandiose arrangements with ease," noted Stephen Thomas Erlewine of *All Music Guide.*

As she entered her sixth decade, San Basilio attracted attention from newspaper writers for her seemingly ageless good looks and also for her atypical lack of any attempt to conceal her true birthdate. In 2001 she made her third appearance in musicals in the lead role of Eliza Doolittle in a Spanish version of *My Fair Lady,* and her 2002 album *Eternamente* (Eternally) was a collection of songs from musicals. She also appeared in a stage version of *Victor Victoria.* Collections of San Basilio hits crowded music-store shelves and Internet retail listings by the mid-2000s, and in 2006 she received a Lifetime Achievement Award from the Latin Recording Academy, presenter of the Latin Grammy awards. That achievement was far from finished, however; San Basilio released a new album, *Diva,* that year.

## Selected discography

*Sombras,* EMI, 1975.
*Dónde vas,* EMI, 1977.
*Ahora,* EMI, 1981.
*Dama,* EMI, 1982.
*Vuela alto,* EMI, 1986.
*Grande,* EMI, 1987.
*Vida,* EMI, 1988.
*Quiéreme siempre,* EMI, 1989.
*Nadie como tú,* EMI, 1990.
(With Plácido Domingo) *Por fin juntos,* EMI, 1991.
*De mil amores,* Capitol, 1992.
*Paloma mediterranea,* Capitol, 1993.
*Al este del Eden,* EMI, 1994.
*Como un sueño,* EMI, 1996.
*Clasicamente tuya,* EMI, 1998.
*Perlas,* EMI, 1999.
*Escorpio,* Sony International, 2001.
*La música es mi vida: 30 grandes canciones,* EMI, 2004.
*Inolvidablemente,* Vene Music, 2005.
*Lo básico,* EMI, 2005.
*Diva,* EMI, 2006.

## Sources

### Periodicals

*Miami Herald,* November 7, 1986, p. D11; March 5, 1991, p. C4; March 17, 1998, p. C1.
*La Opinión* (Los Angeles), May 19, 2001, p. B1.
*Sun-Sentinel* (Fort Lauderdale, FL), March 19, 1993, Showtime section, p. 20; March 19, 1998, p. E3; May 11, 2001, Showtime section, p. 34.

### Online

"Paloma San Basilio," *All Music Guide,* http://www.allmusic.com (November 5, 2006).
"Paloma San Basilio estudió un año de Filosofía y Letras" ("Paloma San Basilio Studied Philosophy and Literature for a Year"), http://es.geocities.com/jeliclejesito/Vida.htm (November, 5, 2006).

—James M. Manheim

# Shivaree

## Rock band

In 2005 California's Shivaree released its third album, *Who's Got Trouble?*, but in many ways, it seemed as though the band had just released its debut. "It does feel like we're starting all over again," lead singer Ambrosia Parsley told Helen Brown in the London *Daily Telegraph*. After the band's well-received debut in 1999, *I Oughtta Give You a Shot in the Head for Making Me Live in This Dump*, many believed that band was on the verge of reaching a larger audience. Shivaree's contract with Capitol, however, proved a mixed blessing when the label refused to release 2002's *Rough Dreams* in the United States. Two years later Shivaree received an unexpected boost when "Goodnight Moon" was chosen for the soundtrack of *Kill Bill, Volume 2*. With the release of *Who's Got Trouble* on Zoe, the band once again reached out to American fans and found its artistic footing.

Shivaree, a name describing the practice of banging pots and pans outside of a newlywed couple's room, formed around the songs and voice of Ambrosia Parsley. Born on June 23, 1971, Parsley grew up in Reseda, California. She learned classic American pop songs from the 1920s, 1930s, and 1940s from her grandmother, known as Da Uke Lady, who lived in an Airstream trailer behind the family home. Parsley performed as a child at the pizza parlor across the street where her family ate dinner four times a week, and at 13 she sang songs like "Toot Toot Tootsie, Goodbye" with a 99-piece senior citizens' banjo orchestra at a restaurant in a nearby town. "It was a helluva a noise," Parsley recalled to Brown. "It was also kind of sad because they kept dying. Banjos, funerals, pizza and beer."

Originally calling itself Junebug, Shivaree formed accidentally in the late 1990s. Parsley had recorded several demos, and received a call, she told Dan Cairns in the London *Sunday Times,* from Danny McGough, a keyboard player who had worked with Tom Waits. "He called me and said: 'Your stuff doesn't suck as much as most people's. If you ever wanted to work with me, I guess I would.'" Parsley and McGough worked on several songs the following week. When they returned to the studio to replay the recordings, though, they were surprised to learn that someone had secretly dubbed a guitar part to one of the songs. They soon learned that the part—which they both liked—had been the work of Duke McVinnie, a guitarist who slept on a camp bed next to the studio.

Still, the trio had no intentions of forming a band. Parsley handed the tape to a friend, however, and soon she, McVinnie, and McGough were receiving offers from record labels. "It was kind of ridiculous," Parsley told Brown. "But I said, 'Hey, why don't we just sign one of these deals.'" Shivaree signed with Capitol and began recording songs in singer-producer Joe Henry's backyard. In 1999 Shivaree released *I Oughtta Give You a Shot in the Head for Making Me Live in This Dump*. The title came from an episode of television's *Green Acres,* in which a cow swallows a radio that continues to play.

Critics praised the album, but seemed perplexed on how to categorize Shivaree and lead singer Parsley's performance style. Brad Reno of *Trouser Press* wrote, "Parsley has star quality to spare—a talent for sometimes surreal southern gothic lyrics, supermodel beauty, hilarious interview patter and a voice best described as a smoky mix of Gwen Stefani, Altered Images' Claire Grogan and the Motels' Martha Davis." Timothy White wrote in *Billboard,* "Shivaree's sound is a bit of a Dole fruit cup: colorful, tart, and surprisingly appetizing for something served at room temperature."

With a successful album behind them, many believed that Shivaree's sophomore release would introduce the band to a wider audience. Released in September of 2002, *Rough Dreams* followed in the dark footsteps of the group's debut, and a number of critics preferred the newer album. Capitol, however, chose to only release the album in Europe, where Shivaree's following was strongest. Because of Capitol's marketing strategy, the band more or less disappeared from the popular music radar in the United States. However, Shivaree toured continuously, while Parsley struggled with chronic stage fright. Interviewed before the filming of a video for "John 2/14," she confessed to Cairns, "I'd rather have nails driven under my eyelids."

In 2004 Parsley turned her attention to politics and radio, performing "Ambrosia Sings the News" on Air

## For the Record . . .

**M**embers include **Danny McGough**, keyboards; **Duke McVinnie**, guitar; **Ambrosia Parsley**, vocals.

Shivaree, originally Junebug, formed in California, late 1990s; recorded *I Oughtta Give You a Shot in the Head for Making Me Live in This Dump,* 1999, *Rough Dreams,* 2002, and *Who's Got Trouble?* 2005.

Addresses: *Record company*—Zoe Records, 1 Camp St., Cambridge, MA 02140, phone: 1-800-768-6337, email: www.zoerecords.net.

America. Each Friday, she would turn the headlines into song lines, penning lyrics that skewered the politics of the day. To meet the demanding schedule, Parsley developed a routine. Each Thursday she sat down with a stack of daily papers at her favorite restaurant, Café Havana. "I sit down, order a bloody mary and huevos rancheros," she told *Paste.* "Then I go through the papers, rhyme it up, go sing it, and they play it on Friday."

Shivaree also received a boost when film director Quentin Tarantino chose "Goodnight Moon" for the closing credits of *Kill Bill: Volume 2* in 2004. The same year, the band released the EP *Breach,* featuring two new tracks and three covers, including Eno's "The Fat Lady of Limbourg." The EP more or less paved the way for 2005's *Who's Got Trouble?* on Zoe Records.

*Who's Got Trouble* used the film *Casablanca* as its touchstone, subtly offering observations on contemporary politics by way of a world view of an earlier time. "The songs are kind of like ghosts coming back at you," Parsley told Philip Shelley in the *Washington Times.* This haunting quality, combined with evocative arrangements, has become Shivaree's trademark.

## Selected discography

*I Oughtta Give You a Shot in the Head for Making Me Live in This Dump,* Capitol, 1999.
*Rough Dreams,* Capitol, 2002.
*Who's Got Trouble?,* Zoe, 2005.

## Sources

### Periodicals

*Billboard,*January 22, 2000.
*Daily Telegraph* (London, England), April 23, 2005.
*Sunday Times* (London, England), June 16, 2002.
*Times* (London, England), September 1, 2000.
*Washington Times,* October 7, 2005.

### Online

"Looking for Trouble: Ambrosia Parsley and Shivaree Get Political," *Boston Phoenix,* http://www.bostonphoenix.com/ (October 24, 2006).
"Shivaree," *Paste,* http://www.pastemagazine.com/ (October 24, 2006).
"Shivaree," *Trouser Press,* http://www.trouserpress.com/ (October 24, 2006).

—*Ronnie D. Lankford, Jr.*

# Sierra

## Christian music group

The music group Sierra has had 15 Top 5 hits on Christian radio; seven of these have hit the number one spot. They have sold more than a quarter of a million albums and have performed for sellout crowds at Christian women's conferences.

Sierra was founded in 1991 in Houston, Texas, by singer/songwriter Wendi Foy Green. Green graduated from Baylor University in Waco, Texas, and moved to Austin, Texas to work at a Christian radio station. While working there she met a record company executive who offered her a solo recording contract. This led to her solo release of an album titled *Finders Keepers* in 1988. For Green, however, the most important aspect of this project was that she met producer Brian Green. They decided that if they could work together to make a record, they could successfully do anything together, and they were married in February of 1989.

### Three-Part Harmony

Meanwhile, Green had become interested in finding other women to form a vocal trio. She had been singing in groups since childhood, when she joined her father, a music minister, and her two sisters to sing religious songs in churches. She told the CMO.com website, "I've always loved the sound of three-part harmony, and I wanted to do it again." Through her husband's work in the Christian music business, Green met two women who, coincidentally, had the same first names as her sisters: Deborah Schnelle and Jennifer Hendrix. Like her sisters, they had grown up in families that combined a love of music and religious faith; all had parents or grandparents who were full-time ministers.

Schnelle, born in Austin, Texas, had sung background vocals on Green's solo album, and they had been friends for several years. Schnelle was delighted when Green asked her to help form a trio. She did not want to have a solo career, so the group was perfect for her. Green met Hendrix through her husband, a producer, who was working on a project with her. Hendrix told CMO.com that when Green called to ask her to join, "I prayed about it and said yes."

The three had a remarkably close blend of voices, similar to that of real sisters. In 1992 they moved to Nashville to pursue their dream. They sang during their lunch breaks at the Baptist Sunday School Board, where they were working, and eventually signed a contract with Star Song. They spent the next ten years touring and performing hundreds of times each year at religious venues and on Christian television shows, including *Life Today With James Robison, The 700 Club, The Crystal Cathedral,* and Trinity Broadcasting Network, as well as on many Christian radio programs.

In October of 1994 the group released their debut album, *Sierra.* It was a huge success in the Christian music market, selling over 100,000 copies in only nine months. Their second album, *Devotion,* had similar success. They released *Story of Life* in 1991.

### "That's Me"

The group's goal was to combine their soaring harmonies with their love of God, in order to inspire listeners to be closer to God. They drew from their own life experience to write their songs. For example, in the song "Tearing Down the Temple," Schnelle wrote about her struggles with anorexia nervosa, an eating disorder. She told CMO.com that the song resonated with audiences: "It never fails, when I sing that song, someone will come up later and say, 'That's me.' And I can pray with them from the heart, because I've been there."

Schnelle left the group, and a new member, Marianne Tutalo, joined for the group's next album, *Change.* After releasing *Change,* the group's members went through their own personal changes. Hendrix had her second child, and group member Marianne Adams got married. Their next album, *The Journey,* reflected these changes. It was lighter, with less emphasis on struggle and tribulation. Hendrix commented on the group's website, "It is almost as if we are looking in the rearview mirror at the past and saying, 'Thank you God', for carrying us through."

Following their release of *The Journey,* Sierra decided to limit their concert appearances to six per month so

## For the Record . . .

Members include **Marianne Adams**; **Wendi Foy Green**; **Jennifer Hendrix**; **Deborah Schnelle** (left group, 2000); and **Marianne Tutalo** (joined group, 2000).

Group formed in 1991; released *Sierra,* 1994; released *Devotion,* 1996; released *Story of Life,* 1998; released *Change,* 1999; released *The Journey,* 2001.

Addresses: *Management*—Soapbox Inspirations, 234 North Easat Alpenview Lane, Bend, OR 97701.

they could spend more time with their families. Although they continued to appear at Women of Faith conferences and Women of Virtue conferences, and hosted a show on the TBN network called *The Sierra Hour,* they made their families a priority. They also decided to spend more time studying the Bible and praying, because they felt all the emphasis on performing had distracted them from their spiritual lives. Hendrix wrote on the group's website that doing this "makes me spend time with the Lord, and it is wonderful. I want it. I need it. That is why I am forcing that time to happen."

In 2002 the group decided to disband. Green went on to pursue a solo career, and Tutalo and Hendrix formed a new worship band, called Abide. "I think change is for the better," Green said on the group's website. "There is constant change. Hopefully it is change for the better—to be more Christ-like, to be more Christ-centered, to be less self-centered." She added, "Ten years ago my writing was lighter, fluffier. I wrote good songs with good messages, but as I mature… I want to paint an aural picture with more colors." She noted, "If you are going to present something, present it from the depths of your soul."

## Selected discography

*Sierra,* Star Song, 1994.
*Devotion,* Star Song, 1996.
*Story of Life,* Star Song, 1998.
*Change,* Pamplin Records, 1999.
*The Journey,* Pamplin Records, 2001.

## Sources

### Online

Christian Music Lighthouse, http://www.christian music light house.com/main/news/sierranews/index.htm (November 2, 2006).
CMO.com, http://www.cmo.com/cmo/cmo/date/sierra.htm (October 24, 2006).
Sierra Official Website, http://www.sierra1.org/Biography.htm (October 24, 2006).
Soapbox Inspirations, http://www.soapboxinspirations.com/resources/wfgreen-artist.html (November 2, 2006).

—*Kelly Winters*

# Sneaker Pimps

Electronic band

**M**anchester, England-based electronic band Sneaker Pimps mixes melodic, electronic pop with flowing vocals. A *Pollstar* reviewer commented, "There's something eerily fascinating about the Sneaker Pimps' music. Their songs have a lurid edge—something that turns the listener into a voyeur. The band reveals the bruised underbelly of the whole trip-hop electronica stereotype without giving away their own secrets."

The band was formed by Chris Corner and Liam Howe, who grew up together in the 1980s in the English town of Hartlepool, and their friend Nick Drake. The three shared a love of the music of Shirley Bassey and Kraftwerk, and in 1992 they began recording their own early efforts to make music on an eight-track machine in Howe's bedroom in Hartlepool. Howe told Isaac Josephson in *Rolling Stone,* "The most interesting thing about Hartlepool is that in the 19th century, the inhabitants hung a monkey because they thought it was a French spy."

Their early work resulted in the *Soul of Indiscretion* LP, which later became known as "trip-hop" for its combination of beats and acoustic sound. The group produced the same sound on another EP, *F.R.I.S.K.*

In 1993 Corner and Howe, calling themselves Line of Flight, released an EP album, *World as a Cone,* on the Clean Up label. However, they were not satisfied with their sound, and wanted to produce music that incorporated vocals with their spacey, instrumental sound. A friend, Ian Pickering, wrote lyrics for them, and they wrote songs that would eventually become the Sneaker Pimps' first album, *Becoming X.* Josephson described their sound as "a catchy fusion of pop, trip-hop and blues." He added, "The album shifts seamlessly between fuzz guitar and crisp, roots blues riffs, all laced with a tawdry electronic sludge... fat bass and Dayton's babydoll vocals," and commented that the Pimps "have managed to produce some of the most accessible trip-hop to date."

They decided that their sound suited a female vocalist best, and when they heard Kelli Dayton singing in a pub, they knew they had found the sound they were looking for. They convinced her to join them, and Sneaker Pimps was born. Secretly, none of them thought the union would last, but they were all willing to give it a try.

Their first single, "Tesko Suicide," featured their trip-hop sound, with lyrics advocating the sale of "suicide kits" in a UK grocery-store chain. According to the group's bio on the One Little Indian Records website, critic Stephen Dalton wrote, "If you can't find it in your heart to love such brilliantly stupid, stupidly brilliant pop stars, the joke's on you."

## Becoming X

*Becoming X* was released in 1996, and it was not expected to sell well; it was viewed as a short-term project, a sort of experiment. The group expected to do many other short-term projects and did not expect widespread success from any of them. Wilson told a BBC interviewer, "At that time we thought it was going to be a one-off short project rather than a career."

In the meantime, they brought in other members: college friends Joe Wilson, who had designed the sleeves for Howe and Corner's earlier releases, and Dave Westlake, a drummer. In an interview on the University of Washington's *Online Daily,* Westlake told Kathryn McGrath, "There've been too many bands recently where you've got two guys with keyboards and a girl in front singing and a tape playing. We did want to get back to being a band." He summed up the band's sound as "basically the sound of five people arguing," because it incorporates threads from each person in the band. "That's how it sounds like different things all running together."

Against all their predictions, *Becoming X* became a huge hit, and they embarked on 18 months of touring. As the One Little Indian Records website described it, "The musical genre they had helped to introduce had become wallpaper, the soundtrack to every pizza café/cappuccino bar in the world. Sneaker Pimps had fallen into a genre trap and only drastic action could help them escape."

After the *Becoming X* tour, seeking a fresh angle and a new sound, they moved their studio from northeastern

England to London. They recorded *Splinter* in 1998, and in 1989 founded their own label, Splinter Records. Among other acts, they recorded Robots in Disguise, Trash Money, and Servant, as well as Placebo and Natalie Imbruglia.

### Bloodsport

In 2002, they went to France, where they recorded *Bloodsport,* following it with a 12-country tour of Europe in the spring of 2001. Before the band recorded *Bloodsport,* Kelli Dayton left the band, changing her name to Kelli Ali to pursue a solo career. Chris Corner took her place, providing vocals for this album. They told David Jack Browning in *Toxic Universe* that this was actually the band's original intention: "We originally did the demos with Chris singing on the songs. We recorded them with Kelli and it sounded right with her on those songs." Of the album, Browning wrote, "These musicians use machines to tell stories through pulses and beats more than rising scales and falsettos that were never meant to be. Corner's voice adds just the right flavor to the mix."

One unexpected result of the band's success was that it became harder for the members to maintain friend-ships with people back home. Corner told Josephson, "You're gone so much. Things change. People think that you've changed. They think you can't relate to them anymore, and they become quite bitter about your success." Howe added, "You don't realize how stupid you look until you get into a group of normal people. Our hair is dyed stupid colors, and we wear silly shirts and sunglasses…. You think 'My god! I've been consumed by this madness.'" After *Bloodsport,* the members of the band decided to pursue other projects.

## Selected discography

*Becoming X,* Clean Up, 1996.
*Becoming Remixed,* Virgin, 1998.
*Splinter,* Clean Up, 1999.
*Bloodsport,* Tommy Boy, 2002.

## Sources

### Online

"Bloodsport," *Toxic Universe,* June 8, 2002, http://www.toxicuniverse.com/review.php?rid+10003322 (November 14, 2006).
"IAMX," *Remix,* October 1, 2006, http://www.remixmag.com/artists/remix/iamx/ (November 14, 2006).
"Interviews: Whisperin' and Hollerin'," *Infinite Star,* July, 2002; http://www.infinitestar.co.uk/whisperinandhollerin_interview.html (November 14, 2006).
"Joe Wilson, Musician," *BBC,* http://www.bbc.co.uk/blast/music/peoplein/joe_wilson.shtml (November 14, 2006).
One Little Indian Records Web Site, http://www.indian.co.uk/sneakerpimps/ (November 14, 2006).
"Sneaker Pimps," *Pollstar,* http://www.pollstar.com/news/viewhotstar.pl?Artist=SNEPIMR (November 14, 2006).
"Sneaker Pimps Become X," *Rolling Stone,* http://www.rollingstone.com/artists/sneakerpimps/articles/story/5922276/sneaker_pimps/ (November 14, 2006).
*University of Washington Online Daily,* http://www.archives.thedaily.washington.edu/1997/051597/051597/SneakPimps.html (November 14, 2006).

—*Kelly Winters*

# Regina Spektor

**Singer, songwriter, pianist**

Paul Hawthorne/Getty Images

A classically trained pianist with an eccentric style of pop songwriting, Regina Spektor made a name for herself at the turn of the century, playing quirky but intimate songs on the café circuit in New York's Lower East Side. Spektor was born and raised in Moscow, in the former Soviet Union, until age nine. After moving to the New York City borough the Bronx, the Jewish-Russian-American musician emerged with a string of independently released albums before signing to major label Sire Records in 2004. *Blender's* Pauline O'Connor described Spektor's music as, "...a weirdly ancient-sounding mash-up of pre-rock and art-school piano delivered in a voice that swoops from whisper to moan and back again." Spektor herself told O'Connor, "My songs take elements of classical music and literature and mix them with an 'I can do whatever I want' punk-rock attitude."

Born at the dawn of the 1980s, Spektor grew up in Moscow, Russia, with her mother and father. After watching her mother play the piano for years, by six, Spektor was ready to play herself. While living in Moscow, Spektor's mother worked as a music teacher and her father was a trained violinist. In 1989 the Jewish family left Moscow to escape religious persecution and immigrated to the Bronx in New York City. When the family moved, they had to leave most of their belongings behind, including the piano given to them by their grandfather. Situated in the United States, Spektor's parents were forced to take any job they could find, leaving the family with little money, and much to young Spektor's heartbreak, no piano. Clearly gifted, even without a piano at home, Spektor continued to practice whenever and wherever she could, including on the piano at her synagogue and on tabletops and counters, until they could afford their own piano.

Without enough money to hire a worthy piano teacher to help the gifted Spektor flourish on the keys, it was her father's chance meeting on the subway where Spektor found help. After chatting with a fellow violinist on the subway, Spektor's father discovered that his new friend's wife happened to be a music professor at the Manhattan School of Music. The teacher saw the talent in Spektor and offered to teach her for free. After years of playing classical pieces, into her late teenage years, Spektor began to write her own songs. Since she had heard little popular music growing up, her songs emerged from putting classical composition into a pop realm. Coupled with Spektor's coquettish voice, the songs had a truly unique style and flair. After graduating from SUNY-Purchase's Conservatory of Music (in three years instead of four) Spektor began playing her own songs.

## Road to Independence

By 2001, with friend and jazz bassist Chris Kuffner, Spektor recorded enough original songs to sell CDs at her shows. Dubbed *11:11*, the jazzy flair of Spektor's

**For the Record . . .**

Born in Moscow, Russia. *Education:* Attended State University of New York's Purchase College.

Self-released *11:11,* 2001; self-released *Songs,* 2002; released *Soviet Kitsch,* Shoplifter, 2003; signed with Sire Records, reissued *Soviet Kitsch,* 2004, released *Begin to Hope,* 2006.

Addresses: *Record company*—Sire Records, 3300 Warner Blvd., Burbank, CA 91505. *Website*—Regina Spektor Official Website: http://www.reginaspektor.com.

songs often took on unusual tempo changes with intriguing storytelling-style lyrics. Befriending other local musicians gigging New York's Lower East Side, Spektor was soon considered part of the extended family of the "anti-folk" scene. Just before Christmas that year, Joe Mendelson, co-owner of the venue The Living Room, offered Spektor use of his studio for one day. Mendelson sort of challenged Spektor to see how many songs she could write and record in one day. On Christmas Day 2001, Spektor recorded an impressive collection of tracks that Mendelson insisted people hear. In the new year, Spektor packaged the Christmas tracks as the album *Songs* and sold copies at her shows.

"I don't have an over all sound," Spektor admitted to EMI Publishing. "I tend to think of each song as its own little world…. It's more fun that way because I never have to do the same thing over and over again." Catching more than a few of Spektor's performances were two industry insiders—Alan Bezozi (a drummer for groups They Might Be Giants and Freedy Johnston) and The Strokes' producer Gordon Raphael. Not really knowing that in 2001 The Strokes were one of the most popular rock bands in America, Spektor respected Raphael's knowledge and she set herself to work with him and Bezozi on her next album. Recording in New York and London, Spektor's new songs were filled out with guitars, bass, and cello. Released independently in 2003, *Soviet Kitsch* was Spektor's first album to spread outside of the New York scene.

"Twisted and misty-eyed all at once, Spektor uses big, pleading choruses and elegant pauses to drag the listener through the emotional ringer with her," *Devil in the Wood*'s Patrick Rapa wrote about *Soviet Kitsch.* The tales on *Soviet Kitsch* were often strange character stories with a dark sense of humor about subjects such as death, divorce, and cancer. "I try to write songs the way a short story writer writes story," Spektor told EMI. "I always thought, 'Why can't I write a song from the point of view of a man or a criminal or an old woman?' Obviously some of it comes from personal things, but it's so much more fun when a concept or idea pops into my head and then I pull on it and out comes this thing that I never expected." The Strokes' frontman Julian Casablancas liked *Soviet Kitsch* so much he asked Spektor to go on tour with his band. Since she wasn't signed to a record label, she had to pay her own way across the United States for The Strokes' sold-out tour. Spektor's tight relationship with The Strokes—she even sang on the rock band's B-side "Post Modern Girls & Old Fashioned Men"—threw Spektor into the spotlight in 2003. The following year, she signed a deal with Sire Records who re-released *Soviet Kitsch.*

After more touring, including an opening slot for rock bands Kings of Leon, in the summer of 2005, Spektor sat herself down to record her first official, record-label-budget album. Spektor spent two months recording her new album at New York Noise Studios with producer David Kahne (Paul McCartney); that was by far, the most time she had ever spent recording. The bigger deadline had a huge impact on the new songs. "I was able to be more playful because it was such a no-pressure atmosphere," Spektor told *Rolling Stone*'s Brian Orloff. "It was just the two of us, me and David, and we were just working like on an art project. It was the first time when I really let go." In the studio, for the first time really, she was able to experiment with her voice and different range of instrumentation that included electronic beats and drums.

With more oomph and other instrumentation, including guitar (The Stroke's Nick Valensi added guitar to the track "Better"), Spektor's new album, dubbed *Begin to Hope,* was glossier and fuller sounding than anything she had recorded in the past. Some songs included trickling electronic drum beats and smoothed-out, pop-friendly tracks, and while Spektor's lyrics were still a bit strange, with *Begin to Hope* she really began to write about herself instead of characters. Almost a year after recording it, in June of 2006, Sire issued *Begin to Hope* to rave reviews. "Less miserable than Fiona Apple, less wacky than Nellie McKay and less hippiesh than Tori Amos, Spektor shows off her gorgeous, fluttery voice, her burgeoning writing chops and her God-given quirks …," wrote *Rolling Stone*'s Jenny Eliscu. Sire also issued the CD/DVD *Mary Ann Meets the Gravediggers and Other Short Stories,* a collection of songs from her first three independent albums.

Brian Garrity of *Billboard* described Spektor's extraordinary style as "…a girlish piano-pop naiveté crossed with an East Village rock sensibility." For Spektor, she's found the perfect middle for her passion. "I always wanted to play classical recitals and concerts, and go from place to place and learn new programs and practice new things and play hours and hours of piano for people," she told EMI. "And now I do that, except instead of playing the compositions of Chopin and Mozart, I play my own."

## Selected discography

*11:11,* self-released, 2001.
*Songs,* self-released, 2002.
*Soviet Kitsch,* Shoplifter, 2003; reissued, Sire, 2004.
*Mary Ann Meets the Gravediggers and Other Short Stories,* Sire, 2006.
*Begin to Hope,* Sire, 2006.

## Sources

### Periodicals

*Billboard,* September 4, 2004, p. 31.
*Blender,* December 2004.
*Devil in the Woods,* June 2005.
*New York,* June 12, 2006.
*Rolling Stone,* March 15, 2006; June 12, 2006.

### Online

"Regina Spektor," Big Hassle Media, http://www.bighassle. com/publicity/a_regina_spektor.html (November 10, 2006).
"Regina Spektor," EMI Music Publishing, http://www. emimusicpub.com (November 10, 2006).

*—Shannon McCarthy*

# Styx

## Rock group

Styx, one of the most successful "arena rock" groups of all time, was born on the South Side of Chicago in the late 1960s. Tradewinds, a trio formed by neighbors Dennis DeYoung and Chuck and John Panozzo, offered a distinctive blend of driving rock 'n' roll rhythms with classical-influenced melodic themes. The group, which formed while DeYoung and the twin Panozzo brothers were in high school, was transformed into TW4 with the addition of guitarist John Curulewski, a fellow student at Chicago State University. In 1970 James "JY" Young, a guitarist with a rival band, joined the group. Not long thereafter the group cut a demo tape that eventually came to the attention of Wooden Nickel Records, a regional label and subsidiary of RCA, with whom TW4 signed a recording contract in 1972; label executives insisted, however, that the group change its name. The band members eventually settled on Styx, mostly because it was the only one of the hundreds of names they'd considered that no one in the group actively hated.

For their debut album, Wooden Nickel recommended the group focus on material written by other people, not their own compositions. Much to Wooden Nickel's surprise, however, the only song from that first album to hit the top 100 was "Best Thing," a track cowritten by Young and DeYoung. Despite this success, the group's record deal didn't enable its members to focus entirely on their music. To make ends meet they still had to hold their regular jobs—DeYoung and Chuck Panozzo taught music and art in the Chicago public schools, while Young drove a cab. They recorded three more albums for Wooden Nickel—*Styx II, The Serpent Is Rising,* and *Man of Miracles*— but grew increasingly discouraged by the label's apparent inability to promote their work. When *Man of Miracles* was released in 1974, Styx was on the verge of disbanding. About that time, however, "Lady," a single from *Styx II,* suddenly began to get intensive radio play in the greater Chicago area and soon was a hit. Before long the rest of the nation caught on, and both the single—written by DeYoung about his wife, Suzanne—and the album became big hits, the single climbing to number six on the *Billboard* top 40.

Seizing the moment, Styx went in search of a new label. It wasn't difficult to find a taker, given the success of "Lady," and in 1975 the group was signed by A&M Records. The band's first self-produced album, *Equinox,* was released that same year. It revealed a maturation and refinement of the group's style, best illustrated by "Suite Madame Blue," DeYoung's allegory for the decline of the United States. It also launched the band as social commentators, a role they would relish for years to come.

Only a week before Styx was to begin its tour to support *Equinox,* guitarist John Curulewski left the band to spend more time with his family. Desperate for a guitarist to replace him, the band tracked down Tommy Shaw, a performer recommended by the group's road manager. He proved to be an excellent addition, his bluesy style nicely complementing Young's screaming guitar licks. More important, the group found that Shaw's songwriting style bridged the divide between DeYoung's mainstream pop/rock sound and Young's metallic leanings. The year after *Equinox,* Styx released *Crystal Ball,* which featured the swinging rock single "Mademoiselle." The group's road tours in support of *Equinox* and *Crystal Ball* totaled nearly 400 concert dates; these helped the band to further refine their "arena rock" style.

With the 1977 release of *The Grand Illusion,* Styx acquired genuine "superstar" status. "Come Sail Away," a single from the album, quickly climbed the charts, helping take *The Grand Illusion* platinum. Next up was *Pieces of Eight,* released in 1978. This album also quickly went platinum, its sales fueled by the popularity of its "Renegade" and "Blue Collar Man" tracks. The group's third platinum album in a row was *Cornerstone,* which was something of a departure for Styx, featuring a mellower sound. Its crowning glory was the single "Babe," a classic ballad that quickly climbed the charts. Other hot singles from *Cornerstone* included "Borrowed Time" and "Why Me." To promote all three albums, the band toured virtually nonstop and was shown in a 1979 poll to be the hottest concert ticket among teenagers between the ages of 13 and 19.

Early in 1981 Styx kicked off a 110-date North American tour to lay the groundwork for the April release of

together a complete story through songs, an elaborate stage act featuring scripted dialogue and multiple set and costume changes, and an eleven-minute film. It told the tale of a renegade's rebellion against totalitarian control by bringing rock 'n' roll to the people. The album and its elaborate touring show featured the techno-rock single "Mr. Roboto," and the trademark power ballad "Don't Let It End." To support the album, Styx took its spectacular stage show on tour.

In 1984, not long after the release of the group's double live album *Caught in the Act,* Styx members DeYoung and Shaw announced plans to leave the band to pursue solo projects. Although the album was well received by the public, the remaining members of the band decided it was time for a much-needed break. DeYoung and Shaw's departure provided the perfect excuse for a hiatus after more than a decade of constant touring. Young put it this way in comments included on the Don't Wait for Heroes website: "We came to a point where we had creatively exhausted ourselves. We needed a chance to refresh and reenergize, a chance to work with other people and explore new areas." Guitarist John Curulewski, who had left Styx in the mid-1970s, died tragically of an aneurysm in 1987.

A number of reunion plans failed during the late 1980s, but in 1990 four of Styx's five members did manage to get back together again. Prior obligations prevented Shaw from joining the group, so singer/guitarist Glen Burtnik was asked to take his place. The reunion album, *Edge of the Century,* featured the hit single "Show Me the Way," written by DeYoung. It climbed to number three on the charts, finding a ready audience in a country preoccupied with the standoff with Iraq in the Middle East. Styx toured in support of *Edge of the Century* the following year, playing to standing-room-only crowds across the country. The tour was one of the most successful of 1991.

Another hiatus followed, as individual group members went their separate ways. DeYoung played Pontius Pilate in the national touring company production of *Jesus Christ Superstar.* Young formed his own group, called simply the James Young Group, which included some of Chicago's best rock musicians. Styx members reunited briefly in the studio to record "Lady" for A&M Records' Styx compilation album *Greatest Hits: Volume 1.* This brief get-together not surprisingly planted the seeds for yet another tour in 1996. Drummer John Panozzo, who had struggled for some years with alcoholism and was unable to join the tour, died in July of 1996.

Styx members continued to pursue their individual solo careers when they weren't on the road with the band. Bassist Chuck Panozzo, diagnosed with HIV in 1990 and successfully fighting full-blown AIDS since the late 1990s, participated now and then in appearances with

*Paradise Theatre,* which spent three weeks at number one on the rock album charts. The album featured two hit singles in "The Best of Times" and "Too Much Time on My Hands," which helped push the album to platinum status, making Styx the first rock 'n' roll group in history to have four consecutive albums go platinum. The band followed up this success with an offbeat concept album entitled *Kilroy Was Here.* By far the group's most theatrical venture, *Kilroy Was Here* wove

the group but devoted most of his time to other projects. In July of 2001 he publicly disclosed his homosexuality, telling *USA Today,* "It's a weight off my soul.".

The group's appearances continued into the new millennium with a two-month tour of U.S. amphitheaters, teamed with the group REO Speedwagon, and a 50-date tour in 2002, also with REO Speedwagon. By 2002 the band's roster included Tommy Shaw (guitar and vocals), James "JY" Young (guitar and vocals), Glenn Burtnick (bass), Lawrence Gowan (keyboards and vocals), and Todd Sucherman (drums). Panozzo played with them occasionally during this period. The band's tours were successful, almost filling the 13,000- to 18,000-seat arenas where they played. Young told Tamara Conniff in *Hollywood Reporter,* "We are climbing Everest for a second time." Conniff noted that although "music snobs turn up their noses at arena rock, fans nationwide are crowding to see Styx." She added, "Live rock music at its best is a ritual, a communal experience. It is an art Styx has mastered."

# Selected discography

*Styx,* Wooden Nickel, 1972.
*Styx II,* Wooden Nickel, 1973.
*Equinox,* A&M, 1975.
*Crystal Ball,* A&M, 1976.
*The Grand Illusion,* A&M, 1977.
*Pieces of Eight,* A&M, 1978.
*Cornerstone,* A&M, 1979.
*Paradise Theatre,* A&M, 1981.
*Kilroy Was Here,* A&M, 1983.
*Edge of the Century,* A&M, 1990.
(Contributor) *Greatest Hits, Volume 1,*A&M, 1995.

(Contributor) *Greatest Hits, Volume 2,* A&M, 1996.
*Return to Paradise,*BMG/Sanctuary, 1997.
*Brave New World,* BMG/Sanctuary, 1999.
*Styxworld,* BMG/Sanctuary, 2001.
*Cyclorama,* BMG/Sanctuary, 2003.
*Big Bang Theory,* BMG/Sanctuary, 2005.

# Sources

### Periodicals

*Amusement Business,* March 13, 2000, p. 5; January 14, 2002, p. 13.
*Daily Variety,* October 3, 2005, p. 9.
*Guitar Player,* July 1981.
*Hollywood Reporter,* June 26, 2003, p. 2.
*USA Today,* July 27, 2001; February 18, 2002.

### Online

"Biography," Glen Burtnik, http://64.91.227.187/glenburtnik/bio.html (February 20, 2002).
"Biography," Lawrence Gowan, http://www.gowan.org/biography.htm (February 20, 2002).
"John Panozzo Press Release," Styx Web Team, http://www.tiac.net/users/Styx/panozzo-press-release.html (February 20, 2002).
"Official Styx Press Package for 1996 Return to Paradise Tour," Styx Web Team, http://www.tiac.net/users/kat/Styx/press-package-96.html (February 20, 2002).
"Styx History," Don't Wait for Heroes: Equal Time for Dennis DeYoung Since 1977, http://www.styxnet.com/deyoung/frontpage.html (April 29, 2002).
Styx Official Website, http://www.styxworld.com/History.cfm (February 20, 2002).

—*Don Amerman and Kelly Winters*

# Sugarhill Gang

## Rap group

In 1979, disco music had reached its peak. Popular music was composed of a mix of performers from singer Rod Stewart to the band the Who to the duo of Peaches and Herb. Their styles were different, but predictable. A backlash against the popularity of disco was brewing and as radio listeners everywhere were turning on the station to hear another Olivia Newton-John song, something very new traveled across the airwaves. It was the sound of men talking fast and rhyming in time to the hit disco song "Good Times" by the successful group Chic. It was the introduction of hip-hop to the American public, and it was done by a group of New Jersey boys under the moniker of the Sugarhill Gang.

The song heard on the radio in 1979 was "Rapper's Delight." It was fifteen minutes long and brought hip-hop and the culture of rap to the forefront of attention. The Sugarhill Gang was composed of Guy O'Brien, Michael Wright, and Henry Jackson who went by their rap names, Master Gee, Wonder Mike, and Big Bank Hank, respectively. The story of their formation and the release and success of "Rapper's Delight" is rife with speculation and intrigue. In some ways it's a rags to riches story, but it's also exemplary of how a genre can be capitalized upon without honoring its true innovators. Brolin Winning wrote about "Rapper's Delight" for *Remix* magazine, "It wasn't the lyrical skills that carried it, nor the revamped disco groove; it was the whole package—a classic example of the sum being greater than its parts."

The Sugarhill Gang was the brainchild of Sylvia Robinson. She and her husband, Joe Robinson, owned a small record label called Sugar Hill Records in Englewood, New Jersey. Sylvia had been a part of the record business since the early 1950s—first as a teenage singer, then as part of the duo Mickey and Sylvia, and then later with her own 1973 hit song "Pillow Talk." During that time she also worked with her husband at their record company All Platinum Records. All Platinum went bankrupt in the late 1970s, and not long afterwards they formed Sugar Hill Records.

### Putting the Act Together

Robinson is said to have come across hip-hop at a party in New York. Impressed by the sound and the audience reaction she decided to put together a rap record. How she ended up with O'Brien, Wright, and Jackson depends on what story you read and who is telling it. As with many origin stories, the facts seem to have been conflated and confused. Henry Jackson may have been discovered at the pizza joint where he worked, he may have been rapping at a party where Sylvia Robinson first heard him, or he may have been a friend of Joey Robinson, Sylvia's son, who they drove by and picked up to fill in for an original pick who never showed up to the studio. One story states that she drove with her son to audition Jackson. As they were sitting in their car parked on the street Jackson rapped over a song they had on a tape player in their car. O'Brien and Wright happened to walk by and they showed off their skills. Robinson picked all three to be the members of the group.

However the group was formed, O'Brien, Jackson, and Wright eventually ended up in the studio to record their first song. During recording, Robinson is said to have pointed at the rappers to cue them when to start rapping. The house band played key samples of the disco group Chic's hit song "Good Times," and "Rapper's Delight" was made. It was 15 minutes long and nothing like it had ever been heard on broadcast radio before. Andrew Drever of the *Age* wrote, "'Rapper's Delight' was the first track to crash through the hostile barrier of commercial radio—radio saw rap as a cheap fad at that time—and into mainstream consciousness." According to Steven Daly of *Vanity Fair,* the record was made on a $750 budget. Robinson explained to Eddie Drury of *X-Press Online,* "I thought it would be big in the northeast area of the United States, but three months after we even held the audition, we're performing in Germany."

The first station to play "Rapper's Delight" was WESL in St. Louis. When all was said and done the single ended up selling more than eight million copies. At the peak of its popularity, 50,000 copies of the song were selling each day. "Rapper's Delight" hit number four on Billboard's R&B charts and made it to number 36 on Billboard's popular music charts. One of the amazing aspects of the song's popularity is that radio stations would play the 15-minute song. As Robinson explained to Drury, "The radio stations would play the 15 minute version, in an era when songs were five minutes long. They could have cut it off, they could have faded it, they could have gone to commercial or whatever but they kept playing it and people would call up and say 'play it again,' and they would play it back to back. So you'd have 30 minutes of uninterrupted rap."

### They'll Always Be the First

The Sugarhill Gang went on to record two more records with Sugar Hill before they disbanded in 1985. Their single "8th Wonder" made it to the number 15 spot on the R&B charts, while their next single reached number 13. The three original members went their separate ways, reportedly working odd jobs here and there outside the music business. In 1990, Joey Robinson, Jr., reformed the group, taking on the name of Master Gee and acting as manager. Since then the group has been touring. They released a children's record in 1999 called *Jump On It!* and donated some of the proceeds to the Boys and Girls Club of America. O'Brien, while not performing with the group, is involved in the music industry again. In 2005, he teamed up with his son Guy O'Brien, Jr., and Wright forming a group called M.G. Squad and recording an album titled *Better Than Ever.*

The Sugarhill Gang will always be known as the first rap group to reach international fame. They brought rap and hip-hop culture to the masses and helped launch a genre that continued to grow and change within its boundaries while also influencing popular music. The group stays busy touring, which takes them across the United States and as far as Australia. Robinson explained to Drever that the time seemed right to reunite when they did, "In the late-'80s we weren't getting much respect from the hip-hop community because of the style of rap that was out at the time. We were party, good-time rap, but everything became much more gangster.... Now things have come full circle. Rap is more fun again … bragging about how many girls they had, what clothes they got, just whimsical, foolish things, fun things." There was also a desire by many to experience what a Sugarhill Gang show was like, a desire by modern audiences to revisit the roots of rap.

## Selected discography

*Rapper's Delight: Best of Sugarhill Gang,* Sugar Hill Records, 1980.
*The Sugarhill Gang,* Sugar Hill Records, 1980.
*8th Wonder,* Sugar Hill Records, 1982.
*Jump On It!,* Rhino Records, 1999.
*Rapper's Delight,* Castle Records, 2002.

## Sources

### Periodicals

*Independent* (London), April 29, 2003.
*Jet,* January 7, 2002.
*Vanity Fair,* November 2005.

### Online

"Father and Sons of Rap," NorthJersey.com, http://www.northjersey.com/page.php?qstr=eXJpcnk3ZjczN2Y3dnFlZUVFeXk2MzgmZmdiZWw3Zjd2cWVIRUV5eTY3MTI1MTAmeXJpcnk3ZjcxN2Y3dnFlZUVFeXk5 (November 4, 2006).
"Sugarhill Gang," *Remix,* http://remixmag.com/mag/remix_sugarhill_gang/ (November 4, 2006).
"Sugarhill Gang," *X-Press Online,* http://www.xpressmag.com.au/archives/000189.html (November 4, 2006).
"They Don't Stop," *Age* (Australia), http://www.theage.com.au/articles/2004/03/26/1079939824819.html (November 4, 2006).

—*Eve Hermann*

# Billy Swan

Singer, songwriter, guitarist

© Henry Diltz/CORBIS

**B**est-known for the 1974 number one hit "I Can Help," soft-spoken Billy Swan has struggled and succeeded through various musical eras, somehow keeping the true roots feel in his best records. A fine songwriter, guitarist, producer, part-time Jerry Lee Lewis-styled piano pumper, and professional jack-of-all-trades, he is simultaneously a living link to the first great era of rock 'n' roll and one of its most credible foot soldiers.

### Bill Black Gave Him His Start

Growing up in Cape Giradeau, Missouri, during the 1950s, Billy Swan initially admired cowboy movie hero Gene Autry. Through his sister's record collection, he was exposed to country great Hank Williams and grew to love the music of Lefty Frizzell, Faron Young, Webb Pierce, and Johnnie & Jack, along with such established pop stars such as Perry Como and Vaughan Monroe. However, it was rock 'n' roll that really turned him on.

Swan began playing guitar when he was 14 years old, and occasionally attempted Jerry Lee Lewis-style piano pumping on his aunt's piano. By the time he was 16, the youngster had added the drums to his repertoire and began gigging with a local band, playing cover versions of tunes by Jimmy Reed, Ray Charles, and Jerry Lee Lewis. Not long after, local singer Dennis Turner provided an introduction to Mirt Mirley & The Rhythm Steppers, the band that facilitated a turning point in Swan's life.

When Mirley and his band went to Memphis to record for Bill Black, they asked Swan to come along. They recorded his single "Lover Please" on Louis Records, though that first version sank without a trace; but Bill Black subsequently put out another version by Swan's friend Dennis Turner. When that record started getting airplay in St. Louis, Mercury Records' producer Shelby Singleton recorded a version with R&B pioneer Clyde McPhatter in 1962. The result was a true pop classic, and the final Top Ten pop hit of McPhatter's career.

Swan, a fan of McPhatter's, recalled just where he was when he first heard his song over the radio. "It was about 12:30 at night and it was snowing in this small town in Missouri," he said in an interview. "When I [heard it], I was so happy that I just started spinning the car around in the snow–;there was nobody out at that time in the morning. I never will forget that."

### Produced "Polk Salad Annie"

Just 19 years old, Swan continued to play gigs with the Rhythm Steppers and another group called the Four Notes. Eventually he moved to Memphis with the idea of writing full-time for Bill Black's publishing company. With no job or further hit songs on the way, the young-

## For the Record . . .

Born William Lance Swan on May 12, 1942, in Cape Giradeau, MO; son of Jasper Ray and Mary Johnson Swan; married Marlu (deceased); children: two girls, Planet and Sierra.

Singer, songwriter, producer, 1959-; played piano and guitar for Mirt Mirley and the Rhythm Steppers, 1959-62; wrote "Lover Please," which became a hit by Clyde McPhatter, 1962; produced Tony Joe White's hit "Polk Salad Annie," 1969; toured with Kris Kristofferson's band, 1971-87; wrote the number one pop and country hit "I Can Help," 1974; formed Black Tie with former Eagle Randy Meisner, 1986; assistant musical director of film *Great Balls of Fire,* 1989; appeared in David Lynch's film *Wild at Heart,* 1990, toured Europe with The Billy Swan Band, 1993-95; recorded as Meisner and Charlie Rich Jr., 2001; has recorded for Monument, A&M, Epic, Mercury, Bench, Varese, and 706 Records.

Awards: Inducted into Rockabilly Hall of Fame, 1999.

Addresses: *Record company*—Collectors; Choice Music, P.O. Box 838, Itasca, IL 60143-0838, phone: 1-800-923-1122, website - http://www.ccmusic.com, http://www.wma.com. *Booking*—Mars Talent Agency, 27 L Ambiance Dt., Bardonia, NY 10954, phone: 561-743-1990, fax: 561-743-1993, website: http://www.marstalent.com, http://www.wma.com. *Website*—Official Billy Swan Website: http://www.billyswan.com.

ster struggled. Fortunately, a chance conversation with Travis Smith, Elvis Presley's uncle and the gatekeeper at Graceland, resulted in Swan renting a room with Smith's family. For a time the aspiring singer-songwriter hung out with Presley's crowd when the rock king rented out movie theaters, skating rinks, or amusement parks.

Drifting, Swan returned to Missouri, before moving to Nashville in August of 1963. Doing whatever he could to keep afloat until he got a break, Swan's career began in earnest with a job at the CBS studio in Nashville, working for producer Fred Foster. "I used to hang out there a lot and play ping-pong with all the musicians," he recalled. "So they offered me this job that they called an engineer's assistant, but basically I would clean up between sessions. I would erase tape and go get food for the engineers."

This seemingly menial position led to a chance to produce a hit recording by swamp blues rocker Tony Jo White. Swan's technique with White was simple: he let the artist use the wah-wah peddle on his funky blues guitar fills. The result was "Polk Salad Annie," which hit number eight on the pop charts in 1969. Subsequently, Swan produced three albums for White, although none yielded any further hit singles.

Finding work as a producer meant that Swan could leave his job as an engineer's assistant. He plugged along during the early 1970s writing songs and working in bands headed up by friend Kris Kristofferson and by Billy Joe Shaver and Kinky Friedman. In 1975 the gift of a compact RMI organ provided the impetus for his greatest commercial achievement. Living in an apartment complex in Nashville and awaiting the birth of his first child, he wrote "I Can Help." "I wrote it in this duplex my wife and I were living in," Swan remembered. "It was one of those songs that came real fast. I wrote the three verses first and I said, Well, I need something to go between the second and third verse. So, I wrote that little bridge, When I go to sleep at night."

Released on Monument, "I Can Help," with its swampy organ and twangy rockabilly guitar fills, became a number one pop and country hit. Swan formed his own band, toured Europe, and hosted an edition of NBC's late night music series *The Midnight Special.* The tune inspired dozens of cover versions, none more important to Swan than those by two of his boyhood heroes, Elvis Presley and Jerry Lee Lewis.

Due to his excessive drinking, Swan lost the focus on his career and on a proper follow up to "I Can Help." One single, "Everything's the Same (Ain't Nothing Changed)," gained favor with country programmers and rose to number 17 on the charts. Although he never enjoyed another major pop music success, Swan didn't really fit the model for a true one-hit wonder. After issuing strong albums on Monument and A&M, he found a niche at Epic Records, where he racked up five Top 40 country hits, including "Do I Have to Draw a Picture," "I'm Into Loving You," and "Stuck Right in the Middle of Your Love." His commercial luck ran out after 1983, although he continued to record without much success for Epic and Mercury before being relegated to independent label status.

### Meisner, Swan & Rich

During the mid-1980s Swan dabbled in films. He worked closely with producer T-Bone Burnett on the soundtrack for the Jerry Lee Lewis bio-pic *Great Balls of Fire!,* and handled the music and tackled a small role in David Lynch's film *Wild at Heart.* Far more interesting for his musical career, however, his willingness to jam resulted in a band affiliation with former Eagle Randy Meisner and Jimmy Griffin from Bread. They went on the road as Black Tie, with Alan Rich later stepping in when Griffin returned to Nashville. Black Tie produced one album. The nucleus of a later edition of the band recorded another album as Meisner, Swan & Rich during the early 1990s, but it wasn't released until 2001. The group's work together turned out a smart fusion of gospel, rock, country and blues that just didn't benefit from enough distribution or promotion to encourage more than a cult following.

The latter part of Swan's career found him returning to his roots for self-produced albums on Audium and 706 Records. An album titled *SUNatra*—Frank Sinatra classics redone in the style of 1950s Sun Recordings—was shopped around to no avail. On the bright side, he continues to do gigs when offered the right opportunity. Moreover, he takes great pride in the accomplishments of his two music-minded daughters, Planet and Sierra. Asked about his daughter Sierra, who now records for the Interscope label, Swan replied, "She gives me advice," he laughed. "I can't tell her much of anything. She's got her own little peers in her age group that she works with and they are all very hip. Hipper than I am at this time of my life. You kind of feel like some things have passed you by, and then you don't, because music, I've always felt, is like gambling. I could probably write a great song when I'm 70 or write a great book or paint a great picture. The arts are that way. You just never know."

## Selected discography

### Singles

"I Can Help," Monument, 1974.
"Everything's the Same (Ain't Nothing Changed)," Monument, 1975.
"I'm Her Fool," Monument, 1975.
"Hello! Remember Me," A&M, 1978.
"Do I Have to Draw a Picture," Epic, 1981.
"I'm Into Loving You," Epic, 1981.
"Stuck Right in the Middle of Your Love," Epic, 1982.
"With Their Kind of Money and Our Kind of Love," Epic, 1982.
"Rainbows and Butterflies," Epic, 1983.
"Your Picture Still Loves Me (And I Still Love You)," Epic, 1983.

### Albums

*Billy Swan,* Monument, 1975.
*I Can Help,* Monument 1975.
*Rock 'n' Roll Moon,* Monument, 1976.
*Billy Swan,* CBS, 1977.
*Four,* Monument, 1977.
*You're Ok I m Ok,* A&M, 1978.
*I'm in to You,* Epic, 1981.
*When the Night Falls,* (w/ Black Tie) Bench, 1990.
*Bop to Be,* Carlton, 1995.
*Billy Swan Live,* Carlton/706 Records, 2000.
*I Can Help / Rock 'n' Roll Moon,* See For Miles, 1997.
*Billy Swan / Four,* See For Miles, 1997.
*Golden Classics* Collectables, 1997.
*Like Elvis Used to Do* Castle/706 Records, 1998; reissued, Audium/Koch, 2000.
*I Used To Be James Dean,* 706 Records, 1998.
*The Best of Billy Swan,* Epic/Legacy, 1998.
*Meisner, Swan & Rich,* Varese, 2001; reissued, Rev-Ola, 2002.
*Greatest Hits,* Columbia, 2005.

## Sources

### Books

Bronson, Fred, *The Billboard Book of Number One Hits,* Billboard, 1997.
Jancik, Wayne, *The Billboard Book of One-Hit Wonders,* Billboard, 1998.
McCloud, Barry, *Definitive Country—The Ultimate Encyclopedia of Country Music and Its Makers,* Perigree, 1995.
Roland, Tom, *The Billboard Book of Number One Country Hits,* Billboard, 1991.
Stambler, Irwin, & Grelun Landon, *Country Music—the Encyclopedia,* St. Martin's Griffin, 1997.

### Online

"Billy Swan," *All Music Guide,* http://www.allmusic.com (November 13, 2006).
"Billy Swan," *Rockabilly Hall of Fame,* http://www.rockabillyhall.com/SwanBilly1.html. (November 13, 2006).
"Black Tie," *All Music Guide,* http://www.allmusic.com (November 14, 2006).
"Meisner, Swan & Rich," *All Music Guide,* http://www.allmusic.com (November 14, 2006).
Additional information for this profile was drawn from a 2004 interview with Billy Swan.

—*Ken Burke*

# Ben Taylor

**Singer, songwriter**

As the son of singer-songwriters Carly Simon and James Taylor, singer Ben Taylor seemed destined for a musical career. His parents divorced when he was three, and his mother raised him. Taylor suffered from a kidney condition at birth, and when he was three he underwent surgery to correct it. He was unable to fit in at a series of public and private schools, so he was eventually homeschooled by tutors. Simon told Steve Dougherty and Anne Driscoll in *People,* "It was the kind of education that, in part, made Ben who he is, which is tripped out." Taylor commented on the Iris Records website that his education was "phenomenal in the most absurd ways. Instead of going to high school, I got independent credit for doing correspondence work. So I was always on a trip, working on the Colorado River or in the Grand Canyon or on a farm in New Mexico, and writing essays about what I'd learned. It was a pretty cool way to get an education." As a teenager, Taylor trekked through Asian and American wilderness areas, activities he had enjoyed with his father. Simon commented, "James did all sorts of outdoor activity with him, which I wasn't keen on. I get cold feet. I mean literally. I have poor circulation."

AP Images

Taylor's education was also musical, as he toured with his father, watching him perform or noting how, after his father spent a great deal of time alone, he reappeared with new songs. He also watched and listened to his mother, who wrote songs more openly, playing her rough drafts and asking for his opinion. He also had musical uncles and aunts, who frequently came to the house to play music.

### Wasting His Time

Despite his family background and the fact that he was, as Simon told Dougherty, "absurdly musical," Taylor did not want to pursue a career in music. He was intimidated by his parents' success and worried that he would either be seen as following in their wake, or as not measuring up to their heritage. He wanted to break away and have his own identity separate from that of his parents, so that he would not be perceived simply as copying their careers. He considered becoming an organic farmer, and worked as a wilderness guide and fitness instructor. However, in 1996, a family friend, Mike Nichols, told him he was wasting his life if he didn't make use of his musical gifts. In 1997, inspired by Nichols's pep talk, Taylor spent ten days in the Caribbean working on songs, enough time to realize that he did have talent he could work with. However, he was not satisfied with his work. As he noted on the Iris Records website, "I was trying to make something totally different from anything a Taylor had recorded before. Ultimately, that meant I was not putting my best foot forward, and we lost the focus we should have kept on the songs themselves. Certainly, I don't blame anyone but myself for that."

He continued to work, however, and Taylor first came to the attention of listeners in 1995 when his version of the Beatles' "I Will" appeared on the sound track of *Bye, Bye Love.* Although Taylor said he was not interested in pursuing a musical career, the song debuted at No. 39.

In 2000 Taylor joined his mother to sing in a commercial for a new perfume by designer Ralph Lauren. They sang a version of the Rodgers and Hart classic tune "My Romance."

### "I Couldn't Be Happier"

In 2003 Taylor released a debut CD, *Famous Among the Barns.* Critics noted that his vocal style was very similar to that of his father, and Taylor told Dougherty and Driscoll, "I couldn't be happier with the comparison. I learned to play guitar by learning my dad's songs. I don't think anybody is going to say I sound like Stevie Wonder." His mother commented, "He's not a copycat. James has been a very strong and wonderful influence on his life. He's inherited a great many of the wonderful aspects of his father."

Taylor followed *Famous Among the Barns* with *Another Run Around the Sun* in 2005. On this album, he was more comfortable with his musical and vocal resemblance to his father. On the Iris Records website he wrote, "This album is a natural progression of who I am and what I've been through. I wanted to make a record that I could tour by myself if I had to—something I could live with night after night." He added that the album is "honest." "There wasn't a whole lot of me in some of my earlier recordings, but this one is entirely me. It's the most self-accepting thing I've ever done." Taylor performed in support of the album and appeared on a variety of television and radio venues, including *The Today Show, The Tonight Show, The CBS Morning Show, Last Call With Carson Daly,* and *Howard Stern.* He also appeared at the Christmas at Rockefeller Center show, the Fox network's Teen Choice Awards and the Bravo network's Songwriters Hall of Fame awards. He also branched out into acting, with a recurring role as Cal, a struggling singer/songwriter, on the NBC show *American Dreams.*

Taylor, who is vegan, believes in promoting a healthy lifestyle and makes sure he balances his recording and performing schedule with regular exercise. He told the *People* reviewers, "When my body is limber and strong, I feel more confident about everything. Kung fu, kickboxing, bicycling, running up mountains—whatever I can find. I love endorphins!"

## Selected discography

*Famous Among the Barns,* Iris Records, 2003.
(With the Ben Taylor Band) "Day After Day" (single), 2004.
(With the Ben Taylor Band) *The Ben Taylor Band* (EP), 2004.
*Nothing I Can Do* (EP), 2005.
*Another Run Around the Sun,* Independente, 2006.

# Sources

## Periodicals

*Adweek Midwest Edition,* January 3, 2000, p. 3.
*Billboard,* April 29, 1995, p. 106.
*Newsweek,* December 14, 1998, p. 100.
*People,* March 10, 2003, p. 105.
*Vogue,* November, 2002, p. 321.

## Online

"Ben Taylor Bio," Iris Records Website, http://www.irisrecords.com (November 6, 2006).

*—Kelly Winters*

# Otis Taylor

Singer, songwriter, guitarist, banjoist

© Jack Vartoogian/FrontRowPhotos

In a genre historically dominated by formulas and fixed musical elements, Otis Taylor has been a blues original. His hypnotic musical structures, with few changes of harmony, have drawn comparisons with blues great John Lee Hooker but resemble those of no other contemporary blues artist. Taylor has avoided using drums in his music, and his instrumentation features such novelties as a banjo or a cello. His storytelling lyrics hark back to the violent, wrenching, tragic world of early acoustic blues, discarding the sexy party themes favored by many musicians who make a living with the blues today. Asked by Mark Wolf of the *Rocky Mountain News* to categorize his music within a blues framework, Taylor responded that it was "Otis Taylor blues. Blues with attitude."

The son of a railroad worker, Otis Taylor was born in Chicago in 1948 to parents who had migrated from the South. Both his father, Otis Sr., and his mother, Sarah, were jazz fans, and "I Just Want to Make Love to You," by blues balladeer Etta James, was among his mother's favorite songs. The Taylors drifted into the orbit of drugs that surrounded the jazz world; Sarah Taylor served time on a heroin possession charge, and after Taylor's uncle was killed in a shooting, the family headed for Denver, where his grandmother offered them a place to live. Taylor himself, having observed these events in his early childhood, never used drugs at all, even though he came of age at the height of the 1960s counterculture.

Wanting to become a musician, Taylor asked his parents for a clarinet but was told there was no money to buy one. He found an outlet for his musical energy at the Denver Folklore Center, five blocks from his family's house. He had no money to pay for lessons, but he asked for them anyway. "Sometimes I'd have to wait a whole day to learn one song, or wait three or four days to get a song when they could get the right time to teach me," he recalled to Lynn Saxberg of the *Ottawa Citizen.* "I think I drove them crazy." The center, he told Mark Brown of the *Rocky Mountain News,* "was so important to my career I can't even express it." Taylor scraped together the money to buy a used ukulele, then a banjo. He liked the haunting and often bluesy Appalachian banjo music of white country musician Dock Boggs, but he later switched to guitar and harmonica because of the banjo's association with racist parodies of African American culture. He did not learn until much later that the banjo, whose history stretched back to Africa, had much deeper roots in black music than it had ever had among whites.

A natural performer from the start, Taylor was featured in a 1964 *Denver Post* photograph that showed him riding a unicycle while playing a banjo. That year he formed a group called the Butterscotch Fire Department Blues Band, which evolved into the Otis Taylor Blues Band. A tape made of Taylor at the Denver Folklore Center in 1967 revealed that much of the unique style that brought him to prominence three

## For the Record . . .

Born 1948 in Chicago, IL; son of Otis (a railroad worker) and Sarah Taylor; moved with family to Denver, CO; married; children: a daughter, Cassie. *Education:* Attended Manual High School, Denver, CO; took music classes at Denver Folklore Center.

Formed Butterscotch Fire Department Blues Band, Denver, CO, 1964; band changed name to Otis Taylor Blues Band; moved to England, mid-1960s; signed to Blue Horizon label but never released album; returned to Denver; performed with bands T&O Short Line, the 4 Nikators, and Zephyr, early 1970s; retired temporarily from performing, 1977; operated antiques business, Denver, 1977—; coached professional bicycle racing team; performed benefit concert, 1995; persuaded by musician and friend Kenny Passarelli to resume career; released album *Blue Eyed Monster,* on own Shoelace label, 1997; released *When Negroes Walked the Earth,* 1998; signed to Northern Blues label, 2001; released two albums on Northern Blues; signed to Telarc label, 2003; released albums *Truth Is Not Fiction, Double V, Below the Fold.*

Awards: Sundance Institute (Park City, UT), composition fellowship, 2000; W.C. Handy Award, Best New Artist, 2002.

Addresses: *Home*—Boulder, CO. Management office—Shoelace Music, P.O. Box 3564, Boulder, CO 80307.

an institution of Denver party music called the 4 Nikators in the early 1970s. By 1977, however, he had had enough. He retired from music and opened a small antiques business. Specializing in decorative arts and furniture of the early twentieth century, and later in slavery-era African-American memorabilia, he had an instinct for antiques, and made a good living searching out stock at junk shops and sales, and was still in business in the new millenium. Taylor was inspired to start an all-black bicycle racing team after reading a magazine story about black cyclist Major Marshall Taylor, who succeeded as a racer despite racial discrimination in the years around 1900. Taylor's team rose as high as fourth in national rankings in the mid-1980s.

Taylor kept in contact with Passarelli, who had toured with stars such as Elton John and who encouraged him to resume his own career. They joined forces with guitarist Eddie Turner in 1995 to play a benefit concert for a friend of Taylor's, and the response led the three to begin performing around the Denver area. In 1997, with Passarelli as producer, Taylor released the album *Blue Eyed Monster,* following it up a year later with *When Negroes Walked the Earth.* In 2000 Taylor worked on new material with the help of a composition fellowship from the Sundance Institute in Park City, Utah. He was signed to the Northern Blues label in 2001 and released *White African.* The following year *Respect the Dead* earned him a best new artist nod at the annual W.C. Handy Awards show, at the age of 53. In 2003 he was signed to the prestigious Telarc label.

Each Taylor album had a slightly different sound. His music might be predominantly electric or acoustic. He used various instruments—a trumpet, mandolin, a steel guitar, or a cello—as brushstrokes on his sonic canvas, and he returned to the banjo with a full understanding of its African roots on the 2005 album *Below the Fold.* Taylor's daughter Cassie joined his band as a bassist and vocalist. Harmonically, Taylor tended toward static repeated patterns that fit the ideas being expressed in a particular song. He used the phrase "trance blues" to describe his music. According to G. Brown of the *Denver Post,* it had "a drumless yet driving groove, reminiscent of John Lee Hooker's one-chord boogie."

The lyrics of Taylor's songs—all originals in a genre where most other singers tend to reinterpret older material—were on the dark side. "I'm not an angry person," Taylor observed to Buddy Blue of the *San Diego Union-Tribune.* "I'm just telling stories and you decide what you think about them. … I'm just good at writing about dark things." Many of Taylor's songs had an element of social criticism, touching on the difficult conditions faced by African Americans throughout their history. Sometimes, as in "Mama's Selling Heroin," he drew on his own family's experiences. "Kitchen Towel," from Taylor's 2003 release *Truth Is Not Fiction,* dealt with a quadruple suicide among a group of Native Americans. Some Taylor songs, such as "Rosa Rosa"

decades later was already in place. In the late 1960s it looked as though Taylor might benefit from the growth in electric blues music that accompanied the mass success of blues-based rock musicians like Jimi Hendrix and Eric Clapton. He headed for England, where he opened for the folk-rock band Fairport Convention and was signed to the Blue Horizon label. His first album was shelved due to creative differences, however, and he returned to Denver.

The Denver scene of the 1960s produced several successful musical careers in addition to Taylor's—rock fretless bassist Kenny Passarelli was Taylor's childhood friend, and Deep Purple guitarist Tommy Bolin was his classmate at the folklore center. Taylor and Bolin joined forces in a band called T&O Short Line. Taylor also played with the band Zephyr and with

(a tribute to civil rights pioneer Rosa Parks), boiled down their subjects to simple phrases that matched the hypnotic quality of his music. "Rosa Rosa," Taylor told Wolf, "just came to me. They all just come to me like dreams."

Hoping to build a new generation of blues musicians and listeners, Taylor has participated in a "Blues in the Schools" program operated by the Colorado Blues Society. His own career has been hampered somewhat by the preference of American blues promoters for upbeat music. "They want party blues," he observed to Curtis Ross of the *Tampa Tribune.* "They say, 'Why are you playing this dark stuff? It gets people upset. How can you play sad blues?' I thought 'blues' means sad. Blues guys have always played stuff like 'St. James Infirmary.' Something got twisted and it went in another direction." But Taylor has built a strong following in Europe; *Truth Is Not Fiction* earned an album-of-the-year nomination at France's national music awards. By the mid-2000s he had emerged as a critical favorite in the United States as well, and was continuing to write new music quickly, perhaps making up for time lost during the two-decade hiatus in his career.

## Selected discography

*Blue Eyed Monster,* Shoelace, 1997.
*When Negroes Walked the Earth,* Shoelace, 1998.
*White African,* Northern Blues, 2001.
*Respect the Dead,* Northern Blues, 2002.
*Truth Is Not Fiction,* Telarc, 2003.
*Double V,* Telarc, 2004.
*Below the Fold,* Telarc, 2005.

## Sources

### Periodicals

*Boston Globe,* August 7, 2004, p. C4.
*Denver Post,* September 20, 2002, p. FF02; March 6, 2003, p. F1.
*Guardian* (London, England), November 10,, 2005, p. 22; April 19, 2006, p. 36.
*Milwaukee Journal Sentinel,* November 5, 2004, p. A2.
*Ottawa Citizen* (Ottawa, Ontario, Canada), July 6, 1999, p. C7.
*Rocky Mountain News,* September 27, 2003, p. D5; April 26, 2004, p. D5; December 7, 2004, p. D10.
*San Diego Union-Tribune,* February 16, 2006, Night & Day section, p. 17.
*Tampa Tribune,* February 10, 2006, p. 20.

### Online

"Otis Taylor—Bio," Otis Taylor Official Website, http://www.otistaylor.com (November 13, 2006).

—*James M. Manheim*

# Justin Timberlake

**Singer**

AP Images

As a member of *NSYNC, one of the most successful groups in music history, Justin Timberlake has sold millions of albums worldwide and even more merchandise. When the singer broke free from the boy band to release a solo album, no one could have expected he would become one of the most popular pop artists in the world. Like Michael Jackson, one of his musical icons, Timberlake is one of the few former band boy members who was able to distance himself from his past and become just as successful on his own. Timberlake's R&B/pop style has earned him fans of all genres, and his songwriting, producing, and dancing continue to wow fans worldwide.

Born on January 31, 1981 in Memphis, Tennessee, Timberlake grew up with a strong relationship with his mother, Lynn, that continues through adulthood. His father, Randy Timberlake, played bass in a bluegrass band with Lynn's brother. After his parents divorced, both remarried and Timberlake was mostly raised by his mom and his stepfather Paul Harless. Timberlake began singing in public at the church where he grew up in Millington, Tennessee. Early on, it was clear that he had talent and soon his mother began to enter him into a string of talent shows. In 1991, Timberlake won the Preteen Mr. American Pageant and sang on the *Star Search* television competition show. After moving to Orlando, Florida, in 1993, Timberlake got a gig that parlayed his singing, dancing, and stage presence into a television job. For almost two years, Timberlake appeared on *The New Mickey Mouse Club* with other future mega stars including Britney Spears, Christina Aguilera, and *NSYNC's JC Chasez.

After his stint with the Disney company, Timberlake received a phone call that changed his life. In 1996, Timberlake joined his friend Chasez, Lance Bass, Joey Fatone, and Chris Kirkpatrick in the new singing group *NSYNC. In the tradition of the Jackson 5 and New Kids on the Block, *NSYNC wooed teenager girls' hearts and stormed the record charts with bubblegum pop songs. After touring in Germany and gaining a strong European following, in 1998 *NSYNC returned to the United States for the release of their self-titled debut album. The return of the boy band was triumphant with record sales of over 10 million.

Only 14 when he joined *NSYNC, Timberlake had little to do with the group's debut. For their follow-up, two years later, both Timberlake and Chasez received songwriting credits on *No Strings Attached*. The group's sophomore record sold a phenomenal one million copies on the first day and 2.4 million in just one week. The group's hit song "Bye Bye Bye" was nominated for a Grammy, giving the group credibility in the pop field. For *NSYNC's 2001 album, *Celebrity*, Timberlake wrote six songs, including the very successful single "Pop."

## For the Record . . .

Born Justin Randall Timberlake on January 31, 1981, in Memphis, TN; son of Lynn and Randall Timberlake.

Joined *NSYNC, 1996, group signed to RCA Records and released *NSYNC, 1998; group signed with Jive Records, released No Strings Attached, 2000; and Celebrity, 2001; signed to Jive as a solo artist, released Justified, 2002; won two Grammy Awards, 2004; released FutureSex/LoveSounds, 2006.

Awards: Grammy Awards, Best Pop Vocal Album for Justified, Best Male Pop Vocal Performance for "Cry Me a River," 2004.

Addresses: Record company—Jive, 2100 Colorado Ave., Santa Monica, CA 90404. Website—Justin Timberlake Official Website: http://www.justintimberlake.com.

## Solo Debut

In 2001, Timberlake and Spears ended their much-publicized romantic relationship that had begun years earlier. The songwriter used his experiences to write songs for a solo album. In November of 2002, Jive released Timberlake's explosive debut Justified. Certified triple platinum in the United States, People's Chuck Arnold called the album, "... soulful inspiration from Off the Wall-era Michael Jackson." With Justified, Timberlake matured into adulthood with a soundtrack to match. Citing artists Al Green, Prince, Stevie Wonder, and Michael Jackson as some of his biggest influences, Justified was emphatically more R&B, hip-hop, and blue-eyed soul than anything he had done with *NSYNC. "All I try to do is just to make R&B music. That's where I shine.... It's what I like to do," Timberlake told VH1.com. As detached from boy band material as possible, Justified crossed over musical genres. Producers like The Neptunes used live instrumentation and a hip-hop and rock mix to fuel singles "Like I Love You," "Rock Your Body," and "Senorita." A big name in hip-hop, producer/artist Timbaland created a field of sonic beats for the autobiographical "Cry Me a River," a song said to be about Timberlake's relationship with Spears.

After taking a 14-piece band on the road and spending the summer of 2003 touring with Christina Aguilera on the "Justified & Stripped" tour, Timberlake decided that it was time for him to take a break. "I was really burned-out on the music," he told W's Robert Haskell. "After that album, I just didn't have any creative juice left. It was my first solo record, and it was kind of like every idea I had about myself since I was a little boy." While the artist did some work, like hosting Saturday Night Live in October and singing the McDonald's jingle "I'm Lovin' It," Timberlake took time to enjoy the simple things in life. "That was amazing for me," Timberlake told Rolling Stone's Austin Scaggs about his almost two-year break. "Just the little things, like sitting home on the weekend or making a Sunday tee time. Play golf, then come back home, have a beer and call it a day."

Timberlake's only major appearances in 2004 included winning two Grammy Awards (Best Pop Vocal Album for Justified, and Best Male Pop Vocal Performance for "Cry Me a River"), and his infamous performance with Janet Jackson at February's Super Bowl XXXVIII. During the duo's performance, Timberlake went to remove part of Jackson's outfit. Unlike in rehearsal, during halftime, Jackson's breast was almost fully exposed. Dubbed a "wardrobe malfunction," Timberlake apologized for the accident, which Jackson later revealed was intentional.

## No Sophomore Slump

After appearing on the Snoop Dogg hit song "Signs"—a direction that clearly showed Timberlake's crossover appeal—the singer had surgery in May to remove nodules from his vocal chords. As the year came to a close, Timberlake began work on is sophomore album at producer Timbaland's studio in Virginia Beach, Virginia. Working more like a freestyle rapper than a former boy band singer, Timberlake would often free-form his lyrics and melodies in the studio, taking musical chances at every turn. "I knew that I needed something new," he told Scaggs. "I wanted to take more of a chance—experiment."

FutureSex/LoveSounds hit shelves in September of 2006. With a distinctly sexier and brasher sound, the album gained comparisons to works by Prince and Michael Jackson. For his new record, Timberlake's songs were less biographical. The album's first single, "SexyBack" (with Timbaland beats and vocals), showed a daring side to the star. "I don't really think I'm bringing sexy back," Timberlake admitted to Scaggs. "But when a twenty-eight-year-old-male or female is standing in a club in New York City at 2:30 in the morning and that f****ing song comes on, I want them to feel like they are. That's what music should do. When I was a kid and I heard 'I Wanna Hold Your Hand,' I wanted to find someone's hand to hold."

Justin Conner of *Interview* wrote "... the album taps into electroclash, disco, and gospel, remixing and matching old sounds to make them modern." *FutureSex/LoveSounds* also contained a mélange of song topics. From the falsetto and heavy synth beat of "My Love" with rapper T.I. to the bold "Losing My Way," a track inspired by a documentary on crystal meth, the album contained all of the emotions and repercussions of sex and love. "... *FutureSex/LoveSounds* is about the very nature of how sex and love are interchangeable and immutable and contradictory and complementary all at once...," wrote Jennifer Vineyard of MTV.com.

In the business for 15 years and in his mid-twenties, Timberlake has had a more successful (monetarily and artistically) career than artists twice his age. Though he loves it, as he told Scaggs, he can't keep doing it forever. "The dream is to be able to have a schedule like I've had in the last five years, to put out a record and tour, then take a little break, maybe do some films. But I don't want to work this hard forever."

## Selected discography

(With *NSYNC) *NSYNC*, RCA, 1998.
(With *NSYNC) *Home for Christmas*, RCA, 1998.
(With *NSYNC) *No Strings Attached*, Jive, 2000.
(With *NSYNC) *Celebrity*, Jive, 2001.
*Justified*, Jive, 2002.
*FutureSex/LoveSounds*, Jive, 2006.

## Sources

### Periodicals

*Interview*, October 2006, p. 112.
*People*, September 18, 2006, p. 47.
*Rolling Stone*, September 6, 2006.
*W*, September 2006, p. S114.

### Online

"Apologetic Jackson Says 'Costume Reveal' Went Awry," CNN.com, http://www.cnn.com (November 10, 2006).
Justin Timberlake Official Website, http://www.justintimberlake.com (November 10, 2006).
"Justin Timberlake: Wanna Be Starting Somethin'," VH1.com, http://www.vh1.com/artists/interview/1472671/06132003/timberlake_justin.jhtml (November 10, 2006).
"Justin's Album Shows off Two Sides: Over-The-Top- Saucy, Unassumingly Sweet," MTV.com, http://www.mtv.com (November 10, 2006).
*NSYNC Official Website, http://www.nsync.com (November 10, 2006).

—*Shannon McCarthy*

# Tripping Daisy

## Rock group

In the middle of the '90s grunge era, all the major record labels were looking for the next alternative act á la Nirvana. Dallas, Texas, rock group Tripping Daisy were just one of the mid-90s bands who got signed to a big record deal and hoped to become the next big thing in alternative music. After signing to Island Records, Tripping Daisy had a hit on their hands with the quirky song "I Got a Girl" in 1995. The band's psychedelic-tinged alternative pop-rock had just touches of the '90s angst, but with an ironic and whimsical sensibility akin to The Flaming Lips. The Texas band's live shows often included films or special effects arousing eager participation from their fans. After leaving Island in 1999, the group lost a member to a drug overdose and effectively ended Tripping Daisy that year.

Formed in 1991 in Dallas, Texas, almost as soon as they started, Tripping Daisy was a local favorite. Singer/guitarist Tim DeLaughter, guitarist Wes Berggren, bassist Mark Pirro, and drummer Bryan Wakeland had their first taste of regional popularity when their song "Lost and Found" was put into rotation at Dallas radio station KDGE. The group's fan base took off after Dragon Street Records issued Tripping Daisy's debut album, *Bill,* in 1992. Major label reps had already been scouring Texas and soon Tripping Daisy signed a deal with Island Records. The label re-released *Bill* (with bonus tracks) less than a year after its initial release, doubling the album's sales.

Before recording the band's next album, drummer Wakeland left the group, with Mitch Marine replacing him. The fresh quartet released the buzzed-about record *I Am an Elastic Firecracker* in 1995. The edgy single "I Got a Girl" was instantly all over the radio and MTV, propelling sales to over 300,000. After a successful tour to support their new album, the band took time off before they embarked on a 57-city tour opening for '80s rock band Def Leppard in 1996. The exhausting tour caused enough friction in the band that they were forced to take time off for a while. "We were almost finished as a band," DeLaughter told *Weekly Wire.* "We were on the road for 6 1/2 years, constantly grinding, and before we knew it we were tapped. But some forces stronger than us were saying, 'No, it can't happen. Cope.' We took time off, regrouped and it made all the difference in the world."

Not only did they take some much needed time apart, but the group's lineup was changed again when additional guitarist/trumpeter Philip Karnats joined and Marine was replaced by new drummer Ben Curtis. For two months in the winter of 1997, the restructured band recorded in an old church-turned-recording studio near Woodstock, New York. Sonically expanded, more melodic and intimate, the band's new recordings showed a maturity in Tripping Daisy. Unlike with the making of *I Am an Elastic Firecracker,* record label executives weren't breathing down the band's neck, allowing them more freedom this time around. "We had really been stifled by big business," DeLaughter told Anni Layne of *Rolling Stone.* "Our label was going through some changes of their own at the time, which took their focus off us while we made the record. We basically had the opportunity to do exactly what we wanted to do without any interruptions. It was the most fun we have ever had making a record." The songwriter also confessed that his songwriting palette had grown and matured since their first Island album; "It's something you just grow into through time and experiences. I found myself writing more about self-worth and the possibilities of human progression."

In July of 1998, Island released Tripping Daisy's third album, *Jesus Hits Like an Atom Bomb. All Music Guide*'s Stephen Thomas Erlewine called the CD "an impressive record that balances punk-pop with art-rock. It's a smart, ambitious and successful album...." Although ultimately dissatisfied with Island's lack of support behind the album, DeLaughter used the outlet to stay as true to his art as possible. "I'm taking advantage of having the privilege to be able to play music, to be able to reach people," he told Marie Elsie St. Leger of *Rolling Stone.* "I'm giving them something that's from the heart, from the soul, that I consider is real, American music."

After *Jesus Hits Like an Atom Bomb* failed to bring in the kind of numbers Island needed, the band and label parted ways. Tripping Daisy started up their own label, Good Records, to release future albums by their band as well as other artists. "You have to become what you despise to be able to have something to talk about,"

## For the Record . . .

**M**embers include **Wes Berggren**, guitar; **Ben Curtis** (1997–99), drums; **Tim DeLaughter**, lead vocals, guitar; **Philip Karnats** (joined 1997), guitar; **Mitch Marine** (1995–97), drums; **Mark Pirro**, bass; **Bryan Wakeland** (1991–95), drums.

Group formed in 1991 in Dallas, Texas; released *Bill*, Dragon Street Records, 1992; reissued, Island, 1993; released *I Am an Elastic Firecracker*, Island, 1995; *Jesus Hits Like the Atom Bomb*, Island, 1998; left Island Records; guitarist Wes Berggren passed away, 1999; disbanded, 1999; released *Tripping Daisy*, Good Records, 2000.

Addresses: *Record company*—Good Records, P.O. Box 140948, Dallas, TX 75214, website: http://www.goodrecordsrecordings.com. *Website*—Tripping Daisy Official Website: http://www.trippingdaisy.com.

DeLaughter told St. Leger of the early days on Island. "I became what I despised; I was part of that marketing scheme. I realized that it wasn't about that. I kind of got back to where I got started in the first place." The band regrouped to record a self-titled album to be issued on their new label. Before its release, on October 27, 1999, founding guitarist Berggren was found dead in his home of an accidental overdose of drugs. The remaining band members announced that with the end of Berggren's life, it would also be the end of Tripping Daisy.

In 2000, Good Records posthumously released Tripping Daisy's self-titled and final album. *Dallas Observer's* Shannon Sutlief called the record "the exclamation point on a career of catchy melodies, hallucinogenic anthems, and shows filled with paper airplanes and bubble machines." *Tripping Daisy* displayed DeLaughter's transition into a grandeur style that explored bountiful harmonies and orchestral arrangements; a method that would come tenfold with DeLaughter's post-Tripping Daisy band, The Poly-phonic Spree. Formed with DeLaughter, bassist Pirro, former Tripping Daisy drummer Wakeland, and around two dozen singers and instrumentalists all wearing gospel-style robes, The Polyphonic Spree released their debut album, *The Beginning Stages of...* on Good Records in 2002. In the wake of his former band, DeLaughter's ostentatious new band actually became more fashionable and popular than Tripping Daisy ever was. Other Tripping Daisy members continued making music, including drummer Curtis who formed The Secret Machines and Karnats who released the solo album *Pleasesuite* in 2006.

## Selected discography

*Bill,* Dragon Street Records, 1992; reissued, Island Records, 1993.
*I Am an Elastic Firecracker,* Island, 1995.
*Jesus Hits Like the Atom Bomb,* Island, 1998.
*Tripping Daisy,* Sugar Fix Recordings/Good Records, 2000.

## Sources

### Periodicals

*Billboard,* September 9, 1995.
*Dallas Observer,* April 2000.

### Online

"Tripping Daisy," *All Music Guide,* http://www.allmusic.com (November 13, 2006).
"Tripping Daisy," Good Records Official Website, http://www.goodrecordsrecordings.com/td_bio.html (November 13, 2006).
"Tripping Daisy," Weekly Wire, http://weeklywire.com/ww/07-06-98/fw_music.html (November 13, 2006).
"Tripping Daisy Finds a New Attitude," *Rolling Stone,* http://www.rollingstone.com/artists/trippingdaisy/articles/story/5918879/tripping_daisy_finds_a_new_attitude (November 13, 2006).
"Tripping Daisy Hits Like an Atom Bomb," *Rolling Stone,* http://www.rollingstone.com/artists/trippingdaisy/articles/story/5922113/tripping_daisy_hits_like_an_atom_bomb (November 13, 2006).
"Tripping Daisy Guitarist's Death Ruled OD," VH1.com, http://www.vh1.com/artists/news/519989/11111999/tripping_daisy.jhtml (November 13, 2006).

—Shannon McCarthy

# Astrid Varnay

## Singer

**F**ew opera singers have experienced the longevity and critical acceptance of Astrid Varnay. From her debut in Richard Wagner's *Die Walküre* in 1941 to her retirement in 1995, Varnay completed 200 performances at the Metropolitan Opera House in New York City and performed at the Bayreuth Festival in Germany for 17 years. While her vocal aptitude was apparent, she also gained a reputation, and set herself apart from her peers, because of her emotional acting style. Varnay initially gained notice performing Wagner in the United States, but during the 1950s and 1960s she branched out to many other roles on the international scene. "A singing actress of great intensity," wrote Elizabeth Forbes in the London *Independent,* "she excelled in roles that allowed her to portray characters in the grip of extreme emotional stress."

Varnay was born Astrid Ibolyka Maria Varnay in Stockholm, Sweden, on April 25, 1918. Her Hungarian parents, Alexander and Maria Javor Astrid, were both singers, and she grew up within the opera world. One story recalled how Varnay, as a child, slept in a drawer in the dressing room of Kristen Flagstad, the great opera singer, during a performance. After World War I, her family traveled to Argentina before settling in New York City. After Varnay's father's death, her mother gave voice lessons to support the family.

Originally, Varnay intended to become a classical pianist, and she studied at the New Jersey Musical College. At 19, however, she decided to become a singer, and studied under her coloratura soprano mother. A year later, Flagstad arranged for her to study with Hermann Weigert at the Metropolitan Opera House (Varnay and Weigert married in 1944).

Varnay made an inspiring if unscheduled debut on December 6, 1941, a month before her official debut as Elsa in Wagner's *Lohengrin.* The 23-year-old opera singer had arrived at the Metropolitan Opera House to practice for that upcoming role with her trainer, Maestro Erich Leinsdorf, when she was asked to report to makeup. Mme. Lotte Lehmann, slotted as Sieglinde in *Die Walküre* had contracted a cold and was unable to perform the afternoon matinee. The more experienced candidates were unavailable, leaving the role to Varnay, a young, unknown singer with no stage experience. She was, however, familiar with the role, and the performance went exceptionally well. "The *Walküre* performance," Varnay later noted in her autobiography, *Fifty-Five Years in Five Acts,* "concluded in a burst of glory for all parties. The generous audience showered us with applause, and all my colleagues welcomed me to the pack."

Because the show was a Saturday afternoon matinee, Varnay and her family had to wait until Sunday for the reviews. The Sunday paper, however, reported the stunning news of the attack on Pearl Harbor. Once they remembered to look at the reviews, they learned that the critics had announced Varnay as an important new voice. Paul Thomason of *Opera News* later called her first singing date "one of the most remarkable debuts in the history of the Metropolitan Opera." Six days following her performance, Varnay replaced Helen Traubel as Brunnhilde in the same production.

After World War II, opera singers could once again travel between the United States and Europe. In 1948 Varnay received an offer to perform abroad at the Royal Opera House in London. In 1950 Wieland and Wolfgang Wagner (Wagner's grandsons) invited her to audition for the opening season of the Bayreuth Festival. She was unable to try out because of her schedule, but the brothers eventually decided—partially because of Flagstad's recommendation—to waive the audition. The following year, Varnay began what would become a 17-year run at the Bayreuth Festival. "I realized that what had once only been a dream somewhere in the back of my imagination, a dream of an integration of music and drama, was becoming vibrantly true."

The mid-1950s brought both personal and business changes to Varnay's career. On April 12, 1955, Hermann Weigert, her husband since 1944, died. She severed her relationship with the Metropolitan Opera House when she learned that the current management was less than enthusiastic about her repertoire. Because of that change, Varnay began branching out to new venues, traveling the globe from San Francisco to Buenos Aires to Mexico City. "Born and raised in the family business of making music," Varnay recalled, "I always regarded being on the road as the essence of life." She traveled to Scotland to perform the lead in Wagner's *Tristan and Isolde* in 1958. In 1968 Varnay played Kostelnicka in Leos Janacek's *Jenufa,* a role she revived when she returned to the Metropolitan Opera House in 1974. "I *would* be back at the Metropolitan, but, poignantly, I wouldn't really be coming home," Varnay later wrote. "There was no more home and family in that city for me to return to."

Because of the vocal strain of her demanding roles, Varnay eventually lost part of the upper range of her voice, moving her from a soprano to a mezzo soprano. This allowed her to sing a number of new roles, including that of Ortrud in Wagner's *Lohengrin* and Klytem-

nestra in Strauss's *Elektra.* "In my career, one season had simply come to a gradual end," Varnay recalled, "and another was getting started."

Varnay chose to retire from the stage in 1995, 55 years after her debut at the Metropolitan Opera House. Over the span of those years, she performed an incredible 58 roles in 47 operas. After retirement she became a professor and taught in Dusseldorf at the Conservatory of Music. In 2000 Varnay published her memoir, *Fifty-five Years in Five Acts: My Life in Opera,* and in 2004, a documentary about her life, *Never Before,* was released.

Because of the demands of her profession, Varnay noted in *Fifty-five Years in Five Acts,* her private life was a quiet one. "To some people," she wrote, "my private life may seem as unglamorous as an empty hatbox, but to me, it provides the balance I need to rekindle my inner flame." Varnay died on September 4, 2006, in Munich, at the age of 88.

## Selected discography

### As singer

(Richard Wagner) Siegfried, Testament, 2006.
(Richard Wagner) Die Walkure, Testament, 2006.

## Sources

### Books

Astrid Varnay, with Donald Arthur, *Fifty-five Years in Five Acts: My Life in Opera,* Northeastern University Press, 2000.

### Periodicals

*Independent* (London, England), September 6, 2006.
*Opera News,* December 2000.

—Ronnie D. Lankford, Jr.

# Wild Strawberries

## Rock group

Canadian husband and wife duo Ken Harrison and Roberta Carter-Harrison have made music as the Wild Strawberries since 1992. Atypical of most touring musicians, Ken and Roberta both hold medical degrees and until the birth of their first child, both practiced medicine while simultaneously playing gigs. In the early '90s, Wild Strawberries emerged as a band that put moody and ethereal electronica noisescapes into a pop context. As the '90s closed out, many bands of a similar genre dropped the programming sounds and moved on, but the Wild Strawberries just expanded on their keyboard and synthesized beats, concocting hypnotic pop grooves for nearly two decades. Residing in a home in Ontario with their daughters Georgia and Ruby, the Wild Strawberries continue to make music at their home studio, on their own terms.

The Wild Strawberries began in Cambridge, Ontario, while Ken and Roberta were attending school, both pursuing medical degrees. Ken was born in Thailand where his parents were missionaries; they later moved to Cambridge where Ken grew up playing the piano and composing his own songs by age 10.

Ken, often called, the "musical architect" of the band, writes the poetic (and often ominous) lyrics, and all of the music for Wild Strawberries while Roberta sings. Ken uses a number of keyboards and sampled beats to create their songs as a two-piece. The band got serious when they won a contest at a Toronto radio station for their 1988 song "Crying Shame." In 1989, the duo self-recorded and released the album *Carving Wood Spectacles,* which sold a staggering 3,000 copies. Ken

emerged from university with a license to practice as a physician, and Roberta graduated with a degree in physiotherapy. The duo followed *Carving Wood Spectacles* up with the album *Grace* in 1992. The pair then established their own record label dubbed Strawberry Records for their 1994 album *Bet You Think I'm Lonely.* The album got a helping hand when A&M distributed it across Canada. The album's success earned the band a Canadian Juno Award nomination for Best New Band.

Vancouver record label Nettwerk, home to Sarah McLachlan, caught on to the technologically savvy musicians and signed the Wild Strawberries to the label in 1995. That year, Nettwerk released one of the band's most popular albums of their career, the Canadian Gold record (50,000 copies), *Heroine.* The album featured musicians from McLachlan's band including drummer Ashwin Sood and bassist Brian Minato. The Wild Strawberries, a full band, toured that summer as part of McLachlan's hugely successful female-minded tour, Lilith Fair.

Building a home recording studio over the years, Ken and Roberta paid some of the expensive equipment bills by practicing medicine on their downtime. Ken worked on and off as a doctor at Toronto's Queen Street Mental Health Centre and Roberta practiced physiology until the birth of their daughter in 1997. "One mandate we had at the very beginning was to build up a home studio so that when and if the record company ever got tired of what we were doing, we could still make music if we wanted and put it out if we wanted," Roberta told *Canadian Musician'*s Cindy Waxer.

After months writing and recording their follow-up to the popular *Heroine,* in 1997, the band turned in a batch of new songs to Nettwerk who in turn gave them back and demanded more mixing and re-writing. Strained by the demands of the record company, Ken and Roberta tried to get out of their deal with Nettwerk, but were bound by contract to stay put. After time, the band and the label split the difference and the album was co-produced in Vancouver by David Kershaw, a former keyboard player for Sarah McLachlan. *Quiver,* released in 1998, marked the writing debut of Roberta as a lyrical co-writer on three songs. While Ken's emotional lyrics moved a bit from the autobiographical ones of the past to more conceptual and character-driven, Roberta helped Ken co-write the songs "Trampoline," "Speak of the Devil," and "Pretty Lip." "I felt confident enough to give it a try and I never actually felt confident enough before," Roberta admitted to Waxer. "I couldn't imagine that anybody would want to hear anything that I had to say."

With sprawling sounds including string arrangements and mixing old equipment like a '70s vocoder with the newest sampling technology of the '90s, *Quiver* had

**For the Record . . .**

Members include **Roberta Carter-Harrison**, lead vocals; **Ken Harrison**, synthesizers, keyboards.

Duo formed in Cambridge, Ontario, Canada, c. 1988; self-released *Carving Wood Spectacles*, 1989; *Grace*, 1992, released *Bet You Think I'm Lonely*, 1994 on Strawberry Records; signed to Nettwerk Records, released *Heroine*, 1995; *Quiver*, 1998; parted with Nettwerk, released *Twist*, Universal Music, 2000; released self-produced and self-financed *Deformative Years*, 2005.

Addresses: *Record company*—MapleMusic, 230 Richmond St. West, 11th Fl., Toronto, Ontario, Canada, M5V 3E5. *Website*—Wild Strawberries Official Website: http://strawberries.com.

what Perry Stern of *Eye Weekly* called, " ... a much more elegant, detached style," than *Heroine*. The album title, as Roberta explained on the Lilith Fair website, came from the idea of something visceral; "We wanted something slinky, something that vibrated," she said. "We were looking for a word with ambivalence—something that suggested both arousal and fear."

By 1999, the Wild Strawberries had enough of corporate labels and were asked to be let go from Nettwerk Records. That year Roberta sang at a wedding for a Warner Music Canada rep, where she paired up with a band which included flamenco guitarist Robert Michaels. Michaels and Roberta's performance inspired the duo to record the song "Wrong to Let You Go," which was released on the compilation *Women & Songs 3*. Recorded and released in 2000, the band's next album *Twist* was put out by their own label, but distributed by Universal Music. "Every time we make a new record we always try and do something different," Ken told *The Gate*. "That was kind of our manifesto on this, that we were gong to and not in any way you might expect it, and not to make it darker but more to twist it like with a twist of lemon."

After meeting with German electro trance-pop artist ATB (DJ Andre Tannenberger), Wild Strawberries spent time writing and recording for ATB and doing shows in Germany for much of 2002 and 2003. ATB had taken Roberta and Robert Michael's "Wrong To Let You Go" and remixed it as "Let You Go." The club track reached number 18 on the U.S. Billboard Hot Dance Music/Club Play chart and number 7 on the German singles chart. "Our fist single with ATB sold more in one week than what we sold during our entire careers in Canada," Ken confessed to *Pop Journalism*'s Robert Ballantyne. "It's just more lucrative in the European market, based on [population] scale."

Almost five years after the last Wild Strawberries album, Ken and Roberta released the completely self-made and financed record *Deformative Years*. Recorded, produced, and mixed in the couple's home studio in New Hamburg, Ontario (about two hours west of Toronto), *Deformative Years* was created simply for the band and its fans. "This record is for all those people who e-mailed us over the years, wondering if we were still alive," Ken joked to Ballantyne. Roberta doubled that sentiment on the MapleMusic website admitting, "It's the first album in a long time that we haven't written for anybody but ourselves. We did it because we simply love what we do."

## Selected discography

*Carving Wood Spectacles,* self-released, 1989.
*Grace,* self-released, 1992.
*Bet You Think I'm Lonely,* Strawberry Records, 1994.
*Heroine,* Nettwerk, 1995.
*Quiver,* Nettwerk, 1998.
*Twist,* Universal Music, 2000.
*Deformative Years,* MapleMusic, 2005.

## Sources

### Periodicals

*Canadian Medical Association Journal,* February 23, 1999.
*Canadian Musician,* July-August 1998.
*Eye Weekly,* April 23, 1998.
*Pop Journalism,* September 10, 2005.

### Online

"The Wild Strawberries," *The Gate,* http://www.thegate.ca/interviews/wildstraw.php (November 4, 2006).
"Wild Strawberries," MapleMusic, http://www.maplemusic.com/artists/wst/bio.asp (November 4, 2006).
Wild Strawberries Official Site, http://strawberries.com/ (November 4, 2006).

—*Shannon McCarthy*

# Andre Williams

## Singer, songwriter, producer

© Jack Vartoogian/FrontRowPhotos

Call him by one of his various nicknames: the Black Godfather, the Father of Rap, Mr. Rhythm. Or there is another common description available—as Williams admitted to Larry Katz of the *Boston Herald,* "They call me the dirtiest man that ever lived." Andre Williams is a rhythm-and-blues wild man, a survivor of the raunchy urban African-American music of the 1950s and 1960s who enjoyed an unlikely career revival at the 20th century's end, when he was more than 60 years old.

Williams was active as a writer and producer in Detroit during the first part of his career, and he was a hidden presence in the early days of the city's famed Motown label. What drew new young fans in his direction later on, however, was the raw sexuality of much of his own music. "I Wanna Be Your Favorite Pair of Pajamas," from his 1998 album *Silky,* was one of his milder efforts. "I'm trying to tell a story. Dig the theme," Williams explained to Gilbert Garcia of the *Dallas Observer.* "We can't all go on the expressway. Sometimes some of us got to take the low road."

### Heard Southern Country, Chicago Blues

Andre Williams was the stage name of Zeffrey Williams, who was born in Bessemer, Alabama, on November 1, 1936. During his childhood he bounced back and forth between Chicago, where his father worked in a steel mill, and his grandparents' home in rural Alabama. "My grandfather was a primitive, sanctified man," Williams told Joss Hutton of the Perfect Sound website. "Him and my grandmother. That means seven days a week in church. No rock 'n' roll on the radio, no smoking or drinking." The music Williams heard plowing fields in Alabama was country, coming over the radio from WLAC in Memphis: Hank Williams, Hank Snow, Patsy Cline. In Chicago, however, where he worked after school (and through much of the night) at Cadillac Bob's Steakhouse on the South Side, he heard the hyper-charged blues of Wynonie Harris and other singers and instrumentalists on the cutting edge of African-American music around 1950.

Threatened with a stint in an Illinois reform school due to repeated truancy, and impressed by the naval adventure film *The Frogmen,* Williams, at age 14, borrowed an older brother's birth certificate and joined the United States Navy. After serving for some months, and singing with doo-wop groups the Cavaliers and the Thrills while in Chicago on leave, he was found out, court-martialed, and imprisoned for a year on charges of fraudulent enlistment. Williams then headed for Detroit with a Navy friend. Wearing the red corduroy jacket he had been given as part of his Navy discharge, he entered an amateur-night contest at the Warfield Theater in the city's Hastings Street black entertainment district. He took home the $25 first prize with a daring dance routine in which he misjudged a jump over the orchestra pit but kept going without breaking stride, and local music executives began to get wind of the brash youngster's talent as he was invited back for subsequent performances. Comedian Redd Foxx dubbed Williams "Mr. Rhythm," and the nickname stuck.

Williams knew that he did not have the voice to compete with Clyde McPhatter and other singing stars of the time, so he tried to go back to musical roots. "I wanted to tell stories!" he explained to Hutton. "I'll tell you somethin' … the first line of communications was the drums. That was in Africa, the Congos, the Mongos, and all them 'gos. When they was doin' communications, it was with the drums. So if I could get a drum rhythm which captivates people and put a hell of a story on top of it, I can't lose. And that's where I went." Signed to Detroit's Fortune label, he released "Bacon Fat" in 1956, drawling over a drumbeat and a doo-wop chorus about a new dance, the Bacon Fat, that was taking hold among cotton pickers in the South. He composed the song while driving to a gig in Tennessee and holding a bacon-and-egg sandwich in his hand. Fortune's engineers thought he was joking when he began talking rather than singing, but a Detroit DJ, Frantic Eddie Durham, was observing the session and realized the record's potential.

## Influenced Funk and Rap Performers

The song reached the national rhythm-and-blues top ten and was picked up for distribution by the major Epic label, but Williams realized few profits from the deal. He released a series of follow-up singles; "The Greasy Chicken" and "Pass the Biscuits Please" reprised the food theme, while "Jail Bait" suggested the sexual content of his later music. These recordings, collected on the 1960 Fortune LP *Jail Bait,* were not big hits but were known to other performers and became collectors' items. "Bacon Fat" helped spawn a tradition of spoken songs that influenced performers up to 1970s funk master Bootsy Collins and beyond. "I wouldn't say I was the first in the world, but that's how the talking thing started," Williams observed to Katz. "Now some people call me the Godfather of Rap."

In 1961 Williams moved to the new Motown label after his barber introduced him to auto-plant worker and music entrepreneur Berry Gordy. He began writing songs prolifically; of his 230 compositions registered with the BMI licensing agency, many date from this period. Among his compositions was Stevie Wonder's very first recording, "Thank You for Loving Me." Williams' biggest hits as a songwriter and producer, however, came with other labels—his relationship with Gordy was tense, and he was fired and then rehired several times after notching a hit with another artist. The rhythm-and-blues standard "Shake a Tail Feather," sung by Ray Charles in the film *The Blues Brothers,* was originally written and produced by Williams, with a group called the Five Du-Tones performing. He also wrote the Alvin Cash and the Registers hit "Twine Time."

In 1965 Williams left Motown after an incident in which he is said to have taken a shot at a stranger who had entered the dressing room of Motown star Smokey Robinson. Working briefly as road manager for singer Edwin Starr, he signed with the Chess label in Chicago and released several moderately successful singles—small classics of early funk such as "Cadillac Jack" and "The Stroke." In the early 1970s Williams was working for the Houston independent label Duke (artists in his producer stable there included bluesmen Bobby "Blue" Bland and O.V. Wright), but this stretch of his career came to an end when his life was threatened by a gangster whose daughter he had become involved with. Given the gift of a plane ticket by a friend, blues star B.B. King, Williams headed for California and signed on with R&B duo Ike and Tina Turner, then in the last stages of their marriage and professional partnership.

## Struggled with Cocaine Addiction

Williams worked with Ike Turner for 18 months, which was long enough to develop a full-blown addiction to cocaine. "You know how your mother would have little porcelain elephants or whatever, on the kitchen shelves, like salt and pepper shakers. Well, every single one of these in Ike's house was full of coke!" Williams recalled to Hutton. "You could either pick the neck down or move a leg and shake a gram out of it. Full of coke! When I went to work with Ike I was weighing 185 pounds. At the end I was 85 pounds!" Williams managed to return to Detroit and recover temporarily, but the rise of the high-tech disco style displaced his lowdown brand of blues and funk from urban music charts.

Things went from bad to worse, and Williams ended up in a Chicago homeless shelter, prey to a long drug addiction. He made a living by panhandling, and recalled one day on which he was forced to sit on a bridge begging for quarters in a 40-below-zero wind chill, wearing five pairs of pants and nine shirts. "I found this little spot in Chicago where all the white boys come off the train with their purple platinum Visa," he recalled to David Kunian of the Best of New Orleans website. "I'd make me $150 by 9 a.m. Then I'd take the bus to the projects and by the time I left the projects at 11, I'd have one dollar and 38 cents. I gave that up one New Year's Eve when I got so paranoid that I threw $290 in the Chicago River, and I almost threw in my coat. Those kind of things are what turned me around."

### Made Surprising Comeback

Williams had no thought of resuming his music career until he was tracked down by rock 'n' roll enthusiasts at the St. George and Norton labels. "I just woke up one morning, went to the bathroom, and all of a sudden the phone rang," he recalled to Katz. "It was, 'Andre, do you want to make a record?' And I said, 'Are you trying to wake me from this terrible dream that I'm nobody? OK, I'll try it.' All of a sudden I'm playing in Europe, at festivals, everywhere. And suddenly I realized I am somebody." Williams released his *Greasy* album in 1996 and then moved to California's In the Red label for 1998's *Silky*.

Returning to his country roots with the 1999 album *Red Dirt,* recorded with the alternative country band the Sadies, Williams mixed classics of deranged country music such as Johnny Paycheck's "Pardon Me (I've Got Someone to Kill)" with originals like "She's a Bag of Potato Chips." Part of the reason for Williams' continuing success in the early 2000s was that he had no trouble writing new material, even as he approached 70 years of age. He told Hutton, "You come up with stuff about what the f**k happened yesterday! Always in life … if you wake up tomorrow, something's gonna happen in that day that the world can relate to. You just got to find that one thing that happened. And then put your own self in it." The experiences Williams sang about in such songs as "Your Stuff Ain't the Same" (from 2001's *Bait and Switch*), were often sexual ones. It was not quite true that, as Garcia wrote, "His music has one message: He's horny and he wants to do something about it," but the characterization was appropriate for many songs. Jeff Gordinier of *Fortune* noted that Williams' "salacious soul workouts are clotted with good, old-school sonic crud; sometimes the mike literally sounds as if it's daubed with griddle fat and carburetor grime."

At the instigation of a Jamaican-born girlfriend, Williams converted to Judaism later in life. Despite the raunchy content of his lyrics, he often professed religious faith in interviews and credited his career resurgence to divine intervention. Entering his eighth decade of life, Williams was making music at a pace that exceeded even his busiest days in Detroit at the Fortune label. He released the *Aphrodisiac* album on the Pravda label in 2006.

## Selected discography

*Jail Bait,* Fortune, 1960.
*Greasy,* Norton, 1996; reissued, 2003.
*Mr. Rhythm,* 1996.
*Silky,* In the Red, 1998.
*Red Dirt,* Bloodshot, 1999.
*The Black Godfather,* In the Red, 2000.
*Fat Back & Corn Liquor,* St. George, 2000.
*Bait and Switch,* Norton, 2001.
*Holland Shuffle!,* Norton, 2003.
*Red Beans and Biscuits,* Soul-Tay-Shus, 2005.
*Aphrodisiac,* Pravda, 2006.
*Movin On: Greasy and Explicit Soul Movers: 1956–1970,* Vampi Soul, 2006.

## Sources

### Periodicals

*Boston Herald,* October 4, 2001, p. 65.
*Fortune,* January 21, 2002, p. 136.
*Wisconsin State Journal,* October 26, 2006, p. 19.

### Online

"Andre Williams," *All Music Guide,* http://www.allmusic.com (November 7, 2006).
"Andre Williams," In the Red Records, http://www.intheredrecords.com/pages/andre.html (November 7, 2006).
"Andre Williams May Be 63 Years Old, But He's Still Agile, Mobile, and Hostile," *Dallas Observer,* http://dallasobserver.com/Issues/1999-11-11/music/music3.html (November 7, 2006).
"Here Comes Trouble: Rhythm and Blues Bad Boy Andre Williams Rings in the New Year in New Orleans," Best of New Orleans, http://www.bestofneworleans.com/dispatch/2001-12-25/ae_feat.html (November 7, 2006).
"The Black Godfather: Andre Williams," Perfect Sound, http://www.furious.com/PERFECT/andrewilliams.html (November 7, 2006).

—James M. Manheim

# Robbie Williams

AP Images

**Singer, songwriter**

After five years with the British boy toy band Take That, Robbie Williams left the group, and was dismissed and discredited by the music press in the United Kingdom. He proved the critics wrong by winning over new legions of fans and selling more albums than any other artist in the United Kingdom in 1998. In 2006, according to Mark Sutherland in *Billboard,* Elton John called him "the No. 1 star in the world."

Robert Peter Maximillian Williams was born on February 13, 1974, in Stoke-on-Trent, Staffordshire, England. Williams thrived in the limelight. While in his teens, he joined the Stoke-on-Trent Theatre Company and performed in a number of productions in various minor roles before landing a small part on the English television soap opera *Brookside.* He dropped out of school at 16 and went to work as a salesperson, a job he detested.

Williams responded to a newspaper advertisement looking for young men who were interested in becoming members of an English boy band that would rival the pop music dominance of America's New Kids on the Block. The advertisement was placed by Nigel Martin Smith, the svengali-like figure behind the band. In 1990, Williams auditioned for the band and was later named the fifth and final member of the Greater Manchester-based band Take That.

For the first year or so, the band traveled across England, perfecting and promoting their image and music. They were signed to RCA and had their first big break in 1992 when they released the single "It Only Takes a Minute." The single cracked the British top ten, the first Take That single to do so. Later that same year they released their debut album, *Take That and Party,* which debuted at number five on the British album charts. Their next single was a cover of the Barry Manilow song "It Could Be Magic." It climbed to the British top three in January of 1993. The following month the song won won the BRIT Award for Best British Single. Take That released their debut album in America in the spring of 1993.

For the remainder of 1993 the group continued to release chart-topping hit singles in the United Kingdom. "Pray" debuted at number one in July. They repeated the achievement in October with "Relight My Fire" and two months later, "Babe" hit the top of the charts. Their sophomore release, *Everything Changes,* debuted at number one in October and was certified platinum in the United Kingdom.

At the BRIT Awards in February of 1994, Take That took home statues for Best Single and Best Video for the song "Pray." Their next single, "Everything Changes," also debuted at number one, making Take That the first band to enter the British charts at number one four times and have four number one singles from their debut album. Their string of consecutive number one debuts was broken in July of 1994, when "Love Ain't Here Anymore" debuted at number three. In October, their single "Sure" debuted at number one in England. The following month, Take That won the Best Group Award at the inaugural European MTV Music Awards.

"Back for Good" was the band's next single. Just as many of its predecessors had done, "Back for Good" debuted at number one in Britain in the spring of 1995. In May, *Nobody Else* debuted at number one on the British album charts. However, despite the tremendous success of the band, all was not well within the group's ranks.

Williams had begun to grow tired of the highly regimented, pretty-boy pop image that Take That had cultivated. He started to sleep with band groupies, take drugs, and drink heavily. His rebelliousness ostracized him from the rest of the band. After cavorting on stage and off with Oasis at the Glastonbury Music Festival in June of 1995, Williams decided that he wanted out of the band. Rather than allowing Williams to exit the band gracefully, Martin-Smith, in effect, fired him, thus

setting in motion a legal suit between himself and Williams.

When he was ousted from the band, Williams immersed himself in alcohol, partying, bitterness and self pity. His previously trim figure ballooned as he drank and ate excessively. He spent the remainder of 1995 and most of 1996 as a professional partygoer, appearing at bars and celebrations everywhere. The British press had a field day with his downward spiral and dismissed Williams as a talentless lout who was full of resentment for his former band and friends.

Williams was unable to record anything until late 1996 due to contract restrictions with RCA. This eventually cost him most of his previous earnings. In June of 1996 Williams signed a recording contract with Chrysalis. He released an updated cover of the George Michael song "Freedom 96" later that year. In comments included at his Geocities website, Williams called the single "more a statement than a single. The lyrics tell my story. After this, I'm going to go away and re-invent myself, then come back with my own stuff."

Collaborating with Guy Chambers and sobering up in the process, Williams began to work on a debut solo record. The album, *Life Thru a Lens,* was released in September of 1997. Commenting on the album's songs, Williams said on the Geocities website that "they're stories about me and my experiences. It's been really good for me to write them, it's been like having my own counseling sessions." The first single, "Old Before I Die," went to number two on the British singles chart, and the album was well received by both critics and fans.

The album's single "Angels" helped push sales of *Life Thru a Lens* to 300,000 copies in Europe and 1.2 million in the United Kingdom, and the record went quadruple platinum in less than a year. In September of 1998 Williams scored his first solo number one single with the song "Millennium," which was taken from his second album, *I've Been Expecting You,* released the following month.

By the end of 1998, Williams had become the biggest-selling artist in Britain, with sales in excess of two million copies. Commenting about his critics, Williams quipped on the Geocities website that "there are still people who can't believe it when they hear me sing. You see them thinking, 'Hey, he actually has a good voice.'"

His success in the U.K. and many other countries seemed to make Robbins a shoo-in for success in the United States. His first attempt at a U.S. solo career began when his song "Angels" reached number 53 on the *Billboard* Hot 100 in 2003. However, after that he struggled to be noticed. He canceled plans for a U.S. tour that year. His 2005 release, *Intensive Care,* and

2006's *Rudebox* were not even released in the United States. According to Sutherland, he once told a British interviewer that "the only way an album of mine is going to be in the States is if I leave it in Tower Records."

By 2006 Williams had sold more than 51 million albums, singles, and DVDs. However, he seemed to be growing weary of the constant push to perform, and was considering a possible new career direction. He told an interviewer in *Music Week,* "I don't know where I stand with it all at the moment. I've had a good run." He added, "What I'm saying is, then, 'Do I take things into my own hands and dismantle this monster and have a good life?'"

## Selected discography

### With Take That

*Take That and Party,* RCA, 1992.
*Everything Changes,* RCA, 1993.
*Nobody Else,* RCA, 1995.

### Solo

"Freedom 96," Chrysalis, 1996.
*Life Through a Lens,* Chrysalis, 1997.
*I've Been Expecting You,* Chrysalis, 1998.

*Sing When You're Winning,* Chrysalis, 2000.
*Escapology,* Chrysalis, 2002.
*Live at Knebworth,* Chrysalis, 2003.
*Greatest Hits,* Chrysalis, 2004.
*The Ego Has Landed,* Chrysalis, 2004.
*Intensive Care,* Chrysalis, 2005.
*Rudebox,* Chrysalis, 2006.

## Sources

### Books

Rees, Dayfdd, and Luke Crampton, *Encyclopedia of Rock Stars,* DK, 1996.

### Periodicals

*Billboard,* October 3, 1998; April 1, 2006, p. 17; July 29, 2006, p. 8; October 21, 2006, p. 31, 32.
*Economist,* January 16, 1999.
*Management Today,* May 5, 2006, p. 53.
*Music Week,* September 2, 2006, p. 2, 3, 12.

### Online

"Biography," *Geocities,* wysiwyg://88/http://www.geocities.... setStrip/Lounge/8286/Biography.htm (January 19, 1999).

—*Mary Alice and Kelly Winters*

# Dwight Yoakam

**Singer, songwriter**

AP Images

Arguably the finest artist to emerge from country music's neo-traditionalist movement during the mid-1980s, Dwight Yoakam skillfully blended a collector's taste for traditional country and rockabilly into a series of now classic recordings. The swivel-kneed singer/songwriter has continued to prove himself as a recording artist, and has also made a name for himself in films as an actor. When not recording, he has earned positive reviews for his roles in such films as the 1996 Academy Award-winning *Sling Blade* and the 2005 hit comedy *Wedding Crashers*.

## Started in Cowpunk

Yoakam was born on October 23, 1956, in Pikeville, Kentucky, but the family moved to Columbus, Ohio, when Dwight was very young. Yoakam first showed an interest in playing the guitar at the age of two, and quickly taught himself to play along with Hank Williams's records. He composed his first song at the age of eight. A devotee of vintage recordings by Johnny Cash, Johnny Horton, Elvis Presley, Hank Locklin, and particularly Buck Owens and his Buckaroos, the youngster started a rockabilly band while still in high school. He worked as a singer in nightclubs while attending Ohio State University, but after two years he left for Nashville in search of a career in country music. Unable to get his career started while living in Nashville, Yoakam decided to try his luck in Los Angeles, where he moved in 1978.

In Los Angeles, Yoakam worked as a truck driver and on a loading dock while struggling to find his musical niche. Latching onto a secure spot in the San Fernando Valley cowpunk scene, the singer eventually began sharing a bill with such emerging local acts as Los Lobos, the Blasters, and Lone Justice. He worked with lead guitarist and roots music visionary Pete Anderson, and the two produced *A Town South of Bakersfield,* a six-song EP for the independent Oak Records label. Hailed as a return to country's true roots, the smart-selling disc paved the way for Yoakam's major label deal with the Warner Brothers' subsidiary Reprise.

## A Major Country Hitmaker

Yoakam's 1986 debut album, *Guitars, Cadillacs, Etc. Etc.,* was well-received by critics and country music fans alike, and spawned a hit remake of Johnny Horton's "Honky Tonk Man" and the singer's own composition "Guitars, Cadillacs, and Hillbilly Music." This first album quickly went platinum, and the next four went gold; Dwight Yoakam had clearly become a major country music star.

Yoakam released four more albums in the next four years—1987's *Hillbilly Deluxe,* 1988's *Buenas Noches from a Lonely Room,* 1989's *Just Lookin' for a Hit,* and 1990's *If There Was a Way*—and managed to keep his

careers of two of his country idols. He enticed Buck Owens out of semi-retirement to record one of the legendary singer-songwriter's early tunes, "Streets of Bakersfield." Not only did their recording hit number one on the country charts, but Yoakam and Owens toured together with great success. In 1992 Yoakam convinced Roger Miller, one of country and pop's cleverest tunesmiths, to write a song with him. The result was the number seven charting "It Only Hurts When I Cry," a final triumph for Miller, who died of cancer a short time later.

Despite this solidification of his country stardom, there were fans and critics who expressed a desire for the singer to expand his musical horizons, abandon his characteristic honky-tonk, rural sound, and adopt a more sophisticated rock-driven contemporary country music sound. Yoakam's response was the 1993 album *This Time,* and he succeeded, according to *Entertainment Weekly*'s Alanna Nash, in "pull[ing] off a near miracle: Staying stone country for his core following, and turning progressive enough for radio, without alienating either audience." Songs such as "A Thousand Miles from Nowhere" and "King of Fools" were especially lauded, and Yoakam himself, in an article by *People* contributor Tony Scherman, characterized the type of music he played as "country rock," but asserted: "I'll never quit playing country music, or at least acknowledging it, always, as the cornerstone of what I am." In a review in *Maclean's,* Nicholas Jennings declared that Yoakam's "songwriting … ranks among the best in country music."

Despite his busy schedule as an actor on stage and screen, in 1995 Yoakam managed to release *Dwight Live,* which consisted of versions of songs that were recorded live during concert performances, and *Gone,* which continued the trend Yoakam had started with *This Time.* Both albums were well regarded by critics and popular with fans. Tony Scherman, writing in *Entertainment Weekly,* called *Dwight Live* a "most satisfying country record." *Guitar Player*'s Art Thompson also offered a glowing review of the live album, and advised his readers that this was "the music of dented pickup trucks and funky bars, not the silly tight-Wranglers scene that dominates today's 'young country.'" Reviews of *Gone* were largely positive, but some critics asserted, as did Alanna Nash in her *Entertainment Weekly* review, that "he's so busy getting the synthesis right that he forgot the soul."

## Branched Out into Films

Yoakam, a country heart-throb whose knee-swiveling on stage antics drew appreciative screams from female fans, had been dabbling in films since his first roles, in 1993's *Red Rock West* and 1994's *Roswell,* His first starring role came as a rodeo clown in the 1994 action feature *Painted Hero.* In 1996 Yoakam earned rave reviews for his portrayal of the abusive, alcoholic Doyle

loyal traditional country music fans satisfied. During this early peak, he was able to briefly revitalize the

in the film *Sling Blade.* He received *Premiere* magazine's Premiere Performance Award in recognition of his "breakthrough performance" in the film.

Following his performance in *Sling Blade,* Yoakam received offers to appear in many more films, but shied away from mainstream features in favor of grittier independent films such as 2000's *South of Heaven, West of Hell,* which he directed and starred in, 2002's *Waking Up in Reno,* which he also produced, and 2005's critically acclaimed *The Three Burials of Melquiades Estrada.*

Further, Yoakam used his multimedia fame to branch out into the prepackaged food business by signing a deal with Modern Foods to manufacture such faux southern-flavored edibles as Dwight Yoakam's Chicken Lickin's and Boom Boom Shrimp.

On the musical front, Yoakam's 1997 release of his eighth album, *Under the Covers,* featured cover versions of songs originally recorded by such diverse artists as The Clash and Johnny Horton, and drew praise from critics who expressed appreciation for the singer's artistic inventiveness and mastery of a wide range of musical styles. Critical response to the album was mixed, with some critics praising Yoakam's creativity and range, while others characterized the work as overdone. *People*'s Amy Linden, who while admitting that initially the new versions were interesting and enjoyable to listen to, remarked that "eventually the production razzle-dazzle and sudden leaps of genre get tiresome." *Entertainment Weekly*'s Jeremy Helligar, however, was enthusiastic about *Under the Covers* and concluded that Yoakam's performance on the album was "inspired as hell and absolutely out of control."

### Returned to Independent Labels

Yoakam's status as a hit recording artist slipped during the late 1990s, although he consistently drew large concert crowds. By 2001 he and Reprise/Warner Bros. had parted company, and the singer-songwriter signed with the hot independent Audium label. Right out of the box, Yoakam proved that his creative fires were undiminished. Aided by longtime producer/guitarist Pete Anderson, 2003's *Population Me* continued to revel in the Buck Owens-inspired Bakersfield sound and self-deprecating Johnny Horton honky-tonk, while embracing guest star Timothy B. Schmidt's connection to the folk-rock sounds of the Eagles.

The alliance with Audium was short-lived. The label folded and Yoakam leased his next efforts to the independent New West label. *Blame the Vain* (2005) was recorded without longtime partner Pete Anderson, who had left to concentrate on his own Lucky Dog label. Yoakam still enjoys a devoted fan base, even when modern radio playlists ignore his works. Robert Loy of *Country Standard Time* expressed it best in his review of *Blame the Vain*: "It's just that radio no longer bends enough to accommodate the always eclectic (sometimes too retro, sometimes too progressive) Mr. Yoakam. And there's probably not anything on his 18th album to make them alter that policy."

## Selected Discography

### Singles

"Honky Tonk Man," Reprise, 1986.
"Guitars, Cadillacs," Reprise, 1986.
"It Won't Hurt," Reprise, 1986.
"Little Sister," Reprise, 1987.
"Little Ways," Reprise, 1987.
"Please, Please Baby," Reprise, 1987.
"Always Late With Your Kisses," Reprise, 1988.
"Streets of Bakersfield," (With Buck Owens) Reprise, 1988.
"I Sang Dixie," Reprise, 1988.
"I Got You," Reprise, 1989.
"Long White Cadillac," Reprise, 1989.
"Turn It On, Turn It Up, Turn Me Loose," Reprise 1989.
"You're the One," Reprise, 1991.
"Nothing's Changed Here," Reprise, 1991.
"It Only Hurts When I Cry," Reprise, 1992.
"The Heart That You Own," Reprise, 1992.
"Suspicious Minds," Reprise, 1992.
"Ain't That Lonely Yet," Reprise, 1993.
"A Thousand Miles from Nowhere," Reprise, 1993.
"Fast As You," Reprise, 1993.
"Try Not to Look So Pretty," Reprise, 1994.
"Nothing," Reprise, 1995.
"Things Change," Reprise, 1998.
"Crazy Little Thing Called Love," Reprise, 1999.
"What Do You Know About Love," Warner Bros., 2000.

### Albums

*Guitars, Cadillacs, Etc. Etc.,* Reprise, 1986.
*Hillbilly Deluxe,* Reprise, 1987.
*Buenas Noches from a Lonely Room,* Reprise, 1988.
*Just Lookin' for a Hit,* Reprise, 1989.
*If There Was A Way,* Reprise, 1990.
*This Time,* Reprise, 1993.
*Dwight Live,* Reprise, 1995.
*Gone,* Reprise, 1995.
*Under the Covers,* Reprise, 1997.
*Come On Christmas,* Reprise, 1997.
*Long Way Home,* Reprise, 1998 .
*La Croix d'Amour,* WEA International, 1999.
*Last Chance for a Thousand Years: Greatest Hits from the 90's,* Reprise, 1999.
*Tomorrow's Sounds Today,* Warner Bros., 2000.
*South of Heaven, West of Hell,* (Original soundtrack recording) Warner Bros., 2001.
*Reprise Please Baby: The Warner Bros. Years* (4 CD boxed set), Rhino, 2002.
*In Others' Words,* Reprise, 2003.
*Population Me,* Audium, 2003.
*Dwight's Used Records,* Koch, 2004.
*The Very Best of Dwight Yoakam,* Rhino, 2004 .
*Blame the Vain,* New West, 2005.
*Live from Austin,* New West, 2005.

*The Essentials,* WEA International, 2005.
*Platinum Collection,* Warner Bros., 2006.

## Videos/DVDs

*Just Lookin' for a Hit,* Warner/Reprise, 1989.
*Pieces of Time,* Warner Bros., 1994.
*Live from Austin,* New West, 2005.
*Dwight Yoakam,* St. Clair Vision, 2006.

# Sources

### Books

McCloud, Barry, *Definitive Country: The Ultimate Encyclopedia of Country Music and Its Performers,* Perigree, 1995.
Stambler, Irwin & Grelun Landon, *Country Music: The Encyclopedia,* St. Martin's Griffin, 1997.

### Periodicals

*Country Standard Time,* July 2003.
*Entertainment Weekly,* April 2, 1993, p. 51; May 26, 1995, p. 86; November 3, 1995, p. 66; December 6, 1996, p. 48; July 25, 1997.
*Guitar Player,* September 1995, p. 119.
*Los Angeles Magazine,* May 1993, p. 165.
*Maclean's,* April 26, 1993, p. 44.
*People,* March 29, 1993, p. 19; April 26, 1993, p. 46; November 27, 1995, p. 22; August 4, 1997, p. 23.

### Online

"Dwight Yoakam," *All Movie Guide Guide,* http://www.allmovie.com. (October 25, 2006).
"Dwight Yoakam," *All Music Guide,* (October 25, 2006).
"Dwight Yoakam," *Internet Movie Database,* http://www.imdb.com. (October 25, 2006).
George Graham Weekly Album Review, broadcast August 6, 1997, on WVIA-FM, http://www.george.scranton.com/yoakam.html.
*The Official Dwight Yoakam Website,* http://www.dwightyoakam.com. (October 25, 2006).

*—Lynn M. Spampinato and Ken Burke*

# Timi Yuro

**Singer**

Hulton Archive/Getty Images

The powerful Jackie Wilson-influenced opening to the 1961 hit "Hurt" led many listeners to mistakenly believe that Timi Yuro was a young black man or—because of the spelling of her name—an Asian. One of the great unheralded female singers of her era, she was blessed with the ability to phrase like R&B stars Dinah Washington and Little Esther Phillip, and she embraced both the supper club soul of Della Reese and mainstream pop. The diminutive songstress was barely out of her teens when she employed impressive operatic histrionics to remake Roy Hamilton's "Hurt" into a Top Ten pop smash. One of her best-known follow-up hits transformed the bitter comeuppance soul ballad "What's a Matter Baby" into an anthem of personal triumph, and turned Charlie Chaplin's standard "Smile" into a heartbreaking confession.

Unable to prolong her string of hits, Yuro's recording career slipped badly during the late 1960s. Still playing clubs and concerts worldwide, she thrived as a much admired cult figure until throat cancer forced an early retirement. Although Yuro never enjoyed a career as successful as her talent seemed to warrant, she remained popular in some circles. Among her many admirers was none other than Elvis Presley, who copied her style for his own version of "Hurt" during his late 1970s concert period.

## Loved Opera and R&B

Born Rosemarie Timotea Aurro on August 4, 1941, she spent her earliest years in Chicago, where her Italian-born mother Edith was determined to have the talented seven-year-old study opera despite the family's financial hardship. After their 1952 move to Los Angeles, one of her vocal coaches was so impressed by Yuro's blossoming voice that she gave the child lessons even when the family was unable to pay.

Opera gave the young singer an appreciation of deeply felt emotion, but thanks to the Houstons, a black couple who had helped raise her mother, she also gravitated towards 1950s R&B. As a result, when Yuro first sang publicly in bars owned by her grandmother, or later in her parent's own restaurant, the youngster was able to draw on tunes as disparate as the Italian standard "Sorrento," the classical "Poor Butterfly," and the Dinah Washington oldie "Long John Blues." Yuro's mother encouraged her pursuit of song, no matter what form it took, although the singer's father strongly disapproved of her predilection for salty blues numbers and often physically punished the child.

Irononically, it was Yuro's penchant for popular music that saved her father's restaurant, Alvoturno's, from going bankrupt. Their high-class eatery proved to be a financial failure, but once the teenaged singer convinced her father to turn it into a rock 'n' roll club—where she sang her mix of R&B and operatic pop every night—the eatery quickly became a success. Eventually a talent scout from Liberty Records signed her to a recording contract in late 1959.

### The Little Girl with the Big Voice

Once they had signed Yuro to their label, Liberty had no idea to do with the eclectic vocalist. Meanwhile, the young songstress was growing impatient. According to author David Freeland in *Ladies of Soul,* after a week of waiting outside Liberty chief Al Bennett's office, Yuro burst into the office and made him listen to what she was capable of doing. Bennett called in producer Clyde Otis, who worked with Yuro to create a performance that stood out from other recordings of the time. "Hurt," backed with "I Apologize," became a solid tri-market hit. Overnight she was transformed from a local sensation to an international recording star. Yet the naked anger of "Hurt's" introductory moments were perceived to be so masculine that Liberty felt compelled to call her "The Little Girl With The Big Voice."

Liberty quickly brought her back into the studio to cut more discs, but they didn't really have a solid creative game plan. Rather than capitalize on Yuro's natural affinity for R&B, they had her record "I Believe" with the down-on-his-luck Johnnie Ray, and followed up with such chestnuts as "Let Me Call You Sweetheart" and "Smile," all in 1961. Her career was further complicated by a tour of Australia with Frank Sinatra, which con-

vinced many of her teenaged fans that Yuro was strictly a cabaret performer.

The only new Liberty recording that suited Yuro's blue-eyed soul style was the 1962 hit "What's a Matter Baby." It was one of the singer's finest soul performances, and her vocals paired the sound of a survivor's self-righteousness with a triumphant teen symphony backing track, courtesy of producer Phil Spector, who took over the mixing Yuro's record when Clyde Otis abruptly left Liberty. Spector, who was also heading up his own Philles label at the time, never worked with Yuro again, and Liberty didn't capitalize on the hit by having the singer record more in the same style, choosing instead to appease the pop crowd with the Burt Bacharach-penned "The Love of A Boy" in 1962.

Yuro recorded four albums in three years for Liberty. Most featured adult contemporary style tunes done in a bluesy manner. The most daring of her early projects was her 1963 LP *Make the World Go Away.* Following the lead of Solomon Burke, Ray Charles, and especially Esther Phillips, Yuro revamped country tunes with soulful vocals using lush country crossover back-up musicians. The title track, also recorded in hit renditions by country great Ray Price and classic pop singer Dean Martin, became a solid hit, and the album is revered as a minor classic. However, without Otis to guide her in the studio, Yuro lost faith in Liberty Records.

### The Lost Voice of Soul

After departing Liberty in 1963, legal and medical problems kept Yuro from immediately recording for her new label Mercury, and the Chicago-based label could not rebuild her chart momentum. Only one single, her overwrought remake of the standard "If," made Billboard's Hot 100, and the label issued only one album, *The Amazing Timi Yuro.* Cutting a mix of Italian songs, pop, and flat-out soul, she was still capable of remarkable work when focused, including a version of Connie Smith's "Once A Day" and the soul offering "Cuttin' In," easily the best soul offering she made at Mercury.

Hoping to recapture past glories, Yuro returned to Liberty in 1968, releasing the album *Something Bad on My Mind,* which, though somewhat overproduced, was an underappreciated gem in its time. Better still was the label's next planned release, *Live at P.J.'s,* featuring Yuro singing a live set of big hits and contemporary cover tunes. Unfortunately, Liberty withdrew the album almost as soon as the released it, and fans would have to wait 30 years to hear the in-her-prime Yuro performing for a live audience.

Aside from a few singles for the Playboy and Frequency labels, Yuro's recording career was over. Her marriage in 1969 and subsequent birth of her daughter Milan, slowed the frequency of her tours until the early 1980s, when she began to gig overseas regularly again. Needing product to sell off the stage, she recorded three albums of material filled with re-recordings of her big hits and solidly delivered cover songs. Released in Holland and parts of Europe, these LPs seldom made it to her fans in the United States.

Yuro's final stab at the big time came via old friend Willie Nelson. The songstress had met Nelson during the early 1960s when he was still a struggling country songwriter. Charmed by Yuro's mother, who insisted on feeding him, Nelson never forgot the kindness he was shown. In 1984, upon learning that Yuro couldn't get financing for an album, he offered to record her at his studio. "He paid for everything," Yuro told Freeland. "He let me stay there and I did that whole album there." Despite the appearance of Nelson as a duet partner, the finished collection of Nelson-penned songs didn't attract a label, and Yuro pressed up discs herself and sold them via mail order. A short time later, the singer learned that she had throat cancer.

Several operations, including a tracheostomy and the removal of a lung, effectively ended Yuro's singing career. She fought hard and lived another two decades, eventually seeing her early recordings repackaged for enthusiastic collectors in Europe, where she is revered as the "Lost Voice of Soul." Timi Yuro died of brain cancer on May 30, 2004.

## Selected Discography

### Singles

"Hurt," Liberty, 1961.
"Smile," Liberty, 1961.
"I Apologize," Liberty, 1961.
"She Really Loves You," Liberty, 1961.
"Let Me Call You Sweetheart," Liberty, 1962.
"What's A Matter Baby (Is it Hurting You)," Liberty, 1962.
"Insult to Injury," Liberty, 1963.
"Make the World Go Away," Liberty , 1963.
"The Love of a Boy," Liberty, 1963.

### Albums

*Soul,* Liberty, 1962.
*Let Me Call You Sweetheart,* Liberty, 1962.
*Make the World Go Away,* Liberty, 1963.
*What's a Matter Baby,* Liberty, 1963; reissued, RPM, 2004.
*The Amazing Timi Yuro,* Mercury, 1964.
*In the Beginning,* Liberty, 1968.
*Interlude* (Original Motion Picture Soundtrack), Colgems, 1968.
*Something Bad on My Mind,* Liberty, 1968.
*Live at PJ's,* Liberty, 1969; reissued, RPM, 2000.
*All Alone Am I,* Dureco, 1981.
*I'm Yours,* Arcade, 1981.
*For Sentimental Reasons,* Arcade, 1982.
*Timi Yuro Today,* Ariola, 1982.
*The Lost Voice of Soul,* RPM, 1993.
*The Voice That Got Away: Timi Yuro,* RPM, 1996.
*The Timi Yuro Album,* EMI, 1976; reissued, 1996.
*The Unique Sound of Timi Yuro,* MCPS, 1997.
*The Amazing Timi Yuro: The Mercury Years,* Universal, 2005.
*Very Best of Timi Yuro,* EMI Gold, 2006.

## Sources

### Books

Freeland, David, *Ladies of Soul,* University Press of Mississippi, 2001.

### Online

"Timi Yuro," *All Music Guide,* http://www.allmusic.com (November 16, 2006).
"Timi Yuro—Feisty white singer with a black soul voice," *The Guardian,* http://www.guardian.co.uk/obituaries/story0, 3604, 1189247,00.html. (April 10, 2004).
"Timi Yuro," *Internet Movie Database,* http://www.imdb.com. (November 16, 2006).
Additional information for this profile was drawn from liner notes for RPM Timi Yuro reissues and compilations.

—*Ken Burke*

# Cumulative Subject Index

*Volume numbers appear in **bold***

## A cappella

Brightman, Sarah **45**
  *Earlier sketch in CM **20***
Bulgarian State Female Vocal
  Choir, The **10**
Cole, Jim **54**
Dixie Hummingbirds, The **41**
Fairfield Four **49**
Golden Gate Quartet **25**
Haden, Petra **55**
  *Also see Decemberists, The*
  *Also see Rentals, The*
Ladysmith Black Mambazo **60**
  *Earlier sketch in CM **1***
Moxy Früvous **45**
Nylons, The **6**
Persuasions, The **47**
Rockapella **34**
Sweet Honey In The Rock **26**
  *Earlier sketch in CM **1***
Take 6 **39**
  *Earlier sketch in CM **6***
Zap Mama **51**
  *Earlier sketch in CM **14***

## Accordion

Buckwheat Zydeco **34**
  *Earlier sketch in CM **6***
Chavis, Boozoo **38**
Chenier, C. J. **15**
Chenier, Clifton **6**
Galliano, Richard **58**
Jocque, Beau **51**
Jordan, Esteban **49**
Oliveros, Pauline **47**
Queen Ida **51**
  *Earlier sketch in CM **9***
Richard, Zachary **9**
Rockin' Dopsie **10**
Simien, Terrance **12**
Sonnier, Jo-El **10**
Yankovic, "Weird Al" **48**
  *Earlier sketch in CM **7***

## Ambient/Rave/Techno

Allien, Ellen **55**
Aphex Twin **48**
  *Earlier sketch in CM **14***
Atkins, Juan **52**

Autechre **35**
Basement Jaxx **60**
  *Earlier sketch in CM **29***
Boards of Canada **44**
Carlos, Wendy **46**
Chemical Brothers, The **51**
  *Earlier sketch in CM **20***
Cibelle **59**
Cinematic Orchestra **52**
Clark, Anne **32**
Collins, Sandra **41**
Cox, Carl **43**
Crystal Method, The **35**
Deep Forest **18**
Dimitri from Paris **43**
Dirty Vegas **48**
DJ Spooky **51**
808 State **31**
Esthero **58**
Frankie J. **58**
Front Line Assembly **20**
Future Sound of London **41**
Goldfrapp **59**
Gus Gus **26**
Hawtin, Richie **45**
Holmes, David **31**
KMFDM **18**
Kraftwerk **9**
Lamb **38**
Lavelle, Caroline **35**
Lords of Acid **20**
Man or Astroman? **21**
May, Derrick **51**
Mouse On Mars **32**
Múm **50**
Neu! **32**
Nightmares on Wax **51**
Oakenfold, Paul **32**
Orb, The **18**
Phoenix **59**
Propellerheads **26**
Röyksopp **57**
Russell, Arthur **50**
Sasha **39**
Shadow, DJ **19**
Sheep on Drugs **27**
Slater, Luke **38**
Tall Paul **36**

Tobin, Amon **32**
2 Unlimited **18**
Underworld **26**
Van Dyk, Paul **35**
Van Helden, Armand **32**
Villalobos, Ricardo **53**
Zero 7 **49**

## Bandoneon

Piazzolla, Astor **18**
Saluzzi, Dino **23**
Troilo, Aníbal **58**

## Banjo

Boggs, Dock **25**
Bromberg, David **18**
Brown, Alison **44**
Clark, Roy **1**
Crowe, J.D. **5**
Fleck, Béla **47**
  *Earlier sketch in CM **8***
  *Also see New Grass Revival, The*
Hartford, John **37**
  *Earlier sketch in CM **1***
Lang, Eddie **60**
McCoury, Del **15**
Piazzolla, Astor **18**
Scruggs, Earl **3**
Seeger, Pete **38**
  *Earlier sketch in CM **4***
  *Also see Weavers, The*
Skaggs, Ricky **43**
  *Earlier sketch in CM **5***
Stanley, Ralph **55**
  *Earlier sketch in CM **5***
Watson, Doc **59**
  *Earlier sketch in CM **2***

## Bass

Brown, Ray **21**
Carter, Ron **14**
Chambers, Paul **18**
Clarke, Stanley **3**
Cohen, Avishai **42**
Collins, Bootsy **8**
  *Also see Golden Palominos*
Dixon, Willie **10**
Fell, Simon H. **32**
Fender, Leo **10**
Friesen, David **41**

Haden, Charlie **40**
  *Earlier sketch in CM **12***
Hinton, Milt **33**
Holland, Dave **27**
Johnson, Marc **58**
Kaye, Carol **22**
King, Chris Thomas **43**
Kowald, Peter **32**
Lane, Ronnie **46**
  *Also see Faces, The*
Laswell, Bill **14**
Lopez, Israel "Cachao" **34**
  *Earlier sketch in CM **14***
Love, Laura **20**
Mann, Aimee **56**
  *Earlier sketch in CM **22***
McBride, Christian **17**
McCartney, Paul **58**
  *Earlier sketch in CM **32***
  *Earlier sketch in CM **4***
  *Also see Beatles, The*
Meyer, Edgar **40**
Miller, Marcus **38**
Mingus, Charles **9**
Ndegéocello, Me'Shell **18**
Parker, William **31**
Peacock, Gary **48**
Silva, Alan **45**
Sting **41**
  *Earlier sketch in CM **19***
  *Earlier sketch in CM **2***
  *Also see Police, The*
Sweet, Matthew **9**
13th Floor Elevators **47**
Was, Don **21**
  *Also see Was (Not Was)*
Watt, Mike **22**
Weber, Eberhard **41**
Wells, Bill **34**
Whitaker, Rodney **20**

## Big Band/Swing

Andrews Sisters, The **9**
Anthony, Ray **60**
Arnaz, Desi **8**
Asleep at the Wheel **29**
  *Earlier sketch in CM **5***
Atomic Fireballs, The **27**
Bailey, Pearl **5**

Blanchard, Terence **13**
Botti, Chris **40**
Bowie, Lester **29**
Brown, Clifford **24**
Bushkin, Joe **54**
Cherry, Don **10**
Coleman, Ornette **5**
Dara, Olu **46**
Davis, Miles **1**
Douglas, Dave **29**
Driscoll, Phil **45**
Edison, Harry "Sweets" **29**
Eldridge, Roy **9**
   *Also see McKinney's Cotton Pickers*
Ferguson, Maynard **7**
Gillespie, Dizzy **6**
Hargrove, Roy **60**
   *Earlier sketch in CM **15***
Harrell, Tom **28**
Hassell, Jon **43**
Hawkins, Erskine **19**
Hirt, Al **5**
Isham, Mark **14**
James, Harry **11**
Jensen, Ingrid **22**
Jones, Jonah **53**
Jones, Quincy **20**
   *Earlier sketch in CM **2***
Jones, Thad **19**
Little, Booker **36**
Loughnane, Lee **3**
Mandel, Johnny **28**
Marsalis, Wynton **20**
   *Earlier sketch in CM **6***

Masekela, Hugh **7**
Matthews, Eric **22**
Mighty Mighty Bosstones **20**
Miles, Ron **22**
Minton, Phil **29**
Navarro, Fats **25**
Oliver, King **15**
Payton, Nicholas **27**
Rodney, Red **14**
Roney, Wallace **33**
Sandoval, Arturo **15**
Severinsen, Doc **1**
Shaw, Woody **27**
Stańko, Tomasz **47**
Terry, Clark **24**
Truffaz, Erik **54**

**Tuba**
Phillips, Harvey **3**

**Vibraphone**
Ayers, Roy **39**
Burton, Gary **10**
Gibbs, Terry **35**
Hampton, Lionel **6**
Jackson, Milt **15**
Norvo, Red **12**

**Viola**
Menuhin, Yehudi **11**
Van der Velden, Mieneke **55**
Zukerman, Pinchas **4**

**Violin**
Acuff, Roy **2**
Alsop, Marin **58**

Anderson, Laurie **25**
   *Earlier sketch in CM **1***
Barton Pine, Rachel **52**
Bell, Joshua **21**
Ben-Ari, Miri **49**
Bird, Andrew **46**
Bonham, Tracy **34**
Bromberg, David **18**
Carter, Regina **22**
   *Also see String Trio of New York*
Carthy, Eliza **31**
Chang, Sarah **55**
   *Earlier sketch in CM **7***
Chung, Kyung Wha **34**
Clements, Vassar **18**
Coleman, Ornette **5**
Cugat, Xavier **23**
Daniels, Charlie **6**
Diamond, David **58**
Doucet, Michael **8**
Dubeau, Angèle **47**
Galimir, Felix **36**
Germano, Lisa **18**
Gingold, Josef **6**
Grappelli, Stephane **10**
Haden, Petra **55**
   *Also see Decemberists, The*
   *Also see Rentals, The*
Haendel, Ida **42**
Hahn, Hilary **30**
Hartford, John **37**
   *Earlier sketch in CM **1***
Haydn, Lili **46**
Heifetz, Jascha **31**

Huggett, Monica **50**
Jenkins, Leroy **39**
Josefowicz, Leila **35**
Kang, Eyvind **28**
Kennedy, Nigel **47**
   *Earlier sketch in CM **8***
Krauss, Alison **41**
   *Earlier sketch in CM **10***
Kremer, Gidon **30**
Lamb, Barbara **19**
Maazel, Lorin **46**
Marić, Ljubica **48**
Marriner, Neville **7**
Menuhin, Yehudi **11**
Midori **7**
Mutter, Anne-Sophie **23**
O'Connor, Mark **1**
Perlman, Itzhak **37**
   *Earlier sketch in CM **2***
Ponty, Jean-Luc **8**
Rieu, André **26**
Roumain, Daniel **54**
Sahm, Doug **30**
   *Also see Texas Tornados, The*
Salerno-Sonnenberg, Nadja **3**
Schroer, Oliver **29**
Shaham, Gil **35**
Skaggs, Ricky **43**
   *Earlier sketch in CM **5***
Stern, Isaac **7**
Tiersen, Yann **59**
Vanessa-Mae **26**
Whiteman, Paul **17**
Williams, Claude "Fiddler" **42**
Wills, Bob **6**
Zukerman, Pinchas **4**

# Cumulative Musicians Index

*Volume numbers appear in* **bold**